Janet ~
with all good wishes
from the author
(Gladys Mary Coles)
25 March '98

THE FLOWER OF LIGHT

Also by GLADYS MARY COLES

BIOGRAPHY AND CRITICISM

Mary Webb: Collected Prose and Poems
Introductions to Mary Webb's novels *Gone to Earth*
    and *Precious Bane*
Introduction to Mary Webb's essays *The Spring of Joy*
Selected Poems of Mary Webb
Mary Webb: a new biography
Walks with Writers (with Gordon Dickins)
Mary Webb and Her Shropshire World

POETRY

The Sounding Circle
Sinerva and Other Poems
The Snow Bird Sequence
Stoat, in Winter
Liverpool Folio
Studies in Stone
Leafburners: New and Selected Poems
The Glass Island

AS EDITOR

Both Sides of the River: Merseyside in Poetry & Prose
Poet's England: Lancashire
Poet's England: Cheshire
Wirral: An Anthology
The Poet's View: Poems for Paintings
    in the Walker Art Gallery, Liverpool

VIDEO

Secret Shropshire (Shropshire Books)

THE FLOWER OF LIGHT
a biography of
MARY WEBB

by
Gladys Mary Coles

Gladys Mary Coles

HEADLAND

Published by
HEADLAND PUBLICATIONS   1998

First published in Great Britain by
Duckworth & Co Ltd. 1978
and in the U.S.A. 1979

This edition published by
HEADLAND PUBLICATIONS
38 York Avenue, West Kirby, Wirral,
Merseyside. L48 3JF

ISBN: 0 903074 98 2

British Library Cataloguing in Publication Data.
A full CIP record for this book is available from the British Library.

Printed and bound in Great Britain
by Ram Print, Derby.

Although it fall and die that night
It was the plant and flower of light.
In small proportions we just beauties see;
And in short measures, life may perfect be.

Ben Jonson, from 'A Part of An Ode'

A burning flower that lights
The hollow world —
Your rosy banner, sweet!
By love unfurled.

Henry B. L. Webb,
from 'To Mary'

AUTHOR'S NOTE

The text of *The Flower of Light*, first published twenty years ago, is reprinted here in its entirety, with bibliographical additions.

This, the first paperback edition, arises from constant demand by readers and students for the biography to be made available again. Its publication marks the seventieth anniversary year of Mary Webb's death and reflects the continuing growth of interest in her life and work.

It is also seventy years since her rise to posthumous literary fame, with Prime Minister Stanley Baldwin's enthusiastic commendation of her writing (April 1928), followed by the phenomenal success of her *Collected Works*, published by Cape (1928-29).

Gladys Mary Coles

Contents

List of Illustrations   ix
Preface   xi
Acknowledgments   xvi
Abbreviations   xviii
Chronology   xix

PART ONE: APPOINTED JOURNEYING: 1881–1902

1. Prelude   3
2. Early Eden: The Grange, Much Wenlock 1882–1896   19
3. No Primrose Path: The Woodlands,
   Stanton-upon-Hine Heath 1896–1902   40

PART TWO: THE SEARED SPIRIT: 1902–1912

4. Anchorhold: Maesbrook, Meole Brace 1902–1909   63
5. Life's Dark Cedar: 1909–1912   91

PART THREE: THE APOCALYPSE OF LOVE: 1912–1921

6. Hiraeth: Weston-super-Mare 1912–1914   113
7. Rose Cottage, Pontesbury – and *The Golden
   Arrow*: 1914–1916   131
8. Chester, The Nills – and *Gone to Earth*: 1916–1917   154
9. Lyth Hill – and *The House in Dormer Forest*:
   1917–1921   176

PART FOUR: THE SADNESS TERRENE: 1921–1927

10. Bayswater – and *Seven for a Secret*: 1921–1923   219
11. Hampstead – and *Precious Bane*: 1923–1926   245
12. The Last Years – and *Armour wherein he Trusted*:
    1926–1927   289

Epilogue   321
Appendix 1: Mary Webb's Shropshire   332
         2: Comments on Mary Webb by her
            Contemporaries   334
Select Bibliography   335
Index   343

Illustrations

Mary Webb (*c.* 1920)   frontispiece
facing page

1. George Edward Meredith   8
2. Sarah Alice Meredith   8
3. Kenneth Meredith   8
4. Leighton Lodge, Mary Webb's birthplace   9
5. Mary Webb at about 15 (*c.* 1896)   9
6. Sketch by George Edward Meredith   74
7. Mervyn Meredith, aged 2, at the Grange   74
8. The Little Wood, Lyth Hill   75
9. Mary's view from Spring Cottage, Lyth Hill
   Westley Farm in the centre   75
10. Maesbrook, the Meredith home from 1901 to 1912
    (George Meredith sitting on the bank)   106
11. Spring Cottage   106
12. 5, Grove Cottages, Hampstead, where *Precious Bane*
    was written   107
13. Facsimile of Stanley Baldwin's letter to Mary Webb,
    14 January 1927   266
14. Facsimile of Mary Webb's reply to Stanley Baldwin   267
15. Henry Bertram Law Webb (1924)   298
16. Mary Webb as Madeline at the Dickens Ball (1924)   298
17. Mary Webb in her last years   299

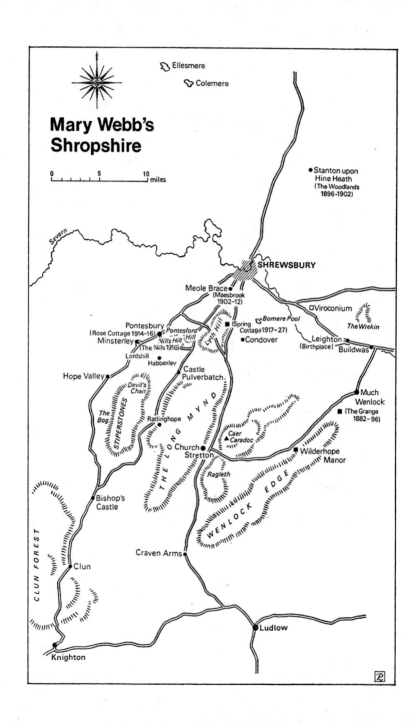

Mary Webb's Shropshire

Preface

The scene was laid for tragedy – not necessarily
overt tragedy, but a drama of the spirit, more
devastating, more searing.

(HDF, 59)

In this study of Mary Webb my purpose is twofold: to tell the
story of her tragic life and to draw attention to a neglected talent.
I hope my interpretation of her life and work will interest both
the general reader and the student.

It may well be asked, as a *Literary Digest* critic asked in 1928,
'Who Was Mary Webb?' Novelist, poet, mystic, lover of nature,
of humanity and the Shropshire countryside with which she was
emotionally and spiritually integral, she has been described as a
'strange genius'. Her intensely creative life ended in 1927 at the
age of forty-six. In a literary career begun during the dark days
of the Great War and cut short as she was reaching her prime,
her output – six novels (one uncompleted), essays, short stories,
some two to three hundred poems, a quantity of articles and
reviews – was fairly prolific, the product of little more than a
decade. Yet though she had a small and growing circle of
admirers in the literary and publishing world, and had won a
coveted award – the 1924 Prix Femina Vie Heureuse for *Precious
Bane* – she had no success with the public and died in obscurity,
feeling that she had failed in both her literary and her personal
life.

Ironically, six months after her death she was 'discovered'
by the wider reading public as a result of Stanley Baldwin's speech
at the Royal Literary Fund dinner (April 1928), in which he
praised the 'first-class quality' of her writing. There followed an
enormous posthumous success, a reputation which suddenly
blossomed and almost as suddenly faded, at its zenith in the
thirties, then dwindling into a literary twilight. But while her

popularity waned, Mary Webb's critical reputation – almost still-born, Baldwin's eulogy having antagonised the academics and intelligentsia – began, very gradually, to move forward. Today, some fifty years after her death, she is attracting a new generation of readers and it is time that a revaluation of her work was made, her place in literature re-assessed.

Although numerous articles about Mary Webb have appeared from 1928 onwards, no major study of her life and work has emerged hitherto. Two early biographies are both short studies: the invaluable *Mary Webb* by Hilda Addison (1931) and Thomas Moult's *Mary Webb: Her Life and Work* (1932). Two semi-travelogues, *The Shropshire of Mary Webb* by W. Reid Chappell (1930) and *The Shropshire Haunts of Mary Webb* by W. Byford Jones (1948), deal with the Shropshire world in which she moved and which was both source and setting of her work. A more recent book, Dorothy P. H. Wrenn's *Goodbye to Morning* (1964) is another brief account of her life.

In my research for this biography, I succeeded in locating documentary sources not available to any of the previous writers (it had been thought that little or no evidence of this kind was extant). A close study of these family diaries, letters and other papers has yielded a vivid picture of her background; her own letters to her publishers, and various unpublished pieces have provided further important biographical material. In addition, I have had the opportunity to integrate a great deal of detailed information from Mary Webb's eldest brother, Kenneth Meredith, and from her first biographer, Hilda Addison, who has given me material she herself did not use since she was writing so soon after Mary Webb's death. Other first-hand accounts (both oral and published) by her literary friends and those who knew her well have added to the mosaic.

Most enrichingly (and essentially) in my quest for Mary Webb, I have spent many months in Shropshire in all seasons, all weathers, immersed in her landscape of hills, woods and meres, exploring the settings of her novels, visiting the houses in which she lived, speaking to those Shropshire people who remember her – and to those who do not. The 'Mary Webb country' is remarkably little changed since her day. This 'solemn land of long-fulfilled desires' as she herself described it, and in particular the hill country of the Welsh border, is much as it was earlier this century – a landscape suggestive of the infinite (and haunted like all borderlands), stretching from Pontesford Hill to the high, superstition-bound Stiperstones with the dark pinnacles of the Devil's Chair, south to Clun Forest, and across the rolling moorland plateaux of the Long Mynd to the Stretton Hills and Wenlock Edge where she spent her childhood. An intimate knowledge of Mary's country-side as much as of her writings in their entirety, is centrally important to any real understanding of her. And my investigations in London where, migrant between there and Shropshire, she partly lived from 1921 until her death, also proved fruitful, so that by careful weighing and sifting of information I have been able to illumine the events of her tragic final phase.

To study her life is to study her work, and conversely, for to an extraordinary degree in Mary Webb life and work are an inseparable whole. Her will to the creative life, to an inner world of experience, was as ardent and strong as her body was frail – in this and in other ways she resembles Emily Brontë, not least as a literary mystic with a heightened vision of her surroundings. Lives lived at such intensity often burn out more quickly. For Mary Webb, with her 'rarely delicate senses', as Walter de la Mare noted, and her pantheistic response to nature, the physical world was 'a place of almost unbearable wonder'. And for her not just the beauty, but the terror and pain of life, were quickened (perhaps intensified still further by the effects of her thyroid disease). This extreme sensitivity and emotionalism was both a blessing and a curse in a nature deeply compassionate, highly complex, strongly pulled by dualities. She also had a keen sense of irony. No one could have been more aware than she of the 'sharp sweetness of human life' (her phrase in *The Golden Arrow*), and all her novels – like her life – are studies in 'the bitter-sweet'. The outlines of her own story are as simple and soul-stirring as those of the border hills she loved. Yet though fraught with suffering and agonising 'dark night', her life was charged with love (her supreme value), joy, humour, spiritual experience – all of which inform her writing. The extravagances of her nature and the refinements of her sensibility are equally reflected in her work, rendering it bizarre, brilliant, intense, sometimes overdone, but never dull. Above all, she was a romantic, using the novel poetically to express her mysticism and her highly individual vision of life and reality.

'Gravity in joy': this phrase captures her quintessential quality, and it is 'in her poetry', as T. Earle Welby pointed out, 'that this finds its finest expression'. Though better known as a novelist, Mary Webb, like Thomas Hardy, always thought of herself as primarily a poet. And while undoubtedly her best work lies in her novels – on these her literary reputation has rested – the poems too represent a definite (if neglected) achievement and have an abiding appeal. They are also richly autobiographical: here we find her most personal utterance; here not only the joys, but also the fears, griefs and despairs that haunted her life are given most immediate expression. While the novels (whatever their defects), embody variously her unifying vision, her sharp perceptions and observations, her passion and her pity, the poems are small crystallisations of the same, and are imbued with the immediacy of her personality. This personality, the presence in the novels, also permeates the essays, articles and reviews in which she speaks directly and with utter integrity: on these too, I have drawn extensively in elucidating her thought and opinions.

Discussions of the novels and poetry are placed in a biographical context in order that the intimate interrelation of Mary Webb's life and art may be seen and one may illuminate the other. It has not been my intention here to make a full critical study, but an approach towards a new assessment, aiming to bring fresh insights and perspectives to her work. In particular I have set out to clarify her central concerns and her methods of conveying them, and to draw attention to certain essential aspects of her writing hitherto overlooked, wherein she transcends the regional to universal significance and can be linked to important literary developments in her period. In examining Mary Webb's evolution as a literary artist, I hope that the nature of her achievement will emerge and the relevance of her vision to the culture and consciousness of the age will be seen more clearly.

There is the danger, however, in portraying a mind in growth, of attempting to expound what Virginia Woolf called 'every secret of a writer's soul . . . every quality of his mind'. I do not intend to deprive Mary Webb's work of all its mystery, but to entice the reader to discover more for himself. Ultimately though, one's response to her work will be a question of individual temperament.

Writing of the art of the literary biographer, Leon Edel says:

'When he has penetrated to the heart of his materials, he throws open a window upon a life and thereby opens it upon life itself. Endless are the views and vistas . . . we can sum up the process of giving such a view in three simple words : understanding, sympathy, illumination'. This admirably expresses my own concept of biography and my aims in this exploration of the life and work of Mary Webb. Yet in capturing the essence of this fine literary artist and extraordinary personality, we find something elusive at the core which cannot quite be grasped and which is the correlative of an irreducible quality in her writing. This wood-bird elusiveness is part of her fascination.

G.M.C.

Acknowledgments

My warm thanks go to the following for their generous help with this biography:

to Susan, Lady Tweedsmuir for her advice and suggestions, for reading part of the manuscript in its early stages, and for permission to quote from her essay 'Mary Webb';

to Hilda L. Addison, who wrote the first authentic account of Mary Webb's life, for the insights she has given me and for her immeasurable support;

to Dame Rebecca West for her personal recollections, kind interest and suggestions;

to Hamish Hamilton for valued encouragement and verification of important facts;

to Stella Gibbons for correspondence clarifying her intention in writing *Cold Comfort Farm* as a parody of the rural novel in general, and not exclusively of the works of Mary Webb;

to Raymond Lister, Honorary Senior Member of University College, Cambridge for invaluable references and encouragement;

to H. Bradley Martin for giving me access to his private collection and for his kind permission to publish this material;

to the late Professor Kenneth Allott for his interest, advice and encouragement at a crucial stage;

to the late Kenneth Meredith, eldest brother of Mary Webb, for providing me with much family information (both verbal and documentary) to the immense enhancement of this biography, and also for his friendship during six years of meetings, conversations and correspondence.

I would like to record my gratitude to the Staffs of the following libraries, museums and institutions: the University of Liverpool Library and particularly the University Inter-Library Loans Service; the Bodleian Library, Oxford; the British Museum; the National Central Library, International Loans; the London Library; the University of Bristol Library; the British Library,

Boston Spa; the New York Public Library; the Library of Congress; the Picton Reference Library, Patents and Periodicals, Liverpool City Libraries; the Department of Local Studies, Shrewsbury Library, Shropshire County Library; Somerset House.

I make full acknowledgment to the following publishers for information and for permission to reprint copyright material :

to the Executors of the Mary Webb Estate and Jonathan Cape Ltd for the many quotations from Mary Webb's works;

Constable & Co Ltd; Hutchinson & Co Ltd; John Lane, The Bodley Head, Ltd; Cassell & Co Ltd; Hodder & Stoughton Ltd. In addition I make acknowledgment to the *Cornhill Magazine*; the *Spectator*; *The Times*, the *Times Literary Supplement*; the *New York Times*; the *Whitehaven News*; the *Shropshire Magazine*.

I am especially indebted to the Liverpool Council of Social Service and the Lundie Memorial Trust for two bursaries enabling me to study and write undisturbed at St Deiniol's Residential Library, Hawarden.

Finally I wish most gratefully to thank all who have given me their time and valuable assistance and who have contributed first hand information, personal recollections, documentary material and photographs. Among these I should mention particularly : Nikki Archer, Headmistress of the King Alfred School; the Headmaster of the Priory School for Boys, Shrewsbury; A. R. Munday, Headmaster of the King's School, Chester; M. P. G. Tolfree for permission to use her excellent Bibliography of Mary Webb (University of London Dip. of Librarianship); Arthur L. Thomas, Reference Librarian, Shrewsbury Borough Library; C. A. Seaton, Librarian for the *Spectator*; Miss E. Hibburd, former Secretary of the King Alfred School; Mrs E. Wicksteed (wife of Mr Joseph Wicksteed, former Headmaster, the King Alfred School); Doreen Bourne and Derrick Bourne (editors respectively of the *Shropshire Magazine* and the *Shrewsbury Chronicle*); Anthony Rota of Bertram Rota Ltd; Percy Muir of Elkin Matthews Ltd, Antiquarian Bookseller; John Beech of Deighton, Bell & Co, Rare and Fine Books, Cambridge; the Mansell Collection; the House of Books, New York; Mrs Tessa Maclean; Mr T. R. Webb; Timothy Cape; Mrs H. M. Bott; Elizabeth Chesterton; the late Ethelbert White of Hampstead; Margaret Hardy; Dorothy P. H. Wrenn; Mrs K. Ryder, Mrs N. Cullis, Mrs Weaver and Mrs

Muriel Teasdale, all formerly of Lyth Hill; Mrs Key of Pontesbury; Mrs Constance Jellicoe-Wall of Meole Brace; the late Mrs Mary Ward of Much Wenlock; Mrs Richenda Acheson of Much Wenlock; Mr S. Hotchkiss of The Grange, Much Wenlock; Mr R. Groves of Condover; Mrs W. Edge of Wem (bridesmaid of Mary Webb); Mr J. Thorne; the Vicar of Holy Trinity, Meole Brace for access to the church log books; Mr R. Poynton, Mrs Jarvis, Miss Olive Sullivan and Mr Hayes for allowing me to see and photograph their houses; and my special thanks to Keith G. Medley, photographer (L.I.P.R.) for his skilful work, especially the splendid prints from old and sometimes faded originals; and to Carol Trotter for her care and patience in typing the manuscript.

G.M.C.

Abbreviations

GA	*The Golden Arrow*
GTE	*Gone to Earth*
HDF	*The House in Dormer Forest*
SFAS	*Seven for a Secret*
PB	*Precious Bane*
AWHT	*Armour wherein he Trusted*
PSJ	*Poems and the Spring of Joy*
51	*Fifty-One Poems*
CPAP	*Mary Webb: Collected Prose and Poems*

Page references are to the Illustrated Edition of Mary Webb's novels published by Jonathan Cape and reprinted in the 1960s; to the 1928 edition of *Poems and the Spring of Joy* and *Armour wherein he Trusted* (Collected Works); and to the 1946 edition of *Fifty-One Poems* (Jonathan Cape).

Chronology

1881   M.W. (Mary Gladys Meredith) born 25 March, at Leighton, Shropshire

1882   Merediths move to Much Wenlock

1887–94   Births of Alice Muriel, Edward Walter Kenneth, George Douglas, Olive Marion, John Henry Mervyn

1895   M.W. confirmed at Holy Trinity, Much Wenlock
Alice Meredith's accident

1895–7   M.W. at Mrs Walmsley's School, Southport

1896   Merediths move to Stanton-upon-Hine Heath

1901–3   M.W.'s first severe illness – onset of Graves' Disease
Begins series of essays in convalescence (later *The Spring of Joy*)

1902   Merediths move to Meole Brace

1902–3   M.W. recovers health

1903–9   M.W. attends Cambridge University Extension Course

1907   M.W.'s second severe illness

1907   October: M.W.'s first published poem, 'The Railway Accident' (*Shrewsbury Chronicle*)

1908   March: Departure of Kenneth Meredith to Canada

1909   5 January: Death of George Edward Meredith
July: M.W.'s first published short story, 'The Cedar-Rose' (*Country Life*)
Series of poems to her father

1910   M.W. sends essays to publishers under title 'The Scallop Shell' – without success

1910–11   M.W. becomes close friend of Henry Bertram Law Webb (H.B.L.W.)
February: Publication of *The Silences of the Moon* by H.B.L.W.
Summer 1911: Engagement of M.W. to H.B.L.W.

1912   12 June: M.W. marries H. B. L. Webb
M.W. moves to Weston-super-Mare
M.W. begins *The Golden Arrow*

1914	Webbs return to Shropshire (Pontesbury). War declared (August)
1915	M.W. completes *The Golden Arrow*
1916	Webbs move to The Nills (nr. Pontesbury)
	April–July: Webbs live at Chester and The Nills
	M.W. begins *Gone to Earth*
	July: Publication of *The Golden Arrow*
	September: H.B.L.W. commences at The Priory School, Shrewsbury. Webbs live at Lyth Hill
	M.W. completes *Gone to Earth*
1917	Completion of Spring Cottage (Lyth Hill)
	American publication of *The Golden Arrow* (May)
	Publication of *Gone to Earth* (*Sept.*); American publication
	The Everlasting Quest by H.B.L.W.
	The Spring of Joy (Oct.)
	M.W. begins *The House in Dormer Forest*
1918	M.W. working on *The House in Dormer Forest*
1919	Kenneth Meredith returns to Canada
1920	February: M.W.'s first published critical writing 'The Core of Poetry' in *The English Review*
	July: *The House in Dormer Forest* published
	M.W. meets the Buchans
	M.W. begins *Seven for a Secret*
1921	January: Webbs move to London. H.B.L.W. commences at the King Alfred School. Webbs live at Bayswater
1922	October: *Seven for a Secret* published
	December: M.W. begins reviewing for the *Spectator*
1923	Webbs move from Bayswater to Hampstead
	M.W. begins *Precious Bane*
	M.W. writes 'Glimpses of Old Shropshire'
1924	30 April: Death of Alice Meredith
	July: *Precious Bane* published
1925	M.W. working on *Armour wherein he Trusted*, short stories and review articles for the *Bookman*
	M.W.'s health deteriorating
1926	Award and presentation of Prix Femina Vie Heureuse of 1924–5 for *Precious Bane*
	M.W. writes 'The Chinese Lion'; articles in *T.P.'s and*

Cassell's Weekly and the *Bookman*

September : short story 'Mr Tallent's Ghost' in *The Ghost Book* (ed. Lady Cynthia Asquith)

M.W.'s breakdown of health

1927 January : letter to M.W. from Stanley Baldwin, P.M.

M.W.'s articles in the *Bookman* (February, June, September)

8 October : M.W. dies at St Leonard's, Sussex

Mary Webb (c. 1920)

PART ONE

APPOINTED JOURNEYING

1881–1902

> ... let us create
> The one thing we were meant to be,
> And make our own appointed journeying.
>
> Mary Webb, from 'Sallow-Catkins'

> Thrice happy he, who not mistook,
> Hath read in Nature's Mystick Book.
>
> Andrew Marvell

I

Prelude

Fair, fierce Life! What will you do with me?
What will you make me?
Take me and break me,
Hurt me, or love me,
But throne me not lonely and safely above thee,
Sweet Life![1]

'To Life' (*PSJ*, p. 42)

Leighton Lodge, Shropshire, 25 March 1881

Snowdrops had come and gone by then. On the lawns of
Leighton Lodge birds had returned, their keen song ringing in
the adjoining parkland of the Hall and rising from tall trees in
the Lodge grounds. Through the dark earth spring flowers were
cleaving, and a mist of green veiled the hedges, giving hint that
apple-blow would not be long, soon the wild rose would hang
upon the thorn. Here, at Leighton Lodge, Mary Gladys Meredith
was born on Lady Day in one of the rear rooms which face
towards the South Shropshire hills. She was the first child of
George Edward Meredith and his wife, Sarah Alice.

Leighton, a tree-hidden village near the coiling Severn, lies at
the southern foot of the Wrekin, that strange, solitary hill. Rising
dome-like from the Shropshire plain, this darkly wooded hump
with its cusp of Pre-Cambrian rock is one of the world's most
ancient hills, an early volcano. Well-known as a symbol of Shropshire, the Wrekin is a brooding presence, visible from many parts
of the county and dominating when viewed from Leighton Lodge.
For Mary it would be one of her 'inviolable places',[1] the 'changeless heights' which physically and spiritually were her hills of
home.

Situated on the road that follows the Severn winding to Build-

[1] All quotations in the following pages are, unless stated otherwise, from
Mary Webb's work.

was and Ironbridge, Leighton Lodge – red-brick and ivy-covered
– is a spacious country house, considerably enlarged earlier in the
nineteenth century when it had been the vicarage. At one side is a
stabling area where George Meredith kept his horses, carriage
and numerous dogs; and beyond this the large coach house of
Kynnersley Hall, its gilded clock striking the quarters, resound-
ing across the quiet dell and into the recesses of the Lodge's
many rooms.

The atmosphere of this house was ideally peaceful for the small
boarding-school George Meredith kept there, preparing boys for
entrance to public schools, Sandhurst and the universities.
Cultured, witty and placid, George was an Oxford M.A. in
Classics.

Described by friends as 'tall and cheerful', he had rather
ascetic features, his nose 'high in the bridge – the kind of nose
that comes of Welsh ancestry', as Mary was to write of a
character in one of her novels – and she herself inherited this
feature as well as the Meredith blue-grey eyes and fine dark brows.
She also derived from her father a deeply sympathetic nature :
George Meredith was remembered at Leighton for his rich sense
of humour and his poetry, but most of all for his kindness to the
old people and children of the cottages often flooded by the
swollen Severn.

He had married Sarah Alice Scott in 1880 – a well-matched
couple from similar backgrounds of moderately wealthy middle-
class society, each with strong Church of England connections.
No longer young, George was approaching forty and Sarah Alice
twenty-nine when Mary was born. She, who came with the
spring, was to be the modern child of nature, an apostle of
wonder. Taken to her christening on an April day, she was
carried through a gate at the end of the garden with its thickly
clustered primroses, into the bird-haunted grounds of the Hall
and to St. Mary's, the small parish church (also private chapel
of the Leighton and Kynnersley families). Here the vicar, William
Wingfield, a close friend of George Meredith, baptised her,
pouring the chill water.

> Radiant, terrible Life ! See now, I offer thee
> Body and spirit.
> Let me inherit
> Agony – wonder :

But leave me not icily, numbly asunder,
Dear Life!

So, years later, Mary expressed in a poem her total and passionate commitment to life; and so it was to be – agony and wonder in full measure.

Mary was the name of her paternal grandmother (Mary Blunt Meredith) and great-grandmother (Mary Ford). But following family custom, the second Christian name was used and she was known to everyone as Gladys, not becoming Mary until some thirty years later, after her marriage (this being the name her husband preferred). Throughout this study she will be referred to as Mary since in exploring her life we are discovering what went to the making, emergence and maturing of the literary artist, Mary Webb. And this emergence was a development through extremes of joy and suffering, love and pain interfusing. For her, then, the symbolical significance of the emergence of dragon-flies from the chrysalis, of which she was to write in *Precious Bane*: 'Once out, they're out for good. It costs a deal to get free. But once free they never fold their wings.'

Although only her first fifteen months were spent at Leighton, here she received her earliest sense-impressions of those Shropshire surroundings which were to be the greatest shaping influence in her life, quickening her sensibilities and fertilising her creative imagination. As an infant, sleeping and waking outdoors in the Shropshire air, she was surrounded by the 'watching presences' of old trees, the sigh and rustle of leaves, the spiritual sound of birdsong rising and falling 'from the green height to the green depth'. And everywhere the pervasive fragrance of flowers, 'the ravelled sweetness in the air'. Woven deeply into the fabric of her earliest consciousness were 'multitudes of soft sounds', nature's music which, as she said in a future essay,[2] 'is never over' – the sound of grass ('the very voice of earth'), of winds and weather, and of running water. Fundamentally Mary Webb was the product and expression of Shropshire, the changing moods and unchanging essence of the landscape, its 'echoing past', physical aspects and, above all, the unique spirit of the place.

There was much in her father too that had developed in

---

[2] 'The Joy of Music', *PSJ*, pp. 151–9. 'Nature's silences are pauses not conclusions'.

response to the Shropshire countryside. Of humans, it was he who exerted the deepest formative influence upon her – a man of fine, sensitive, if over-generous nature whom she adored. It would be difficult to exaggerate the impact of his personality upon her : in their relationship he was a remarkable blend of parent, friend, tutor, loving mentor, kindred soul.

George Meredith had a great love of his native Shropshire and, like many Salopians, was proud of his Welsh descent, the Celtic vein in his nature very pronounced. Imaginative, sympathetic, perceptive, his emotions were strongly felt, his romanticism tinged with both humour and melancholy. In Mary this Celtic strain was potent, inherited from both parents : her mother was Scottish, the only child of a rich Edinburgh surgeon, Walter Scott, of the same clan as his great namesake.

Mary's ancestry was clerical as well as Celtic : on the Meredith side, her grandfather and great-grandfather were vicars, and her father, born in 1841, first son of the Reverend Edward Meredith, had been expected to follow family tradition. But George Meredith was too sincere to take Holy Orders without a vocation – unlike many sons of Victorian clerics. Educated first by his father (then Headmaster of Newport Grammar School) and later at St. John's, Oxford, George, after graduating, returned to Shropshire and took up tutoring. He became the chief support of his ageing father who was, by then, Vicar of Longdon and finally, of Ightfield. Family tradition, meanwhile, was taken up by his cheerful, sporting brother, John Blunt Meredith, who enthusiastically pursued an ecclesiastical career – and the hunt.

Significantly, George Meredith's deepest interests were literary and artistic – and together with these went an intense love of nature. Sensitively appreciative of Classical and English literature, he was proud of his library in which an eager Mary was to spend hours of her childhood and youth reading extensively. Moreover, George was an accomplished artist and a fairly prolific poet from a line of poets, inheriting the gift from his mother and grandmother.[3] The discipline of classical scholarship is evident in his verse and he is said to have known the derivation of every word

[3] The unpublished letters and poems of George E. Meredith are part of a collection owned by the present author. Among the mss is 'The Dame and Her Pig – an old story versified and dedicated to George E. Meredith by his Grandmamma'.

in the English dictionary. Yet his second son, Douglas Meredith, has stressed: 'While Father was not of the parson type, neither was he by any means exclusively studious . . . Although he loved his books . . . he spent a large part of his time out of doors.' Passionately interested in all growing things of garden and countryside, in livestock, poultry farming and bee-keeping, George Meredith shared these enthusiasms with his wife, of whom a friend said, 'every plant thrived that she handled'. One of George's favourite anecdotes about himself, recalled by his eldest son, Kenneth, reveals much in a single glimpse: gardening one day at Leighton Lodge in his usual outfit of oldest clothing and a cap, George noticed a tramp looking over the hedge who, thinking he was the gardener, enquired hopefully, 'What's t'maister like o' that big 'ouse?' To which George gave a characteristic reply: 'I don't know. You'd better go and see.'

Kenneth Meredith also recalled that letters used to arrive for his father incorrectly addressed 'the Reverend George Edward Meredith' – a mistake which always amused George but which reflects his genuine 'goodness', the impression he gave. Not that he was dull, self-righteous or priggishly pious in any way – quite the reverse. His immensely quick sense of humour was a distinctive quality (expressed in witty verses and a delight in punning); and other characteristics were irritating to his strait-laced wife – excessively easy-going, notoriously unpunctual, he was generous 'almost to a fault' with his money, his time and the trouble he would go to in helping others. A born teacher, he had endless patience and (in Kenneth's words) 'a way of putting things so that you never forgot what he said'. In tutoring young people he was doing something which he enjoyed, at which he excelled and which also gave him ample opportunity to lead the life of a country gentleman. As with Abel Woodus in Mary's second novel, *Gone To Earth*, 'all his means of livelihood were joys to him'.

Mary spent the first three decades of her life in the Meredith home. The tone and quality of that home environment was crucial to her development as a person and a writer, and the kind of writer she was. This tone and quality arose directly from the personalities of her parents and the all-pervading influence of the Shropshire countryside.

It was her father who fostered in her from an early age a keen awareness of the natural world : they shared hours immersed in the green wild of Shropshire fields and woods, out on the 'slumbering steeps' of the hills or in their 'dark, shelving forests'; and sometimes wandering along the Severn : 'By the rushy-fringed bank/Where grow the willow and the osier dank' – lines from Milton's *Comus* which George Meredith often quoted. His own philosophy and beliefs owed much to his study of Milton, and this he impressed upon the young Mary – for instance, the Miltonic view of death as 'the gate of life'. Equally he was influenced by Wordsworth, particularly the spiritual integrity and meditation of *The Prelude*. Like this great poet, he experienced a mystical desire to penetrate the secret meaning of nature, the truths glimpsed in those fleeting moments of vision, 'a sense sublime/Of something far more deeply interfused'. Shaping, colouring George Meredith's attitude to life and religion was a mystical temperament which Mary very definitely inherited. In her this was developed so intensely that it was to lead her beyond and outside orthodox beliefs to a pantheistic mysticism which would mould her life and permeate her writing.[4] While George undoubtedly felt something of this oneness with universal life, in his first child it was to be a central, creative passion. Already during childhood and adolescence, Mary would respond to nature with a rapture 'as keen as pain'; already she would see, as Wordsworth saw, with 'that inward eye/Which is the bliss of solitude'; and later, in what was virtually a sacramental union with her countryside, giving as much as receiving, she would go far beyond the spiritual yearning that was her father's response to his Shropshire environment. As Amiel said, 'Un paysage, c'est un état d'âme'.

A Victorian romantic, George Meredith not only understood but knew the Wordsworthian 'love of nature leading to love of man' – here we come at once to the ambience of Mary's life. And it was, no doubt, George's quality of affirmative love that

---

[4] The validity of mystical experience is not in question here, neither are any explanations – psychological, pathological, religious or otherwise – under discussion. Mysticism is a word currently over-used and sometimes abused. But it applies to an aspect of human experience known throughout the ages and with considerable individual variation; it is not otherworldly, but is essentially a type of consciousness, and of this life. In discussing Mary Webb as a literary mystic, I am not presuming to analyse her experience, but see it as part of her creative impulse, thought and vision.

1. George Edward Meredith

2. Sarah Alice Meredith

3. Kenneth Meredith

4. Leighton Lodge, Mary Webb's birthplace

5. Mary Webb at about 15 (*c.* 1896)

attracted Sarah Alice Scott when, after a chance meeting with him at a Birmingham railway station, she made an entry in her diary (29 November 1875): 'We went to Birmingham in the morning and fell upon George Meredith at the station. He was come to the Poultry Show where he had some fowls. He offered us tickets but we had not time to go. He is very nice looking and I am sure very *good*.' The progress of the relationship that developed subsequently can be traced in Alice's diaries for 1875–9, a fortunate survival, giving us insights into her mind, background and character, and a detailed account of her life before marriage.[5] A picture unfolds of a Victorian young lady of independent means caught up in a social whirl that failed to satisfy her, and longing to find someone who could be her 'all in all'.

Sarah Alice Scott, born 6 May, 1852, was very young when her father died, and the dominant influence on her childhood was her mother – the reputedly formidable authoritarian Harriett Marian, a typical Victorian who made sure that the prime consideration in Alice's upbringing was 'a religious education'. Like the Dodsons in George Eliot's *The Mill on the Floss*, Harriett Marian – a rich widow but a sick woman – saw the necessity of leaving 'an unimpeachable will', providing carefully for her daughter's inheritance, maintenance and education.[6]

Alice's diaries reveal how closely her upbringing had complied with the spirit and letter of Harriett Marian's will, and the profound effect this had on her personality and outlook. They give evidence too of qualities in Alice which Mary inherited – and which made their relationship, at times, a difficult one : intensity, energetic thoroughness, love of exactitude, remarkable memory for detail, a fearless critical faculty, obstinacy and strong will-power (the cause of many a spirited clash). Her first biographer,

[5] The diaries of Sarah Alice Scott are in the author's Meredith & Webb collection.

[6] In her will of 1861, made in Worcestershire where she was then living, Harriett Marian designated her own mother and sisters as guardians of Alice, her only child. The trustees were given instructions on how the Scott estate was to be used for her maintenance and education, and by a codicil to the will, Alice's minority was extended to twenty-three. She was 'to be educated by some Lady who will make religion the first consideration of her education'. The Scott inheritance was considerable – later it was known as the Scott Funds from which the Meredith children were each given an annual allowance.

Hilda Addison, gives us an amusing glimpse of the infant Mary, revealing the determination of this small being who when placed by her nurse Kathleen in the nursery chair before a plate of bread and butter, promptly licked off the butter, firmly returned the bread to the plate and said, with a mischievous if greasy smile, 'Ta-ta bread'. Cheerfully tenacious. Like her father, Mary had a lively sense of fun combined with quick understanding and compassion. Here was a fundamental difference between daughter and mother, Alice being rather dour, bitingly sarcastic, unfortunately lacking in imaginative sympathy and tolerance. The widely differing characteristics of her parents met and fused in Mary, and to this synthesis she brought what was uniquely her own. In her complex nature there were many conflicting traits, extremes which others found bewildering, exasperatingly difficult.

In Alice's diaries, the sharp comments indicate that while her earnestness was a typical Victorian quality, her critical cast of mind and preciseness were inborn characteristics. Occasionally her judgments could be harsh and arbitrary. For instance, of the Fords (relatives of her companion Elizabeth Blunt), she said : 'Georgie, a very odd girl with great eyes; her elder sister writes, therefore is peculiar.' A significant comment when seen in relation to Mary Webb. Neither did Alice spare churches or clergymen ('The service was not well intoned' . . . 'The Bishop gave a terribly long, dry sermon' . . . 'A sallow, grey man, more of a scholar than a parish priest'). This criticism is interesting in view of her daughter's future lack of reverence for Church and clergy, satirised in her novels and particularly in *The House in Dormer Forest*. Firm opinions, trenchantly expressed : in this Alice and Mary were alike, and it was often to lead to tensions between them.

Yet her upbringing accounts for much of the stiffness in Alice's nature. And it is clear from the diaries that her religious zeal did not spring from deep spiritual feeling – unlike that of George Meredith – but was part of the Victorian moral attitude imprinted so rigorously upon her. She had a ready supply of Biblical quotations and sanctimonious homilies appropriate to each situation, sayings such as 'Out of our mistakes God builds up His completeness' (vital ingredients in a Victorian 'religious education') — and these she used to advantage later when enforcing her authority as

'Mother'. In the diaries, though, we see the real Alice struggling
to emerge.

Small, slim, with dark eyes and a firm chin, Alice at twenty-
three was a wealthy young woman maintaining her own house-
holds at Chester and Richmond Park with her cousin-companion,
Elizabeth Blunt (future godmother of Mary).[7] But in spite of the
social whirl of her life at that time (of which churchgoing was
an important part), she was an inwardly lonely, sad being, with
no special place of her own, no special person. Serious, longing
always for 'deep talks', Alice hid a rather pathetic, yearning self
behind her prim and precise exterior. She was seeking – and perhaps never ceased to seek – some deeper satisfaction, something
complete, more than endless 'kettledrum' gatherings, the cultural
attractions of London, visits to various vicarages, peregrinations of
the country, tours of the Continent, or even church services could
give her. If anyone fulfilled her need for an 'all in all' it was
George Meredith. But the fundamental desire for her own wholeness was a strong, insistent call in Alice, although she herself
would not have recognised or understood it as such; and of this
there was to be an even stronger urge and striving in Mary, for
whom it would be both substance and shadow, reality and dream,
her privilege and her doom.

As a prelude to Mary's life-long love affair with Shropshire and
the richly wrought novels which arose from this, it is interesting
to see in the diaries her mother's first impressions of the county.

The Devil's Chair, black outcrop of rock, legendary throne of
the Devil on top of the high Stiperstones, was to hold a profound
significance for Mary and draw her to it again and again : a place
of overpowering elemental atmosphere, it took the centre of her
imagination and was to be both setting and symbol in her first
novel, *The Golden Arrow*. On the 'long mammoth-like' ridge,
the Chair loomed 'dark as purple nightshade', or 'like a black
pearl in a troubled sea of mist', or hidden in fog, 'like some black
altar when curtains are drawn for an unholy rite' – Mary's

---

[7] Elizabeth Blunt was the daughter of Sarah – Harriett Marian's sister who
had married into the Blunts. She was the same age as Alice and, like her,
motherless from adolescence; also cousin of George Meredith (whose mother
was Mary Blunt) – and it was due to this connection that he came to know
Alice Scott.

descriptions in *The Golden Arrow* reflect both her close observation and the singular fascination the Chair held for her :

> So the throne stood – black, massive, untenanted, yet with a
> well-worn air. It had the look of a chair from which the occupant
> has just risen, to which he will shortly return. It was understood
> that only when vacant could the throne be seen. Whenever rain
> or driving sleet or mist made a grey shechinah there people said,
> 'There's harm brewing.' 'He's in his chair.' Not that they talked of
> it much; they simply felt it, as sheep feel the coming of snow.
>
> (p. 41)

In July 1877, the unreceptive Alice had made her first (and
probably last) visit to the Devil's Chair on a Geological Society
outing from Worcestershire. She records caustically :

> . . . We were finally deposited at the foot of some hills which
> we climbed and were enveloped in mist. When we reached the top
> however, the object of the day was achieved, i.e. to look at some
> rocks called the Stiperstones. We walked some way through
> heather and then met the carriages which took us to the station.
> We were very wet and having had nothing to interest us, felt
> anything but pleasant when we arrived back at 11 p.m.

Alice, however, was more readily appreciative of Shropshire
during a week she spent there in September 1879 as the guest of
her prospective husband, the cultured country gentleman who not
long afterwards made her a proposal of marriage and was
accepted. George Meredith was delighted to show her his countryside, driving in the carriage from Leighton Lodge to places in
which, a few years later, he would immerse his acutely receptive
first child. And to this Shropshire district around her birthplace
Mary was to return many times, especially to Viroconium, the
Roman city at Wroxeter, five miles from Leighton. Her father
may well have wondered as she gazed fascinated by the ruins,
what the future would hold for this child with her air of dreaming eagerness. Of this city near the gleaming Severn, founded in
the first century, becoming a centre larger than Pompeii but
sinking back to a wilderness with the collapse of the Roman
empire, Mary was to write :

Virocon – Virocon –
Still the ancient name rings on
And brings, in the untrampled wheat,
The tumult of a thousand feet.
                    (*PSJ*, pp. 53–4)

And she would write of it more than once, in prose as well as in
poetry. Like Wilfred Owen she was entranced by its atmosphere,
by the visible past and the felt unseen past in hedgerows, fields
and ruined silent walls:

> And still the breaking seas of grain
> Flow havenless across the plain :
> The years wash on, their spindrift leaps
> Where the old city, dreaming, sleeps.

In resonant evocations, Mary would recreate in her writing the
past of her county, give 'memoried glances' of distant ages now
but a murmur within our own.

A short distance southwards from Leighton Lodge is Buildwas
Abbey : here George took Alice to see the grey shell once peopled
by white-robed Cistercians, lawned cloisters near the Severn
where it curves and flows beneath an iron bridge which, in 1879,
was the original Telford structure. Buildwas once had monastic
links with the large Welsh Abbey, Strata Florida – and knowledge
of these abbeys was to contribute, years later, to Mary Webb's
close weaving of her last novel, *Armour wherein he Trusted*, a
medieval story of struggle between the physical and spiritual self,
'being the say of Lord Gilbert of Polrebec, afterwards the Holy
and Pious Abbot of Strata Florida'.

And up the steep, wooded flanks of the Wrekin, topped by a
hill fort (an early settlement of the Cornovii), George Meredith
took Alice for a picnic on a splendid early autumn day. From
here they could view the far reaches of the Shropshire countryside, the expansive plain below, and in the western distance 'the
quiet, misty dales/Towards the hyacinth hills of Wales'. To
George's claim, always made with a touch of humour, that his
Welsh forebears were descended from Prince Llewelyn, Alice Scott
would add, always with a touch of pride, that she was of the clan
of the great Sir Walter. She knew that among George Meredith's
favourite books were the Waverley Novels; and Sir Walter Scott
had written of the Shropshire border country, making it the

setting of *The Betrothed*. But neither George nor Alice could have imagined then, on that September day in 1879, that this landscape stretching far in the autumn air would become known, half a century later, as 'the Mary Webb Country' . . .

> A solemn land of long-fulfilled desires
> Is this, and year by year the self-same fires
> Burn in the trees. The untarnished colours keep
> The sweetness of the young earth's infant sleep :
> Beyond the plain, beneath the evening star,
> The burnished hills like stately peacocks are . . .
>
> (*PSJ*, p. 46)

The Wrekin is a constant inspiration to Shropshire people – 'To all friends around the Wrekin' is the traditional county toast. And for Mary, born beneath it, this lonely hill, heavy with old memories, thickly cowled in legend and folklore, would exert an unending fascination. From her first days she was steeped in its atmosphere, which is the atmosphere of Shropshire – a curious deep sense of presence, a strangely mysterious quality as if 'far gone in spells'. Although her life was not to be eventful in external circumstances, inwardly Mary would live in a vivid realm, her 'land within', vital, illumined, clear and keen, rich with impressions, observations and responses born of her intimate relationship with her landscape. And in the poems and novels to come, she would not only depict with almost uncanny accuracy and lucidity, the physical features, details and moods of the Shropshire countryside, but imbue this external world with symbolical meaning. In her writing her countryside is transmuted, undergoes a 'sea change', its physical qualities become symbols of human experience.

Alice, who had led such an unsettled life, feeling roots nowhere, going endlessly from place to place, probably never understood how and why her first child could so totally absorb, so poetically express 'spirit of place'. But Mary was also – and more completely – Shropshire's child : this was the essential in her life and art, and it was something she herself understood thoroughly as she shows us in this penetrating comment in *The Golden Arrow* :

> For the personality of a man reacting upon the spirit of a place produces something which is neither the man nor the place, but fiercer or more beautiful than either. This third entity, born of the

union, becomes a power and a haunting presence – non-human, non-material. For the mind that helped to create it once, it dominates the place of its birth forever. (p. 222)

The Shropshire countryside with its feeling of secrecy, of static profundity 'deep in the drift of time', is a landscape of contrasts : the vast 'multiple-tinted' plain; the sudden mounds of 'shadow-coloured hills' . . . 'hump-shouldered, kingly-headed/Or eel-shaped'; the circular meres set darkly in rings of lichened trees and frequently mist-shrouded. Ethereally lovely and sometimes eerie . . . here are felt emanations of good and evil, opposites which would occupy the forefront of Mary's consciousness. It is a particularly lonely landscape even today and still more so in late Victorian and Edwardian days when the population was sparse (with fewer women than men), when isolated cottages, remote farms and villages were connected by only the roughest of tracks and narrow winding lanes.

Alice Meredith is known later on to have found living in some parts of the county too isolated. She never desired a close intimacy with nature, and certainly not with nature in all its moods and truly wild – so different here from her husband and first child. But whatever her impressions of Shropshire and Leighton Lodge may have been in September 1879, it was not long after that she decided to marry George to whom she seemed 'the heaven-sent bride'. Her diary comes to a close as George, as it were, takes over : so it is with 'George and I' – riding, boating, walking to Kew, going to church 'at 8, 11 and 7' – that the diary ends and, for Alice, the new life begins.

After their wedding at Richmond on 27 April, 1880,[8] they

---

[8] George Meredith's wedding speech conveys something of the flavour of his personality. Making use of political terms and issues of the day (he was a strong Conservative) he parodied the style of 'public utterances' speaking of the 'Programme' he and his 'Colleague' (Alice) hoped to 'carry out' in matters of 'Domestic Legislation' : 'My Co-member will doubtless endeavour to maintain the principle of *Woman's Rights* with a vigour not unworthy of so noble and so good a cause; while I, for my part, shall be not a whit behindhand in seeking to establish a firm and beneficent *Home Rule*. Should the strength of our convictions prevent us, on occasions, from yielding to a policy of *"Peace at any Price"*, we shall strive, so far as may be, that our conferences be conducted in a spirit of mutual conciliation, and thus bring them to a wise and happy issue resulting in *"Peace with Honour"*. We shall strongly repudiate a *"Repeal of the Union"* which has been ratified today between us . . .'

spent a short time in London before coming to Leighton Lodge, 'our home in the country', as George called it. A well-loved figure in the district, he was often seen striding along the lanes surrounded by dogs and pupils. In his rich speaking voice he gave frequent 'Penny Readings' of his amusing verses and at the village hall helped the Rev. William Wingfield to entertain the children with Magic Lantern shows and Christmas plays which he wrote, such as 'King and Troubador', and in which he acted and sang. He was remembered by many for his 'clever humorous songs' at 'entertainments for charitable purposes'. When member of an Acrostics Club George enjoyed the verbal exercise involved in 'subtle riddle', but eventually he ceased to compose and received a letter of rebuke from the club's secretary. To this he replied in characteristic fashion:

> ... Who can draw water when the well is dry?
> Who without wings can ever hope to fly?
> Who looks for harvest if no seed be sown?
> Who can write verses when the muse is flown?
> Or to Acrostic heights presume to soar
> And make quotations when he lacks the lore? ...

Later George wrote verses for family anniversaries and the birthdays of his children, also using this method of communication when reprimanding them – a short rhyme to the offender, usually signed 'your very affectionate Father', would be left on his or her chair (this in contrast to Alice's sharp rebukes).

Although not of any special artistic merit, George Meredith's poems stand in interesting relation to Mary's: he was obviously a strong influence on her early work, and in his serious, contemplative poetry comes close in mood and theme to poems of her mature achievement. The perennial theme of human transience is, of course, central, as in his 'Obsequies': 'For me – when death shall claim me as his own/Let friendship raise no monumental stone./For me – whom living, Nature best could please –/Enough that she perform my obsequies.'

Always attentive to form, George's preoccupation with metre and rhyme possibly inhibited his deeper lyrical impulse; powerful though his feeling for nature was, he did not (or could not) often give expression to this in nature imagery. Here we find a significant difference between his poetry and Mary Webb's with its sensuous immediacy, intimacy of observation and strong sense of personal relationship with nature. Yet in a few poems George does reveal his attitude, how he saw in nature an allegory – and he taught Mary from an early age to read and interpret all its signs, the 'occult script', as she said in an essay, one of her first mature writings.

The atmosphere of the home in which Mary's poetic imagination was nurtured, her vision of life given initial shaping, was created largely by the mind and personality of her father. His poems and letters clearly show him to be the original of John Arden, the central character in Mary's first novel, *The Golden Arrow*, a work permeated with autobiographical elements, although very much what George Eliot called 'experience . . wrought up'.

Into the character of John Arden, a Shropshire shepherd, Mary worked her father's qualities – his insight, tenderness, 'large humour' (which occasionally had a wry edge), and mystical tendency. Moreover, the close, sympathetic understanding between John and his daughter Deborah (who undergoes intensities of love and suffering), was drawn directly from the central, formative relationship in Mary's own life. And in John Arden's relationship with his practical wife, Patty, who chides him acidly for his lack of time-sense, his generosity and tolerant attitude, we find a reflection of George's relationship with Alice (whom he always referred to affectionately as his 'Ally').

In depicting John Arden's 'self-giving love', his conviction that 'the end of man's life is love – to give it and take it', Mary was portraying what to George Meredith was the prime reality. Yet such love can involve sharp pain, and it was this kind of love – her own way of loving – which, as we shall see later, Mary dramatised and symbolised in *The Golden Arrow*.

During her early life and young womanhood, she evolved the vision of oneness and of unifying love which she was to embody variously in her writing – and which eventually was the core of her personal tragedy. This vision, with its related themes and ideas, gives unity and coherence not just to her imaginative world but to the entire output of her short, concentrated literary career. Flame-like as the flight of a delicate, brief-lived dragonfly, imaged in water.

To quote from Walt Whitman in 'A Song Of Myself' : 'Before I was born out of my mother, generations guided me.' No one could have been more aware than Mary Webb of all that such a statement implies in terms of individual and collective heritage, those intangibles of existence which, as she herself said, 'have grown slowly by gradual accretion', elements inherent in parents and countryside, in dialect, myth and folklore – present expressions of a cumulative past. She was to receive all that her environment could give. And she brought to it that innate gift referred to by Goethe as 'exact sensory imagination', impelled to intimate her sense of life's mystery and the meaning she felt in nature . . .

> As a pale moth passes
> In the April grasses,
> So I come and go,
> Softlier than snow.
> Swifter than a star
> Through the heart I flee,
> Singing things that are
> And things that cannot be.
> I whisper to the mole
> And the cold fish in the sea,
> And to man's wistful soul
> Life sendeth me . . .   (*CPAP*, p. 95)

With exquisite wonder, mystical inwardness and joy perilously close to anguish, she would submit herself to life with all the passionate sincerity of her eager spirit. No matter what the cost. For Mary this was the inevitable path, following always that inner necessity urging to still fuller life, to deeper experience, striving to grasp what Dostoevsky called 'the inmost essence of truth'. And not just to grasp but to communicate her vision of reality, both outer and inner. The novels to come – very much her unique world – would be at once inspired yet flawed, controlled yet extravagant, mystical yet sharply concrete, infused with vivid humanity.

Leighton Lodge, folded in among trees, birdsong, water, and near the mysterious Wrekin, was an especially appropriate birthplace for Mary Webb. Her early years however were not lived there, but further south and west of her county, in a green valley where the ridge of Wenlock Edge slopes down towards 'the ancient borough' of Much Wenlock.

2

Early Eden
1882–1896

The Grange,
Much Wenlock

There are the pastures of sleep
And creatures at rest;
A mountain enchanted and steep
Floats on the west.

And there, like a blossoming tree
On a dew-drenched lawn,
My playmate is waiting for me
In the luminous dawn.
(CPAP, p. 101)

As a child I remember standing awe-stricken at the strange
beauty of a well-known field in the magic of a June dawn.
(PSJ, p. 197)

The Merediths, more prosperous than at any subsequent period,
bought The Grange, a fine country house, with its lodge, outbuild-
ings and nearby farm. The next fourteen years were spent there,
and during this settled phase another five children were born.

The Grange, Much Wenlock and the magnificent countryside
around Wenlock Edge was the setting of Mary Webb's childhood
and adolescence – her early Eden. In many ways, idyllic: 'All
was so changeless, quiet, fair/All swam so deep in golden air' –
so it was to seem, looking back. A childhood of gentility in the late
Victorian world, of country lore and farming, lessons and legends,
the Bible and the Mabinogion, of bluebell woods and snares,
spring blossom and the autumn hunt, jackets red as berries and
blood. Implanted then were the seeds of joy – and of pain.

Mary's father called her, when she was still very young, his
'precious bane', quoting from Milton's *Paradise Lost*: an expression which would have central significance for her. She would

find 'the core of sweetness in much bitter', and it was the days of her childhood which both prepared her for and held within them an inexorable legacy of suffering. Irony hovered deep as the shade of yew trees in the grounds of The Grange.

This house stands large, red and isolated in the green meadows. Mary looked from its windows to her well-loved fields extending to hillsides more wooded then than now. The Grange, enormous to a child, held its own enchantment, grounds thick with copses and secret places, a rookery, orchard, wide lawns, a pond and long tree-lined drives. The small Merediths' favourite playground was the stable area with its hidden corners and leafy crevices around the coach house over the archway of which was a fine old clock in a belfry. In this cobbled courtyard Mary loved to linger where a fig tree clings to the stable wall, and where she could see the activity in the kitchen and laundry.

A child with wind-flower charm, shy, slender, serious, elfin in appearance, eager in manner, Mary gave the impression of being always on tiptoe. She combined physical resemblance to both parents, having her father's darkness, fine features and candid eyes, her mother's firm chin and smallness. Rather precocious, full of zest and a delightful curiosity, 'little Gladys' was from her earliest days her father's darling. And he was the sun in her world.

Mary was an only child for six years, the youngest member of the household, alone among grown-ups and schoolboys. Apart from her father's companionship, she had 'sworn friends' among the flowers, and was comrade to the grey pony in the stables, the dogs and cats and her own pet ducks given to her as a gift 'for her special care'.

The ducks swam in the little pond by the drive and Mary used to watch them closely, fascinated by their characteristics. Always she was to be an acute observer of life in all forms and everything was part of her exploration. While, as a small child, much of her perception was still unconscious, she was nevertheless absorbing a great deal. The little pond reflecting the sky, 'water the colour of light' . . . eyes of the child water-gazing, eyes of the future mystic who, deep in contemplation, would look long into the dark and silver meres, into the chill dew-pond and into 'the opaque and fathomless pool' within her own being.

From an early age aware of the symbolic in the real, she

noticed the crosses set in the exterior brickwork of the house, crosses repeated in doorstep 'threshold patterns' (a superstitious Shropshire custom to ward off the Devil), crosses imprinted everywhere in nature, in the tangle of branch and thicket, in the heart of flowers. Inquisitive, alert, she was not long in asking her father 'the meaning of the cross'. He can be pictured explaining (like John Arden) in 'unhurried utterance'. In the same earnest tones he gave a Bible reading before family and school prayers, morning and evening. Mary was to convey perfectly, in describing John Arden, her father's characteristic way of praying: 'He was always a syllable behind the rest, tasting each word, very emphatic.'

At The Grange, George expanded his boarding school and became, at the same time, a gentleman farmer. The Meredith farm was across the meadows, a little further up the road towards Wenlock Edge. Managed by his bailiff, it was not just a pleasant interest for George but a source of produce to feed his large household. He took a keen interest in his stock as well as the assortment of dogs and cats (especially his greyhounds and beagles). Years later he referred to his days as a gentleman farmer in a mildly satirical verse: 'He took to farming, days gone by,/A kind of pastoral lullaby/To soothe his troubled nerves and keep/Him occupied with cows and sheep.'

Occasionally a cow would be brought to the rear of the house on George's instructions and he would sit in the courtyard sketching the animal, watched by a fascinated, admiring Mary. Cousin to the artist David Cox, George's own talent was not inconsiderable and while Mary inherited this artistic eye it was to be expressed in verbal description. Yet she liked to paint and sketch, especially flowers or plants.

At The Grange, a world in microcosm, Mary observed a multiplicity of human foibles and facets – a lively community, populated by family, servants, pupils and a perpetual train of visitors. There were farming and hunting associates of the Merediths, friends from far and near, and relatives such as the Rev. John Blunt Meredith who would vie merrily with his brother in the telling of reminiscence and anecdote, and who, reputedly, was so fat that 'he hadn't seen his toes for years'.

Alice Meredith's energies were directed to the organisation of this large household, said to be one of the 'best conducted' in the county. A strict time-keeper, she made sure that the bell on the roof of The Grange was tolled summoning the boys to lessons and meals. A strong corrective influence over George's slipshod punctuality, she would rebuke, in her sharp manner, any who dared to be late. The cook, Mrs Tilley, recalled years afterwards how strict Mrs Meredith was, 'all the meals being served to the minute'. The school was flourishing and George Meredith's reputation as a tutor spread, 'his method being very sound and thorough'.[1] An extant report of a pupil, St John Trevor, for the Easter term, 1889, reveals a fairly wide curriculum – Maths, French, History, Geography, English, Music, Drawing and Drill as well as Scripture and Classics (on which at this date many small schools concentrated to the exclusion of all else). And for those intending an Army career, the 'sword-exercises' given at the school were an asset.

George Meredith, in the mould of Thomas Arnold, tended the development of his pupils' characters as carefully as the flowers and plants in his garden.[2]

When she was old enough Mary was taught by George himself as well as by her governess, Mrs Lyons, a lady of Dutch origins who was the friend and companion of Alice Meredith.

Apart from receiving her first lessons from her father, Mary was learning from him all the time, seeking information by unceasing questions, avid for his replies, trying to imitate his ways, write poems. He told her 'Read, Mark, Learn'. This she did, looking to him for guidance, fun – and tenderness.

Frequently the two would go for long walks in the fields and

---

[1] *Shrewsbury Chronicle*. Obituary of George Edward Meredith, January 1909.

[2] One of the poems in George Meredith's mss gives a humorous account of 'A Private Tutor's Lamentation':

I've a set of fifteen scholars	Spite of rules and timely warning
And I'm subject to what follers:	Consequently every morning,
Base neglect of *mat* and *scraper*;	*Bad* translations, *badder* grammar,
Tearing-up of *bits of paper*;	All along of last night's clamour.
Contradicting, laughing, talking;	Follows then, on these conditions,
Scampering instead of walking;	Cane or birch or impositions.
Door locks spoiled and windows broken	In these troublous little parties
Garments mudded, stockings soaken;	'Nondum *didicerunt* artes'
Running over beds of flowers;	Which, of men make *moral* heroes
Idling in the silent hours	'Neque sinunt esse feros'.

woods near The Grange, or for drives in the pony-trap along
Wenlock Edge from where the Shropshire countryside unfolds
gloriously on both sides of the high wooded spine. In all seasons
they went there, driving along the tree-bordered road first cut in
the Middle Ages by Stephen and Henry II, a road climbing up
and over the top of the rugged ridge of limestone, descending
eventually towards the Stretton hills. They picnicked in the woods
on the Edge and from various places the Shropshire hills, the 'hills
of home' so vitally significant in her life, were visible : the Wrekin,
distant solitary mound; the Long Mynd, vast windswept tableland, highest point between England and the Ural Mountains;
Caer Caradoc, crested, mysterious.

To these hills and to the Stiperstones, those bleak heights behind the Long Mynd that look towards Wales, they came, George
recounting to his willing listener the numerous legends and superstitions associated with the landscape. In this way Mary first heard
the legends of the foreboding Devil's Chair, a focal point of lore
and superstition. She heard, too, tales of Wild Edric, a Shropshire
hero at the period of the Conquest, said to haunt the Stretton
hills and Stiperstones in various forms with his legendary bride
Godda, especially when great disasters or wars are imminent. And
she saw, on Wenlock Edge, the Major's Leap – a sheer drop
where during the Civil War a Shropshire Cavalier, Major Smallman, evaded his Roundhead pursuers by leaping his horse out
over the steepest part, and escaped when landing below in the
trees although his horse was killed. Mary was riveted by this
story of a man hunted down like a fox, hurtling in desperation
over the precipice. As her sense of pity developed, so in proportion did her sensitivity to cruelty, and already she was experiencing a growing revulsion to bloodsports, especially fox-hunting in
which so many people around her, including her parents, were
involved. She knew there was horror in it, terror and savagery;
she felt immense pity for the hunted creature, extending this to
all victims of cruelty, human or animal. These were the beginnings
of her life-long, passionate revolt against suffering. Years later,
writing the ending of her second novel, *Gone to Earth*, she
extracted an idea from the story of the Major's Leap and wove
her tragic climax as the doomed Hazel, clutching her pet fox, is
pursued by the 'deathpack', and hurls herself over the edge of a
quarry.

Mary's involvement with folklore was intrinsic to her intense involvement with her surroundings. Living in an area where legend and superstition abounded,[3] she came to an early understanding of how these were deeply rooted, folklore being a natural growth integral to the environment from which it springs, yet so often expressive of universal and timeless realities, embodying primordial truths common to mankind. West Shropshire and particularly the hill region bordering on Wales is rich in folklore and superstitious belief, and Mary, in her novels, was to draw extensively on this aspect, as indeed on every other of her local heritage. Like Thomas Hardy in his Wessex novels, she used legend and superstition as an important element, integral to plot, structure and meaning, influencing character and action. So successfully did she incorporate this mythic material which heightens the atmosphere of her fictional world, that sometimes it is not possible to tell when she is imaginatively using traditional legend and belief, and when she is creating from her own fancy.

Already during childhood she was understanding 'a permanence, a continuity in country life which makes the lapse of centuries seem of little moment', as she tells us in her Foreword to *Precious Bane*. From her earliest days she was saturated in the peculiar and distinctive atmosphere of her county, an atmosphere which became part of her and from which eventually she could not bear to be separated. In the same Foreword she states explicitly how fortunate she was 'being born and brought up' in the 'magical atmosphere' of Shropshire, 'a county where the dignity and beauty of ancient things lingers long'; fortunate, too, she emphasises, to have 'the companionship of such a mind' as her father's: 'a mind stored with old tales and legends that did not come from books, and rich with an abiding love for the beauty of forest and harvest field, all the more intense, perhaps, because it found little opportunity for expression.'

So as a child, highly imaginative and intelligent, she became increasingly aware, by his instruction and her own intuition, of the continuously creative nature of existence, and of the collective past embedded in the human mind and spirit as well as in the

[3] L. H. Hayward, 'Shropshire Folklore of Yesterday and Today', *Folklore*, XLIX, 1938, pp. 223–43; Michael M. Rix, 'More Shropshire Folklore,' *Folklore*, vols 71–2, 1960–1, p. 184; Michael Peele, *Shropshire in Poem and Legend*, 1923; Charlotte S. Burne, *Shropshire Folklore*, 1883.

ancient rocks, trees and meres of her landscape. Past in the present, present in the past, both in the future . . . she saw 'them all as long gone by/Returning in futurity'.

Discussing the young Dickens, Graham Greene suggests that 'the creative writer perceives his world once and for all in childhood and adolescence and his whole career is an effort to illustrate his private world in terms of the great public world we all share'.[4] To some extent this is true, and true particularly of Mary Webb. Certainly these fourteen early years at The Grange in the heart of the Shropshire countryside were vital in her development : here we find the source of so much in her life and art, in the individual vision she expressed as a creative artist. Above all this period was for her, in effect, an early experience of Eden, a personal paradise which enveloped her – literally in the Shropshire landscape, her 'hills of heaven' as she always thought of it. And in this Garden of Eden her adored father was the central figure. Such was the harmony, the sublime feeling of wholeness and changelessness in her relationships on the one hand with nature, on the other with this utterly close, fine and reliable human being, that for the rest of her life she would strive to regain the inner totality she experienced then. For inevitably life expelled her from that Eden – and, also inevitably, while she was to camp at its walls and even re-enter it at times, she would experience regression and disillusionment. Yet she was never to cease in her striving to attain and retain wholeness. Whether obliquely or directly she would express this vision in all she wrote.

While environment was to influence her writing in the most intimate and elusive of ways, there were also some obvious assimilations from this period at The Grange, certain characters and incidents in her novels and short stories drawn from stored memories. To take one example, Owd Blossom in the story of that name (*AWHT*, pp. 213–21), was based on an old cowman at the Meredith farm. Fascinated by his 'unket look . . . wispy hair and rheumy eyes', Mary intuitively understood, young though she was, this apparent simpleton : 'Beneath the smile, into the grave, wistful soul of the man, nobody ever thought of looking.' With such country people who seemed almost emanations of

---

[4] Graham Greene, *Collected Essays* (The Bodley Head, 1969), p. 106.

the landscape itself, Mary always had a close affinity, and in her writing conveyed brilliantly their rural aura. Another, more elaborate version of Owd Blossom is Enoch Gale, the earth mystic in *The House in Dormer Forest*.

Mary made a vivid impression on those who knew her during her childhood : already it was thought that there was 'something different' about her, and that this somehow was associated with the intensity of her preoccupation with nature. Since it was usual for country children in the late Victorian period to be absorbed in nature studies, most of the wonder in life still centring around the changing seasons, it is all the more a measure of the intensity of Mary's involvement with nature that this was thought to be extraordinary by the children who knew her at Much Wenlock, and many years later was still remembered.

Although a rather delicate child, never robust, she spent as much time as possible outdoors. Senses acutely tuned to every sight and sound, she knew when each bud unfolded in the garden, and watched the movements of birds and insects for hours at a stretch, particularly fascinated by bees on which her father was something of an expert, keeping his own hives. On 'bees in their refectories' she would reflect deeply, like Maurice Maeterlinck, the Belgian philosopher-mystic, drawn by 'the spirit and perfume, the atmosphere and mystery'.

And it was during these days at The Grange that Mary developed her life-long habits of eating meals outside whatever the weather (in spite of her mother's disapproval), and rising before dawn, slipping out of 'the sleeping house' across the quiet lawns into the meadows to feel herself completely alone with nature, alone with her perceptions. A few years later, in her first significant writings – the essays which became *The Spring of Joy* – she tells us

If you will go out on some June morning, before the earliest bee comes droning by, when the stripes of sunrise lie right across the awakening earth, you will know the fascination of shadows. On such a day they are almost as blue as chicory. As a child, I remember standing awe-stricken at the strange beauty of a well-known field in the magic of a June dawn. It had a line of tall trees in its eastern hedge, and if you watched while the sun rose, you saw what had been a wide, grey expanse suddenly spanned by swart, prostrate giants. It was as if, with one movement, every tree had flung itself upon its face – Mahommedan-wise – at the muezzin of sunrise.

(*PSJ*, p. 197)

She watched at dawn; and she watched at dusk:

Evening after evening, in the summer, I have gone to see the white clover fall asleep in the meadows. Kneeling and looking very closely, as the dew begins to gather, one sees a slight change in the leaves . . . those who are early enough may see them wake and rise in the morning – multitudes moving in slow, unfaltering unity.   (*PSJ*, p. 141)

Here we are already in the world of *Precious Bane*.

One of her brothers recalled how Mary used to lie 'for hours and hours' in the fields near The Grange watching the fitful sunlight, the ever-changing clouds, wind rippling the corn. Intuitive, spontaneous, totally receptive, she was predisposed to respond to and interpret experience in a particular way, never ceasing to enlarge and refine her perception, a development as sure, as inevitable as the upward movement of a plant to the light. In her essential poetic nature she was what the Shropshire countryside made her; and already her apprehension was that of the mystic, conscious of a 'beauty unseen' immanent in material form yet ineffably beyond it. As Hilda L. Addison observed: 'Undoubtedly it is true to say that from early adolescence, even from childhood, she had an unusual perception of the indwelling of the eternal in the temporal, of spirit in matter. She was a born mystic.' And this basically determined her emotional and intellectual attitudes. Not always to her comfort.

Always attuned to what Wordsworth called 'the still, sad music of humanity', Mary felt urgent stirrings of pity when she began visiting cottages near The Grange and in Much Wenlock, confronted by poverty, illness, misery in the homes of agricultural labourers and old people.

Brought up in comfort and affluence, sheltered from the grimmer aspects of Victorian life, she was all the more shocked by what she saw – here having experience of another and harsher reality. While it was one of the conventional 'good works' of the Victorian middle classes to visit the old and sick, a duty which began young after the fashion laid down in *Ministering Children*, for the tender-hearted Mary this was traumatic. She was gripped by pity and it was a grip nearly as powerful as her passion for nature. One young girl who went visiting with her never forgot her strong reactions, her angry recoil at certain incidents and scenes. Mary was appalled – the contrast between life at The Grange and life in the stone-floored cottages with their damp ceilings and peeling walls was sharply before her. What became for her a virtual morality of compassion grew years later into a fervour which eventually held tragic consequences.

Already as a girl, her realisation of human suffering impelled her to creative expression – at first in little practical ways. Every Bonfire Night she invited the cottage children to The Grange where there would be a large blaze in the meadow, turnip lanterns and a supper for all. At Christmas she prepared a list of the children's names – a present for each was carefully wrapped and placed on the Meredith Christmas tree decorated with fruit and candles. The children were invited and George himself would distribute the gifts dressed as Father Christmas. Mary helped him to devise tableaux and little plays to entertain them, and when she was older she wrote the plays herself. On her birthday too, she insisted that the children were invited to her tea party. George Meredith would entertain them with 'magic', having a repertoire of amusing tricks such as the surprise 'glow-worms' he released out of match boxes. A vivid picture springs to mind of the tall, placid country gentleman with 'his clear, noble profile and far-seeing eyes . . . his endless patience, his large humour that had room for all', and the bright, elf-like girl, eager, thoughtful.

We are given a glimpse of Mary's active compassion in her short story 'Many Mansions'. The setting is Much Wenlock, an historic town which even today retains its air of belonging to those distant ages which brood in the stones of hills, in the hearts of old trees. A 'Rip-van-Winkle' of a place, as Mary said of it, 'Somewhere in the Middle Ages it had fallen asleep.' In the twelfth century church of Holy Trinity, George, Alice and Mary, and in term time the boys from the school, occupied a pew each Sunday; here Mary was confirmed. Nearby are the ruins of St Milburga's Abbey, surrounded by tall trees. Stories and legends grow in such a place, and Mary knew all of them including that of St Milburga : 'She sleeps in Wenlock Priorye/Holie fragraunce markes the spotte.'

Approaching Much Wenlock from The Grange, Mary saw it 'in the pool of hyacinth made by the valley shadows and the gentle smoke of hearth fires'. In one of the ancient cottages known as the Bull Ring lived old John Lloyd, the church beadle. When Mary was ten, and John 'something verging on one hundred', she used to visit his 'dusky cottage' each week to read the Bible to him. Her impressions of these visits were woven years afterwards in the cameo 'Many Mansions' (*AWHT* pp. 189–93). The story, descriptively rich, brings before us a scene of her childhood, its chiaroscuro like a Rembrandt. We see the slender ten-year-old going up 'three hollow steps' into the shadowy, firelit room 'silent as one of the porches of eternity', and facing the feeble old man 'in his Windsor chair, his great black Bible . . . ready on the deal table'. This was the bible from which Mary read and which was 'so heavy' that it made her thin arms ache. Humdrum though it was to read the same passage every time when there were so many other parts which interested her, nevertheless 'because John liked what he called "the Many Mansions piece" . . . when it was his turn to choose he chose that. And when it was my turn to choose, remembering that this was John's party, I was in honour bound to choose that also'. And so 'the book always fell open just there'. The details she recalls reveal that her memory was as sharp as her observation.

Mary's character during childhood is clearly conveyed in this keenly incised autobiographical fragment – her eagerness (looking upon each of these visits as 'a great adventure'), generosity of spirit and ready sympathy. Dreamy yet purposeful, she overcame her longing to loiter on the brown country road 'between its sloping fields of miraculous green' where she found in the hedgebanks wild flowers and 'the largest most brightly-coloured snail-shells' then used for the game of conker. She offered John a prize shell, but as the old fellow said, he was 'past conker'. Mary had a collection of them, kept in what she called her 'faery house'. While she was fascinated by glass marbles and boxes, and had a musical box model of a grand piano complete with silken interior and a mirror on the inside that reflected her large eyes as she raised the lid, such special attachment to 'things' was rare. Always – throughout her life – it was the minutiae of nature that held the deepest significance and value; in fact, all that lived and grew.

During these years Mary felt an increasing abhorrence of bloodsports. It was a severe shock when two of her father's dogs were shot accidentally by a friend of the family who had come for a 'shoot' in the Rookery. Incidents such as this undoubtedly contributed to her loathing of 'sport' and she became passionately opposed, even though both her parents, like most Victorian country-house people, were enthusiastic about hunting, and George Meredith was a member of the South Shropshire Hunt. Did this lead to any tension between Mary and her father? Perhaps, but according to members of the Meredith family, no real shadow ever fell between them – while Mary was firm in her own attitude, she tried to be forebearing when her father and brothers took part in a meet or a shoot. However she was developing a characteristic independence of spirit and held tenaciously to her very definite views, proving that she was no mere imitator of her father or anyone else, and was influenced only where her own innate tendencies lay. Neither was she hesitant, even as a girl, in making her views known to the close circle of family which comprised her world : she had an equally fierce aversion to the killing of animals for food, and refused to eat meat when it was put on her plate, verbal tussles with Alice showing only who had the stronger will. So when very young, Mary became a vegetarian and always remained one, idealistic-ally pronouncing in an essay that she longed for the day when 'the corpses of the defencless will be seen no more on the tables of those who profess the gospel of love'.

And hunting led to a disaster in the family. Near Wenlock Edge in 1895, Alice fell from her horse during a hunt and suffered fairly serious spinal injury. After this accident Mary's position as eldest daughter became one of real responsibility, especially when her own schooling was completed. Five children had been born to the Merediths in the seven years between 1887–94 : Alice Muriel in 1887; Edward Walter Kenneth in 1888; then George Douglas, Olive Marion and, lastly, John Henry Mervyn. While Mrs Meredith was fully engaged in nursery and household, she did not have time, nor, it seems, much inclination to develop a close relationship with Mary; and Mary, on the other hand, so secure in her father's love, neither needed nor demanded much from her mother. She became very devoted to her young brothers and sisters, taking a maternal, protective attitude towards them. Sharing with her father his 'unfailing delight' in the children, they would discuss together the development of the young ones, and the little incidents that occurred during the day. Throughout the remainder of her girlhood Mary, as Kenneth Meredith put it, was 'helping to teach and guide them, plan treats, make fun, ease away any tensions and small troubles'.

Alice's injuries were serious enough to keep her in bed for many long months and even when she recovered sufficiently to move about her room, it was in a wheel-chair. She remained more or less an invalid for the rest of her life, often an invalid in mental attitude as much as in physical condition. At this period she stayed resolutely in her bedroom for five years, this partly a psychological withdrawal. Consequently the children saw very little of her, a remote mother, held in awe and feared for her stern, sharp manner. Every morning and evening they would be paraded solemnly into her room for formal greeting and inspection; never outwardly maternal, she became increasingly formidable, questioning or scrutinising them with her penetrating, critical stare. In spite of being confined to her room Alice had an uncanny knack of knowing when the children had done something wrong!

To the little Merediths Mary seemed 'a mother and sister combined', as Kenneth in particular never forgot. We see this in a retrospective poem she wrote in 1919 for the birthday of 'Duss' (George Douglas), recapturing an incident from his boyhood when a 'birthday photograph' was taken:

> I see you stand, a sturdy little lad
> In your new suit, the sunlight on your head,
> Watching the camera with your earnest eyes;
> For thence would come (the photographer had said)
> For good boys, sweets. But soon your eyes grew sad,
> And soon you frowned in puzzled, pained surprise.
> You had been so good a boy, quite free from blame,
> Yet from the obstinate camera no sweets came!
>
> In such an hour, so bitterly deceived,
> Did it comfort you that one stood by and grieved?
> Someone who thought the sweets well-earned, and knew
> Whoever was in fault, it was not you.   (*51*, p. 51)

Dressing the children, planning their games, writing little plays for them to act, and stories and poems to read to them, Mary loved to be the organiser. Only one of her first stories has survived – 'Clematisa and Percival', written when she was thirteen, 'in a neat and confident script'. Often she was seen in the drives with her troupe of little followers. Each year she took them to hunt for the first snowdrops clustered under the trees :

> Ah, hush ! Tread softly through the rime,
> For there will be a blackbird singing, or a thrush.
> Like coloured beads the elm-buds flush :
> All the trees dream of leaves and flowers and light.
> And see ! The northern bank is much more white
> Than frosty grass, for now is snowdrop time.
>
> (*PSJ*, p. 39)

There were picnics in the woods on the Edge, Mary pointing out the different wild flowers, birds, trees. The bluebell picnic was a favourite. While the children ran at hare-and-hounds and other games, Mary sat watching in the hyacinthine grasses. No doubt she reflected then on 'blue . . . the rarest colour' which, as she writes in her essay 'The Beauty of Colour', is 'only lent to earth' in 'blue expanses – reflections in water, the cobalt of distance'. Looking to the sky she found 'endless, satisfying blue . . . in impalpable space', the 'roaming-place' where 'the mystic . . . launches his spirit'. Expressing the intense yearning she experienced then, initial mystical intuition and desire, she tells us :

> Often a flash of sapphire in water, a shade of turquoise in the sky, will strike across the heart with an inexplicable pang. It is not sorrow; it is more than joy; it is at once the realisation of a perfect thing, the fear that we may never see it again, and the instinct that urges us to ascend through the known beauty to the unknown which is both the veil and the voice that summons beyond it. (*PSJ*, p. 207)

Keenly, and at an early age like Keats, she experienced this 'realisation of a perfect thing'; and keenly too she felt already the contrasts in life, that which stood in stark opposition to beauty and which she sensed in her own landscape – those sometimes tenuous, sometimes powerful emanations of what seemed menacing, primeval, and perhaps evil at once. So, in the woods of the

Edge, the children ran at hare-and-hounds, innocent and un-
aware in the mock hunt; so, in these same woods, the wild savage
music of the real hunt resounded, striking a chill echo within her.

Towards the end of the Merediths' period at The Grange Miss
Edith Lory joined the family as Governess, taking over from Mrs
Lyons, who then devoted herself to Alice as lady companion. Miss
Lory, a young South Country woman of Scots descent, combined
a fund of common sense and firm kindliness with seemingly
inexhaustible reserves of patience and energy : in short, exactly
the type of governess required for the young Merediths. She
would eventually teach all six of them. Muriel and Kenneth
were already about to begin formal lessons, while it was thought
that Mary, then in her eleventh year, would benefit from the
guidance of a younger governess with a more vigorous approach.
   At first Mary was reserved though polite to the new governess.
Recalling, years afterwards, these first impressions of 'little
Gladys', Miss Lory said :

> I saw at once that she had a very sweet nature, and, next to the
> father whom she adored, she was the most unselfish of a fine-
> natured household. She was devoted to her younger brothers and
> sisters, and her care of them gave her an old-fashioned motherly
> way as a girl. I helped her with her studies for the next four
> years. She was always ready to learn.

Always ready to learn – and equally, always ready to be outdoors
in the fresh meadows under wide Shropshire skies, as Miss Lory
realised before long. If her lessons went on after class time, the
governess would notice 'a pair of frank eyes' staring with dis-
concerting steadiness.
   'What are you looking at Gladys?' she would ask.
   'The clock. It's several minutes after twelve, when we were to
stop.'
   'But I wish to finish this point before we leave the lesson this
morning . . .'
   The gaze was unwavering, eyes staring fixedly at the clock.
Mary, like her mother, could be irritatingly exact and precise
when it suited her, although on other occasions she seemed, like
her father, to have no time sense at all. These traits became more
accentuated in adult life. Miss Lory observed her eldest pupil's

unusually independent spirit and the streak of obstinacy which often emerged in dealings with her mother. Mary, for instance, would water the flowers and plants because she liked to, but when Alice ordered her to do it she rebelled against 'being *told* to do what she would have done anyway' – and so, contrarily, she would not do the watering until later when she relented.

It was Miss Lory's love of good literature and Mary's eagerness to expand her own knowledge of it which unquestionably helped their relationship to develop in the early stages. 'Gladys would sit by the hour while I read Shakespeare to her, and she grew to love the plays more than anything in literature,' Miss Lory recalled, and certainly this 'regard for Shakespeare' helped to 'foster her writing'. Shyness overcome, when Mary was 'drawn out', especially discussing literature or history, she could be remarkably fluent and penetrating. *Extempore* she could quote at length from the major poets.

The smaller Merediths, unable to pronounce Miss Lory's name (they were born tongue-tied), called her 'Mi-Noni', and this was adopted by everyone as her nickname. In a similar way Mary (Gladys) had become 'Gagga'. Gradually the two developed an affectionate friendship. The good-natured Minoni, although a conventional middle class governess, 'sensible and unsentimental' in outlook, had a sense of humour which greatly appealed to Mary's own – and this, of course, was an important factor in bringing them closer.

Admiring her pupil's creative work even then, Minoni became the proud possessor of an album containing some of Mary's first poems (written from the age of six) and a few paintings (signed Gladys Meredith). She had vivid recollections of Mary's creative zeal – arranging charades and plays to amuse her brothers and sisters, boldly ransacking her mother's wardrobes and chests for silk clothing in which to dress them as fairy characters or flowers – poppy, primrose, forget-me-not, daffodil. An appropriate verse would be pinned on the child, who would be encouraged to learn and recite it (not always successfully). A photograph of Mervyn on the rear lawn at The Grange, shows a bright, happy face above one of Mary's improvised costumes. Sometimes she arranged the children as characters from *Alice in Wonderland*, and Miss Lory remembered how charming they looked – 'exactly like Tenniel's drawings'. Even when forbidden by her mother to raid the wardrobes, Mary forged ahead, cheerily disobedient, determined to get what she wanted, emerging in amazing outfits.

A photograph taken when she was fourteen or fifteen was an excellent likeness according to Miss Lory and members of the family. It captured perfectly her expression – showing sensitiveness, integrity, a hint of humour – and determination. Mingled in her highly wrought nature were qualities which would not make life easy. Blessed or cursed with the finest of sensibilities and apprehensions, she was compounded of dualities (later reflected in her writing), seemingly contradictory extremes particularly irritating to her mother who could neither understand nor cope with them. Sometimes Mary's burning sense of fairness led her into difficulties. Exceedingly conscientious herself, she expected the same from others – once when one of her young sisters complained of being 'not very well' and was excused from lessons only to be heard playing in an upstairs room, Mary insisting this was 'not fair' demanded action from Miss Lory and was satisfied when her unfortunate sister was dosed with quinine. Yet she was desperately anxious to be needed, eager to be of service, and concerned if the feelings of others were hurt. Once, after a harsh scolding from Alice, Kenneth had hidden himself away sobbing bitterly, 'nobody cares'. Then, sensing Mary sidling up to him softly (this was her characteristic movement), he heard her words – 'Somebody does'. And when her governess was tired, she liked to surprise her with a cup of hot milk, or tea and biscuits. In some aspects of her nature, Mary resembled Keats who, in the words of his friend Bailey, 'allowed for people's faults more than any man I ever knew'. Mary's swift insight made her quick to see faults and equally quick to allow for them.

As Mary grew older, her friendship with Minoni deepened; and it was to Minoni she came, years later, her health broken, emotionally and spiritually devastated, death near. But there was no note of pain in these early days. Only a vulnerability latent in her total responsiveness to life, her open eagerness for experience . . . 'Take me and break me/Hurt me or love me/But throne me not lonely and safely above thee/Sweet Life!'

Minoni did a great deal to widen Mary's literary horizons at a very impressionable age. At least two of the writers she introduced were to have an important influence on Mary's style and thought: Thomas Hardy, whose novels, especially *Tess of the*

D'Urbevilles, Mary admired and came to know thoroughly; and Richard Jefferies, whose spiritual autobiography *The Story of my Heart* (1883) became one of her best loved books during youth, his lyrical writing greatly appealing to her, since nature was his inspiration.

Minoni taught Mary for nearly four years until it was decided that she should go to boarding school, to one of the girls' 'finishing schools' which were becoming increasingly popular among the middle class in the late Victorian period. These establishments are typified (although allowing for some exaggeration), by Miss Twinkleton's seminary in Dickens's *Edwin Drood*, or Bush House in Mrs Ewing's *Six to Sixteen* – schools run without much imagination, the emphasis on social graces rather than learning (which tended to be parrot-fashion). Mrs Walmsley's Finishing School at Southport, apparently rather better than the average, was recommended to the Merediths by a friend of the family. Mary was sent there at fourteen or thereabouts.

How was she affected by this first experience of separation from home and countryside? Unfortunately we have no evidence. But it cannot be doubted that she missed acutely the immediate family circle at The Grange, set in her larger charmed circle of Shropshire surroundings. And Southport, a flat coastal town, with vast beaches like desert plains and the distant grey horizon of the Irish Sea, presented her with a complete contrast to the 'hills of home'. Here she would have to seek harder for beauty; here was no green world. There were no woods brimming with birdsong and secret life; and the only hills were sandhills over which sounded poignantly, intermittently, the call of gulls. Yet her senses, delicately pitched, exquisitely exercised during a childhood spent around Wenlock Edge, were quick to catch any glimpse of beauty: 'Among the most desolate sandhills you may find in July acres of wax-white pyrola . . . covering the plains between the lonely ridges of harsh, grey grass.' This she wrote later in an essay. Her imaginative power was developing and she stored her fresh perceptions – the seeds of imagination which were later to germinate and flower in simile and metaphor.

It is impossible to gauge how much or how little Mary gained intellectually at Mrs Walmsley's, though she is known to have astonished her teachers by her mental energy and thoroughness – remarkable even by Victorian standards. She excelled at French and won a special prize; but on one occasion her marks were so consistently high that they were queried by the teacher and, on coming back to The Grange, Mary, who so loathed unfairness, was fiercely indignant, telling her parents how she had been suspected of cheating. This, in itself, is a bleak comment on Mrs. Walmsley's, and at the same time it gives some indication of Mary's reaction when her honesty was questioned, her sense of justice outraged.

One of the happier aspects of Mary's Southport schooling was the development of her first close relationship outside the family – with Beatrice Cannon, a school companion with whom she often stayed at Southport. The two remained good friends for many years, until Beatrice's tragically early death. They enjoyed organising the kind of musical evening which was the delight of Victorian families, Beatrice, who sang beautifully, accompanied by Mary who played the piano moderately well (especially Beethoven sonatas).

When travelling through Liverpool to and from Southport, Mary thought of the slave ships which, in the previous century, had anchored there, human cargoes unloaded across the Atlantic (renewing her characteristic response of passionate pity on reading *Uncle Tom's Cabin*). At the Walker Gallery she saw a painting which gripped her imagination – Sir Edward Poynter's 'Faithful Unto Death', depicting a Roman guard standing at his post while Pompeii falls under the red hot lava. Vividly expressive of the pathos of humanity, compelling admiration for the soldier, loyal to the last yet with fear in his dark eyes, Poynter's painting, so suggestive of doomed humanity triumphing in spirit, was for Mary a pictorial experience she never forgot. Many years later, writing the novel *Seven for a Secret*, she used her impression of the Roman soldier's face and character in her portrayal of Robert Rideout, the staunch, self-sacrificing lover who was prepared to give all, even life itself, for the self-absorbed immature Gillian :

> On the way they looked into shops, and Gillian saw a picture of a Roman soldier standing in a glare of light. Underneath was written : 'Faithful unto death' . . . She bought it. 'Look ! It's like you, Robert !' Robert looked into the face of the soldier . . . It comforted him . . . to dream that there might come a time when he would stand amid the red ruin of his life defending the helpless, childish soul of Gillian.   (pp. 82–3)

A somewhat idealised hero; and a somewhat idealised conception of love. Tragically Mary was to learn the truth of the words of Mechthild of Magdeburg, a medieval mystic, that 'the higher the love, the greater the pain', that the highest love is also the rarest, that what to her was actuality, to others was only concept or ideal. Herein her peak, herein her dark ravine.

Before Mary had completed her schooling at Southport, George Meredith decided to sell The Grange. Already after a phase of poor health he had closed his boarding school and retired from teaching. Rather unwillingly also, he had sold the farm. The cattle were sent off for auction and unfortunately for the Merediths their untrustworthy bailiff collected the proceeds of the sale and was never seen again. This blow plunged George into despondency. Since Alice's accident things had fallen somewhat apart for him : her brisk efficiency and thriftiness in household affairs had been crucial as he always found it difficult to keep money, generously disposing of it on all sides. This facet of his nature was drawn by Mary in the character of John Arden who, like his prototype, 'was very sensitive about his business faculty, not having any'. Mary herself was, in this respect, a curious mixture of both parents – endowed with her mother's business ability and a generosity that surpassed her father's; like Alice, firm about her rights, and like George, giving away what was hers to give. Before leaving The Grange, George wrote a short verse regretting the closing of this period :

> Times grew hard as time went on
> And Health and Wealth and Hope were gone.
> His head was sick, his heart was sore,
> His dream of life was fled.
> So 'Farmer George' exists no more
> For 'Farmer George' is dead.

The Grange was sold in 1896, the Merediths moving to another large but less expensive country house at Stanton-upon-Hine Heath, north of Shrewsbury and some fifteen miles from Much Wenlock. A sad departure from the familiar home and its surrounding loveliness : for Mary especially as her fourteen years at The Grange had been richly formative – the vital nurturing period when a fusion of influences, an ever-increasing awareness, brought her to the threshold of mystical consciousness and to her essentially poetic vision of life.

Always she was to be drawn back to the South Shropshire hill country, but she was never to know again the complete security that had been hers at The Grange. The gradual ejection from Eden had begun.

3
No Primrose Path
1896–1902

The Woodlands,
Stanton-upon-Hine Heath

'We go to plant sweet love,' she said,
'In pain's deep forest.' Then she pointed where
The dark trees loomed. I cried – 'Oh, soul – not so!
No spring of joy is there.'
She answered – 'None the less, at dawn we go.'

(*51*, pp. 26–7)

The mystical life is no primrose path but a continual struggle.
Roger Bastide (*The Mystical Life,* p. 83)

The Woodlands, now known as Harcourt Manor, tucked away in remote fields near Stanton, was described later by one of the Merediths as 'five miles from anywhere'. Approached by narrow lanes, it lies cupped in a fold of undulating pasture land – a square Georgian house with Victorian additions, built of pale stone, facing South towards the far blue outline of hills which threaten always to disappear into distance and mist.

From the top of the incline where a long drive slopes down through the estate, banked on either side by woods, the Wrekin can be seen in 'glass-clear weather'. The drive branches off behind the manor to an impressive block of stables and coach house, and at the front to a lawn with an ancient mulberry which was the favourite swinging and climbing tree of the young Merediths. Now its boughs are supported by stout staves like an old villager on crutches. An enclosed garden gave a feeling of hedged secrecy in what was otherwise a very open aspect.

At The Woodlands, serene and pastoral though it seemed, a series of catastrophies both of major and minor proportions occurred, bringing drama and upheaval to the Merediths and to

Mary in particular. Here, during the years from adolescence to young womanhood, she came to her first severe test of suffering and, as a result of this, to her first significant creative achievement.

Not long after the move to Stanton, Mary returned from Mrs Walmsley's to take her position as eldest daughter assuming a fuller responsibility and an increased share of duties. With Alice Meredith continuing her invalid's life upstairs, Mary was active in the management of the household, as well as helping her father and Minoni with the tuition of her brothers and sisters, though she found the keeping of discipline a strain. Physically she was developing into an attractive young woman, wearing her thick dark hair in a bun, a style which set off to advantage her fine straight features and expressive eyes. She was small – no more than five foot two – and her slimness was accentuated by the long skirts and high-collared blouses then fashionable. Frequently she wore her favourite mauve, a colour she described as 'neither of earth nor heaven'.[1] Becoming very aware of her appearance, she was pleased to be regarded as good-looking, though she had a secret longing for golden hair (as she told an interviewer years later, who asked what were 'the aspirations' of her youth).[2]

Mary's life at The Woodlands was fairly strenuous, not only teaching the children, but expending herself in their general care, always looking for new ways to amuse them. The charades and plays continued, and as each birthday came, she would organise everything around 'the little King or Queen of the day'.[2] There were explorations of the comparatively flat countryside around Stanton – sometimes on foot, sometimes in the ponytrap she had learned to handle expertly. And nearby, Hawkstone estate brimmed over with 'magic' in its extensive woods, small hills,

---

[1] Mauve – from 'The Beauty of Colour', *PSJ*, p. 205: 'I had two great aspirations. One was that one day I should be able to write real poetry, and the other that I might grow very beautiful and have golden hair, so that all the choir boys would fall in love with me': *T.P.'s and Cassell's Weekly*, 25 June 1925, p. 274. It is interesting that in her novels she sometimes makes 'yellow hair' emblematic of weak character – Lily in *The Golden Arrow*, 'straw coloured', lacking emotional depth, avid for the 'small change of sex', who tries to seduce Stephen (also golden-haired); the blonde Jancis in *Precious Bane*, envied by Prue. This prejudice, which Mary humorously acknowledged, also creeps into her reviews.

[2] Kenneth Meredith's recollections of Mary Webb: ms in the author's possession.

ruins, lake and a mysterious Grotto[3] – the original of the strange Grotto with shell-covered walls in *The House in Dormer Forest*. On winter evenings she would read stories to the little circle, frequently her own.

Always a light sleeper, she rested little, up before sunrise, determined not to miss 'the dove-grey' time before dawn and spending 'long, solitary hours', continuing that ardent communion with nature which had begun at Wenlock Edge, impelled now by a growing need. Wanting to explore further, she was delighted when her father bought her a bicycle. In the 1890s the 'safety bicycle', an improved speedier model, was becoming very popular, bringing a thrilling new freedom for young women – thereby liberated from chaperones and unnecessary petticoats. With great enthusiasm Mary pedalled along the lanes to and from The Woodlands, enjoying the exhilaration of the down-hill run to the house, and setting off with a sense of anticipation on journeys to remote parts of a remote countryside. 'Gladys has gone off on her own' became a familiar Meredith expression, implying also an acceptance of her independence as eventually no one questioned her whereabouts. A few years afterwards, when in her twenties, she would go away to the meres or the South Shropshire hills, sometimes for two weeks at a time, taking writing materials with her and nobody except her father would know quite where she was. Alice, however, did not understand Mary's need 'to disappear' into such 'lost and forgotten places' (to use the country phrase) – and to go unchaperoned was both dangerous and unconventional.

'The full woods overflow/Among the meadow's gold . . .' In her Shropshire Eden, keen sensory awareness heightening her response, Mary was utterly absorbed, taking in the subtlest qualities, the minutest details. Later on, when she met leading writers and critics of her day, those who came to know her personally were always astonished by the sharpness of her senses. Walter de la Mare, for instance, described them as 'rarely delicate',[4] and Martin Armstrong commenting on this 'microscopic keenness',

[3] The Hawkstone Grotto was described by the eighteenth-century Shropshire poet John Salmon, with its 'rocky mantled dome', fossils and 'various shells from every shore'.

[4] Introduction, *PSJ*, p. 15. 'She could – most rewarding of feats – seize the momentary.'

affirmed that she could 'detect an exquisite perfume in flowers which, for most of us, are scentless'. He related that she told him she 'had never taken to smoking because she was afraid she might lose the power of enjoying the scent of flowers'. Of trees she could discern the different odours, 'the perfume thrushes smell'; of flowers every slight gradation of movement – in her own words, each 'pale shadow of a gesture . . . as lovely, as inevitable as the flight of swans'. And always she watched birds intently, listening, distinguishing their 'songs that pass and come again'. Hers was an ever richer understanding and receptivity – and few can have been so exquisitely equipped to receive.

Henry James's comment 'To live over other people's lives is nothing unless we live over their perceptions, live over the growth, the varying intensity of the same – since it is by these they themselves lived' is of particular relevance here. In delineating the evolution of a creative artist such as Mary Webb, it is important to discern the point at which perception became the bridge to creative reality. At this critically formative stage of late adolescence, her cumulative perceptions led directly to creative fruition, her potentialities, literary and spiritual, developing towards a synthesis.

When years later she described Amber Darke's response to nature in *The House in Dormer Forest*, Mary was unquestionably speaking of her own 'going out into the green world' which 'had in it something of a religious rite'. And from this she knew that 'the understanding of beauty is a priesthood' (p. 274). This she had learned very early on. Going beyond her initial conscious perception of the transient 'beauty seen', she reached an apprehension of the imperishable 'beauty unseen', a beauty which, she assures us, 'is not less real because its revelations are subtle and its essence beyond the reach of the senses'. Nature was her book of revelation, a spiritual revelation through spontaneous response to the loveliness of the physical world – and this, for Mary, meant Shropshire. A highly specialised personality, she was what Shropshire made her: in her life and art so much stemmed from the intimacy and intensity of this relationship, a relationship at the deepest level of her being, as vital and powerful as a love bond with a person, a union which was to endure for life. This fact is central to an understanding of her. As Hilda L. Addison tells us, Mary's passion for Shropshire 'absorbed her so completely that everything was in some way related to it – her understanding of physical as of spiritual experience, her gift for friendship and her grasp of religion. Every by-path in her mind led finally to this centre' (Addison, p. 82).

Here too was the source of her developing mysticism, which began as nature mysticism. During this stage at Stanton, she was developing an inward hearing like that of Ruysbroeck and Emerson, listening, as she said, 'not with the ear but with the soul'. So she attained 'a vision of the Soul of the World' – the immanent reality. All things around her in nature were at once symbol and embodiment of a living, creative truth which she still thought of, at this period, as the living God.

Also fascinated by the factual realities of nature (the intellectual counterpart of her intuitive penetration), Mary was avidly curious, using every reference book available, learning the scientific terms for the species of flowers, herbs, plants, as well as the country names. Much of her conversation with old cottagers, herbalists and gardeners concerned nature and country lore; already at Stanton she was acquiring a specialist's knowledge (seen later in her reviews of natural history books for the *Spectator*). And throughout her future literary work, as any page of the novels and poems reveals, her naturalist's eye serves the concerns of her poetic imagination. The effectiveness of her descriptions is augmented by detail precisely observed and charged with poetic feeling.

This area around Stanton was excellent fox-hunting country, and at The Woodlands Mary was brought into even closer contact with the hunt, with all the ferocity of the scarlet and black, and the sounds which she described later as 'some of the most horrible of the English countryside'. In fact the meet often assembled at The Woodlands itself, hounds, horses and a concourse of huntsmen milling around the courtyard. On one occasion, a hound found its way into the kitchen and reappeared with a leg of mutton in its mouth, whereupon George Meredith, quick to make a pun, told the Master of the Hounds: 'If they've come for the meet, they've got it.'

The pack was kept not far north of Stanton and each day at feeding time the barking and yelping which rose to a crescendo could be heard quite distinctly from The Woodlands. And to

Mary this baying seemed to rouse 'the shivering echoes', to be like 'the death-pack', the phantom hounds of legend raging in the darkness, streaming by with the mythical Black Huntsman. In reality too, death did come in the night, ironically to the Keeper of the Hounds: he was torn to pieces and his bones picked clean by the dogs when he went out in his dressing-gown to check on them. George Meredith, telling the family about this local tragedy, explained how the pack had turned on the Keeper by mistake. To Mary, some twenty years before writing *Gone to Earth*, hounds and the hunt already were symbolical of savagery and fear, of primitive collective frenzy, the frenzy of the pack – any pack, human or animal. Emphatically she saw the hunt as representative of cruelty, and cruelty she now equated with evil. Later she was to react passionately against the cruelty and suffering of the Crucifixion, rejecting the doctrine of spiritual redemption through sacrifice. Like Hazel Woodus in *Gone to Earth*, she refused 'to be died for', refused to accept that sin could be 'washed white' by shedding of Christ's blood. But at this date, although developing her own views, she was not yet in rebellion against Church dogma and the central concept of a crucified Christ. And she had not yet worked out her views about good and evil – a central preoccupation and theme later on.

This Stanton period was, in fact, Mary's most devotional. A regular communicant at St Andrew's, the sixteenth-century parish church, she sang there with her father in the mixed choir and took a class at Sunday school. The Merediths two or three times on Sunday occupied their pew, Mary at one end, her father at the other, the children between them, faces shiningly clean, wearing their stiff 'best'. But immersed though she was in the institutional religion which had played so dominant a part in the lives of her parents and grandparents, nevertheless those characteristics which in George Meredith had led him to resist a career in the Church were in Mary already pulling her in a direction that would lead, before long, to a total abandonment of orthodoxy.

In spite of innate shyness, Mary went visiting around Stanton, spending many hours in the cottages, and distributing the parish magazine to outlying parts. Gradually gaining confidence in her own literary ability, she contributed articles and poems to this magazine – and these represented her first small successes. Encouraged, she continued to write, though she also continued to tear up most of the poems, unsparingly critical of her own efforts at a time when she was steeping herself in the major poets. Only one of these Stanton poems is extant : entitled 'Spring' and dated 1898, it reflects the overwhelming effect the season has upon her.[5] A picture is given of the quiet, pastoral setting of The Woodlands which recalls Goldsmith's scene of Auburn before the desertion. There are 'hoary apple trees', the scent of blossom is 'mixed as in a dream', sounds are intensified – 'the drowsy hum of bees', 'the laughter of some children gathering flowers', and from Stanton village 'a far distant bell . . . chiming the hour'. The young poet Gladys Meredith, trying to impower her words with her feeling for nature is, at the same time, concerned with form, concentrating on rhyme and metre. In this example of her early work we see her learning her craft, and though immature, the poetic emotion presses through, anticipating the power of her later poems, as this stanza illustrates :

> Now suddenly there breaks upon the ear
> The bleating of the sheep upon that hill –
> With sunlight fair;
> And then (so low that we can scarcely hear)
> Comes from more distant fields the answer, till
> It fills the air.

The sheep referred to in this poem were those in George Meredith's flock which he acquired soon after moving to this sheep-raising area, loving 'the sad eyed ewes' and the lambs with their 'small palpitating bodies'. Undoubtedly it was this aspect of her father that influenced Mary's future depiction of him as the compassionate shepherd, John Arden, who thinks of God as 'The Flockmaster', a personification of love, whose fold includes all. And to Deborah Arden her father is 'a symbol of The Flockmaster' : just as for Mary her own adored father was a human Flockmaster. She relied increasingly on his love – 'the great affirmative' – for her the central, meaningful relationship, satisfying, enriching, secure. He was her lode-star. Here was oneness, wholeness.

As Kenneth Meredith said, Mary and her father were 'twin souls', at one in their poetic and imaginative response to life, and almost constant companions at this period. We see George Meredith as he was in later years, in Mary's remarkably vivid descriptions of John Arden – 'spare and tall with blue gaze and white hair', his eyes 'like cwm water', his brown face running 'into kindly smiles as easily as a brook runs in its accustomed bed'. With her father, Mary went to Ightfield where they tended the graves, to Leighton, visiting Kathleen Powis, the Meredith nurse and, most often, to Shrewsbury where she was to learn much of the heaven and hell of life. Mary loved this old town ringed by the liquid horseshoe of Severn. Already she knew it well, the narrow, twisting streets and leaning black-and-white 'gossip gables', the sandstone castle, statues of Charles Darwin and Robert Clive – and, not least, 'the busy market'. She was intrigued by Shrewsbury's ancient past, her father's talk of its Celtic, Saxon and medieval origins kindling her imagination and firing still more that strong affection for the 'Silverton' of her future novels and poems. While Mary was eagerly immersed in 'the vivid present', as she put it, she was always, at the same time, keenly aware of what Henry James called 'the conscious past'.

Mary's sense of the flow of history, of being immersed in a continuum, intensified as the nineteenth century drew to its close, the new century dawned, and Queen Victoria died in the bitterly cold January of 1901 – mourning was observed everywhere with muffled pealing of bells, black drapes stark against the snow, the prevalent feeling both loss and anticipation, poised at the end of the longest reign in British history and at the beginning of the Edwardian era. Mary had a strong intuitive feeling for history and such a feeling is a subtle transmutation of a feeling for life. She was to express explicitly in the Foreword to *Precious Bane* this sense which permeates her entire work: 'The past is only the present become invisible and mute . . . We are tomorrow's past. Even now we slip away . . . we, that were the new thing, gather magic as we go.'

In the words of François Mauriac, 'childhood and youth alone is enough to provide a born novelist with an immense amount of literary nourishment. Nobody can stop the flow of the river that flows from us.' An observation which can be underlined when applied to Mary Webb, the environment of her childhood and youth carried into adult life. Although always a poet, she did not become a novelist until her mid-thirties: given a rich nurturing, her fictional art was to be imbued with her fine apprehensions, her pointed perceptions, the texture of her life informing her writing throughout. And 'the flow' in novels, once untapped, was not to be quenched, a creative uprush from the deepest levels and from foundations set in Shropshire, in all that her surroundings could give.

During those first years at The Woodlands she was blissfully happy at the centre of a close-knit family group to which she was entirely devoted. Life, for Mary, would never be dull 'five miles from anywhere'. Though she could be very good company, she did not like, and tried to avoid, social occasions. As Hilda Addison has emphasised, 'she did not easily transfer her affections outside her home circle . . . Utterly selfless and anxious to help others, she was at the same time slow to break through her reserve and admit newcomers into the confidence of real friendship' (Addison, pp. 10–11). Having her father's companionship she neither needed nor looked for any other. Yet this love for him was perilously acute and strongly focused. What of the future? And how would this extraordinarily deep attachment influence her love relationships in years to come? For the present, while she was needed so thoroughly by those most important to her, she found complete contentment and fulfilment in her golden sphere of home, father, countryside.

Yet Mary was coming ever closer to 'pain's deep forest'. The note of approaching disaster sounded first with the drowning, in a pool near the house, of six lambs from George Meredith's flock. This upset everyone and seemed an ill omen. Then came the 'death' of Mrs Lyons, a macabre episode, when the Merediths went into mourning, a gloom and sorrow on the entire household. For the children this was their first confrontation with death. Arrangements for the burial were made. Then, shortly before the funeral, Mrs Lyons twitched her little finger. Fortunately this slight movement of the 'corpse' was noticed and a doctor summoned. He announced that she was not dead after all, but in a deep coma. Mrs Lyons was removed from the coffin and later recovered consciousness, living on for another ten years. Her 'death' subsequently became a family joke, yet at the time when it occurred was a traumatic event and one which stayed vividly in Mary's memory. Writing *The House in Dormer Forest* some twenty years later, she inserted the incident, adapting it adroitly and with humorous effect into the typically gruesome-comic dialogue of an old country-woman servant, Mrs Gosling, an expert in the laying out of 'good corpses'. Mrs Gosling, one of Mary Webb's brilliantly suggested and vivified minor characters declares:

> 'I'd liefer a funeral than an outing! I mind when old Mr Mucklewick deceived me sore that way. He went into a swound, and they took un for jead. So they made un a coffin. He was allus bone-idle, was Mr Mucklewick, and he stayed in that swound till they came to nail un down. It was touch and go, then! But he stirred the little finger, so they knew their trouble was for nought.'
>
> (p. 270)

The next crisis at The Woodlands had more serious repercussions and distressed Mary acutely since it concerned her eldest brother Kenneth, with whom she was close in spite of the seven years difference in their ages. Lively, fun-loving, he often teased her about her 'iron pony' – the bicycle she kept in the stables. He himself preferred real ponies and was an excellent young horseman, very proud of his dapple-grey on which he enjoyed cantering ahead of his father, who would follow in the horse and trap. One fine afternoon Kenneth's pony bolted. Kenneth, unseated, his foot caught in the stirrup, was dragged along the stony road for a few miles before the pony was pulled up at a farm. George Meredith followed, horrified to find the semiconscious Kenneth covered in mud. Tenderly he brought the boy home in the trap and a doctor was called from Wem. Kenneth was desperately ill for a time – he had concussion and seven stones were removed from his scalp which had to be stitched where the pony's hoof had driven in. The doctor called twice a day during the fortnight that followed. Fortunately Kenneth was a tough, wiry eleven-year-old, and he survived. Covered in plaster from head to foot, he was tended by an anxious, sympathetic Mary who, when he was feeling better, read to him and encouraged him to eat. Alternately she looked after her brother and tried to comfort her father who was devastated.

The near-tragedy affected Mary deeply, giving edge to her awareness of the unpredictability of existence. 'Gaunt foreboding', that sudden dread and sense of insecurity, later to haunt her increasingly, had begun to take hold. She was learning from experience that in the continual flux of life only change is certain.

Not many months after the accident it was decided that Kenneth and Douglas should be sent to boarding school. Ellesmere College was chosen, a Shropshire school of good reputation in 'the meres district', some ten miles north of Stanton. This decision was symptomatic of a change in Alice Meredith's outlook. The children were growing up rapidly, neither George Meredith nor Mary were disciplinarians, and it seemed to Alice that an increasing unruliness prevailed which even Minoni was ineffective in curbing. And probably she had never forgotten the occasion some years previously when she had chastised the younger children for, as she thought, pretending not to know· their work, only to be confronted by a defiant Mary, upset by their tears, arguing that since Alice was not *inside* of them, how could she possibly know they were pretending?

Without the slightest hint or warning Alice reappeared at the breakfast table one morning, suddenly terminating the five-year retreat in her bedroom. From this time onwards she would resume her position as Mother in the centre of family life. The apparent arbitrariness of her 'recovery' had behind it that characteristic thoroughness in action once a decision was made. Having made up her mind to take a firm grip on the household again, Alice lost no time in doing so. It was a psychological readjustment rather than a return of physical health, as she remained a partial invalid for a number of years afterwards. But her abrupt reappearance greatly surprised, even shocked, the children. A frigid atmosphere seemed to descend at once, her severe attitude having a dampening effect on everyone's spirits and her 'economies' making life less interesting as well as less free than it had been when Mary was in charge. Any small extravagances were now stopped. One of the first changes the children noticed was in puddings, Mrs Meredith ordering the cook to make them 'plain but wholesome'.

Whatever the general effect of Alice's resumption of control, for Mary it involved a definite shift in personal focus. She was relieved of tasks she had regarded not as onerous duties but joyful undertakings. She had been the centre of a busy round world of her own creation. Now this was disrupted, the circle broken.

And though their relationship did not alter, her father now had less time to spend with her.

Mary, at nineteen, became increasingly solitary, serious and quiet. She had come to that crucial phase of development, the *fine pointe* of moulding, in which her mature personality – and her literary art – would evolve from a matrix of influences: forces of her inner being working from within; the pressure of circumstances acting from without. Her basic disposition intuitive, emotional, mystical, was moving her into positive channels, inward towards a new circle of wholeness. While to those around her she seemed ever more shut up inside herself, in actuality this 'land within' was a world of ineffable unity, a unity or wholeness experienced in oneness with nature, a unity lost in the multiplicity, fragmentation and uncertainty of everyday life. But at the same time she was heading precipitously towards her first serious physical collapse.

Nervously strained by the build-up of crises, emotional shocks and pressures of family life combined with the other activities into which she flung herself so whole-heartedly, Mary – never physically strong – was becoming very thin and pale, her appetite even poorer than usual. For passionately-held reasons, as we have seen, she was a vegetarian, with no concern for her bodily needs. Already anaemia was developing, but she ignored all signs, all warning signals. Spending longer periods in her bedroom writing, reading, she was living, with increasing intensity, a life of the imagination and spirit. As her impulse towards poetic expression and the articulation of her inner experience was deepening, so was her acute joy and absorption in her Shropshire surroundings, in the timeless beauty of nature there, this 'beauty with its deathless seed of love'. And love is the key to her mysticism: for her, beauty and love are synonymous, expressions of eternal truth. She was responding with a pantheistic mystical rapture to the indwelling creative force she apprehended in all living things. This experience of ephemeral oneness produced an 'inexhaustible desire' for more permanent oneness, an unquenchable yearning – essential in mystical progress – for ever closer, more lasting union with that absolute reality or beauty or love. These were total re-entries into Eden, but a fleeting Eden. Such fervid extensions, beyond the senses, in touch with areas of being normally inaccessible, were life-enhancing. Life-enhancing but also exhausting. The ardour had to be paid for. Mary's emotional and spiritual intensity took an early toll on her frail body and at the outset of adult life she began to pay the physical penalty.[6]

The first severe illness took hold soon after her twentieth birthday. It was early spring 'and the pointed leaves/Came swiftly in green fire to meet the sun' – in this awakening Shropshire world, Mary was gripped by that 'mysterious mingled joy and pain', a pitch of exaltation. She was cycling further – too far. Once absorbed 'deep in leaf and blossom', invariably she stayed for hours then would cycle home at a furious pace, this overstraining the last in an accumulation of stresses that caused her delicate health to break. She collapsed. And the disease from which she was to suffer for the rest of her life now showed itself devastatingly.

Her heart and gastric system were seriously affected, the underlying cause being the onset of Graves' Disease (thyrotoxicosis or exophthalmic goitre), about which little was then known. At that date there was no cure for this endocrine disorder in which the thyroid gland becomes overactive causing high temperature, nervousness, quickened metabolism, gastric difficulties. The visible effects are equally distressing : the enlarged thyroid gland seen as a lump or goitre at the base of the throat, and together with this, a condition of exophthalmos – eyes prominent, protruding with a frightened staring look.

No stretch of the imagination is needed to understand Mary's horror on realising these alterations in her appearance. At first, however, she was too ill to know, so critically ill she was thought to be dying. The next six months were desperate – a complete prostration. Long periods of fever exhausted her and she was unable either to eat or drink properly, sometimes a cube of ice on her tongue all that she could take. There was little the doctors could do to help her, and George Meredith spent many anxious hours at her bedside in the late spring and summer of 1901.

When eventually she felt slightly stronger, she was brought downstairs on to a couch in the drawing room where she could look out to the distant hills of her childhood. She would gaze for

[6] Roger Bastide discussing pathological and psychological theories on mysticism stresses that the true mystics 'are not to be explained by their ailments . . . they are not active *because* of their ailments but in *spite* of them.'. *The Mystical Life*, pp. 179–80.

a long time then lapse into a sleep. On warm days the couch was brought out on the lawn under the trees. She would lie for hours, absorbing the scene around her, watching delicate movements of wings in the sunlight, listening intently to the silence and the stirrings of nature within it, to the leaves with their rise and fall like a never-coming tide. Gradually – very gradually – she felt restored.

Confined to her couch in the long convalescent stage, her thoughts ranged . . . days at The Grange, walks on The Edge, picnics, shouts echoing in the woods, the bluebell haze . . . and she read again her favourite books, and when she was tired Minoni would read aloud Shakespeare, her father the Bible.

Deeply distressed by the physical changes her illness had wrought, she was appalled and could not be comforted or reassured by anyone. Not even her father could convince her she was not the hideous figure she believed herself to be. There was indeed a disfiguring effect, her eyes now noticeably protrusive, a goitre low in her throat which though small would, she feared, grow larger as time went on; and her skin was pallid, her body excessively thin. Ultra-sensitive, she exaggerated in her mind these defects and always, from this time onwards, she was haunted by a deep sense of physical inferiority believing her 'ruinous mortal dwelling', as she called it, to be repulsive to others. She – so keenly appreciative of beauty – would have a dire struggle to come to terms with this marring of her own person.

She tried desperately to disguise the malformations. High-necked collars and frills covered her goitre and later, when the fashion changed, she would conceal it beneath enormous bows and tulle scarves. Wide-brimmed hats sheltered the upper part of her face and her dark hair was drawn low over her forehead to divert attention from her eyes. Impossible for her to know then that there would be long periods in future when, health improved, these visible effects of her disease would be scarcely noticeable. Her grey eyes, large and anxious, brimmed with life and expression – the degree of protrusion was to vary considerably according to her state of health. But though her features were still attractive (her smile warm and tender), Mary persisted in regarding herself as utterly unlovely. Shy, reserved, as she had been before, now she became painfully self-conscious, shutting herself away, fearing the shocked glance, the embarrassed recoil.

What were the long-term effects of the illness on her outlook and personality? It would be easy, of course, to depict melodramatically a bitter, warped woman, morbid, morose, tortured – and this at least one writer has done. But such an assessment of Mary would be an unjust falsification of the evidence supplied both by those who knew her closely and by her own writings. ' "We go to plant sweet love," she said/ "In pain's deep forest"...' If she shunned company, it was not because of self-pitying morbidity but rather that she was reluctant to offend by her appearance, wishing neither to give pain nor receive it; if she became a semi-recluse, it was not because she turned against humanity but rather that she turned increasingly to nature with an ever deepening dependence – here she found, as she expressed it, her 'sure harbour'. Unquestionably, though, she was ever after extremely vulnerable and insecure in her emotional life. And possibly this disease did (as some have thought), heighten her already acute sensibilities; most certainly it heightened her sensitivity, also depriving her of some of that spontaneous cheeriness (though not her wit and sense of humour) which was so marked a characteristic during girlhood. At first she felt despondency, the lassitude which follows a severe illness, particularly one of this kind in which recovery is slow. And in addition she was no longer able to go out at dawn or roam the fields at will – no one could have felt this deprivation more keenly.

Yet the virtual cutting off from nature helped to crystallise her thoughts about it: the positive was brought out of the situation, feelings of self-pity gradually yielding. From nature she had received already so deep an infusion of spiritual vitality and to nature she turned now in her mind. Using convalescence to write as well as read, she began to express in essays her thoughts, perceptions, observations – the creative result of her impregnation in Shropshire. Soon this became an impassioned flow, indirectly the product of illness and suffering: herein that ironic logic, leitmotif in her life.

A burning sincerity lay behind her desire to communicate, to extend somehow to humanity, a desire all the stronger because she was now physically withdrawn from outside contact. Minoni, an unfailing support, encouraged the writing as she knew how important this creative outlet could be at such an absolutely crucial stage to one so highly sensitive and imaginative. But while

Minoni was immensely impressed by Mary's literary ability, she could not have guessed then the ultimate outcome of this development: in writing these essays, Mary was discovering not just a life-line but her life-force.

As so often, the life leads us at once to the work, the interweaving of the fabric of her life and art having its real commencement from this period of suffering. And Mary's life from this time onwards was frequently one of desperate struggle. The next decade in particular would be chequered by illness – like Orpheus she was a singer because a sufferer. And it was in prose rather than in verse that she sang first what was her individual song in her individual voice.

The essay was, for her, a particularly satisfying medium. Here, in prose, she was not inhibited as in poetry (influenced by her father's style and the struggle for technical mastery). She found ample scope for her descriptive power and was able to express, directly or obliquely, her poetic vision. Caught up in prose writing, ideas long incubating within her poured out and she worked at the essays throughout the later part of her convalescence and afterwards. Although begun at Stanton, they were continued and revised at Meole Brace where the Merediths lived subsequently, and the series of nine related essays which she finally selected for publication can be regarded as her first complete prose work. It was eventually to be published in 1917 under the title *The Spring of Joy* – after she had become known as a novelist.

These essays, if looked at fairly closely, can contribute significantly to our understanding of Mary Webb. Even the briefest reading will reveal that here is a writer of unusual integrity, of compelling ardour. She has set out to illumine the way to neglected sources of vitality and inner strength, her own path to healing and wholeness. The central theme is indicated in the title of the opening essay, 'Vis Medicatrix Naturae': the 'healing power of nature', which is a 'spiritual healing'. Her touchstones are Joy, Beauty, Laughter. In the descriptive studies of motion, music, fragrance, form, shadow and colour, she reveals everywhere her remarkable poetic and spiritual intimacy with nature and the vision she was to embed later in her prose fiction.

This 'little book of healing' (her sub-title), is reminiscent of the work of Richard Jefferies, but the individual view she expresses, the spiritual discoveries she describes, are entirely her own. She is especially concerned for those who, like herself, have been 'smitten with some incurable disease', physically circumscribed but with powers 'unimpaired'. We are given glimpses of her suffering:

> How deep in the desolation, when a sad soul looks out anxiously, through eyes that cannot reflect its beauty, watching for an answering smile, and meeting only a look of swiftly concealed repulsion!

Such desolation can be overcome – as she herself overcomes it – by fusion with nature:

> The leaves do not hesitate to finger and kiss any face, however marred, that looks up into their dwelling. No distortion of body frightens the birds if the heart within loves them. . . . Out in this world the spirit that was so desolate, lost in the strange atmosphere of physical inferiority, may once more feel the zest that he thought was gone forever.　　　　　(pp. 131, 134)

The first step is awareness, the following of pure intuition, 'the sudden sense – keen and startling – of oneness with all beauty, seen and unseen'. A great rush of joy sweeps 'into the mind and into those recesses of being beyond the conscious self'. Those who achieve this, whatever their physical condition, are 'in the land of consolation, beside the healing water-courses . . . in this land (no visible country)', there can be a healing of 'the worn spirit' (pp. 127, 220–1).

In reflecting so abundantly this stage of her intellectual and spiritual development, the essays are valuable autobiographical writings. And the attitude to life permeating the series was one she maintained throughout her twenties. The tone is remarkably buoyant. Vehemently she affirms 'In nature . . . life's values right themselves again' . . . 'in whatever way and to whatever extent people are set aside from the world they can make their lives magnificent . . . No accident of environment or circumstance need cut us off from Nature . . . one violet is as sweet as an acre of them.'[7] There are many lovely amplifications here and in the poems and novels to come.

---

[7] *PSJ*, pp. 129, 221; Bastide, cf. 'Looking into the world of nature from sickroom or garden, one finds out how lovely the near things are; the one

Certainly Mary succeeds in imparting something of her own breadth and depth of vision achieved in a restricted sphere; and it is equally clear that her understanding of truth, the mystical apprehension she is endeavouring to put into concrete terms, is pantheistic. To Mary, 'the complex life of Nature . . . is the life of God'; so the person 'who holds direct intercourse with the cosmic life through his heart and mind' has, like herself, 'a purpose in waking each morning, a reason for existing – he clings to the beauty of earth as to a garment, and he feels that the wearer of the garment is God' (pp. 131–2).

Everywhere in the essays it is evident that her 'longing (almost a torment)' for union with the soul of nature makes the world for her 'a place of almost unbearable wonder', vibrating with clear vitality. And she brings to her literary depiction of it the complete wealth of her inner being. One can feel her presence, an intimate sense of personality, of unceasing wonder, and a joy cleaving like pain.

As with all Mary Webb's prose the effect is cumulative and cannot adequately be conveyed by isolated quotation. So many passages spring forward, but the following – watching plovers on 'a wide stretch of ploughland' – will convey something of both her vision and the incisive descriptive power she was already capable of in her early twenties :

> . . . up and down the furrows gleamed the white breasts of plovers. In a moment they rose with a flashing of underwings in the light, and their plaintive cry came down through the thin air. United to the soil by all the ties of life, being its very essence, they were yet much more; they were the soul of the field – gifted with music and motion and the freedom of the sky. So, at first, the patient watcher of earth sees only inanimate beauty, voiceless, without initiative. Then suddenly there is a clapping of wings, a flash of immortal radiance, a strange, haunting cry – and he has had a vision of the Soul of the World.   (p.222)

And the closing paragraph of 'The Beauty of Shadow' illustrates how her acute, sensuous awareness of physical life constantly mingles with and merges into visionary apprehension – a swift fusion from one level of reality to another :

tree or field will reveal depth on depth of beauty to the long, concentrated gaze.'   (*PSJ*, p. 216)

When we look down into the blueness of some little pool,
rejoicing in the birdlike passage of the clouds, and then look up
to the wide sky, we realise that the finite is like a lake which, as
far as its capacity allows, mirrors the infinite; and when we see
the foreshortened image of a poplar stretched in pale colouring
beneath it, we have a sudden vision of time as the faint,
straitened shadow of eternity.   (p. 201)

Mary had reached that creative plane of being which the Sufis
call the constructive spirit lying behind the world of the senses.
So the uprush of ideas carried her forward and the more she
wrote the more passionately she desired to give back something
of the magic she had received, to convey the 'enchantment',
although she knew that what she was seeking to express is beyond
complete expression in language.[8] Even at this early stage of her
literary career she was convinced of the significance of what she
had to say, these essays a confident if at times over-didactic and
over-written declaration of faith in her spiritual experience.

It is clearly evident in these early writings that Mary's attitude
to existence is that of a creative mystic not that of an analyst –
herein the essential source of her artistic feeling and striving as
well as her involvement with nature. Her impulse is not, and
never would be, primarily intellectual but is a blend of the truly
poetic and the truly religious in the sense that her deepest concern
is with the mystery of life – the ceaseless search of man for meaning – and with beauty as both ideal and reality. Far more than
nature studies, these short prose pieces, like nature itself, are full
of poetic suggestiveness, extending the mind and spirit of the
reader by endless associations. No one after reading *The Spring
of Joy* is not the richer for it.

Apart from their biographical importance as a key to Mary's
thought and personality in the third decade of her life, the essays
deserve wider attention and recognition for their intrinsic loveliness – small masterpieces of nature writing which place her in a
direct line of literary descent from Gilbert White and Izaak
Walton. As one critic said, years later, the essays 'are indeed
poems in prose'.[9] To quote Walter de la Mare, 'Mary Webb being

---

[8] 'With literary artists who are also mystics the power of aesthetic creation
cannot be dissociated from mystical experience . . . the symbolic development
is spontaneous.' Bastide, pp. 200–1.
[9] *Boston Transcript* (Book Section), 27 April 1929, p. 5.

a poet is always a poet when her interest reaches a certain creative intensity . . . The mere statement of facts that she was interested in is poetical in effect . . .' Wilfred Gibson, writing of *The Spring of Joy*, emphasised 'the delicate and luminous quality of the writing' and said of these 'prose lyrics' that 'their truth is not merely the truth of the naturalist, but the truth of the poet . . . Mary Webb though the acutest of observers, with all her senses trained to the most exquisite pitch of apprehension, was something more; she was a mystic of the kin of Vaughan and Traherne.'[10] Another critic, Grace Chapman, in the *London Mercury* (Feb. 1931, pp. 364–71), described her as a writer 'with the soul of a poet and the observation of an artist', an assessment applying as much to the youthful essays as to the major prose works of a later date. And such is the thematic cohesion of her work that in the essays the same intensities and preoccupations are found which are at the heart of her fiction.

When Mary's tragic life is seen as a whole and her literary work viewed in retrospect, the bright optimism of the essays has an added poignancy, her occasional naivities and excesses an increased wistfulness. Life was yet to teach her other lessons, bring other dark griefs: to these she came closer when her parents decided to move to Shrewsbury. She was still very much a convalescent when The Woodlands was sold late in 1901 and George Meredith bought a lovely old Mill House in the village of Meole Brace.

---

10 'The Poems of Mary Webb', the *Bookman*, February 1929, pp. 269–70.

PART TWO

THE SEARED SPIRIT

1902—1912

The seared spirit must have silence.

(*PSJ*, p. 219)

Deepening and widening our conscious experience . . . we have two great Scriptures of the world: the Bible of Nature and the Bible of Pain. (Sufi saying)

4

Anchorhold

1902–1909

Maesbrook,
Meole Brace

Was there a sound of leaves here once, and streams
Gurgling on pebbles? (In dreams, my soul! in dreams).
'The Land Within' (*PSJ*, pp. 114–15)

Only through the bravery of the root, its determination to
suffer rather than die, does the flower dance in the light.
(*PSJ*, pp. 240–1)

The brook, gleaming and rushing, flowed beneath a white
wooden bridge to join the waters of the weir. Tall trees sheltered
the banks, fresh, cool, green, before the large house set on a grassy
rise above. Here at Maesbrook, the Old Mill House, the next ten
years were a crucial period in Mary's maturing when she
struggled to recover from and come to terms with her disease; to
develop the creative force she had found; and finally to overcome
negation, a 'dark night of the soul' that almost swamped her. She
came as Mary Gladys Meredith. She would leave as Mary Webb.

The waters, the mill-race, gave Maesbrook a heightened atmosphere, an invitation to all the senses. A compelling place for
Mary and her father with their specialised vision of nature – and
for the Meredith boys in quite a different way. Dating back to
the seventeenth century, the ivy-covered house was known locally
as Hiles Mill. Its elevated position gave commanding views over
the surrounding meadows: Mary was often seen at her window
looking out thoughtfully across the gardens and fields. On one
side the windows faced towards Pontesford Hill with its sil-
houetted line of larches resembling a spiky-maned primeval beast

– an outline powerfully beckoning to Mary since it marks the beginning of the hill country she loved, stretching across to Wenlock Edge and The Grange.

Coming from the remoteness of Stanton, the Merediths found the red-brick and sandstone village of Meole Brace a closely clustered community only two miles from Shrewsbury yet in the countryside. They would have approached their new home along what was then a narrow, tree-lined lane passing the village field and the sandstone church with ancient graves huddling round it, old yew trees growing near the graves, and sheep grazing between church and Vicarage – a scene which reminded George Meredith of the churchyard in Gray's Elegy. Then on to the black and white gates of Maesbrook, into the leafy grounds, hearing the endless water music. The house with its many rooms was intriguing, the drawing room on the first floor where a door gave access to the upper garden and tennis court. All the Meredith children developed deep affection for Maesbrook, their favourite home : the grounds with their woodland atmosphere and the mill-race cast a spell that mingled with the spell of youth, security, united family life.

Gradually Mary recovered her strength during the early months there, walking slowly in the gardens, watching the brook, the little waterfalls, in 'absorbed preoccupation' with the movements of birds, insects, water-life. And sometimes resting during long 'dream-rich' days in a hammock her father had put up for her among the trees – here she watched the squirrels and listened intently to the birdsong, for Maesbrook was thronged with birds : 'Silver-throated birds came all day long/And haunted it with ecstasies of song.' Along the banks she found the first snowdrops, early primroses, wild daffodils. To venture beyond the gates was still unthinkable – for this she had neither strength nor inclination. But with a glad, grateful receptivity she absorbed the beauty of her new surroundings.

These were momentous days for her, her zest returning. And she came with her perception sharpened still further, with what she referred to as 'the undimmed vision of the soul'. A short poem she wrote at this time celebrates her reunion with nature and, though slight, conveys her joy with an immediacy and spontaneity that point to her best work :

Nature has opened her gates again!
Her gates of gold and green;
Has opened them wide to welcome me
Back to her glorious liberty,
To her wholesome grass and sun and rain,
Through her gates of gold and green.

The infinite sky bends close to me
With a great protecting calm,
And wave upon wave of its peace profound
Steals on my spirit and circles me round
With the stillness of eternity
And a great protecting calm.

                                    (*CPAP*, p. 97)

She used this poem as an introduction to the essays on which she was continuing to work, experiencing in the isolation, the sanctuary of these surroundings that 'great protecting calm'. Even when strong enough to go about the lower garden and adjoining meadows daily, Mary would not go into Meole Brace, fearing scrutiny in the small community where villagers were curious to see 'the eldest Miss Meredith', the strange invalid who, when they called to the house, would evade introduction, shutting herself in her bedroom until they had gone. Acutely self-conscious, she was not yet ready to face the world again – always to be, as she said, 'in the world but not quite of it', in a 'land of Betwixt and Between', a borderland. Yet ironically it was because of this, as she showed later through the experience of the afflicted Prudence Sarn in *Precious Bane*, that she found 'the glory that comes from the other side of silence', her mysticism 'the core of sweetness in much bitter'. At this period in Meole Brace, leading an 'enclosed' life, Maesbrook was her anchorhold. But while the life of a recluse was essential to her at this time, as it was to be at others, her compassion still reached out, at once a plea and her own first answer.

Within the 'anchorhold', Mary extended to an immediate focus in her sisters and brothers and most of all her adored father. On recovery from the long illness she showed her gratitude to everyone in the family, and to Minoni by the gift of a book – Harriet Eleanor Hamilton's *The Sermon in the Hospital*, enclosing this in stiff covers on which she embroidered a sampler in purple, green and gold. She also copied out for Minoni some poems written during her 'forced unwilling leisure' including 'Elsewhere' dedicated to 'The Soldiers of Suffering'.

Outdoors sometimes the entire day from dawn to 'deepening dusk', Mary shared many hours of convalescence with her father who with 'utter comprehension' knew her essence and understood how – though possibly not the extent to which – nature was for her both refuge and church, solace and spring of renewal. At the brook, humorously observing the antics of birds, they watched the 'dipper' at his 'knee-strengthening exercises', the young bullfinches hanging on stalks 'like inexperienced and rather stout trapeze performers'; and here 'swift and free' came the water ousel of her poem, 'with such a flight/As archangels might envy'. In this, one of the best known of Mary's early poems, the water ousel hearing 'a presage in the ancient thunder/Of the silken fall' prepares herself for the day when

> Two little ousels shall fly with her down-stream,
> And even the poor, dumb shadow-bird shall flit
> With two small shadows following after it.
>
> (*PSJ*, p. 26)

There is always now this awareness of shadow. Undoubtedly Mary would have understood Katherine Mansfield's quality of grievous gaiety, and the truth behind the words of this writer (incurably ill with tuberculosis): 'And then suffering, bodily suffering . . . has changed forever everything; even the appearance of the world is not the same – there is something added. Everything has its shadow.'[1] So Mary's laughter as well as her love had a special intensity, a tension which sprang from her awareness of the frailty of human life – such laughter might at any time slip 'into a sob' and fail, her humour turn swiftly to pathos and tragedy, be 'folded in stiff sadness like a dead moth's wing'. Foreboding is never far away; her crystal glass might crackle inwards at any moment.

Often she joined her father in his study where he sat reading the Bible – like John Arden frequently 'dreamy from his favourite passage in Revelation'. Here George was surrounded by dusty calf-bound volumes, Shakespeare, Dickens and Scott prominent,

---

[1] Letter of Katherine Mansfield to John Middleton Murry, 1920.

and tattered books much used when he was a tutor. Now in his sixties, George was spending more time indoors, but still worked in the grounds helped by Mr Downes, the resident gardener. A suggestion that a high hawthorn hedge bordering one of the fields would have to be cut down, brought a passionate outburst from Mary. Minoni, recalling the incident, wrote: 'I remember . . . how distressed she was. She implored her father, she pleaded with her brothers to help her to save the hedge. It would break her heart, she said, if the old hawthorn were cut down.' George understood, knowing how every living thing for her had transcendent spiritual value, even the smallest flower holding all the beauty of creation. The hawthorn was reprieved.

She was delighted when her father planted saplings – alders in The Spinney which she was to watch in their growth each year. The joy of this brought its wake of pain when, years later, after George Meredith's death, Mary sadly observed 'the increasing shade/Of trees he planted by the waterside'. Maesbrook was to be, for Mary, very much a storehouse of memories of her father as there was evidence everywhere of his 'shining thought' and 'stable deed'. He liked to be busy in the rambling barns or feeding Alice's prize poultry[2] or looking at his small herd of cows and the horses he kept in the meadows where Mary would join him when she was well enough. Here they would explore the upper stream near the weir, listening to 'the low sonorous sound' as of the monotone of many bees. At times, especially after heavy rains, this watersound rose to a roaring like a distant incoming sea.

From her bedroom at the front of Maesbrook, Mary saw the meadows under flood, a shining grass lake of indefinite limits, a green mere. Sounds and effects of water fused with those of birds and trees, inner resonances pervading the depths of her being, summoning both conscious and unconscious response. In such states of outward-inward apprehension, time and space ceased to exist. She did not need 'wide experience', for in this fervid inner experience she was at one with an 'immense freedom'.

More than a decade later, writing her third novel, *The House*

---

[2] George Meredith in a letter to Olive wrote amusingly about this responsibility: 'Mother and Muriel propose returning from Pedmore tomorrow. I am in sole charge of the precious poultry and find my hands full of work and my soul full of anxiety: a few chickens have died, but on the whole, I think I am managing pretty well'.

in Dormer Forest, Mary projected herself back in memory to Maesbrook, and with the selecting eye and ear of a literary artist, she extracted innumerable details and impressions, assimilating these into her descriptions of Dormer Old House, Dormer Brook and the Four Waters. As at Maesbrook, so at Dormer, water-song heightens the mood and atmosphere. Much of her life at Meole Brace is recalled here, blended, as in all her novels, with past and later experience, but it is always experience transmuted by her creative imagination, merging imperceptibly with pure fiction.

In the spring of 1903, Mary began to go out beyond Maesbrook, at first in her ponytrap (a present from Mrs Lyons); then walking with her father in the quiet village; and eventually, when she felt physically stronger, in busy, gabled Shrewsbury. During those early excursions, Mary greatly needed her father's reassurance: his tacit understanding, 'the wordless glance that defies fate', gave her courage when she feared to meet people, dreading the expected recoil. Hyper-sensitive, she developed the habit of looking downwards or sideways as she hurried along the streets, head bent, darting furtive bird-like glances. This very different from the Mary who was seen in the countryside, walking across fields waist-high in grasses,[3] fey, preoccupied in the woods and lanes, holding silent discourse with flowers, birds, the 'humming honey folk' – only in the freedom of nature was she truly herself, liberated. And now gradually she began to explore again.

Immeasurably important to her was the discovery of a place of 'almost intolerable loveliness', a place which more than anywhere else was to become essential to both her physical and her spiritual existence: Lyth Hill, to which she could walk from Maesbrook following a route over the meadows. She came out from narrow lanes on to the high extensive plateau of Lyth Hill, lonely, windswept, wooded, covered in bracken, where an old windmill swung its creaking sails and the Shropshire landscape stretched below like a vast flat paten catching the sunlight, contained by a mountainous rim. Walking along the ridge path

[3] Mary always went directly across fields (even when wet), never following a path. She is remembered by farming people who provided her with produce, arriving often with skirts soaked to the waist.

known as the Rope Walk, standing wind-blown at the plateau's
edge, looking down at the plain and 'the meadows dear and low',
she knew she had found forever a haven for her 'fugitive spirit'.
Here at Lyth Hill she was 'caught into the primal beauty of
earth', and presented with all the hills of her childhood and her
future, from the Wrekin away on the left, across the long line of
Wenlock Edge to the Strettons, the tableland of the Long Mynd
and on the right the high crags of the Stiperstones, with the
'little hill' of Pontesford in the foreground.

Lyth Hill was part of the Condover estate, and at this date two
keepers' cottages stood at the gate to a dense little wood at its
southern end. The steep slopes of the hill falling sharply to the
plain were also thickly wooded, but it was the coppice or 'little
wood' beyond the white gate which compelled Mary. This was
a world apart, a green enchantment, the trees lichened, twisted,
many of them ancient oaks and hawthorn. It was of this wood
that she wrote later in 'Green Rain':

> Into the scented woods we'll go
> And see the blackthorn swim in snow.
> High above, in the budding leaves,
> A brooding dove awakes and grieves.
> *(PSJ,* p. 23)

Honeysuckle roped the branches, and in spring bluebells in
abundance covered the spaces among the tangled roots. It seemed
held in a special magic.

Day after day Mary returned here, often leaving Maesbrook
early in the morning, taking a pencil and notebook and staying
for hours. On intensely hot days such as those of August and
September 1906, she would cross the parched fields wearing her
light summer dress and a large shady hat, walk along the plateau
looking down across the 'sapphire-circled plain', and go to the
cool wood where, in shafted sunlight midges whirled, bees
hummed, doves called 'in deep voices, velvet-warm'. Here she
was steeped in loveliness and afterwards in memories of loveliness.

At this date there were only a few cottages on the hill and
Mary came so frequently that some of the cottagers became her
friends – the Barretts of Coppice Gate, in particular. Mary visited
this family regularly, sometimes arriving in her ponytrap with

enough home-made scones and cakes for afternoon tea, and talking to the children about flowers, insects, birds, and the legends of the countryside.[4] Mr Barrett, a shepherd, preached fiery sermons at the little chapel on the hill: his strong personality and individuality greatly appealed to Mary, and years later she worked something of his character into Jonathan Makepeace in *Seven for a Secret* and Eli Huntbatch in *The Golden Arrow*. Equally she admired the homely simplicity of Mrs Barrett. The knowledge of human nature gained in friendships with Shropshire country-people such as these, with whom she was warmly spontaneous, extended her insight and gave the authentic material she drew upon later to vivify her characters (especially the sharply observed minor figures). And to the cottagers and their children, 'Miss Meredith' was someone very 'different' in a way they could not define. The vivid impression she made lasted undimmed in their minds, becoming living myth.

The wooded isolation of Lyth Hill never ceased to beckon Mary and to inspire her poems. She responded keenly to its atmosphere : here the peculiarly compelling spell of Shropshire is intensified, as if spilling over from the 'dark profundities' of the hills into the plain. This is evoked in the lines: 'There is a presence on the lonely hill, / Lovely and chill : / There is an emanation in the wood, / Half understood . . .' (*PSJ*, 44).

Very gradually Mary began to take part in the life of Meole Brace, going to bridge parties (she excelled at this game), playing croquet, accompanying her parents to tea at the vicarage, and her father and Moo-Moo (Muriel) to concerts at the Lion Hotel, Shrewsbury. The Merediths, with their clerical connections, had quickly been integrated into the Church of England community becoming friends of the vicar, William H. Bather, and his wife; George Meredith, very involved in parochial affairs, was elected People's Warden. Probably much too soon for her frail health, Mary took over her mother's parish work, especially the visiting which Alice had always disliked.

She called, complete with flowers, on the old and sick, particularly at Cross Houses Workhouse, where she was deeply moved by the plight of workhouse women sitting in greyness, 'completely sundered from their past lives' (this directly influencing her short

---

[4] For this and other information about Mary Webb and Lyth Hill, I am indebted to Mrs Nellie Cullis, daughter of the Barretts.

story 'Blessed are the Meek', *AWHT*, 241–53). And she took a class at Meole Brace Sunday School, enjoying this weekly contact with the children. She is remembered teaching dressed in white high-necked blouses, her dark skirt always belted with a silver buckle at her narrow waist. Confidence renewed, she helped to arrange Christmas tableaux for the 'schools' entertainment', having the entire cast to tea at Maesbrook when the 'fittings' took place. 'Making enough toast for a choir tea' was one of her expressions based on experience.

Although increasingly since her illness conventional religion ceased to have the meaning for her that it had held in her devotional days at Stanton, she still kept up observances at nearby Holy Trinity.[5] But the long period of illness had resulted in an underlining and clarification of something she had for long implicitly known : that to go beyond and outside organised, conventional religion was not to enter chaos; it was not in church but in nature that her soul had awakened to its own life and vitality. This is explicit in an untitled poem she wrote at this period, beginning : 'I worship the earth and the airs that blow! / Churches and creeds are nothing to me, / I have my church where the daisies grow, / Under a whispering sycamore tree' (*CPAP*, p. 100). This echoes the pantheistic mysticism of her essays. At this time spiritually renewed in what was, for her, a God-filled nature, Mary had developed her own personal religion (which she referred to humorously as 'home-brewed') increasingly convinced that dogma sets up narrow walls around the soul. If she kept up an appearance of orthodoxy this was largely because of unwillingness to distress her father; and because she still responded to the 'homeliness' of the parish church, felt a keen aesthetic appreciation of the atmosphere, the 'externals' and, as she said in a future article, 'the poetic beauty of the Liturgy' (*CPAP*, p. 45). Always she would feel the poignancy of human aspiration.

These years at Maesbrook were a period of immense importance in her intellectual as well as spiritual development. Going regularly to Shrewsbury Library, she read avidly, sometimes two books a day, interested especially in the anthropological and semi-

---

[5] There is a brass plaque attached to the pew where Mary used to sit with the rest of the Meredith family. It states : 'Mary Webb worshipped here : 1902–12'

scientific writings which had been influencing thought during the late nineteenth century. Sir James Frazer's encyclopaedic *The Golden Bough,* the works of Darwin, Huxley and Haeckel absorbed her for many months. With her brother Douglas, 'a very serious-minded youth', she had long discussions about *The Origin of Species* and *The Riddle of the Universe.* Douglas wrote: 'I followed her eagerly. In all my studies I was greatly helped by her . . . and when, later, I went out into the world, we continued our discussions by correspondence. Another book I especially recall in her reading is *The Birth of Worlds and Systems,* because we had lots of arguments about it. The result of all this proved to be a pagan one.'

She admired Walter Pater's style, and the writings of 'Fiona Macleod' (William Sharp). Mary was less influenced than stimulated by this Celtic writer with whom she had an affinity, but at this stage the poetry and 'prose-rhythms' of Fiona Macleod had a self-revelatory effect on her similar to that of Niels Lyhne on Rilke, opening the image world of his soul.

The metaphysical writers of the seventeenth century also appealed to her greatly, with their eloquence and ardent thinking about love and religion: she valued in particular Sir Thomas Browne's *Religio Medici.*

Inevitably she was intrigued by Charlotte S. Burne's *Shropshire Folk Lore* (1883), a monumental work, the first major collection of the folk-lore of an English county. Mary had, of course, already heard many of the legends, much of the lore and countless superstitions intrinsic to Shropshire life, either from her father or during her own explorations and talks with cottagers. And she was well versed too in the Mabinogion of what she called 'my ancestral country'.

Mary's understanding of the growth of legend, the psychological source and significance of myth, was inherent in her mystical disposition, in the swift, intuitive apprehension which brought her to a unity with the collective past embodied in nature – animate, inanimate – the collective past and the collective future. Here, as said later in an article, she was 'in touch with the deepest life of the race' of which mythology and folk-lore are integral – accretions as natural as rock strata.

Study of Darwin, Huxley, Haeckel, although of consuming interest, did not fundamentally mould her thought. Her intuitions made her automatically selective, directing her thought-life: hence her concern was less with origins than with development, less with theories of beginnings than with realities of accumulations. There is no evidence in her writings that she was influenced by the theory of evolution; rather the reverse. As a naturalist, she never ceased to wonder at the perfection of creation; as a mystic she was filled by an 'inexhaustible desire' for oneness with that 'ultimate Beauty, which is the meaning of all symbols'. For her, life always retained its mystery: 'Life – the unknown quantity, the guarded secret – circles from an infinite ocean through all created things, and turns again to the ocean' (*PSJ*, p. 127).

Mary is reminiscent of Emily Brontë in her metaphysical grasp and creative intensity, her pantheism, her deep reserve and devotion to her family circle; but unlike Emily, the more intensely she experienced mystical unity with nature and universal life, the more desperately she needed an emotional centre in 'the world', a oneness of love and understanding with another human being. Emotionally, psychologically, she projected to a centre in her father; but she had still to learn that ultimately she must stand alone.

How far George Meredith saw into the depths and darknesses of Mary's complex personality we cannot know. Certainly he knew her as no one else did. Among his manuscripts is a short verbal portrait. Describing his daughters in a poem, 'The Three Sisters', he depicts Mary:

> One, sitting silent, and with thoughtful mien
> Seemed to be busy with a world unseen.
> No stern recluse, indeed, from daily life;
> Nor base deserter from its passing strife;
> Yet oftentimes I marked her liquid eye
> Upturned, as if to penetrate the sky.
> While, lost in reverie, her eager ear
> Revelled in music others might not hear.
> Her brow, engraven by affliction's tool
> Spoke of hard lessons learnt in sorrow's school,
> But the calm attitude of perfect rest
> Told also that her schooling had been blest.

In a few words he has portrayed perfectly her contemplative look – that of a 'dove woman', the inner madonna whose intuitive vision and immense compassion for mankind has been deepened by her own suffering. In her writing she strove consistently to communicate this feeling for humanity – often synthesised with her feeling for nature – but at this stage she was still aspiring rather than achieving. Showing to her father only the few poems she considered to be effective, it was in the hope of his 'word of praise'. And when this was given she felt fulfilled. Much of her work she destroyed in dissatisfaction with her attempts. Her apprenticeship in poetry was to take longer than in prose where, as Martin Armstrong has said, she was soon 'a master-craftsman'. During the early Maesbrook period she was still struggling with formal restraints, and there were definite derivative traces in her poems, influenced as she was by Keats, Blake, Swinburne, the Rossettis, Browning and others she was studying at this time.

At Meole Brace she found a friend with similar literary interests – a former schoolmistress, Miss Southern. Mary was invited to bridge parties at her home, The Corner House. Miss Southern greatly enjoyed her company, thought her 'uncommonly clever in talking and writing' and admired her ability to 'sit down and write a first-class essay straight away on any subject you set her' (Moult, pp. 102–3).

When a series of Cambridge University Extension Society lectures on Literature and History began in 1903 at St Chad's School in Shrewsbury, Mary and Miss Southern attended together, going in Mary's ponytrap. There was a vigorous branch of the society in Shrewsbury at that date, the preparatory work for the course done at local study circles. Those who studied with Mary and heard her papers were impressed by her literary talent, her critical powers and particularly her sensitivity to latent meanings. When she was ill and could not attend a lecture, Miss Southern used to give 'Miss Meredith's apologies for absence' to the lecturer who would then send Mary a note about the next subject on which she was required to write.[6]

The Meole Brace study circle (known as the Literary Society) was held in a parish room, described by one of the members, Flora McLeod, as 'small and remarkably ugly – a little red-brick

[6] Byford Jones, *The Shropshire Haunts of Mary Webb*, p. 39. The lecturer in English Literature, Mr Burns, regretted Mary's absence, telling Miss Southern, 'I am sorry she is ill because her papers are of uncommon merit'

"To be or not to be" (BACON)

6. Sketch by George Edward
   Meredith

7. Mervyn Meredith, aged 2,
   at the Grange

8. The Little Wood, Lyth Hill

9. Mary's view from Spring Cottage, Lyth Hill (with Westley Farm in the centre)

chamber roughly colour-washed inside, with a rusty fireplace always overfilled with coal and either smoking sulkily or else blazing . . . fiercely.' Flora McLeod remembered their first meeting in October 1903. She noticed Mary at once:

> an eager girl sitting at the end of the table near the door. In all her movements, in the quick question, the emphatic comment, the searching enquiry, one could not but recognise a mind hungry for knowledge and really capable of appreciation.[7]

Shocked by the signs of Mary's recent illness – her swollen throat, strange, brilliant eyes, her pallor and thinness – Miss McLeod did not know then what a supreme effort it was for her to take part. Mary's 'fearful self-consciousness' (Kenneth's words), was, at this time, a greater strain on her than the intensive study and writing, already so integral to her personal world.

Mary attended the Extension Courses for the next three or four years. Unfortunately none of her papers has survived, but in a letter of 1 December 1906 her father made a reference to one of them:

> Gladys has been writing a wonderful essay or paper upon 'George Meredith' (the novelist not your humble servant) and she is to read it on Monday at a meeting of the Literary Society which is held in the village. She gave us a rehearsal in the Drawing Room this evening and we all thought her writing exceptionally good.[8]

This is interesting in view of Baldwin's speech in 1928, when he compared Mary Webb with George Meredith:

> It is curious to see how birth and rearing in that border country with a Celtic ancestry seems to give that writer some of those peculiar gifts of her far greater namesake, George Meredith.

Mary Webb was to develop in her own novels certain elements characteristic of Meredith's – for instance, extensive use of related

---

[7] Flora McLeod, *Talk to Shropshire W.I.* (Shrewsbury Library) 'Mary Webb As I Knew Her', p. 1.

[8] She also wrote papers on Jane Austen, using the copy of *Pride and Prejudice*, a present from her father in 1903 for her twenty-second birthday. He wrote in it 'Read, Mark, Learn'. The annotations in this copy were those she made on the course and which she used years later when writing a critical article on Jane Austen for the *Bookman*.

images and emblematic symbols associated with character and incident. This is particularly evident in her early novels, but in her later work these consciously devised allegoric symbols (sometimes too obviously contrived) are replaced by a less obtrusive, more spontaneous symbolism springing from the deeper levels of her consciousness.

The years from 1903 to 1907 were a great formative period of Mary's thought and style, a time of assimilation and preparation. Yet there was a fine balance between stimulation and fatigue. The intense mental energy and enthusiasm she brought to all she did, began to take its toll, and early in 1907 her health was deteriorating seriously again. As we have seen, her first significant writings, the essays, had set the pattern of her creative life – written while she was still physically weak, yet rich in verbal vitality. Mary's extraordinary volitional power was part of a creative ardour impelling her on at the expense of her frail body. In this she was to resemble other writers caught up inspirationally yet suffering physically – the consumptives Katherine Mansfield and D. H. Lawrence, or the epileptic Dostoevsky.

The usual warning signals – high temperature, exhaustion – were ignored. Her father watched her anxiously, fearing she was overstraining herself: he knew as no one else did, how totally she expended herself on life. In a letter of February 1907, his concern about her tiredness after a late night at a bridge party seems an intuition of the coming collapse. Intense intellectual activity was allowing her no rest[9] and at the same time her mystical fervour intensified – spring was approaching and always she responded to spring with every fibre of her being:

> Soon will come the strange, heart-lifting season
> When through the dark, still dawns, where nothing was,
> Steals the mysterious whisper of growing grass;
> And a joy like pain possesses the soul, without reason . . .
>
> (*PSJ*, p. 82)

For her, as for William Blake, joy and pain were 'woven fine'. April especially brought this 'joy as keen as pain' – 'those gleamy

---

[9] She was still attending the lectures, as George Meredith's letter of 8 February 1907, proves: '. . . (Gladys) has to attend the weekly "Extension Lecture"; she writes a paper every week and so far has secured the highest marks obtainable!'

April days' which hurt her soul 'with too much bliss'. She found
it difficult to sleep, restless to hear 'the cries of birds across the
lawns / In dark and teeming April dawns'. Always she identified
with birds, symbols of the spirit, and in spring, 'the air is full
of wings . . . so all day from dusk to dusk there is music'. In her
essay 'The Joy of Music', defining the various 'ethereal whisper-
ings' and 'liquid notes' of individual species of birds, she describes
the blackbird's song giving 'to all the silent breaths and pulses of
April a voice . . . sweeter even than the singing of those wondrous
birds of Rhiannon . . . fourscore Aprils seem a very little time to
spend in listening; and while you are in the charmed circle –
though your eyes may be full of tears – there is no remembrance
of sorrow at all' (*PSJ*, 158). Mary did not know then that she
was to have little more than half those 'fourscore Aprils . . . to
spend in listening' or that the time would come when the doves
would echo her woe.

The fervid pitch of her mental, emotional and spiritual life
once again caused her health to break, and before April was over
she reached a crisis, desperately ill with high fever followed by
extreme exhaustion which was to last for many months and con-
fine her on her back in her narrow white bed, hearing but not
seeing the birds, listening to the constant undersong of water.

Physical suffering she could endure quite cheerfully. She had
her 'heritage of joy':

Dull? . . . When the full moon slips in silver past my window
pane,
Just as she slipped by the porphyry arch and shone on Sappho
dreaming;
And winds that howled round Ninevah's walls and brought old
Babylon rain
Come, like ravens with wide black wings, to waken me with their
screaming?

Sad? . . . When my saffron crocus holds a brown bee in its cup,
Just as on Hybla's purple hill, where the honey was warm and
yellow;
And every day in my quiet room the crystal light stands up
Pure and sweet as on Olivet when the autumn days grew mellow?
(*CPAP*, p. 103)

Not yet for her 'dark weather'. But dire spiritual suffering, agony of great lack and loss was still to come, a test of quite a different kind which would mould her evolution as a creative artist, shaping her into the poet she knew herself to be.

In 1907 she still had the security of her relationship with her father – the stable centre of her world – sustaining her by his silent presence and by the peace of an understanding so deep that no words were needed, an understanding she was to yearn for in years to come. So when writing *The Golden Arrow,* her mind reached back and she invested with authentic detail and feeling the descriptions of John Arden's patient 'watching' over his stricken Deborah.

During the last week of April, George was relieved when the wave of illness seemed to be receding and she was able to get up for a short while each day. He told Olive (5 May):

> Dear Gladys is still making, I think, very satisfactory progress and has a better appetite, I think, today, than she has felt for a considerable time. She gets up a little every evening now, though at present it tires her a good deal.

The effort was too soon; the strain too great. On 13 May, the full onset came:

> Our thoughts have been almost exclusively taken up with poor Gladys since last Monday, when the sickness returned and she has been extremely weak and ill, though slightly better, I think, today. Poor dear girl! How much she is called upon to suffer! and how wonderfully good and patient she has been and is under her heavy cross! Quite a bright example to us all.

Mary remained very ill throughout the wet summer of 1907. The heavy rains and violent thunderstorms which ruined the harvest in the district, caused the brook to swell and overflood its banks and so the unceasing water-song called all the more insistently during those months of her illness. Unable to move, she could see only the topmost branches of a nearby tree which, she said, 'caught the stars in its meshes'.

Her father refused to leave her side for very long, insisting that he 'must stay with dear Gladys'. Other visitors came regularly. Flora McLeod, who made weekly visits, recalled that in

spite of illness Mary was still reading as many books as possible.
Miss McLeod admired this tremendously:

> '(Mary) . . . opened the door to me into the world of books
> which she knew so much better than I, though I had always loved
> the craft of words. For books had been all her life. . . . Nothing
> would have hindered her from reading.'

Their discussions inevitably included religion, Flora McLeod
discovering to her regret that Mary's views had already diverged
from her own and that 'the churchly life in which she had been
reared seemed cramping and ineffectual'. A firm believer in 'the
orthodox faith of the Church', Miss McLeod was disappointed to
find that Mary 'denied its intellectual foundations' and 'despised
it as a second-hand thing'. She admitted that Mary knew the
Bible 'from cover to cover', but in Miss McLeod's opinion she
knew it 'always on the one hand as emotion, on the other as
literature, with only an imperfect conception of its meaning as a
revelation of God'.

Mary explained, in her forthright way, the spiritual significance
of her communion with earth rather than church, that the beauty
of earth and the soul of earth are in the eye and waking soul of
the perceiver, that nature, for her, was not 'enthroned as God'
but revealed God, revelatory of an immutable vitality in all
created things, animate and inanimate – in them but also beyond
them. To her conventional friend however, this was difficult to
accept since she was adamant that God could only be found in
church and through the orthodox faith. Miss McLeod, in later
years, was probably further dismayed by Mary's comments in
her writings: of the Book of Common Prayer, 'the folklore of
the soul'; of Christ, 'the love-martyr of Galilee'; of Judas, 'if he
had started away from his set part in fear we should none of us
have been saved'; of the cross, 'it may be that if Christ had not
died, the meaning of the cross would have been revealed in some
other way'.

Yet Mary sought for long to include within her pantheistic
mysticism the Christ of orthodox belief, and often God is personified in her writing as a vague Christ-like figure. For instance in
'The Vagrant', a poem belonging to this period of her development, she depicts a mystical presence in nature and universe:
'Silent, without a footprint, no shade throwing. / Infinite worlds

his shadow : all things growing / Stir with his breathing, follow as
he passes' (*PSJ*, 109–10). There are verbal echoes of Francis
Thompson's 'The Hound of Heaven', but here the voice of the
poet is that of the pursuer not that of the pursued. She is striving
to grasp the elusive personality she feels everywhere in nature,
in 'the wet lilac' and the tawny furrows, in 'the dark aspens' and
the 'golden weaving' of the blackbird, a presence with 'fathomless
eyes' and a 'wild music' which comes 'like spray upon the
shingle / Low to the heart like doves when rain is falling.' She
conveys an intense yearning to retain these ineffable glimpses, to
hold and prolong the mystical apprehension which inevitably
fades :

> Then the green river
> Dimmed like a misted mirror; blossom only
> Whitened it, on the covert water lying.
> Westward along the willows ran a sighing.
> Herd-like the clouds went home and left me lonely.

Again the wistfulness, a temporary sense of loss after visionary
unity. 'The Vagrant' is important in a study of Mary Webb's
inner life – Hilda Addison tells us 'she always considered this
poem more truly representative of her spiritual position than any
other'.

It is in this later Maesbrook period that her poems become
infused with mystical intuition. 'The Lost Orchard', for example,
written during this long illness :

> Never in those lonely meadows lingering,
> Shall I see the twilight any more;
> Never hear the golden water fingering
> Pale tansy shadows from the shore;
>
> Never, when the dark thorn hedge is quickening,
> Watch the white narcissi upward steal :
> Nor, in the pink orchard's hazy thickening,
> Hear the early bird-song thrill and peal.
>
> Yet within my heart, where none can ever see,
> Blows the apple tree and flows the stream :
> Through the violet fields I move, as shadowy
> As a fish within the water's gleam.

(*51*, 56)

This is one of the most important of Mary Webb's earlier poems, marking a transition from the first youthful expressions of ecstasy in nature towards the more profound and illumined poems of her maturity, anticipating these in its allusiveness, the impression of shadows within shadows, the intimation of a personality powerfully present yet just beyond grasp, beckoning yet eluding; like a vessel never to be filled and never to be emptied.

In these and other mystical poems, Mary Webb can be compared with Emily Brontë whose finest poems were inspired by her experience of union with the soul of nature, the yearning to remain in or recapture that spiritual dimension of being. Neither of them was a 'religious' mystic : each conveyed an intensely personal vision, not in Christian terms but in imagery drawn from nature into which she longed to be absorbed. Mary's attitude to death also was similar to that of Emily Brontë. When at her weakest, she seemed to her family to be 'near the shadowy gates' (as John Arden said of Deborah); but close to death as she undoubedly was, Mary had no fear – this was eliminated, as she herself tells us, by her 'consciousness of Mystery'. Just as Emily Brontë, desiring her soul's release from its 'dungeon of clay', in her moments of rapturous union thought of death fearlessly, so too Mary regarded it, emphasising 'absence of morbidity' (this being characteristic of mystics) :

> One who has lived under the large arbitrament of earth ceases to question . . . Death is no longer the supreme disaster or the supreme desire, but an incident – the swinging back of the gate on the skyline. *(PSJ,* p. 220)

While this concept recalls Spinoza whose *Ethics* greatly interested her, it also owes much to the optimistic beliefs of her father whose fundamental influence is discernible throughout *The Spring of Joy.*

It is a pity that more of Mary Webb's poems from this later Maesbrook period have not survived : she was writing throughout that time of illness which was a time of inner advance, this slowing her recovery, the stimulation hampering her physical progress, leaving her tired and nervously exhausted.

Kenneth Meredith admired immensely his sister's determination and courage in an illness for which there was no cure.

Resembling his father in physical features and in his affectionate, fun-loving nature, Kenneth always succeeded in cheering Mary by his brightness: 'So young he is, so dear to me, / With ever ready sympathy / And wistful eyes and cheerful smile' (*PSJ,* 90). Full of vitality, Kenneth, like Jasper Darke in *The House in Dormer Forest,* had the 'élan of a growing plant'. His affinity with Mary was close – a lover of earth, fascinated by bees (already he possessed his own hives), by animals, flowers and all growing things. She enjoyed his quick humour, knew beneath the banter his extreme sensitivity, realised how keenly he suffered from his mother's criticisms. Alice Meredith had remained rigidly Victorian in many ways, with little tolerance for the restlessness of youth. Not understanding Kenneth's numerous hectic pursuits, she would say as he prepared to go out again, a sarcastic 'Whither away?' or other acid remark. Detesting Kenneth's 'bad habit' – smoking – she would sniff the air after he had been in a room – 'Smoke?' she questioned sharply. To avoid nightly tensions on this topic Mary, with a typical thoughtfulness and tact never forgotten by Kenneth, had arranged a special room for him to relax in when he returned from work. She converted the former school-room into what she called the 'smoke room', hanging a notice on the door. This helped to silence Mother and gave Kenneth the freedom so necessary to him. Mary's consideration went even further: as Kenneth said, 'she thought of everything' – little ash trays placed strategically around (and emptied by her each day), a comfortable chair and foot-stool for him and one for his dog.

Visiting Mary's bedside each day during the illness, Kenneth was returning something of that loving care. He would be deeply concerned on finding her propped up by pillows writing in a creative ferment which obviously was impeding her recovery. As Miss Southern said, 'she was an invalid longer than she ought to have been . . . so active, mentally and physically, that she got no proper rest when she was ill'. But a cycle or life pattern now established was never to cease – intense inner life, creative outpouring, exhaustion, illness, renewal of creativity – never to cease until she was finally physically wracked beyond recovery: 'Let Life come bringing Death on his heels if need be; but let him come!'

Gradually the illness receded and by October 1907 she had recovered sufficiently to go out again with her father for short drives in the countryside. The autumn of that year was warm with long spells of sunshine. George Meredith knew that as soon as she was strong enough physically, part of her renewal would be to see again her countryside, splendid in the bright and deepening colours of early autumn. She insisted, at first, on going in the small trap pulled by the pony, Master Billy. Later, her father was very pleased when she agreed to go in the large trap with the horse pulling – this was a sign that 'her nerves must be stronger', as he told his other 'dear old girlie' Olive.[10] George was also delighted to report that Mary had been able to accompany him and Muriel to hear a performance in Shrewsbury by the great violinist Kubelik.

In this month of her recovery – October 1907 – her first published poem appeared in the *Shrewsbury Chronicle*. It was the result of a tragic circumstance.

At 2.30 a.m. on 15 October, the L.N.W.R. night mail from Crewe to the west of England crashed at Shrewsbury station, killing eighteen people and injuring thirty or more. This disaster – one of the first major railway accidents – shocked and horrified Shropshire people. In the seclusion of her room Mary wrote a compassionate poem which subsequently Kenneth found on her writing table. He was very impressed, and impulsively put the poem in his pocket. If published it might, he thought, give comfort or stimulate help. And underlying this was his conviction that Mary's literary talent was exceptional. Admiring her gift, he regretted that she tore up and burnt so many of her poems. With typical brotherly pride and good intentions, he took Mary's 'railway poem' to the newspaper offices. It was published on 18 October, alongside a report of the accident :

[10] Letter of George Meredith to Olive (October 1907): 'Do you know that Gladys (at her own special request) has been for two drives with me in the large trap? – one to Upper Pulley a few days ago, and the other this morning to a place called Betton Strange about three miles away – she said today that her nerves must be stronger as she does not now dread going with the horse, as she did some time ago : I hope she will continue the drives as the air is very refreshing to her when moving through it at a fair speed, and this Master Billy cannot do'.

A night wind soughed around the speeding train
Unsatisfied, complaining,
Demanding something – someone for its own :
None heard, for sleep and laughter drowned its moan.
'Lamps lit, blinds down, what matter if 'tis raining?'
In the foreboding wind the lights were straining. . . .[11]

Even though it was anonymous, Mary was appalled to see her poem – all five verses – in the *Shrewsbury Chronicle*. An outpouring from her deeply felt pity, not revised, untypical of her work – not a poem she would wish anyone to read, least of all the general public. Yet there it was confronting her on the printed page.

Kenneth, returning from work that evening, saw Mary at the gates of Maesbrook waiting for him with a stern expression on her face. He admitted, on being questioned, that he had taken the poem for publication. 'Yes! It was too nice to burn.' Mary's reply burned in Kenneth's mind : 'Well! I'm very annoyed with you. It was not fit for publication!' He was upset by her distress yet felt that her temporary annoyance with him was well worth it, for letters of appreciation of her poem poured in to Mary, forwarded by the editor. And he noticed that after this Mary was writing with increased confidence.

In 1908 Mary took a long holiday on Lyth Hill in 'the dream/ And hush of summer', accompanied by Muriel and lodging at a cottage where 'holiday boarders' were welcomed. The sounds of life in the plain rose up, magnified in the still, warm air of summer : the pealing of Sunday bells across 'the lonely meadows', the thrumming of steam-driven trains bound for 'the squalor of big cities', the howling and baying of the hounds as the hunt from Condover passed the wooded base of the hill – reminding Mary of other aspects of reality. Though immersed in nature's symbols – 'Submerged within their beauty, I/Transcend my poor mortality' – it was to humanity 'with its limitless desires, its weak small hands' and to the everyday world that she always 'returned' with compassion, attuned to what Matthew Arnold called 'the eternal note of sadness' in human life. And during those leisurely days of the Edwardian era when, for Mary, Maesbrook was a

[11] *Shrewsbury Chronicle*, 18 Oct. 1907; in the *Shropshire Magazine* – article by Margaret Hardy, 'The Poems of Mary Webb', July 1967, pp. 22–3.

world of laughter and warm affection centred around her father, and Lyth Hill the very 'heart of enchantment', she was nearing the traumatic and tragic realities of her own life.

Changes were to come relentlessly like 'the wind . . . walking in the shaken wood'. Mary saw that her father was ageing; she felt intuitively the approach of personal disaster and disintegration, her heart gripped by 'tremblings chill'. This became a pain within her joy, calling ever more insistently, more keenly, as she sensed the inevitable flux :

> Within my heart a little sorrow crept
>   And wept, and wept.
> Below the lilt of happiest melodies
>   I heard its sighs
> And cried : You little alien in my heart,
>   Depart. Depart !
>
> (*CPAP,* p. 106)

One of the first major changes at Maesbrook – a deeply felt loss to Mary – involved Minoni. Her services were no longer needed with Olive at boarding school and young Mervyn at a nearby preparatory school, The Limes.[12] Muriel, returned from finishing school, was now at home while the two older boys had both left Ellesmere College : Kenneth, working in a Shrewsbury bank, had grown into a good-looking, adventurous young man, although to Minoni it seemed only yesterday that as a schoolboy he stood at family prayers with pet white mice crawling up inside his jacket and out around his neck; Douglas had gone to London to train as an engineer in one of the telegraph companies. Her work with the Merediths finished, Minoni took a post in the South. A sad wrench for all of them. But she never lost contact with the Merediths and corresponded regularly with Mary, having a special affection for 'little Gladys'.

The next member of the family to leave was Kenneth. Christmas 1907 was his last at Maesbrook. Mist lingered around the brook and meadows on Christmas Day; Pontesford Hill

---

[12] George Meredith paid Miss Lory an implicit tribute when he wrote in a letter to Olive, newly arrived at St Winifred's, Bangor, for the autumn term, 1906 : 'I feel sure that you have been thoroughly *well-grounded* at home, and that you will do your level best to profit by it under your new conditions' (his italics).

could not be seen; the Meredith family circle – gathered round the Christmas tree, singing carols which Mary played on the piano – was complete for the last time. Early in the New Year Kenneth announced his intention to emigrate to Canada. He had decided that he must 'sing his own song', break out from the cage which the bank had become for him, seek freedom, adventure across the Atlantic.

This was a time when there was a great influx of immigrants to Canada from Britain, building up from Victoria's Diamond Jubilee climactic focus on the Empire. The *fin de siècle* 'Empire-frenzy' was carried forward after the turn of the century in waves of emigration which both answered and promoted the undercurrent of Edwardian restlessness. Kenneth Meredith was a typical young man of his generation, refusing to be stifled by the backwash of Victorian attitudes, eager to be part of the spearhead of a new age in a new world. He had the individuality of outlook, proud independence and enormous physical zest of which pioneers are made. Mary too had these qualities differently directed in a delving to ultimate truth, exploration of an inner world, development of the individual self, extending the tip of awareness in her writings.

She understood that to Kenneth a career in banking seemed like a prison sentence. In his quest for self-realisation, he needed an outdoor life, close to the soil. His primal needs were those of Jasper Darke in *The House in Dormer Forest:* 'I want myself. I want to be let alone and have room to breathe ...'

It was a shock to the family when they heard of his plans to go to Canada and find work on the vast farms. Alice Meredith was stunned – 'Whither away?' had now assumed an unexpected significance. Various other careers were put forward . . . the Church, the Navy. But Kenneth was emphatic about Canada. Mary, though anticipating the sense of loss that his going would create, knew that he must be allowed to sing his own song, that the time had come for him to sing it.

A sad George Meredith and Douglas (on leave for the occasion), accompanied Kenneth and his luggage to Liverpool in March 1908. He sailed out on the Cunard liner, not quite twenty, full of youthful hope and vitality. At Easter he was writing home that he had begun his first job on a farm twenty-two miles from the nearest town. Kenneth was greatly missed at Maesbrook, particularly by Mary: 'However far he travels on, / Thought follows, like the willow-wren / That flies the stormy seas again / To lands where her delight has gone.'

As Kenneth was departing from the shores of home, his ship steaming out of the Mersey, the flat coastline receding, he had an overwhelming intuition that he would never see his father again.

George Meredith had been declining physically since 1906, increasingly frail, his tall form stooping, energy and enthusiasm for life slipping gradually away. Mary was deeply anxious about the change in him, the difference she saw over two years. In 1906 he had been the same amusing, active man, interested in Church, local and national affairs. A sidesman at Holy Trinity, a leading member of the Church Defence Committee, he enjoyed meetings at which topics such as 'Godless education' were given lively discussion; and his patriotic poem, 'Topics for the Times', was printed by Wildings of Shrewsbury and widely circulated.

In the later part of 1908, George Meredith, then sixty-seven, was too unwell and depressed to go out, feeling old age creeping upon him. Nothing seemed to arouse his interest, not even the news about the rearrangement of Meole Brace charities which had at one time concerned him very much.

He wrote melancholy verses about the transience of human life, the 'growing away' of his children – reflecting on change, thoughts of death came upon him stealthily like dark wings of shadow birds. The writing of poems may have helped to relieve his depression.

Mary was his constant companion and as he had tended her in her long illness so she, in turn, sat with him, gently trying to cheer him, stir him from the lethargy. One of his poems, 'Bereft', indicates the depth of his dejection:

> Draw down the blinds! – the landscape seemed so fair
> When all my boys and girls were playing there :–
> Making the homestead almost Heaven to me –
> Now all are gone! not one dear form I see :–
> I ne'er shall look upon their like again!
> There is a mist upon the window-pane!
> Draw down the blinds!

Yes! draw them down! – I hear the passing-bell
Of Life's most cherished dreams which sounds the knell!
No stars, no moon reward my straining eye,
Nought but a sorrow-clouded canopy :
Draw down the blinds!

At Christmas 1908, he did not write his usual bright verse to
greet the season. The depleted family circle brought his attention
still further to the passing of life. Only two years ago on
Christmas Day the whole family had gone to communion on a
brilliant day of cold sunshine, and at night the snow had fallen,
a layer of three inches covering the village, contrasting with the
red stone of the buildings. On 27 December, 1908, snow fell
again, all day whirling thickly around Maesbrook, curtaining
off the meadows, covering the grounds with a blankness, as if
prophesying negation. For Mary, the experience of utter negation
was at hand, stealing as softly and surely upon her as the silent
swirl of snow.

As the year drew to a close, George Meredith, feeling a little
better, decided to do some manual work in one of the rambling
haylofts. Not really strong enough, he fell from a ladder in the
loft and was very badly shaken. Worse still, the fall caused a
blood clot in his leg. He was very dangerously ill – the doctor
told the family that the clot could move to his heart. Mary sat
by his bedside keeping vigil over him, her whole being tight with
fear, 'And the stark future, stripped of all delight / Loomed up
so near . . .'

On New Year's Day she brought an alder branch 'already
bravely budded' from one of the trees he had planted in the
garden, and set it in a vase by his bed :

> He smiled, but hardly cared to turn his head
> And see how close the purple spheres were studded,
> Wherein the April leaves lay slumbering.
> He spoke of leaves that rustled by his pillows,
> More golden-sweet than airs in summer willows.
> I did not know he would not see the spring.
>
> (*51, 22*)

For Mary, loss was closing in, an icy pall; joy flickered out and she was faced by a fearful reality. On the night of 2 January, he had a dream which caused him to quiver with a 'great yearning joy':

> You heard a strange, sweet voice, that sang and sang
> Within a vaulted chamber – low and dim
> And vaguely shadowy; and the shadows rang
> With the continual beauty of the hymn.
>
> You thought the music came from overhead,
> From some high gallery whence it rose and fell:
> But who the singer was, and what he said,
> Although you longed to know, you could not tell.
>
> (CPAP, p. 111)

As she soothed him and he told her of the dream, Mary saw at once the interpretation – for her no note of infinite joy, only the stark truth of imminent death.

She could not in those few remaining hours share her father's quiet faith – 'There's an answer to every question and at long last the light shines' – as with John Arden, George Meredith's lantern of love was never dimmed. To the last he believed in his God of love – 'Lead, kindly Light'. Mary, sitting by his side throughout the final night, bravely carried on with her embroidery, bending her head low to conceal her face in case it revealed the immensity of the void opening before her.

How to continue without her father's golden presence, the 'word of praise' that had illumined her world, given purpose to her creative expression?

> On that last night, embroidering by his bed,
> I often paused, his loving smile to meet,
> And hear the tender approving words he said:–
> 'Your work is very beautiful, my sweet!'
>
> The embroidery stays unfinished; Life's design
> Must yet be stitched. How can I raise my head –
> And no smile there? Lest sudden tears of mine
> Should stain the cloth, and dull the silver thread.

For when the work is spread before his eyes
It must not seem too sadly incomplete.
So he may smile and say in glad surprise,
'Your work is very beautiful, my sweet.'

(*CPAP*, p. 107)

He died on 5 January, with Mary and Alice by his bedside.

5
Life's Dark Cedar
1909–1912

> ... to know the cosmos as nothing but impersonal force is to dwell in an intellectual hell compared with which the Christian's hell is Nirvana. *(HDF,* p. 257)
>
> ... Life's design
> Must yet be stitched.

George Meredith was buried on Friday, 11 January 1909, snow still covering the fields and hedgerows as the burial procession in deep black travelled from Meole Brace to Ightfield where the funeral service took place in his father's former church. 'All colours from the frozen earth have died / And only shadow stains the cold, white snow.' To Mary, utterly desolate, the world now seemed merely 'a ball whirling through the void'. Everything had lost its identity. Nothing mattered. Nature, too, was part of this nothingness.

A large number of people came from far and near, and many more sent wreaths, including Miss Lory and Miss Southern. The genuine grief and sympathy evoked by his death, showing how highly he was regarded and loved, was not a comfort to Mary at this time, but intensified the pain of loss. The words of the clergyman, however well intended, sounded hollow, afforded no solace.

Of George Meredith's qualities, the Rev. William Bather said:

> Devout, unselfish, ever ready to give his help, kindly, open hearted, humble-minded almost to a fault, with a cheery word of greeting for all, he never failed to wake in those with whom he came in contact a feeling that they were better for his friendship.

As he had died on the eve of the Epiphany, this was the basis of the sermon, but to Mary the optimistic phrases – 'that our loss is his gain, that a great Epiphany has indeed come to him . . . and all mists are now removed' – seemed facile, meaningless; neither could the prospect of a 'grand and new Epiphany, an Epiphany of Comfort, Hope and Grace and Strength' reach through the complete negation. She had come to a dark night, her first dark night of the soul.

And now Mary's only consolation, her only relief, was in her poetry. Here she could express her loss, her dark night, writing to a silence, for she knew no 'word of praise' could come again: 'Since he departed, Silence lays her finger / More heavily on this house than on his tomb.'

In the tragic series of poems that followed, the edge of pain is acute:

> Not for the dear things said do I weep now;
> Not for your deeds of quiet love and duty
> Does my heart freeze and starve since you endow
> Cold death with beauty.
>
> Just for the look of utter comprehension;
> The dear gay laugh that only true hearts know;
> For these I would from life's severe detention
> Arise and go.   (*PSJ*, p. 88)

Mary's grief was of such intensity and so prolonged that, in the opinion of her family, it 'took years off her own life'. The strain certainly undermined her health still further, and during the next three years she suffered long spells of illness. Her poems reveal how constantly she mourned – like Heine, out of her great sorrows she made her little songs.

The spring of 1909 brought no joy – this 'seemed fled forever'; it only emphasised 'The Difference':

> I walk among the daisies, as of old;
> But he comes never more by lane or fold.
> The same warm speedwell-field is dark with dew;
> But he's away beyond a deeper blue.
> A year today we saw the same flowers grow –
> Last May! Last May! A century ago.
>
> Above the speedwell leans the rosy tree
> From which he plucked an apple bough for me.
> Not all the blossom on the branches left
> Can fill the place of that sweet bough bereft;

And none can fill the heart that loved him so
Last May! Last May! Eternities ago ...

(PSJ, p. 87)

This experience of unassuaged sorrow gave greater emotional immediacy to her poetry. Grief, here, was a powerful extender.

All the extant poems of the 1909–10 series (*CPAP*, pp. 106–15) reflect her struggle in the abyss of loss. In 'Treasures' (For G.E.M.) a tribute to her father, there is again the sad catharsis:

These are my treasures : just a word, a look,
A chiming sentence from his favourite book,
A large, blue, scented blossom that he found
And plucked for me in some enchanted ground,
A joy he planned for us, a verse he made
Upon a birthday, the increasing shade
Of trees he planted by the waterside,
The echo of a laugh, his tender pride
In those he loved, his hand upon my hair,
The dear voice lifted in his evening prayer.

How safe they must be kept! So dear, so few,
And all I have to last my whole life through.

(PSJ, p. 86)

The impact made by her father's death cannot be over-estimated. After this she was never to be really secure again. This traumatic period saw her final rejection of institutional religion and marked an important step in her literary development. As her sense of insecurity deepened, to write became – even more than before – a condition of life. At this time she was indeed 'one to whom life was pain, and death a charnel house', but out of her personal chaos she brought something positive and more mature. The suffering extended her range of experience and ultimately had significant creative results, first in her poetry and later in her prose fiction. Not only was it part of the motivation behind *The Golden Arrow* – creating in this first novel a portrait of her father – but she also used her experience of 'an intellectual hell' in the development of Stephen Southernwood in the same novel and of both Jasper and Amber Darke in *The House in Dormer Forest.*

Stephen Southernwood's crisis is a crisis of faith when he casts away the 'ready-made code' and dogma which formerly he had preached, and faces, in his agnosticism, 'the horror of emptiness, utter negation – that modern ghost, more ghastly than medieval devils or the ancient gods of slaughter' (*GA*, p. 230). His inner conflict is vividly depicted as, seeing death, 'the Dark Keeper', everywhere in the autumn landscape, he confronts the antithesis of life and death, of the infinite as opposed to man's pathetic brevity. In the sense of spiritual abyss she conveys here, Mary Webb is a modernist writer.

And again, Amber Darke's state of mind believing her brother Jasper drowned, is expressive of Mary's own after her father's death. The effectiveness of these passages in *The House in Dormer Forest* lies in this evocation of the devastion experienced in 1909, and so keenly evident in her poems of that date. Occasionally the same imagery is used in both, emphasising the link between the personal experience expressed in her poetry and then, at a later date, embedded in the imaginative world of her novels. So she imbues with emotional intensity the passages in *The House in Dormer Forest* in which Amber Darke faces (as she herself has faced) 'the old inveterate antithesis', when 'the soul perceives simultaneously the life of man – its small comforts, its upholstery of everyday – and the infinite; when it asks, bemused and anxious, "Which is the dream?" They cannot both be true, it seems, for they are in flat contradiction . . .' (p. 255). In describing how to Amber life seems unreal and nature itself a mockery, Mary is voicing her own ineluctable spiritual despair, the desolation of her dark night of the soul :

> . . . there were no homely things. This was no longer a forest of familiar trees, carpeted with friendly flowers, under known skies. It was an unknown country – that which encircles the world of fact, holding it as a demon might hold a crystal glass. (p. 256)

In this period of spiritual wilderness, Mary had entered fully the second part of her inheritance. Her life hitherto had been 'one long sigh of wonder' in response to her Shropshire world, her apprehension of spiritual beauty immanent in nature : 'Let me inherit / Agony – wonder : / But leave me not icily, numbly asunder, / Dear Life !' Now agony filled her days and nights as she saw nature in its 'complete indifference' : no longer God-filled, 'merely naked life – nothing but matter, motion and heat'

(*HDF*, p. 257). In this living nightmare, nature had, temporarily at least, lost its meaning, her symbols their significance – hers was a darkness of double vision which could only become light again when the two visions had fused as one.

Whereas before she had found solace, refuge, spiritual fulfilment in nature, now, far from consoling, it offered a deeper horror. Her previous reading in Darwin, Huxley and Haeckel was recalled, plunging her still further into agonised doubt, into the 'intellectual hell' of an impersonal cosmos empty of god – a view which appalled her, colouring everything. She felt, as Thomas Hardy did, the full impact of this negation, the pathos of humanity blindly struggling in a meaningless, mechanical universe. In 'The Door' she depicts humanity as 'children at their father's door, who wait / . . . They only long to climb on father's bed / And cry their terrors out in father's arms. / And maybe, all the while, their father's dead.' (*PSJ*, p. 113)

Mary did not know then that she would emerge to a new understanding, to a renewal of her pantheistic mysticism, to a synthesis of the polarities which were clamouring and contending in seeming opposition, in paradox. Yet by her intuitive extension towards truth she knew that she must totally experience the bleak reality of 'dark night' in which she found herself. How far would she be able to integrate this to achieve a new wholeness? It is certain that she gradually, if painfully, emerged out of this spiritually fallow period to greater strength, her inner progression tending inevitably to literary progression although it was to be another five years before *The Golden Arrow*. This would not be written until she had been renewed by a love comparable to that she had known with her father – the 'ring of pale fire'. Love was to come and illumine reality even more than before. Until then she was still involved in the struggle out of the chrysalis.

Minor literary successes marked this emergence. She sent a short story, 'A Cedar-Rose', to *Country Life* and was greatly encouraged by its acceptance. It appeared on 10 July 1909, under her pseudonym 'Lady Day' – a step in her development towards major works of prose fiction (*CPAP*, pp. 3–6).

'A Cedar-Rose' is a charming vignette about two elderly Victorian spinsters living in a 'fortress-like house' with an enclosed garden dominated by a large cedar tree. The effectiveness of this simple story owes much to the graceful lyricism of the descriptions and particularly to the pathos brought to the character of Miss Adalia, for whom the cedar-rose has symbolic significance. Here the completeness and the use of symbolism indicate aspects of Mary Webb's future achievement in the novel, and some of the similes and metaphors are forerunners of those which animate her later writing. It is reminiscent of Katherine Mansfield's more tender stories, e.g. 'The Aloe', later retitled 'Prelude' – and Mary Webb can be compared with this writer in the pointedness of her perceptions and in her handling of imaginative detail (always relating the carefully selected particulars of setting and season to the emotional mood of her story).

This tale sprang directly from Mary's experience 'visiting' – ever responsive to the poignancy of life, 'the sweet keen trouble of living', she often drew upon her knowledge of actual events, people and incidents for the germ of her short stories. Aged, lonely, sad beings are frequently the subject of these stories and occasionally of her poems.

It is appropriate that this little country story initiated her career as a published writer of fiction, for it closes with a sentence ironically prophetic of her own life and achievement – 'Her life's dark cedar will bear its immortal flower.'

During those bitter months of grief and throughout the snowy spring of 1909, Mary 'came through' by channelling some of her intensity into her literary work: in this she was encouraged by Flora McLeod who had, by this date, become a fairly close friend and who, when 'A Cedar-Rose' was published, shared with Mary 'the excitement and the joy'. Miss McLeod, then working on her own first book, offered to type manuscripts for Mary and they occasionally spent an evening together.

One evening especially was remembered by Miss McLeod: she was reading from her own book about a pilgrim to Mary, quick to grasp the inner meaning of parables and express herself allegorically, as 'A Cedar-Rose' shows. Miss McLeod describes how they 'sat together in the warm firelight, under the glow of the lamp, and then she left me to go out (as she wrote to me next day) into the storm and rain, the cold and dark, which seemed to her a type of her search for life and truth'. After her first confrontation with a great negative – the death of her father – Mary

needed in her 'search for life and truth' to know the full reality
of 'the storm and rain, the cold and dark'. It was an intuitive
search into darkness – reflected later in Deborah Arden's ordeal,
plunged into 'the unknown', facing her own worst fears,
struggling, in her vision of opposites, to reconcile good and evil.

Not long after the publication of 'A Cedar-Rose' Mary decided
to prepare her collection of essays to send to publishers, and Flora
McLeod typed the manuscript. The whole tenor of these essays,
as we have seen, is to direct those who suffer, whether physically
or spiritually, towards a healing: she was one of those who
having suffered terribly herself, desires, ever after, to be a healer,
one like Prudence Sarn in *Precious Bane*, who because she 'had
no lover . . . would lief have been the world's lover'. And love
would always be her supreme value. Each essay was introduced
by a short verse, and under its title, 'The Scallop Shell', her first
complete prose work was sent off to publishing firms.[1] Ultimately
it was to be published as *The Spring of Joy*, but in 1910 it was
rejected by publishers some of whom, in letters of praise, gave
recognition of its quality although they were not prepared to risk
anything on an unknown writer. Eventually, unable to face the
disappointment of further rejections, Mary put the work aside.

During this period of renewed creative impulse, as she was
experiencing these initial hopes and disappointments of her
literary career, there came to live at Meole Brace the man on
whom she was to centre her life and her gift of love.

> Thunder is on the fields, and fear;
> No thrushes sing and no bees hum:
> But my heart's belfry rocks (oh, hear!)
> My lover's come! My lover's come!
>
> (51, p. 57)

Henry Bertram Law Webb had taken up a teaching post in
January 1908 at 'The Limes', the preparatory school near Meole
Brace at which Mervyn Meredith had been a pupil. Graduating
from St Catherine's, Cambridge, in 1907 with a Law Special
and B.A., Henry had decided to teach, returning to Shropshire,
his native county. In fact, 'The Limes' had been his own first

---

[1] The title was taken from Sir Walter Ralegh's poem, 'The Pilgrimage':
'Give me my scallop-shell of quiet,/My staff of faith to walk upon,/My scrip
of joy, immortal diet,/My bottle of salvation . . .'

school where he spent a year, 1898–9, before proceeding to public schools : King Edward's, Stratford-on-Avon (1899–1902) and St Edmund's, Canterbury, going from there to St Catherine's with a classical scholarship in 1904.

The Webb family came from the east of Shropshire, from Dawley and Broseley where Henry's father, Dr Thomas Law Webb, had a medical practice. They were well known at Dawley since Henry's uncle, Captain Matthew Webb, was a national hero, achieving a world-wide reputation in 1875 as the first man to swim the English Channel and gaining further fame in 1883 by his unfortunate if spectacular death at Niagara Falls. Henry (Bertie), born on 23 November 1885, was quiet, charming, cultured, a scholar and philosopher. Soon after graduating he began to write his philosophical ideas developed at Cambridge. Nature notes and observations made at The Limes were interwoven with these to become the book of philosophic essays entitled *The Silences of The Moon*.[2] Meeting a better fate than Mary's 'The Scallop Shell', it was published by The Bodley Head early in 1911 when Henry was twenty-five.

Henry Law Webb came to live in Meole Brace itself in December 1909, when his father, recently retired from medical practice, bought Brent House opposite the Vicarage. The family soon became known in the village : Dr Law Webb was much respected and Henry noted as an outstanding scholar, fluent in seven languages. Before long the Webbs met the Merediths, and Ethel, Henry's sister, became a friend of Muriel Meredith during 1910, visiting Maesbrook. Henry heard from her about 'the eldest Miss Meredith' – Gladys – 'a great reader' and almost a permanent invalid at this time, deeply affected by her father's death, and spoken of by Meole Brace inhabitants as someone unusual, afflicted, a semi-recluse and a poet. He heard of her also at Miss Southern's Corner House where the Literary Society held meetings. Mary's ill health throughout 1909 prevented her from attending, but Miss Southern often spoke admiringly of her, much impressed by the fact that many of Mary's papers which acquired such high marks on the Extension Course were written immediately after getting up from a game of bridge.

It was when Mary, feeling stronger, began to attend again the

[2] This is shown in Henry's annotations to his own copy of the book. I am indebted to Mrs Tessa Maclean for the loan of this and permission to use it.

literary gatherings in the Corner House that she and Henry came to know one another. The attraction between them was immediate and powerful. Discussing literature, they found a great deal in common : Henry began calling on Mary at Maesbrook where they had long talks, walking slowly in the lower garden by the mill-race and in the fields beyond the weir. Soon the walks extended to Lyth Hill where she took him to her Little Wood, already aware that here was the man who might hold 'the keys of her life, of her heaven and hell'. As she wrote later of the meeting of Amber and Michael in the Birds' Orchard : 'They looked at one another, and their look was that of friends who have met a long while since, in other lands, to the sound of wilder music, but with the same remembered ecstasy.' (*HDF*, p. 191.) Such was the nature of their impact on one another – it seemed 'they had always known each other', that 'already he held the essence of her personality within his own'. The relationship of Amber and Michael in *The House in Dormer Forest* is based on Mary's own with Henry, and much of the detail directly autobiographical.

She was experiencing companionship and understanding such as she had known only with her father. Could Henry occupy the gap at the centre of her world, the void left by her father and filled by his memory? With mingled joy and fear she wondered had she found her 'dear acquaintance', 'the candle of her eye'?

Immensely curious about her, Henry was compelled by her sad-sweet intensity, her unusual personality – at once shy yet eager, timid yet spontaneous, dreamy yet precise, fragile yet with boundless mental energy and, at times, physical energy beyond her strength. Here was a woman with a mind as stimulating to him as any he had met at Cambridge – he was strongly drawn by what Walter de la Mare later described as her 'gentle yet ardent company' (Intro. *PSJ*, p. 19), and wanted more of it. Mary 'brought her own quietness into a room' but could talk brilliantly when she had confidence in her companion. Frank, lucid, witty, amusing, she had, like Amber Darke, 'a little goblin of humour' delightfully in tune with Henry's. In her rather deep musical voice, talking of country things and country people, her conversation became especially vivid and lively, often bringing in Shropshire dialect, revealing to Henry a close knowledge of cottagers, how they lived and thought – a depth of sympathy and understanding which contrasted with the hermetic image of 'a semi-recluse'.

And equally Mary was compelled towards Henry, whose kindness, patience, refinement and culture were most attractive qualities to her, so strongly reminiscent of her father. He combined these with boyish appeal and considerable personal charm – tall, rather thin, good-looking, his hair very thick and dark, his eyes, though short-sighted, keen with 'an energy of vitality not of physical origin', laughter lurking in their depths. Although almost five years younger than Mary, Henry thought nothing of the age difference; nor was he deterred by knowledge of her recurring illness which had left its signs. He was increasingly fascinated – Mary, on their walks, striding out across the wind-blown uplands, cheeks flushed, hair dishevelled, large eyes shining, seemed 'all steeped in radiance'.[3] Her intimacy with nature, 'the changing seasons which she knew like a rosary', and the hyper-acute senses through which this special relationship with nature had developed, were admired profoundly by Henry, himself a professed nature worshipper. Undoubtedly they discussed nature as a source of symbols and analogies, as well as the pure fascination of it as, in Mary's words, 'a fairyland of actuality'; and in 1910 both were submitting their essays on these themes to publishers.

Previous studies of Mary Webb have not taken into account Henry's *The Silences of the Moon* which is of central importance to an understanding of his mind and personality, and, intrinsically, of their relationship. It gives eloquent evidence that 'his mind had the qualities of flame', as Mary said later in portraying him as Michael Hallowes in *The House in Dormer Forest*, and also that he and she had a wide area of intellectual as well as emotional rapprochement. A close comparison of *The Silences of the Moon* with *The Spring of Joy* reveals considerable similarity and overlapping of thought.

Consisting of three long essays, *The Silences of the Moon* is written in a graceful style, with a great deal of classical reference and allusion. The limpid quality of Henry's writing recalls the Aegean waters with their calm blue expanse. His dedication is to

[3] Amber Darke seemed to Michael Hallowes 'as lovely as a sun-drenched petal in which neither colour nor texture can be seen, all being steeped in radiance'.

W. Compton Leith, whose highly regarded book, *Apologia Diffidentis*, had made a strong impression on him. Henry's title was taken from a line in the Aeneid: 'A Tenedo tacitae per amica silentia lunae', words which, he says, are 'among my most priceless possessions . . . set high among my mind's Penates'. It is interesting to note that W. B. Yeats, from whom Henry quotes in *The Silences of the Moon*, was, in 1917, to use the same words from the Aeneid as the title of his philosophic essays (*Per Amica Silentia Lunae*).

Throughout Henry's discussion which turns fundamentally on his contention that 'the great test question for every philosophy is, "How does it come into line with Nature" ', he refers to the Greeks, especially to Plato, and also to the Neo-Platonists who, together with the Christians Mystics (also discussed by Henry), were at that time receiving renewed scholarly attention.

Henry's range of reference extended from the Presocratics to Swedenborg. His thought has cohesion and penetration. He expresses his viewpoint unequivocally : like Mary, he has rejected utterly conventional religion, the accretions of Christianity, a personified God, maintaining that dogma is 'in its rudiments nothing more than an encrusted symbol'; and he upholds animism as 'the first and last of religions'. While he was deeply imbued with the classical spirit and found the Hellenic world a source of beginnings, nature was his canon. Declaring himself to be 'a whole hearted idolater', he elevates nature so that he is virtually a worshipper : 'such as love Nature for herself cannot choose but worship her' (pp. 5, 26). Henry, in *The Silences of the Moon* declares persuasively that he is a lover of nature, while Mary, in *The Spring of Joy*, fervently yet implicitly is a lover. Although Henry understands what he calls 'the symbolic spirit of Nature', it is not with Mary's intuitive awareness or her unblinkered and unsentimental recognition of all aspects of nature – the indifference, 'the red in tooth and claw', as well as the beauty. One feels in reading *The Silences of the Moon*, that Henry's appreciation of nature has grown, not as Mary's did by total realistic immersion, but from an idealised view developed in the study rather than in the fields and forest. Henry's 'love of earth', of natural beauty, was primarily intellectual, a blend of perception and reason rather than a mystical rapture, a dilation of consciousness. While Mary attained to ecstatic union, Henry talked aesthetically about it: such is the difference between the true mystic and the mystic philosopher.

Much that in Henry's work is made explicit discursively, in Mary's is expressed implicitly in nature imagery, is cloaked in metaphor. Where Henry explains symbol, Mary uses it. Mysticism he sees as 'a tracking of the footsteps of this same idea of Beauty along one of its numberless paths'. Central to his system of thought is his idea of symbol:

> Symbols are the fairest blossoms of all thought, even of philosophical thought, wherein they are exotic; they are alien to logic, hand in hand with imagination. They are the foundation of every attempt to explain deity by religion or philosophy or the arts; they lie at the root of all beauty expressible or inexpressible by words.   (p. 39)

While he expresses with clarity insights such as these, in other passages Henry reveals himself as a naive young idealist as yet untried by the harsher realities of experience. Mary, no doubt, felt the pathos of his rather blithe statements on death – 'Let us, then, go to death as the gulls swoop to the waves after stormy weather – with a cry of "The Sea!" and the laughter of a soul long pent inland', this significantly underlined (in Henry's own copy of the book) by Mary with the wistful annotation: 'A wonderful ideal, only possible for the strong.' Concerned with the shaping of one's soul in this life, Henry interprets 'the death of the beloved' as a blessing since it ejects the lover into an isolation essential for the growth of his soul; he proclaims 'by adversity we learn to stand alone', emphasising 'the very best fate that can befall us is to be deserted by those upon whose aid we rely and betrayed by the hearts which have beat against our own'. A cool and stoical philosophy indeed. Would he be able to apply it in the actuality of his own life? And what was Mary's reaction to such a viewpoint?

Certainly Henry influenced Mary in the early stages of their relationship, his opinions helping to support and shape hers especially in this period of doubt. He had deep, far perspectives, a detachment, almost a remoteness like the hills he describes 'whose eternity passes like a dream'. Mary writes of his sustaining influence in her poem 'November', admiring his 'sadness of unflinching sight'.

These essays are reminiscent of Richard Jefferies' *The Story of my Heart* which as an 'autobiography of the soul' voiced something of both Henry's and Mary's experience – there is spiritual autobiography in both *The Silences of the Moon* and *The Spring of Joy,* inner growth, deeper soul-life their theme, but Henry's essays are nearer than Mary's to Jefferies' intellectual romanticism, thick with declarations. Henry avers, following Jefferies: 'If I want a definition of the infinite I shall go not to a priest but to a hill-top from which I may look down into the eyes of dawn'.

Henry's descriptions of birds delighted Mary who marked and annotated them. Next to his 'Have you once heard the birds' song in dark Spring dawns?', she comments, 'How perfect the word dark is here! It does everything for the picture.' Excelling, herself, in such exact, vivid description, Mary, as she showed later in her reviews of natural histories for the *Spectator,* was highly critical of anything less than accurate or bordering on the sentimental where nature was concerned.

Henry Webb's little-known essays give us an invaluable insight into his ideas and character, making clear what Mary says of him in a love poem – 'There is so much of beauty in your mind'. Throughout his writing he reveals his calm, aesthetic temperament, and the closing passage (again underlined by Mary) is typical of the whole:

> Now the light has gone and the wind has gone; candles are lit, the bats are squeaking round the fir-tops, and the moon is alighting upon the Welsh hills with the same noiseless tread as when she stole over the slopes of Mount Latmos in search of young Endymion. How, think you, has the world changed since those days of Indra and Vritra, Dian and Endymion? Just as much and as little as it has changed since I lit my candles, so far as I am concerned: for did I not love before the dawn of Time and do I not love still? (p. 139)

'Thrilled and thrilling', their admiration for each other grew to an intensity of feeling. For Henry, to use his own words, love had come 'riding upon a gale' and lifted him 'from clay to magnificence'. Such was his experience with Mary, their love fusion deepening to what she described later in *Gone to Earth* as 'a fervour of mind for mind, a clasp more frantic than that of the arms, a continuous psychic state more passionate than the great moments of physical passion . . .' (p. 201), a passage which can be read alongside Henry's 'Alas! for the mind which has no other to read its unwritten periods and understand its silences'. So they understood (and discussed) Donne's 'interinanimation' :

> When love, with one another so
>   Interinanimates two soules,
> That abler soule, which thence doth flow,
>   Defects of lonelinesse, controules . . . ('The Extasie')

These 'defects of loneliness' were more Mary's than Henry's. While her father's death had been crucial in her maturing process, as we have seen it had left her ill and insecure, sharply attuned ever after to what she called 'the loud discordant sounds of fate.'

Hilda Addison has drawn attention to a resemblance between the Webbs' relationship and that of the Brownings. There are some obvious similarities : those of age difference, delicate health, avid interchange of ideas and writings, a marriage of minds, mental ardour growing to passionate love. Like Browning with Elizabeth Barrett, Henry was patient and understanding with Mary, aware of her keen sense of physical inferiority, the insecurity this caused and her extreme sensitivity in company. She knew that some people would regard theirs as a curious match – herself over thirty years old and a semi-invalid; Henry twenty-six, handsome and eligible.

Among her love poems to Henry, the short 'Reflections' alludes to her painful consciousness of facial defects :

> No beauty is mine, and yet I saw today
> A lovely face within my mirror glassed;
> For you had looked upon me as you passed,
> And still there lingered, as you went away,
> Reflections of your grace in mouth and eye –
> Like those rare dawns that paint the eastern sky
> And mirror forth
> Their beauty even in the hueless north.
>
> (51, p. 35)

Yet Mary's face, although marred, was not, as she thought,

unlovely.[4] Photographs show her attractive features, quiet
strength, dark intentness. Such was her radiance that Michael
Hallowes' words to Amber Darke – 'Your spirit shines so, I can't
see your features' – might well have been Henry's to Mary. Their
love, like that of Amber and Michael, was metaphorically the
'ring of pale fire'. In Mary, Henry had found his Beatrice.

They became engaged during the summer of 1911. In a letter
to Flora McLeod, telling her of the engagement, Mary wrote:

> Pray for me as you kneel in your curtained alcove, for though
> I am so happy, so incredibly and unexpectedly happy, I am also
> somewhat afraid.

After her father's death and the long struggle to regain some
equilibrium, once more she was giving all – and risking all – in
a comparable love. This love brought pain as acute as joy for it
sharpened her awareness of transience, gave a keen edge to her
happiness. Suddenly she had again so much that was precious;
and just as suddenly it could be gone. So the fear of loss loomed
spectre-like to haunt her, and was to remain her dark companion
to the end. Henry, her 'verray parfit gentil knyght' brought her
'the peace of being understood'. But as she wrote in 'Lilies in the
Valleys', she was irrevocably to trust all 'in a love that laughs and
a love that grieves'.

They decided to marry in 1912. In marrying Henry, however,
she had to relinquish Shropshire : he had accepted another teaching post, this time in Weston-super-Mare on the Somerset coast.
The passage in *The House in Dormer Forest* in which Michael
Hallowes asks Amber Darke whether she is prepared to leave her
home – the valley, forest and surrounding nature – and come
away with him, is autobiographical. Amber's reply can be taken
as Mary's own to Henry :

> 'You love me enough to be willing to go?'
> 'I have said so.'

---

[4] There is an unfortunate error in Michael Howard's *Jonathan Cape:
Publisher* (Cape 1971) in which it is stated that she had a harelip, this mistake being due to a confusion between Mary Webb and Prudence Sarn, the
central character of her novel *Precious Bane*. Claud Cockburn in *Bestseller*,
taking his information from *Jonathan Cape: Publisher,* perpetuates this error.

The date chosen for the wedding was 12 June: Mary's tribute to her dear Kenneth – this was the date of his birthday and he was coming from Canada to 'give her away'. With delighted surprise he had read Mary's letter telling of her engagement, and was eager to meet the man who had succeeded in breaking through her shyness and who, he realised, must resemble George Meredith: none of lesser quality could have filled the emotional vacuum in Mary's life. On returning to England Kenneth found Henry watching over Mary with tender care: once again she had been struck down by a severe crisis of Graves' Disease. Her exaltation, renewed by spring and love, together with excitement at the proximity of the wedding, had proved too much for her delicate system.

She suffered long bouts of delirium, head pain, high fever and weakness. Henry tending her was, in effect, her nurse (for she would have no other), an unconventional situation in those days but one which shows how little the two deferred to codes as well as to creeds, brushing aside accepted propriety – they had no intention of 'being crushed by conformity', an attitude which Mary was later to express most energetically and imaginatively in *The House in Dormer Forest*.

Her health began gradually to improve, Henry's soothing presence, his constant nearness, helping to strengthen and restore her. Yet it was doubtful whether she would be recovered in time for the wedding: the overactivity of her thyroid gland left her extremely fatigued, she was anaemic and, as the wedding date drew closer, remained in a condition of dire weakness. Fortunately – the Merediths' usual doctor being away – a young locum was called in who had made recent researches into glandular activity and disturbance. He suggested a course of capsules which were a new treatment. Mary's stubborn resistance to this was overcome when she was assured that the suspiciously red coloured capsules contained concentrated fruit and herbal extract. In reality they consisted of dried sheep's extract and undoubtedly would have been abhorrent to her, had she discovered their real composition. She took the capsules and, greatly to everyone's relief, her condition improved beyond expectation.

The strain of it all was too much for Alice Meredith who had become ill and retired to her bedroom, exasperated by the wedding arrangements which were, in her opinion, as bizarrely

10. Maesbrook, the Meredith home from 1901 to 1912 (George Meredith sitting on the bank)

11. Spring Cottage

The cottage where she lived in Hampstead when writing the reviews.

12. 5, Grove Cottages, Hampstead, where *Precious Bane* was written

unconventional as they were typical of Mary. However, she had realised years ago that it was useless to argue with her eldest daughter or to try to alter her mind once she was set on her course : and Mary was most emphatically set in her unusual choice of wedding guests.

Telling Kenneth about the arrangements, Mary had sidled up to him in a gleeful way which he never forgot and with her characteristic sidelong glance and delighted smile, announced that the seventy guests were to be old and destitute people whom she knew, most of them from the Women's Ward at Cross Houses Workhouse.

Together with these, as Hilda Addison has described, were other aged and lonely ones, including 'an old herbalist who had endeared himself to her by his knowledge of plants, a poor old fellow who only possessed one sound eye, and a decrepit organ-grinder'.

She had chosen as her bridesmaid the three-and-a-half year old daughter of the gardener, Tom Downes. Little Winifred had been born at Maesbrook and Mary had always taken a special interest in her (often giving her presents, a *Bubbles* annual for instance, or playbricks); recalling Mary years afterwards, Tom Downes emphasised : 'She had a lovely disposition. I've never in all my days met anyone with a more loving heart.'

Certainly she gave joyful expression to this at her wedding, seizing the opportunity to bring happiness to others on her own 'grave, beautiful day'. How gladly she had made her plans, knowing what a rare treat and outing this would be for the workhouse women whom she so greatly pitied, enclosed in their grey walls, and for the old men who loved a 'do', and for the little bridesmaid who would wear for the occasion a new white dress of broderie anglaise and a small bonnet to match. Mary was determined that they would all be given a day to remember.[5]

June 12 was bright and dry. A marquee had been set up on the lawn of the upper garden at Maesbrook where the wedding breakfast was to take place. The workhouse guests were brought from Berrington in a large trap, Mary having made a special arrangement for their transport with Thomas Sheffield, a Meole

[5] For the following account of the wedding I am indebted to Kenneth Meredith, and for additional information, to Mrs W. Edge (Winifred Downes) and Mrs C. Jellicoe-Wall.

Brace resident whose two daughters she taught at Sunday school.

Mary herself was a vision of radiant simplicity. Her white muslin dress was adorned only by a sash of specially chosen, symbolic blue: 'a holy colour; the Sufis wore it with this significance. . .'[6] Later, in her novels, there were reflections of her own marriage in those of Hazel Woodus and Amber Darke who both wore white muslin, and in Hazel's strange wedding guests – cat, rabbit, bird and pet fox, Foxy, 'a loving though incompetent bridesmaid'. Mary's comment on Hazel in *Gone to Earth* aptly describes herself: 'Not many brides think so little of themselves, so much of small pensioners.'

Flora McLeod, then in Italy, had sent orange blossoms from a palace garden near Sienna, these exotic blooms contrasting with Mary's own choice of fragile wild flowers. The Meredith wedding procession which proceeded from Maesbrook along the winding lane to the church included Alice Meredith who, fortunately, had recovered in time but who, though reconciled to the situation, still did not relish the thought of entertaining Mary's destitutes. At Holy Trinity the odd assortment of wedding guests in their shabby, 'sad-coloured' garments crowded the pews together with numerous parishioners who followed the ceremony performed by the Rev. William Bather. Little Winifred, fascinated by the red hassocks, insisted on sitting on one in the chancel, and then caused some amusement by dragging it with her to the altar as she followed Mary and Henry up the steps. The best man, H. B. Gooding, Henry's friend, handed him the ring, which he placed on Mary's finger. So they came out into the sunshine:

> In her short life there had not been many moments of such rose and gold . . . for she looked to him as flowers to warm heaven, as winter birds to a fruited tree.   (*GTE*, p. 118)

Afterwards Henry and Kenneth amusedly shared Mary's delight in seeing the workhouse women and old men enjoying what to them was indeed a feast. Mary may have reflected how her father would have understood perfectly her desire to share the happiness of her wedding day with these unfortunate ones;

---

[6] *PSJ*, p. 207. Muslin was Mary's choice of material – wishing to have the simplest of dresses, muslin, as she knew, was the usual material for wedding gowns of country girls.

and he would certainly have appreciated the humour, especially when an old man, asked whether he would like another slice of the cake, replied: 'Ay, and this time give us a piece that dunna bend.' A large and decrepit boot adorned the cab which took Mary and Henry away from Maesbrook. This was Kenneth's characteristically impish contribution to the joyful day.

PART THREE

THE APOCALYPSE OF LOVE

1912–1921

There are many among us who become transparent through the light of their imagination : who, when they mould images of thought and dream, reveal their true selves with an insight that is at once beautiful and terrible.

William Sharp

6
Hiraeth
1912–1914

Weston-super-Mare

... the courses of life flowed on to their undreamed-
of endings, from their mysterious source. (*GA*, p. 262)

For the nearer we be to our bliss, the more we long
after it.

Julian of Norwich[1]

The honeymoon was spent at a cottage in the remote Ashes
Valley deep in the folds of the Long Mynd. It was loaned to
Mary and Henry by a relative of Flora McLeod – an ideal place,
isolated, the lonely green plateaux bathed in light stretching away
on every side. Here they could walk on the grassy heights for
miles, absorb the wild beauty, at one with nature and each other.
A brief idyll, when the hawthorn was 'white over', blossom and
shadow falling on the steep lawned slopes where sheep cried loud
and low. Here they crossed the airy tableland, followed the stream
up grey-green Carding Mill Valley, stood on the high rounded
summits looking down across the Stretton Hills to distant Wrekin
and the plain.

A good deal of the atmosphere and surroundings of their
honeymoon was to go into *The Golden Arrow* with its setting of
the Long Mynd and Stiperstones. It was, in fact, the experience
of physical separation from Shropshire subsequent to the honeymoon which, acting as a catalyst, impelled Mary to recreate her
landscape in a world of imagination. With Henry she left Shropshire for Weston-super-Mare where he was to return to his

[1] Julian, Anchoress at Norwich, *Revelations of Divine Love*, ed. Grace
Warrack, pp. xxvıv, 96.

teaching post at Brynmelyn, a boys' boarding school in Lande-mann Circus. And the break with Maesbrook had a poignant finality because Mary knew, before her departure, that Alice Meredith had sold the house and would be leaving Meole Brace to live permanently at Chester. In future there would be no Meredith home to return to in Shropshire. The drastic effect of this on Mary was intensified by the knowledge that the new owner of Maesbrook, Miss Lowe, planned to pull it down and build another house on the site. The well-loved home, rich in associations with George Meredith, soon would disappear forever. Demolition began on 23 September 1912, at a time when Mary was adapting to her first married home – 'Penrose' – and to the grey coastal town on the Bristol Channel.

During the wet autumn of 1912, Mary explored Weston, walked the wide sands, saw solitary ships edging the horizon and the islands of Flat Holm and Steep Holm like dark stationary whales in the bay. Here she would watch the westward sky flame over the sea and the sun drop behind a watery horizon; here no muted, misted hills, no dear known humps, no trees and meres set in dimpled green. 'Penrose', a tall, solid, semi-detached residence built in the grey stone of the district, was a considerably smaller house than she had been used to, and had no grounds around it. The rear windows looked out to the sky-spanned sea; the front to a gravel drive, grey walls. Neighbouring houses also were in-habited by staff from the two rival boys' schools in the Circus, making this, in effect, a campus. For Mary, these congested, stony surroundings were an abrupt change from the seclusion of the Old Mill House, tree-sheltered with its constant threnody of brook and birdsong. She felt *hiraeth* – the Welsh word she liked to use, meaning an intense yearning, more ardent than ordinary homesickness – *hiraeth* for Shropshire, *hiraeth* for nature. This was to become increasingly acute the longer she was away.

Continuing her habit of going out in the early morning, she found the way to Weston Woods which crest the craggy hill – here, among the trees, although not Shropshire trees, she could commune. As she wrote later in *The House in Dormer Forest*:

> those that feel within them the stir of a growing soul . . . fly from the house of man to the forest, where the emotionless silence always seems to be gathering, as waves mount and swell, to the disclosure of a mystery.   (p. 19)

Before long she and Henry were welcoming their first visitors from Shropshire. Among these was Flora McLeod who has described 'Penrose':

> the white paint against the red carpet ... the pleasant drawing room with its books and flowers and glowing fire; the dining room in its pre-war dignity of white napery and glass and silver.

Miss McLeod noted Mary's pride in this first home, and that she seemed 'full of gladness': what she did not perceive, however, was that the harmony and happiness, real though they were, held for Mary an enclosed, gnawing fear. Mary had written: 'Though I am so happy, so incredibly and unexpectedly happy, I am also somewhat afraid.' Those words applied even more after her marriage than before. Her poems of this date, 'Isolde' and 'Today', reiterate her fear, expressing with immediacy the intensity of her love and of her insecurity in that love. As in 'Isolde', the 'bitter surf' of loss was ever before her:

> Safe in his arms, one moment I abide
> Above the sinister waves. For him, for me
> Dawns a brief peace, a fleet eternity.
> Our silence drowns the full and threatening tide,
> And we forget how many loves have died,
> How stealthy comes the dark and ebbing sea,
> When one, arms empty, calls on vacancy
> And hears the echoes mock on every side.
>
> (51, p. 40)

The imagery here is drawn from the scene around her at Weston, the inexorable sea evoking in her a feeling of menace. So 'the sinister waves', 'the full and threatening tide', 'the dark and ebbing sea' represent metaphorically the 'stealthy' fate which she fears, will snatch Henry from her, sooner or later, by one means or another. The second stanza is explicit:

> How brief is our warm joy, how soon to end!
> Let us hold close and spend our interval
> In heaven! But busy stranger, eager friend
> Break in, and – never knowing – steal our all.
> Then, even as a cynic fate denies
> Our love, the bitter surf is in our eyes.

Mary's anticipation of 'the bitter surf' in the poems written early in her marriage, has tragic implications – a response to experience permeating her attitude and outlook, a pessimism arising from the effect of her father's death (from which she had not recovered and perhaps never recovered), a complex, inverted expectation of suffering. In 'Isolde', her comment on what she considered to be universal truth is a sharp *cri de coeur*, poignantly prophetic of her own fate. In 'Today', which gives us an important insight into her state of mind and attitude to life at this time, she begins by expressing spiritual doubt – 'Beyond the darkling sea, if no fair shore/Lies, where low flutes play, where the bitter surf/Is all forgotten, and the deep sea roar' – and concludes, 'Here is our heaven, in one another's eyes' . . . insisting on the here-and-now, a finite heaven. Both poems are infused with Mary's quintessential grave tenderness, sadness and joy mingled, ecstatic love on a precipice of fear.

This was the tragic flaw: the greater her unity and harmony with Henry, the more it was shot through with fear of loss. She wanted to shut out 'the world', be cocooned with him under their own roof-tree. So she resented, and came to resent still more as the years went on, the intrusion of outsiders into her home – this seemed to her a violation of 'the nest of love', as she called it. 'Busy stranger, eager friend' were not encouraged. She refused domestic help for the same reason, even though the Merediths had always employed a household staff of at least two maids and a cook. The only welcome additions to the home were two cats, which soon became four.

Cut off from her countryside, Mary concentrated on widening her knowledge of literature and sending short stories and poems to journals. In this she had Henry's enthusiastic encouragement. Studying the books in his small personal library which contained philosophical and poetical works, and writings of the Christian mystics, Mary found Dame Julian of Norwich's *Revelations of Divine Love*, a fourteenth-century account of mystical experience. This made a profound impression on her, 'sank deeply into her mind and remained, though more cherished at certain periods than others, one of those subtle influences which, abiding gently in the heart, become at length indelibly outlined there'.[2]

---

[2] Addison, p. 28. The 'Revelations' were recorded by Julian, anchoress at Norwich in 1373 and were published in the version taken from the British Museum MS, ed. Grace Warrack, by Methuen, 1901.

In this medieval mystic's sixteen 'shewings' or visions of love, Mary understood much that had been her own spiritual experience. Not only in Dame Julian but in the lives and writings of other mystics too, Mary found a great deal that she recognised but also much that she had gone beyond, for unlike the Christian mystics she was not bound by a theological framework, having passed outside fettering orthodox patterns and, as she expressed it later, 'cast away the old religious phraseology', as her mysticism developed in response to nature itself. Yet studying Dame Julian in 1912–13 during her own continued crisis of dark night, she may have drawn some strength from the anchoress's affirmative revelations.

Mary became interested also in John Millington Synge. Apart from the Anglo-Irish idiom which, as used by Synge, gives his language a singular beauty, there is his strength as a dramatist in unfolding events in a way which intensifies the sense of inevitable doom, yet still renders the inevitable unexpected. A similar masterly shaping of fate in *Gone to Earth* and *Precious Bane* makes the tragedies of Hazel Woodus and Gideon Sarn so strongly compelling. There is a similarity too in one of the central and most characteristic concerns of both Synge and Mary Webb: the struggle of the individual to create an individual self against opposing inimical and negative forces which seek to stifle and crush it.

Synge's use of Gaelicised English with its subtlety of cadence conveying the feelings and thoughts of peasants with roots deep in the Irish past, may well have influenced Mary to use in her novels a fusion of Shropshire dialect with everyday language. But while she admired Synge, Fiona McLeod and Thomas Hardy, her own work was in no way a pastiche of theirs. Mary Webb in her writing was uniquely herself from the beginning and was not made by affinities or influences. Similarly, while she enjoyed the short stories of Theodor Storm at this time, she did not model her own stories on these, neither was the characteristic humour in her work imitative of Dickens, although she admired his novels.

From the foundation of Henry's encouragement in her literary work, the stimulus of their mental companionship and the small successes of occasional publication of her stories and poems, Mary advanced towards the idea of writing a novel. She now had a fullness of emotional experience she needed to express, and she was to interweave these personal feelings and thoughts with long-stored observations and perceptions drawn from that concentrated area of Shropshire countryside she knew so minutely, which she loved and was then missing so intensely. As Rilke said of Russia, 'How much do I not owe to Russia! It has made me what I am. There I began to be, there is the home of my instincts, the country of my soul'. So might this be said of Mary Webb and Shropshire, for there indeed was the country of her soul. John Buchan's words in the Introduction to *Gone to Earth* apply as much to Mary herself as to the central character, Hazel Woodus: 'She is at once the offspring of the mysterious landscape and the interpretation of it.' Separation from that landscape, her feeling of exile intensified by the knowledge that there was now no Shropshire home to return to, was the vital factor in her genesis as a novelist. Having lost her natural environment so essential to her being, she sought to regain it creatively: the country of her soul became the country of her imagination; Mary had found another way of re-entering Eden.

At Weston she began a series of notes on Shropshire settings, on characters and ideas, a careful preparation for the novel which was to be *The Golden Arrow*. Approaching her mid-thirties, she was coming to novel-writing fairly late, yet as with George Eliot, Joseph Conrad, Arnold Bennett and others, this was an advantage, for she was bringing to her prose fiction a mature vision, a richly stocked mind and an already developed evaluation of life. She intended to present this evaluation of life at once on a realistic and a symbolic level. She was not an innovator in technique: this would be a traditional, chronological novel. At narrative level it would be a realistic story of country people in a South Shropshire setting; and underlying this the deeper meaning – her thematic revelation or 'apocalypse of love'. How convincingly and effectively would she fuse the realistic and symbolic aspects of her fictional art? Enquiry in this direction will illumine her development as a novelist, bringing out some important strengths and weaknesses, successes and failures. Her total work was to have cohesion – unity of vision and themes; in her novels from first to last she was a visionary aiming to transmute realistic material.

She was similar to Emily Brontë in that her experience, though not wide, had been deep; in fact it was the deeper for being circumscribed. Mary, having found her creative force during prolonged confinement in illness, said in an essay, 'It does not matter how shut in we are. Opportunity for wide experience is of small account in this as in other things; it is depth that brings understanding and life' *(PSJ*, p. 129). Again like Emily Brontë, she neither desired nor needed any other environment than her own compact country region. In both novelists, physical limitation brought concentration and intensification, not restricting but enlarging; powerful imagination and strong individual vision combined in a transcendence of the regional, reaching another level of reality, universally significant.

A. R. Reade, assessing Mary Webb in *Main Currents in Modern Literature*, made the following discerning comment: 'Her range is much less wide than that of many other writers, but her intuitions about life are truer . . . and within that range there was little she did not know.' Certainly it was to be one of the strengths of her writing that she did not need – and did not attempt to go – outside the range of her experience. At the outset of her career as a novelist, she began by a process of selection and extraction from that experience, aesthetically ordering and shaping her material. In a personal schematisation of reality, she was planning her characters, selecting incident and detail, aspects of landscape and local folklore, for the significance, the symbolic value these could yield. While too obviously contrived and overdone in her early novels, this is more finely and delicately wrought in her later works written when she was reaching her artistic maturity.

As in many first novels, there is much autobiography in *The Golden Arrow*, threads of her past and present life interwoven. Her own inner conflict – the stress between her mystical nature and the recent negation – was projected into one of the chief themes of the novel and embodied in the characters of John Arden and Stephen Southernwood, the one being a mystic who has 'visionary moments', the other a young man who experiences a crisis of faith which plunges him into a living hell of unreconciled agnosticism.

John Arden, the first of Mary's major figures, is also the first of the mystics who are central characters in her novels: through these she projects her vision. An apt beginning is made with John Arden who endowed his daughter Deborah with his mystical nature, as George Meredith did to Mary herself. Through her mystics, particularly Amber Darke in *The House in Dormer Forest* and Prudence Sarn in *Precious Bane*, Mary is revelatory of her own mystical experience (and as we shall see, the development from John Arden to Prudence Sarn is implicitly Mary's own spiritual progression). Prudence Sarn speaks for her when she says : 'Not that my soul was anything to show, but yet I greatly desired to show it' (p. 157). Language is the enabling instrument – as a literary mystic Mary felt impelled to transmit her spiritual landscapes, attempt expression of the inexpressible, necessarily by verbal symbol – images which, like nature itself, are at once voice and veil, revealing yet still concealing. Her urge, like that of all creative mystics, was to communicate the vision of truth, reality, love, even though, as she says in *The Golden Arrow*, 'in success or failure the seer knows the impossibility of explaining himself' (p. 337). So John Arden, after a moment of deep pantheistic vision when crossing the high plateaux of Wilderhope, tells Deborah that he sees 'summat as there's no words for' (p. 32).

In the singing, homely country speech of John Arden there is a wistful simplicity : the pantheistic nature mysticism he represents had been, as we have seen, Mary's spiritual experience since at least adolescence (expressed earlier in her poem 'The Vagrant') – an optimistic pantheism coloured by Christianity, from which, after her father's death, she had temporarily regressed. We find in some of John's sayings a compound of Mary's mind, the Bible and Dame Julian. He is described in his 'visionary moments' as one who 'travelled into regions where thought stopped', and his religion – 'earthy, fuller flavoured than any formulated creed can be' – is 'deep pantheistic Christianity', 'not chapel nor Church Christianity. Just home-brewed.' For John Arden – as for Mary – God is nature with soul, but his pantheism has a focus in the metaphysical personality he refers to as 'The Flockmaster'[3] (a variation on the Good Shepherd): 'all creatures cry out after him'.

Though Mary herself, at this stage of her inner development, no longer believed in such a beneficent presence ('. . . God is far withdrawn/And heaven a palace fallen in the sea'), she still

---

[3] Her poem, 'The Flockmaster', was written in 1916 (*CPAP*, p. 121).

responded spiritually and creatively, experiencing those ineffable moments in which the soul feels one with nature, and in this oneness gives itself fully. Mary's pantheistic mysticism is expressed in her novels not just through the characters who are mystics, but also in her descriptions of the natural world (which occupy quantitatively a great amount of her writing) – never mere descriptiveness but full of implications. The effect, building up throughout the novel (and from novel to novel), is cumulative. And indeed, through her entire work – articles, poems, novels – runs this fundamental theme of an essential secret enclosed in the heart of earth, accessible to man through contemplation.

Yet there is a danger in stressing this mystical aspect of Mary Webb's work of giving the wrong impression of it: there is nothing abstract or 'religious' about her writing. The novels are not spiritual tracts but warmly human stories, richly alive in their depiction of human passions, the tragedy and comedy of life. A sense of fun is never far away, and the deeper meaning well embedded in a concrete world. An outline of the story of *The Golden Arrow* will indicate its human interest and the characteristic simplicity of the plot.

The love story of Deborah Arden both begins and ends at her parents' stone cottage on Wilderhope, 'in the midst of the hill plateau'. She lives there with her father (the shepherd John), her mother (the sharp-tongued, practical midwife, Patty), and her brother (the stolid, unimaginative Joe). Into her quiet life comes Stephen Southernwood, a dynamic, golden-haired young preacher who desires and pursues her. Immature and impulsive, Stephen persuades her to leave her parents and live with him in a cottage he restores on the opposite ridge (Diafol), beneath the Devil's Chair. He is unconventional, a free-thinker, but is 'lost within' – having cast away the dogma in which he was reared, he abandons his ministry and takes a job as foreman in the mines at Diafol. He does not believe in God, in an after-life, or in marriage. Deborah loves him totally with a self-giving, fear-fraught love. Entwined in their lives are Joe Arden and Lily Huntbatch (the shallow, selfish daughter of hellfire preacher Eli), theirs being the parallel, lesser love story. While Joe and Lily, who have a limited relationship, marry ('the ring hallows all'), Deborah and Stephen, who have potential greatness, do not ('love hallows all'), living in illicit union. Both Lily (unhappily) and Deborah (joyfully) become pregnant.

Deborah, feeling insecure, presses Stephen into a legal marriage but does not reveal her pregnancy.

As autumn draws in over the lonely landscape, Stephen becomes increasingly restless and depressed, feeling tied both by Deborah's way of loving and by the marriage. The countryside acquires an 'apocalyptic' quality for him : he is unnerved by the presence of the 'taciturn' quartzite throne, unalterable, primeval, and by decaying nature all around. In despair he attempts to detonate the Devil's Chair, but the explosion makes no impression on it. Deborah also loathes the Devil's Chair, not because of its 'everlastingness', but because in her superstitious, country way, she fears it, believing it to be evil, believing the legends and ghostly lore associated with it. In her unconscious mind she identifies with this darkness and the threat of evil. She dreads 'black harm' will come to Stephen and in voicing these fears (not knowing of his own), pleads with him to give up the mine and be home all day with her, keeping a sheepwalk as her father does. Stephen, feeling trapped still further by her dependence, is horrified by her distress and disgusted when Lily tries to seduce him. He makes up his mind to leave, and as the first snows of winter are powdering the ranges, he secretly plans his departure, arranging with a farmer to take a herd of Shropshire shorthorns to America. He deserts Deborah on St Thomas' Day – demented, she spends this 'longest night' in a grief-stricken frenzy, burning their home and belongings, and identifying with all the legends of the Devil's Chair (on St Thomas' Eve Shropshire ghosts are said to gather there to elect a King). Deborah staggers in the darkness to her parents' cottage on Wilderhope, drawn (and saved) by her father's lantern (the 'kindly light'). In the weeks that follow, she is near death and suicide, surviving with the help and sustaining influence of John Arden who is finally instrumental in reuniting her with Stephen, after the birth of her child. Stephen, redeemed by his own suffering, returns in June when 'the thorn's white over'.

While, at surface level, this is simply a romantic, sensational tale of lovers broken and made whole by love, Mary Webb is also presenting her view of life, using the novel as a poetic medium (following Hardy) to express her personal values and attitudes which she intends to be meaningful and illuminating. Her artistic intention clearly is not to write realistic rural stories, or entertainments, but illustrative, poetic fables integrating her deepest preoccupations. Product of her ardent, passionately responsive sensibility, all her novels have a warm emotional tone (not to be confused with sentimentality), but in her earlier works, and particularly in this first novel, lack of restraint sometimes leads her into emotional excess and over-simplification. In *The Golden Arrow*, although she proceeds with certainty of touch and pace, she makes too much didactic assertion and commentary, too little dramatisation and demonstration. The weaknesses and flaws are evident, but also abundant promise. She has already learned to present her theme through setting, structure and symbol, using environment and local lore to project and promote the novel's total meaning, selecting from her landscape those features which appealed most to her imagination and which could be adapted aesthetically to present her vision. This was to become a distinctive feature of her writing, but the first novels tend to be too tightly woven and manipulated, and she is prone to lapse into exaggerated feeling in her treatment of character.

In her life Mary had no rein on her imaginative sympathy, and to an interesting degree her writing reflects the depths, strengths and the weaknesses of her personality. The major characters are not intellectual, but are imbued with her own intuitive and sensory awareness; the minor characters, more sharply realised, often lively and humorous, have much of the salt of her personality.

It is also interesting, at this point, to note that not one of Mary Webb's novels is set in her contemporary countryside. They are usually placed in late Victorian-Edwardian days, decades of her youth (apart from *Precious Bane* and the uncompleted novel, set in earlier historical periods). Undoubtedly this retrospection in setting increased the security and wholeness she felt in creating these closely knit, self-contained worlds where everything interrelates : through her creative imagination she was reaching back to the stability and unity of that period in her own life when her father was alive and at the centre of her round world.

And undoubtedly in creating John Arden she was preserving something of her father in a literary portrait. If then, John Arden appears to be idealised, it must be remembered that this was, in fact, Mary's view of George Meredith : the relationship in the novel of John and his daughter Deborah, one of very strong affinity, can be seen as a dramatisation of Mary's relationship with her father and of the vision of life they shared, a vision she had lost at his death and then regained in her relationship with Henry. Reinforced and extended in her marriage, this vision was her 'apocalypse of love' – the power of love to illumine different levels of reality, to unify polarities so that good and evil are seen as blended.

The struggle of opposites (in particular between spiritual and material values, good and evil variously manifested) if unresolved divides individuals within themselves, individuals from each other. This major concern in Mary Webb's work arose from her personal striving towards wholeness. At the end of *The Golden Arrow* the tension of opposites is resolved as Deborah arrives at a new understanding, seeing terror and beauty mingled, the two antithetical visions – the wholly good and the wholly evil – as one.

John was intended, even in the initial stages at Weston, to be a figure of major symbolical significance, representative of the achieved revelation towards which all was to tend and which was the total statement of the novel, namely a reconciling, unifying love, 'the great affirmative', which neither judges nor denies; a vision which, while it looks to infinity, always relates back with 'infinite compassion' to the finite world. John has no orthodox moral code – Mary summed up his essence in a memorable aphorism: 'Those that dwell in the lands of the sun do not need fires.' It was important that John, embodying this apocalyptic love, should be convincing as a naturalistic portrayal – on this was to depend not only the total effect, but the ultimate plausibility of the novel, which ends like a moral fable. In this characterisation Mary successfully avoids a danger: that the more a protagonist is made to stand *for*, the less he *is*. It is generally agreed that John Arden is one of Mary Webb's most effective characters – here she achieves a successful coalescence between realistic substance and thematic function. While he is an epitome of her own values, he is fully individualised and, it should be noted, is one of the few 'good' figures in literature who is not a bore. Not all the major characters in her novels were to be as 'round' as John Arden: throughout *The Golden Arrow* his character is revealed through dialogue and action, and unlike the other central characters, he never becomes stiffly allegorical. The detail with which his character is invested, the foibles and idiosyncrasies which give him human depth (in Henry James' phrase, the 'solidity of specification') went far to giving the colour and substance of real life not only to John but to the novel as a whole.

Yet while many particulars were drawn from George Meredith's personality, John Arden was not based simply on imitation from life. In this portrait, as elsewhere, Mary Webb adjusted personal material and autobiographical experience to her artistic purpose. As Charlotte Brontë aptly said in a letter to Ellen Nussey, answering a criticism that the characters in *Shirley* were direct portrayals of real people : 'We only suffer reality to suggest, never to dictate.'

In John Arden, Mary Webb created a 'moral' centre, establishing the pattern of the novel as the other characters either rise or fall short of his standard. He functions as a touchstone or yardstick, particularly for the two couples ('the four who had life to face'), whose interwoven stories carry the narrative forward : the main story of the relationship of Deborah Arden and Stephen Southernwood, who eventually attain, after suffering, to John's revelatory love and understanding, is offset by the lesser story of the couple who do not, namely Joe Arden and Lily Huntbatch. This contrasting parallel is based on an interplay of opposites sufficiently complex to have required thorough working out in Mary's preparatory notes. The interplay of similarity and difference is something she had learned from her great exemplars : in using polar balancing of characters as a main structural feature of *The Golden Arrow*, she followed conventional narrative procedure which, no doubt, she had studied in the works of novelists from Richardson onwards, but perhaps especially in George Eliot and Thomas Hardy.

The other major characters – Deborah Arden and Stephen Southernwood – are representative of two further aspects of the apocalypse of love. Deborah's increasing fear in Stephen's absence ('the pulse of life stops at parting'), is the expression of Mary's gnawing anxiety over Henry, her dread of losing him; Stephen's fear in his *via negativa*, confronting 'dark, hard reality', seeing death as 'complete annihilation' and life 'like the hum of insects round carrion', is the expression of Mary's spiritual agony in the void of 'utter negation'. The tension of the narrative rises through a series of crises, the stress of the two characters intensifying as each is involved in the inner conflict which must be resolved. Ultimately both survive near-tragedy, suffering being the index of their development to an understanding comparable with John's. Here we find another of the binding themes of Mary Webb's work – the significance of suffering – this arising, as we have seen, from her personal experience.

Deborah Arden is very much Mary's self portrait, the forerunner of Amber Darke and Prudence Sarn – dark haired, intuitive, 'warm hearted', possessing 'the rare, sad, godlike faculty for seeing the end of a thing in its inception'. Capable of giving herself spiritually in 'large measure', she has great tenderness – 'the vague, illimitable love in her – vague as rings in water, widening eternally'. Loving Stephen with 'self-giving love', she overcomes her physical inhibition and fuses within herself 'the red fire of physical passion' and 'the white fire of love', realising that 'in unity both were pure'. Mary's total way of loving is Deborah's. As Deborah says, 'When a man or an 'ooman feels like that . . . they're not to be cured, not this side of silence . . . it's the bones of them and the blood of them. As soon cure folks of breathing' (p. 240).

The relationship of Deborah and Stephen, their sexual union before marriage, estrangement after it, and final re-union, is illustrative of one of Mary's central concerns – the struggle between spiritual and physical realities (she had a keen consciousness of both). For her the spiritual and the physical must always interpenetrate : here is a connection with her response to nature, as in her nature immersion she apprehends the material form around her as spirit, and as a mirror image of man's spirit. Her concept of love does not exclude the normal view but is inclusive of it : the highest peak is the union of spiritual and physical love, but it is on the spiritual grasp of love that lasting happiness depends. This is an obsessive major theme in her work, from first novel to last. Deborah expresses this conviction to an uncomprehending Lily :

> If your man inna the lover of your soul . . . you've missed the honey and only got the empty comb . . . for it's only when a man's the lover of your soul and wants you so as he's nigh beside hisself, as you're his 'ooman, right and true. I'm thinking it's only then as you've a right to be called his wife and sleep along of him.
> (p. 245)

Here Mary is repeating the Shelleyan view of marriage that it is immoral to be bound together if love fails. This was Henry's attitude too, and in writing *The Golden Arrow* she was incorporating ideas and ideals they held mutually at that time.

At first Stephen's passion for Deborah is physical, he is not 'the lover of her soul'. It is the progress of his increasingly troubled consciousness which moves the narrative forward, as he has 'so much to unlearn, to give up, to suffer'. Finally his development is intended to show that for such despairing agnostics, even when 'facing blank nothingness', self-giving 'love and pity' can effect a reconciliation making human existence meaningful, and be both means and end. Stephen is brought by suffering to a realisation that love is 'the great affirmative', but his realisation applies solely to this world, to the here-and-now : because of 'this new burning force in him', he can face 'the infinite void'. The apocalypse of love, in his case, is intended to be *imprimis* an apocalypse for those who confront 'the horror of emptiness, utter negation'.

In this character, Mary not only incorporated the expression of her own spiritual devastation of 'dark night' and her renewal through love, but also depicted a crisis of faith experienced by many when they throw away, as Stephen does, the 'ready-made code'. Here, too, she was reflecting a human problem increasingly acute since the mid-nineteenth century, arising from a change in outlook which had been accelerating under the influence of Post-Darwinian scientific thought and the new psychological insights.

While Mary designed her major characters to illustrate her themes, she was also to demonstrate the emotional and spiritual development of these characters by showing them in constant and intimate relation to their environment which was, of course, the Shropshire countryside, and specifically that high region of haunted borderland. Her treatment of environment therefore was of fundamental importance for her novel's themes as well as being a chief element of style. It is well known that her use of natural scenery is an outstanding feature of her prose fiction – as John Buchan said, 'no one of our day has a greater power of evoking natural magic . . . Mary Webb need fear no comparison with any writer who has attempted to capture the soul of nature in words . . .' Evocative description was certainly one of her strengths, but in her early novels she tends to overdo her effects, to overuse metaphor, suggestive detail and atmosphere, making her writing too high-pitched; at times superheated. This is true particularly of *The Golden Arrow* and *Gone to Earth*.

Mary's perceptive handling of the interaction between the human and the animate and inanimate in the landscape owes much to her reading of Thomas Hardy, but also to her own understanding of the ways in which external circumstances of environment could shape individual lives, and to the exercise of her acute senses during more than thirty years immersed in the Shropshire countryside (senses which served her in the choice of sharp simile and metaphor).

Even in the preparatory stages of this first novel, she made a careful selection of aspects of the south-west Shropshire landscape which, while especially compelling to her, would provide a vividly realistic setting and at the same time lend themselves to the symbolical expression of her contrasted themes of good and evil, peace and conflict, known and unknown. She chose as her setting the area where she and Henry had spent their honeymoon – the parallel ranges of the Long Mynd and the Stiperstones – giving these appropriate names, Wilderhope and Diafol. The opposing heights confront each other with a 'hammock-like' valley between. Wilderhope (the Long Mynd) with its sheep, pasture, hawthorn blossom, fragrance and light is representative of that which is good, peaceful, positive, harmonious and spiritual: here is beauty and joy. To John Arden these 'vast expanses' are 'as air to a swallow'; to Deborah it is the known country. In complete contrast, Diafol (the Stiperstones) with its black rock (the Devil's Chair), charred heather, dead trees, mist and storm represents forces of evil and chaos, that which is negative, conflict-torn, shadowed. Here is ugliness, terror, dark superstition. To Stephen it becomes 'the embodiment of his own mind' when he is consumed by fearful doubt; to Deborah it stands for the darkness and unknown which she dreads.

By a fortunate (and undoubtedly deliberately planned) turn of events in Mary's life, she was soon to gain a more intimate knowledge of the Long Mynd and Stiperstones than she possessed already. She was to use this knowledge of the ranges later when in full flow of composition, extracting details of the contrasting visual and atmospheric aspects, investing these with symbolical value – so, as in all her novels, the natural scenery reflects, amplifies and influences the moods and thoughts of her characters, and helps to move the action forward. Mary's aesthetic adaptation of her landscape and the natural environment is characteristic of her habit of allegorising experience. In her novels the settings are often identifiable, the Shropshire countryside realistically presented, vividly evoked in concrete detail; yet this is very much her own world, seen through what Thomas Hardy called 'the idiosyncratic mode of regard'. As Hardy said: 'Art is a changing of the actual order and proportion of things, so as to bring out more forcibly than might otherwise be done that feature in them which appeals most strongly to the idiosyncracy of the artist.'[4]

Although in her notes (written and unwritten), Mary had gone a long way in the preparation of her novel, she was not to embark on the actual composition until the whole of it had been deeply considered and worked out. Her writing would then be done in compulsive 'rushes', inspiration welling up spontaneously, to be neither summoned at will nor, once in flow, checked or diverted. This was always to be her method. Long germination. Careful nurturing. Then to await the creative efflorescence. Weston, however, could not provide the right soil or climate.

Mary's inspirational source at the core of her being was her oneness with the Shropshire countryside which she needed now in order to fulfil herself as a creative mystic. Not just an intimate knowledge and love of place, but unity with the spirit of the place wherein her consciousness had deepened and dilated. One critic considering her novels remarked that 'probably no other modern writer has been so moved to write and so moved in writing by her environment as Mary Webb'.[5] This was because her synthesis of literary talent and spiritual genius was intrinsic to mystical response in those surroundings with which she had become integral. So her creative imagination awaited the activation only Shropshire could bring.

At this point the wishes of Henry coincided with the needs of Mary. As Flora McLeod observed during her visit to the Webbs: 'Already another note was beginning to creep in. The sound came not from her but from her husband' – Henry was finding the boys at the school 'incredibly dull and unimaginative'. If Mary was

[4] Florence Emily Hardy, *The Life of Thomas Hardy, 1840–1928*, pp. 228–9.
[5] James Carr, 'The Novels of Mary Webb', *Papers of the Manchester Literary Club*, vol. 63, 1937, p. 2.

unhappy away from Shropshire and longing – the *hiraeth* intensifying – to return, Henry too was discontented with life at Weston. The decision to return to Shropshire and specifically to the hill country, was a mutual one arising from their need to be nearer to nature, to devote themselves to writing unrestricted by the demands of timetables and the social pressures of the middle-class community in which they were then living.

Ideas Henry had expressed in *The Silences of the Moon* leave no doubt about his own attitude to nature : he was now creating the opportunity to apply his philosophy, to live it ('My creed cannot be recited or put into a book, but only pondered and lived'). A Shropshire lad himself, the pull of the county upon him was stronger at this time than at any other. Added to this, he wanted to concentrate on his own literary work. Translation of the poetry of other languages was to be a major preoccupation for many years to come, and he hoped to prepare an anthology. He had also begun a long narrative poem about Gilgamesh. Henry was always to be first and foremost scholar rather than teacher, happiest in the private world of study.

And so, seeking individual freedom, they embarked courageously on a 'simple' way of life, new to both of them but regarded by both as the ideal existence : close to nature in a quiet country house, growing their own food and working at their writing without intrusion from the outside world. For Mary it was a return (to use her own words about Deborah) to 'the land of great hills and wide pastures whose child she was'; for Henry a relief from the time-consuming demands of the classroom. But it was with the disapproval of his family (who had come to live at Weston) that Henry resigned his teaching post and returned with Mary to Shropshire early in 1914.

7

Rose Cottage, Pontesbury – and *The Golden Arrow* 1914–1916

> When I am from him, I am dead till I be with him;
> when I am with him, I am not satisfied, but would
> still be nearer him. United souls are not satisfied
> with imbraces, but desire to be truly each other;
> which being impossible, their desires are infinite, and
> must proceed without a possibility of satisfaction.
> Sir Thomas Browne, *Religio Medici*

Henry and Mary rented a rather isolated, detached house with a wide gasden at Pontesbury, a village nine miles south-west of Shrewsbury, near Pontesford Hill, at the foot of the ranges of Long Mynd and Stiperstones. Now Mary's 'interval in heaven' became a reality as never before : to be back in her own country-side, near the hills, and with Henry who would be home all day. This was a 'here-and-now' of bliss. They intended to live on Mary's annual allowance from the Scott funds, this £100 being not inconsiderable in those days, and to supplement their income, if possible, from the proceeds of writing. They would grow their own vegetables and fruit, and keep bees for honey as well as for the fascination of observing the life of the hive.

The triangular garden of Rose Cottage was large enough to provide produce and flowers in abundance. It was situated on a bank leading to a small railway bridge over which the single track went between Minsterley and Shrewsbury. Only the clicking of an occasional passing train disturbed the deep quiet of the garden and 'the silver song of birds' in the surrounding trees. Mary set to with zest, digging hard every day, helped by Henry. But she was concerned that he should not dig for too long or too strenuously as he was suffering from a back injury first incurred when rowing at Cambridge in his undergraduate days. Mary's maternal feelings never ceased to extend to Henry protectively and were all the more intense and concentrated since was she childless.

'Not At Home' – this was the notice which frequently hung from their gate at Rose Cottage to discourage callers.[1] They asked only to be left alone to write, take long walks in the hills and spend hours together undisturbed or gardening as they wished. Speaking of the freedom they experienced at this period, Henry said years afterwards : 'We were two people who felt at home in old clothes, corduroys, or, in Mary's case, a faded sunbonnet. The people of Weston-super-Mare would have felt far from home in them' (Moult, p. 39).

The two years at Rose Cottage were to be among their happiest. Mary was deeply contented, loving the light airy house and its peaceful setting in a country lane where 'two rows of larches lean, / And lissom, rosy pines with wild black hair- / One slim, bright-fingered chestnut in between' (*PSJ*, pp. 100–1). Her life was illumined, transfigured by love :

> To give – to be with her man – to be so utterly at one that no explanation was ever necessary – to work, laugh, sleep and watch the splendid seasons together, being in other things than sex free and equal, and in sex so mutually generous as to forget self and rights . . .   (*GA*, p. 183)

This autobiographical passage in *The Golden Arrow* is eloquent of her fulfilment at this period in such a love – 'the sweetest flowering of which humanity is capable'. And as she wrote later, 'the mystic understands sex better than the sensualist.'

In those first months at Pontesbury, Mary was preparing her novel, building up towards the moment of creative flight and song like a bird in the inspirational instant of winging out from branch into air. She was tentatively reaching towards the literary sphere which was soon to become her central and consuming preoccupation. One step in this direction was her application to the *Liverpool Post* to do book-reviewing. She applied several times and was delighted when the Editor eventually agreed to employ

---

[1] I am indebted to Helen M. Bott, niece of the (then) owner of Rose Cottage (now Roseville) for details of the Webbs' tenancy; and to Doreen and Derrick Bourne, the present owners.

her. According to Caradoc Evans, the Welsh writer, who years afterwards in London became her friend, this editor was possibly 'the first . . . who backed his opinion of Mary Webb with orders for her goods'.[2] This early experience of reviewing helped to establish her confidence. Soon she became a familiar figure in Pontesbury Post Office posting her review articles, sending out poems, short stories and the occasional article (although without much known success).

Gathering creative momentum with every week that passed of this renewed immersion in nature, she was living closer to the soil than she had ever done before. This, for her, was 'The Happy Life':

> No silks have I, no furs nor feathers,
> But one old gown that knows all weathers;
> No veils nor parasols nor lace,
> But rough hands and a tanned face.
> Yet the soft, crinkled leaves are mine
> Where pale, mysterious veins shine,
> And laced larches upon the blue,
> And grey veils where the moon looks through;
> The cries of birds across the lawns
> In dark and teeming April dawns;
> The sound of wings at the door-sill,
> Where grows the wet-eyed tormentil;
> The ripe berry's witcheries –
> Its perfect round that satisfies;
> And the gay scent of the wood I burn,
> And the slap of butter in a busy churn.
>
> (*PSJ*, p. 32)

The uplands of the Long Mynd and the craggy heights of the Stiperstones beckoned Mary continually. Frequently she was seen trailing along dreamily behind Henry, sometimes rainsoaked, muddy or dusty, always holding wild flowers, returning through the village from walks in the hills. 'One feels that the rapture, the passion, the grief of the mountains are in her soul' – her words, written later about Helen Prothero Lewis (*CPAP*, p. 54), are in fact a distillation of her own essence.

Often they went up Pontesford Hill, the larch-maned mound

[2] Caradoc Evans, 'Mary Webb', *Colophon*, new series III, Winter 1938, p. 63.

which looms over Pontesbury like a huge dormant beast with a
primeval soul. Its brooding presence, timeless, compelling, was
felt constantly by Mary at Rose Cottage where the garden and
front of the house face directly across to the hill. She was caught
in the spell of this 'little' hill 'ringed by the misty shire'. There
(she wrote in a poem), 'some calm Presence takes me by the hand'.
Its fascination was heightened by the local custom and legend
associated with it. She spoke to old villagers who remembered
having taken part during their youth in the Palm Sunday tradition when, early in the morning, a race used to occur up the hill
to pick a spray from the old yew tree on the summit. After this
they sought the legendary golden arrow, said to have been lost in
a battle there in 661, and finding which supposedly brought great
fortune, although no one was sure what the arrow was. This
custom and the wake which followed it, apparently had died out
after 1855. Mary was captivated, reshaping the legend in her
imagination and weaving it into the fabric of her novel. She
wrought her own interpretation of 'the golden arrow' as symbol
and legend, and it is her version which is remembered today
rather than the obscure custom recorded by Charlotte S. Burne.

The integration of this legend gave the novel cohesion as well
as a title, the golden arrow being symbolic of that unifying love
which brings to those who seek and find it 'a charm on 'em, and
sorrow, and a vast of joy' (p. 104) – this being, in effect, the
novel's total statement. It is a love which both wounds and heals,
breaks and makes whole, brings renewal and peace out of stress.
Considered from every viewpoint, the golden arrow is an
immensely effective metaphor for the concept of love the novel is
illustrating. Deborah, the self-giving lover, is Mary's mouthpiece
when she says to the shallow Lily, incapable of love : ' "Seems to
me, loving's like the Golden Arrow – bright and sharp, and him
that finds it'll keep it against the 'orld." ' This, taken with Lily's
acid rejoinder : ' "Take care the arrow dunna prick you !" '
(p. 246) while it is an epitome of the story, is also ironically
prescient of Mary's own future pain in her relationship with
Henry. As *The Golden Arrow* eloquently shows, pain is intrinsic
to Mary's philosophy of love and is fully anticipated. She believes
that love is 'forever martyred and forever gladsome'; for her, the
true lover is 'the eternal martyr' and 'the eternal reveller'. Love
is always crucified. This, to Mary, is the central meaning of

Christ: to be a 'love martyr' is the essence of Christianity shorn of all accretions. Constantly aware of what she calls, in this novel, 'the sharp sweetness of human life', throughout her own she reached out in eager receptivity, prepared to take 'the bitter along with the sweet'. Yet tragically, towards the end, she was to know far more of bitter than of sweet.

This inseparable duality of experience, agony-wonder, joy-pain, bitter-sweet, is a threnody sounding throughout her writing. It is echoed in certain symbolic motifs in *The Golden Arrow*, namely hawthorn and blossom ('the thorn's white over'), honeysuckle ('pain is the honeysuckle around the door') and rose berries ('Deborah shivered suddenly. "There's a thorn in your necklace, Stephen!" '). These appropriate motifs reiterate and underscore the meaning of the major symbol – the golden arrow. The symbolical meaning of the golden arrow, referring to human love, is amplified by the Flockmaster's signpost, symbolical of infinite love and compassion. The signpost 'that rose in the midst of the westward tableland', is depicted as a white cross, 'like a crucifix under the troubled sky'.

Appropriately John Arden in *The Golden Arrow* tells the story of the legends, as it had been his prototype George Meredith who first recounted them to Mary. Allied to setting, these legends are carefully worked out and worked into the narrative: on this Mary had brooded during hours spent crossing 'the great plateaux' of Long Mynd (Wilderhope) in the 'lustrous air' and climbing the wild heathery slopes of the Stiperstones (Diafol) to the Chair itself. From this jagged throne, at a height of 1,800 feet, counties and ranges can be seen in clear weather extending like a 'tesselated plain' into vast distance, while below, to the right, Pontesford Hill appears like a small verdigris dome. The quartzite Chair, a foreboding massive outcrop 'blackened and hardened by uncountable ages', dominates the landscape and gathers the storms which move 'from far Cader Idris'. There are vivid evocations of it throughout *The Golden Arrow* – this, for instance, in which the Chair is introduced into the narrative:

> In the plain this pile of rock and the rise on which it stood above the rest of the hill-tops would have constituted a hill in itself. The scattered rocks, the ragged holly-brakes on the lower slopes were like small carved lions beside the black marble steps of a stupendous throne. Nothing ever altered its look. Dawn

quickened over it in pearl and emerald; summer sent the armies of heather to its very foot; snow rested there as doves nest in cliffs. It remained inviolable, taciturn, evil. It glowered darkly on the dawn; it came through the snow like jagged bones through flesh; before its hardness even the venturesome cranberries were discouraged. For miles around, in the plains, the valleys, the mountain dwellings it was feared. (pp. 40–1)

Weather and atmosphere combine with its physical features to reinforce the superstitions and legends which have grown up around it. The Devil's Chair is the focal point of Diafol as the Flockmaster's signpost is of Wilderhope, and the human drama, influenced by environment, is played out between the two. The setting in this novel has an importance comparable with that of the moors in *Wuthering Heights,* the Forest in Hawthorne's *The Scarlet Letter,* or Egdon Heath in Hardy's *The Return of the Native.*

The physical features and atmosphere of these ranges are representative of opposing qualities powerfully pervasive in the Shropshire countryside – on the one hand, keen ethereal beauty, on the other, inimical, creeping menace – and in both one feels emanations from a deep past, suggestive of good and evil. This is a landscape where, as Mary said, 'the lapse of centuries' seems 'of little moment', saturated in a feeling of stillness, of primeval mystery. Her writing, so expressive of her Shropshire environment, conveys all its aspects with crystal clarity. While this keen ethereal beauty is evoked in descriptive passages, there is also, in every novel, a sense of unknown threat usually focused in a central place or feature of the landscape – the Devil's Chair in *The Golden Arrow,* Undern Hall and its surroundings in *Gone to Earth,* the Beast Walk and Dormer Old House in *The House in Dormer Forest,* 'the unket place' near Dysgwlfas in *Seven for a Secret,* Sarn Mere and its 'thick, blotting woods' in *Precious Bane,* and 'the witchen house' associated with the strange Nesta in *Armour wherein he Trusted.*

Mary herself was superstitious 'like all country women', as she acknowledged later in a letter to her publisher. Thoroughly she understood the strong vein of superstition in the people of her county: into *The Golden Arrow* she wove approximately thirty legends and superstitions, while in *Precious Bane* almost two hundred are included, building up the atmosphere of superstitious country life in nineteenth century Shropshire. She selected legend and superstition, integral to environment, as carefully as she selected features of landscape and natural scenery in the interests of her central themes.

In view of her passionate life-involvement, Mary Webb's work must be looked at against its social background since the emergence of her themes in prose fiction is intrinsically related to the traumatic circumstances of her time. *The Golden Arrow* while reflecting the inner stresses Mary experienced, also reflects the outer stress of upheaval, the plunge into chaos and the unknown in the period during which it was written – the First World War.

The Golden Arrow and to an even greater extent *Gone to Earth*, her second novel, written when the tragedy of world conflict intensified, reflect obliquely the influence of war on her sensitive spirit. Though writing a rural novel populated by only a few country people, she was attempting nevertheless to transmit her intuitive philosophy to a war-torn humanity. Always acutely aware of the pathos of human life, she was activated in her pity by the tragic predicament of the Great War, and this was another shaping force impelling her to literary expression.

The war had begun not long after she and Henry had moved to Pontesbury. That summer of 1914 had been an uneasy one throughout Europe, the entangled political alliances finally culminating in open conflict. German troops crossed the Belgian frontier on 4 August, the British ultimatum was rejected, 'a state of war' declared. It was the end of an era, those changes towards a more modern society which had formed the Edwardian undercurrent, now to be hastened in the urgent measures of wartime. There began a mobilisation of manpower, minds and resources on a scale more massive than any known before. Men were summoned from every walk of life, countryside as well as towns being depleted. All over Shropshire young men volunteered for the Shropshire Yeomanry and the King's Shropshire Light Infantry, which were promptly ordered abroad.

Mary's intense relief when Henry, after medical examination, was declared unfit for the services, can readily be understood. Her three brothers, however, all in the Army, were sent to the Western Front. Although she was living in the depths of the countryside, there could be no escape for one of her compassionate nature from awareness of the horrors and consequences of war. And even in the countryside there were reminders everywhere – evidence, as she said in a poem, of 'a world so black with hate' – the improvised labour force of women and boys in field and farm, reports of dead and wounded which came to the most isolated villages, the terror of Zeppelin raids, headlines in newspapers and literature of every kind reflecting the war.

During the autumn of 1914, Mary wrote a poem showing the effects of war on country people (reminiscent of John Masefield's 'August, 1914'). One of her few war poems, 'Autumn, 1914' discloses the acuteness of her own response. Here is an extract:

> He's gone, her man, so good with his hands
> In the harvest field and the lambing shed.
> Straight ran his share in the deep ploughlands –
> And now he marches among the dead . . .
> His son comes in like a ghost through the door.
> He'll be ready, maybe, for the next big war.
>
> O world, come in from the leasowes grey
> And cold, where swathes of men are lying,
> And horror to shuddering horror crying!
> Come home
> To the wisdom of those that till the loam,
> And give man time for his working-day!
>
> ('Autumn 1914', *CPAP*, p. 117)

Deeply anxious about her brothers, Mary was reminded of them when seeing soldiers home on leave from the Front or thronging the streets and railway station at Shrewsbury, boarding troop trains which would speed them south, probably to injury or death. Often their poignant singing drifted from carriage windows of the trains passing across the plain. Mary's compassion for the soldiers extended to humanity as a whole.

Ten years later she was to tell G. Wrenn Howard, the partner of Jonathan Cape: 'It was all so heartrending that I just hibernated in the beauty of Nature'. In this 'confession', the word 'heartrending' is as revealing as 'hibernated'. Sharply sensitive to the tragedy of war, her hibernation was a conscious attitude and later produced feelings of guilt that she had not done more in the way of practical war effort. Yet it was essential to her at that time to renew her relationship with nature. In so doing, her inner being was renewed. Even though the waste and pity of war caused her keen distress, Mary, at one with her Shropshire surroundings, gradually experienced a healing of her spirit. She felt a reconciliation and unification within herself. Her emphasis in *The Golden Arrow* on division and fusion, on stress and ultimate reconciliation through a unifying love, was influenced by the 'scarlet wars' then disrupting life; her imagination was fully engaged in compassionate desire 'to soothe a world so small, so loud', as she expressed it in another war poem, 'A Night Sky' (1916).

In this respect the origins and genesis of *The Golden Arrow* as the product of her vision are of major importance biographically. The inner forces which give rise to a creative work indeed are the province of the biographer – an understanding of these forces can illumine an understanding of the work itself and its relation to the times in which it was written. As Leon Edel, Henry James's biographer, has it:

> Surely the writing of a literary life would be nothing but a kind of indecent curiosity, and an invasion of privacy, were it not that it seeks always to illuminate the mysterious and magical process of creation. That process belongs to the inner consciousness, those deeper springs of our being where the gathered memories of our lives merge and in some cases are distilled into transcendent art.
>
> *(Literary Biography, p. 3)*

For Mary 'the mysterious and magical process of creation' took over on a wet summer morning in 1915 when she felt compelled to begin writing her novel and was then swept along inspirationally at the rate of some 6,000 words a day, her first draft being completed in three weeks. It was a virtual outpouring, her creative method in itself a direct expression of her personality. Informed accounts, written by literary friends with whom she discussed her work when living in London during the 1920s, all verify her habitual method of long consideration then rapid composition. Adrian Bury, critic and artist who was connected with *The English Review* when he first met her, wrote in his 'Impression of Mary Webb':

> She pondered on a story for many months, constructing, revising, and inventing in her mind. Indeed, I gathered that the whole

book was practically created before she set pen to paper. She would then write as one under a spell, for hours and hours at a stretch, rising at length completely exhausted from her task.

Martin Armstrong, when literary Editor of the *Spectator*, gained first-hand knowledge of her method :

> Her novels grew out of a long brooding. She slowly gathered together the substance and circumstances of her theme . . . before a word had been written, until in a ferment of imaginative excitement she at last set herself to write out the now mature work. It was, in fact, a process of accumulation and elaboration. Her novels weld into coherent artistic form a central experience and a mass of appropriate poetic detail.

Armstrong saw that *au fond* her literary impulse sprang from feelings 'intense to the point of mysticism'. She was a creative mystic as spiritually heightened as her medieval forebears, yet expressing herself in a modern literary form – the novel.

Interviewed in 1926 about her method of composition, Mary said : 'I don't write at stated times . . . I think a lot over my work first, and then I go at it until it is finished.'[3] And talking to Caradoc Evans about her art, she told him 'how hard' she worked at her poems in contrast to her novels which, she said, 'just come to me and I write them without thinking and often I'm surprised at what I've written, so strange it reads'. At such times of spontaneous composition, of sudden quickening, there was no distinction between her living self and her writing self, her conscious and unconscious, integrated in creative wholeness. Virginia Woolf, referring to such intuitive or 'unconscious writers' describes how they 'seem suddenly and without their own consent to be lifted up and swept onwards. The wave sinks and they cannot say what has happened or why . . .'[4] To which can be added Mary's own comments in a review of *The Art of Thought* by Graham Wallas : praising his study of the creative mind, she emphasises his understanding of 'the strange necessity for the subconscious, for using "foreconscious processes for conscious ends" ', and she stresses the 'all-importance' in the creative process of what she calls 'the

---

[3] *T.P.'s and Cassell's Weekly*, 25 September, 1926, p. 106.
[4] Virginia Woolf, *The Common Reader* (Second Series), p. 247.

dim waiting' between preparation and incubation, and illumination – 'like the dark waiting on Easter morning. The experience is garnered, the life lived, the death died. What then? We wait by the sealed tomb for the clap of a wing . . . the starting of immortality from its silent nest. It is the one thing needing . . . The poet is a listener on the shelving shores of the subconscious . . . Hardly ever does he do any conscious thinking. He listens; then he writes. Often he is greatly astonished at what he writes' (*CPAP*, p. 58).

These insights into her own creative process are interesting when we consider them together with the statements of her literary friends about her method. Martin Armstrong commented: 'The way in which she composed her novels accounts for their richness and intensity though not for the sharp and delicate style of so much of her writing.' He – and others – noted her combination of spontaneity and exactitude, amazed that this sensitive manipulation of words and precise imagery sprang as she wrote, entailing very little revision; hers was, as Armstrong said, an 'intuitive rather than conscious' technique: 'Down everything went pell mell, and though she sometimes spoke of revision, I don't believe the revision ever amounted to much.'

Henry Webb, years afterwards, speaking of the compulsive flow of Mary's writing confirmed this account, adding that when she read over her day's work for possible revision, she found that the best passages were those most rapidly composed. These needed the minimum of correction – as one of her publishers stated, 'the pages most typical in her manuscripts have fewest changes'. Henry also humorously disclosed, in discussing her swift pace of composition, that on one occasion he surprised her by a gift which was just what she needed – the latest kind of fountain pen, said to supply ink 'at accelerated speed'. Nothing was allowed to interrupt her once she was in the midst of what she herself described as 'a "rush" – ideas coming too fast for the pen'. She wrote spasmodically when and where the ideas came, no matter the time or place, seizing the nearest scrap of paper, the backs of envelopes and bills. But always she preferred to write outdoors in her garden. The spontaneity of her method accounts for the finer, inspired passages as well as the flaws.

While *The Golden Arrow* certainly exemplifies her 'imaginative energy' as Robert Lynd called it, or in the words of a more recent

American critic, Charles Sanders, 'the dynamic verve with which [she] composed', it also evinces immaturity of technique. The weaknesses in this first novel are obvious enough : primarily, a failure to delineate effectively human motivation. At times, manipulation in the interests of the central theme is too thinly disguised : for instance, the thematic function of the major characters, Deborah and Stephen, becomes increasingly conspicuous as the narrative progresses – the two are less convincingly portrayed as they are manoeuvred by the author towards their destinies, and the novel as a whole loses verisimilitude. Mary Webb is attempting here to assimilate too much (a weakness common in first novels) – her own background and relationship with her Shropshire environment, the profound influence of her father, the vision of life she had lost and refound, her spiritual crisis, the new evaluation at which she had arrived since her marriage.

However, in *The Golden Arrow,* she is, as it were, tuning her instrument. Faults there are, but finer elements of her future writing are also present and certain characteristic features of her style at its best. She impresses in similes and metaphors which are as sharp and evocative as any in her later work. Like Hardy, she draws upon nature for her most effective imagery, the keen observation of a naturalist combining with poetic perception.

She enhances descriptions of her characters by analogies with the animate and inanimate in their natural environment, thereby promoting the unity of the world she is creating. Deborah, whose hair is 'brown as a bark-stack', having 'the soft sheen of a woodlark's wing or a hill foal's flank', is depicted at her parents' cottage 'cheering up like a wet bee in sunshine'. Stephen, feeling insignificantly small and helpless faced by the immensity of the ranges, returns at night from Lostwithin coming 'up the rime-whitened hillside, like a gnat on a huge sealed hornet comb'. When Eli Huntbatch, the fiery, sarcastic dogmatist, speaks, it is 'with the acidity of raw sloes'. And conversely, she often portrays nature in human and animate terms. Of the lonely hill country, she says :

It was only in the summer that the hamlets could link hands over the ridges, the white blossom flow up from the plains till it

almost met on the summit, the farmer's wife on one side of the
ridge walk over to see her sister on the other side.   (p. 18)

This suggests the extent to which the people of the ranges are
an integral part of their environment, moulded by dependence on
natural conditions and elements. It also suggests the underlying
theme of division and fusion. Thereby her imagery, functioning
on a number of levels, is unifying, helping to integrate her world.

Certainly a critical assessment of *The Golden Arrow* could be
made which would underline Charles Sanders' contention that
this novel 'has been regarded too long as merely another pledge
of what Mrs Webb was to achieve in her more masterful *Precious
Bane*'. One aspect of *The Golden Arrow* which merits detailed
attention is the structural and stylistic handling of parallel and
contrast : it may well be said of this novel what Hardy said of
Jude the Obscure : 'The book is all contrasts.' And fundamentally,
intrinsically important to everything is her treatment of the
Shropshire landscape – utilised as a *paysage moralisé*, imbued
with symbolical significance, harnessed to idea (even the seasons
adapted dramatically to the action), yet nevertheless evoked in
primary vividness : here, where her imagination is most richly
engaged, she is at her most successful and convincing.

The writing of this novel marks Mary Webb's emergence as a
literary artist : she had now found the literary form most suited to
her talent, giving her fullest scope for expression, and there was
much that she was burning to say. Yet only twelve years of life
remained to her and almost her entire output was to be concentrated in those years. Like a meteor, luminous, atmospheric, her
life force involved life expenditure in a consuming course towards
extinction.

She progressed, after *The Golden Arrow*, to an enrichment of
her art and to greater technical perfection, but her total *oeuvre*
has its own completeness, and the significance to the whole of her
first novel, rudimentary though it is in some ways, is that here,
as the German critic Irene Marinoff perceived, 'the ground-tone
is struck to which all the following works are tuned'.[5]

Writing such as hers requires interpretation rather than

---

[5] Marinoff, 'Die Romane Mary Webbs', *Anglia*, LX (June 1938), p. 440:
'In The Golden Arrow ist der Grundton angeschlagen, auf den alle folgen-
den Werke abgestimmt sind'.

analysis. Concentration on her unities of interest and expression, her overarching continuities, what Proust called 'the constants', will establish the essential nature of her intention and her achievement. Yet the significance of these 'constants', certainly not perceived by critics in her own day, has continued to be overlooked. E. M. Forster's words on visionary writers can be applied to Mary Webb and to her work looked at as a coherent whole :

> 'Everything comes to them in a rush, their arms are filled at once with material for a life's work and their task is to sort and re-sort what they have, rather than to seek fresh experiences.'
> (*Abinger Harvest,* pp. 97–8)

Each of Mary Webb's novels has what Forster described as a predominant 'sensation of a song or of a sound' tending always towards unity. And so, too, a chord is sounded in the reader that reverberates on long after her work has been read. According to Forster, the novelist of 'prophecy' is 'irradiating nature from within so that every colour has a glow and every form a distinctness which could not otherwise be obtained' (*Aspects of the Novel,* pp. 129–50). The light in Mary Webb's work is defined by Chesterton as 'a light not shining on things but through them. It is that mysterious light in which solid things become semi-transparent, a diffused light . . .' (*G.A.,* p. 12).

And it was the intensity of her own inner life, her spiritual, sensory and emotional experience which was both source and substance of her art. Impelled to express the spiritual reality she apprehended in, through and beyond the material form of nature, unceasingly she sought verbal images which would implicitly correspond with this reality. In her novels it is not her intention to reflect the richness and variety of life, the harsher, cruder realities of everyday rural existence. She creates an essentially poetic world which is uniquely her own, self-contained, in which all interweaves and interacts – and she compels us into it.

Her mode not surprisingly, therefore, is the hazardous one of naturalistic allegory and in this she can be likened to Nathaniel Hawthorne, the New England allegorist, especially in his major works, *The Scarlet Letter* and *The Marble Faun*. There are in Mary Webb's novels elements essential to 'the Romance' as envisaged and written by Hawthorne, in particular the creation, vitally significant, of what is described in the Preface to *The Marble Faun* as 'a sort of poetic or fairy precinct'. In such a symbolical world, outer and inner, actual and visionary, fuse indefinably, occur as one.

From the outset, in *The Golden Arrow*, Mary Webb's 'poetic or fairy precinct' is established, the actual geographical location being her hill country, the border region of south-west Shropshire, once part of the old Kingdom of Powys, a mid-way realm in the Marches of Wales where Saxon and Celt intermingle in blood and mind, language and myth. It is a region which she described later, at the beginning of *Seven for a Secret*, as 'the country that lies between the dimpled lands of England and the gaunt purple steeps of Wales – half in Faery and half out of it . . .' This, for her, becomes a symbolical borderland between spiritual and material, where nature is both veil and image. Her 'land of Betwixt and Between', as she finally defined it in the last novel, is an irreducible inner-outer realm of heightened awareness in which ultimate reality is half-glimpsed, felt at a distance yet all around, apprehended yet eluding grasp. Perhaps the abiding appeal of her writing lies in this exquisite allusiveness and a Euripidean quality of 'linked sweetness long drawn out'. Her novels reflect and express both her individual vision and the essence of her personality – mystical and precise at once.

The 'poetic or fairy precinct' which she creates, peculiarly both in and out of a particular time and place, is not seen, as it were, in the broad, hard light of noon, but in the ethereal gleam of dawn and the diffusive mystery of twilight. It is sparsely populated, and the major figures who inhabit it are primarily concerned with a higher order of things than the ordinary details of rural life, for they undergo an entire orientation of inner being towards either self-hood or self-loss, salvation or destruction, renewal or ruin through processes of love, suffering and sacrifice. And initially in *The Golden Arrow*, Mary Webb succeeds in drawing us into this intensely individual and integral world in which everything interrelates, is relevant to the whole and in its appropriate place.

Appropriately too, *The Golden Arrow*, her 'apocalypse of love', is dedicated 'To A Noble Lover, H.L.W.'. She completed this novel in the summer of 1915, typed and submitted it for publication. It is not known whether she tried any other publisher before

Constable, but we can imagine her exhilaration on its acceptance by that firm, her eager anticipation of publication. This was a success indeed, as it had become even more difficult to have a novel accepted during the war period when publishers were forced to cut down their lists, paper and money being in short supply.

Before long, Mary began to think about the plot and details of her next novel, *Gone to Earth* – again an impassioned presentation of her vision of life, clothed in vividly dramatised scene and incident, saturated in the mysterious light and darkness of her landscape. It was another 'intercourse with the world', to use Hawthorne's phrase, an intercourse activated by pity as the tragic waste of the Great War increased.

During this period too, she was attempting a more obviously practical (though not, to her, mundane) intercourse with humanity – at Shrewsbury Market. Her marketing venture, undertaken while living at Pontesbury, may well have helped to fire her imagination when writing *The Golden Arrow*. She was fascinated by Shrewsbury Market. A number of factors influenced her decision to have a stall there.

The primary factor was the war itself. Prices were rising steadily, food supplies were short and Mary wanted sincerely and passionately to 'do something' for the war effort. She began by deliberate self-denial, a dangerous procedure in view of her delicate physical condition, for 'living ascetically' as she called it, ultimately was to bring tragic consequences. At this period, however, and indeed since her marriage, there was no threat of a recurrence of her disease.

Thoroughly enjoying the outdoor life, she worked hard in her garden and was well rewarded by its 'benign and wistful yield' of vegetables and fruit. There was more than enough for herself and Henry, as well as for old people and beggars whom she always supplied generously with homegrown goods. Rather than waste the surplus, Mary decided, for reasons of practicality, to sell it. At first she took seasonal vegetables, fruit and flowers to Shrewsbury Market, selling very cheaply to the stall keepers who then charged what they wished to customers. But this did not satisfy the precise and practical in Mary's nature: with that thoroughness and decisiveness so like Alice Meredith's, she made arrangements to have a stall of her own in order to sell her goods directly to customers and charge the very low prices which, she felt, were all they could afford in those days of hardship.

Joyfully, and with wholehearted enthusiasm, Mary undertook this physically exacting occupation. She and Henry rose before dawn, sometimes as early as three or four a.m., to gather and bind the flowers, and select the vegetables and fruit. Henry usually remained at home while Mary set off on Saturdays for Shrewsbury, although occasionally he took a barrow around Pontesbury selling the surplus fruit to cottagers. His mother and sister, hearing of this, were outraged that Henry, a Cambridge graduate and a gentleman, should be so debased: feeling that Mary's influence was not to Henry's good, they built up still further a wall of resistance against her. The Webb family knew virtually nothing either of the deep mutual understanding of Mary and Henry, and their shared outlook on life at this period, or of Mary's reasons for marketing, the enormous physical effort it cost her and the sheer delight it brought her.

Often she walked the entire nine miles to Shrewsbury and then nine miles back again at the end of the day, observing the countryside as she went 'by slanting ways, in slanting sun'. Her poem 'Market Day' illustrates the exhilaration she experienced: 'We take our roots and country sweets/Where high walls shade the steep old streets.' Occasionally she detoured and cut across the fields to Lyth Hill taking the path across the plateau – this hill never ceased to draw her with the enchantment of its Little Wood and wide view over the 'multiple-tinted' plain to the mountains, ever varying, constantly compelling.

At Shrewsbury Market Mary sold her vegetables and fruit and offered roses at a halfpenny a bunch which had grown over the front porch at Rose Cottage; and in spring, on her wooden trestle table were the primroses she had picked on the way. She is remembered sitting at her stall in 'wet muddy skirts', her dark bun dishevelled, looking 'so different' from the ruddy, raucous farmers' wives. Frail-looking, quiet, she sat among them as they shouted their wares, and when she told the price of her own, it was in a 'low voice' and 'cultured tones'.

After the publication of *The Golden Arrow* she was pointed out by those who knew of it, as 'Mary Webb the novelist' and she became something of a local curiosity. If anyone stopped to talk to her about the novel she was delighted and answered questions eagerly, taking a spontaneous pleasure in their interest. This child-like eagerness to discuss her own work, and her unaffected joy on hearing it praised, were characteristics she never lost and which, later, brought the supercilious scorn of certain sophisticated literary women with whom she mixed in London (notably Vita Sackville-West).

At the close of market day, stall empty, produce usefully disposed of, she emerged again into the town, passing through the Square with its statue of Robert Clive and the clusters of brown shield-shaped cabs awaiting hire. Then out of Shrewsbury towards 'the shadow coloured hills'. Henry recalled years afterwards :

> Although I don't think she earned more than five shillings before she set out in the evening on the nine miles' walk home, she was never dissatisfied. Indeed, she came back looking much brighter : she felt she had done something beautiful.
>
> (Moult, p. 137)

Mary saw in marketing a certain timelessness and 'the beauty of common transactions', as she expressed it in *The Golden Arrow*. Yet she was not romanticising. She took in every aspect of market day. It was a deep pleasure to her when she saw the fresh goods of the earth laid out for sale : 'These simple things, all recklessly cheap, gave to their sellers something of the large dignity of Nature herself' (p. 175). Perhaps in this statement is the key to one aspect of the fascination market held for her. Another was her determination to mingle with Shropshire country people. She felt rewarded when they talked freely with her in the local dialect she loved. When visiting country cottages she was sometimes disappointed that the cottagers were inhibited in her company, feeling her to be 'a lady'. The market stall fulfilled the purpose of bringing her into close contact with these country people as one of themselves. Here she could observe and listen, absorb impressions of the individual and the throng, in a milieu so rich in human interest. This was not consciously calculated writer's research. The descriptions of 'Silverton' market which vivify her novels are informed by a lively and loving perception, the details drawn from actuality – for instance in *The Golden Arrow*, the People's Dining Saloon with its 'long trestle table where the market folk sat with noses nearly touching, like parrots in a cage', and the plate glass door which bore 'a superannuated legend . . . "Christmas puddings piping hot" '. There are classic descriptions of market in this novel which can hardly have been surpassed. Especially memorable is her realistic appraisal of the more gruesome features. While her opinion that 'beauty was everywhere, except in the meat market', was not an entirely objective view, as she was revolted by the slaughter of animals for food, nevertheless, in her day, butchers shops and stalls were particularly repulsive, hygiene at a minimum, carcases piled high, blood everywhere:

> There slow bluebottles, swollen and unwholesome, crawled and buzzed; men of a like complexion shouted stertorously, brandishing stained carving-knives; an unbearable stench arose from the offal, and women with pretty clothes and refined manners bought the guts of animals under such names as 'sweetbreads' or 'prime fat kidneys', and thrust their hands into the disembowelled bodies of rabbits to test their freshness.   (p. 175)

Undue prominence was given to Mary's marketing after she had become posthumously famous. It was grossly exaggerated, not put in perspective as a brief wartime measure. Nevertheless the significance of the light it throws on her character should not be overlooked. First, it underlines her complete disregard for social status, and in this Henry must be included too, both of them refusing to 'conform' or pander to 'appearances', for market-gardening, even in wartime, was not a pursuit of the strata of middle-class society in which they had grown up. Neither was Mary's marketing a sign of eccentricity, nor a pose. Edwin Pugh, the novelist and critic who, a few years later in London came to know and understand her well, made an astute assessment when he said:

> She was unaffectedly, sincerely unconventional. She seemed to have no awareness of what others might think or say about her. And though a little odd, a little queer, as she might appear, she never posed. It was something in the style of her dress, perhaps, something in her manner and poise, that moved strangers to stare at her.[6]

[6] Pugh, 'Mary Webb', *The Bookman* LXXVI, July 1928, p. 194.

Those who recall Shrewsbury Market at this period remember its extreme hustle and roughness. To mix with market folk at their own level was not an easy step for one of Mary's gentle background and self-consciousness. Courageous determination carried her forward here, as it did when she visited cottages. This urgent need to reach out to people, an impelled extension to humanity, was as intrinsic to her mystical temperament as her equally necessary withdrawals.

Since their return to Shropshire from Weston, and the renewal of Mary's relationship with nature, Henry was realising the degree to which her total being was bound up in her countryside, how her highly specialised personality had been shaped and her imagination fertilised by these surroundings. He became aware that Mary's passion for Shropshire was more than animistic and pagan love, more even than nature mysticism, but was part of a rare spiritual process of inner growth. Though Shropshire was not essential to him in such a potent, all-infusing way, Henry during the years at Rose Cottage, understood of Mary how and why, like Deborah Arden, she belonged 'to this country of mountains'.

But to live 'the simple life' is easier to write about than do, even for one imbued with what Henry referred to as 'passionate nature spirit'. This he was finding in 1916. Their financial situation, as the war years went on, was becoming increasingly precarious, prices rising steadily, Mary's £100 allowance devaluating. Neither of them was what is known as 'a good manager'. Henry, throughout their years together, left the finances entirely in Mary's hands – but while it was she who bore most of the pressure of their financial difficulties (the strain of debts one of the stresses which eventually led to the ruin of her health and the deepening of her personal tragedy), in fact it was her own extraordinary generosity to destitutes and children that involved her in this desperate financial worry. And it was during the war, with cases of poverty, hardship and distress proliferating, that she became impelled by wild compassion into an inordinately generous giving which often left her own needs unsupplied.

Bills had to be paid, including the rent of Rose Cottage which at £36 a year was not low. There was little money left for anything beyond the most basic necessities. Of furniture they had hardly any – while Penrose had been a furnished house, Rose Cottage was not and would have been stark indeed without the flowers Mary put everywhere. She did own a grand piano – one of three pianos the Merediths had at Maesbrook – but she could no longer afford to have it tuned. Yet she continued to play and could not bear the thought of selling it. Besides, with a cloth spread over the top, the piano was eminently useful as an improvised table since they didn't possess one. Here they sat to eat and write.

Mary, 'good with the needle' – especially embroidery – made her own clothes or more often mended and 'turned' her old ones. Sadly she reduced her cat family as this had increased to nine (three cats and six grown-up kittens) and it was difficult to feed them all. Henry did not wish to return to teaching but tried to improve their financial situation by occasional tutoring, and for the same reason took a part-time job as a rate collector which he found to be rather distressing. Frequently the people he called on were in the same plight as themselves for he and Mary were having increasing difficulty each quarter day raising the money to pay the rent of Rose Cottage.

She dreaded Henry's absence when he went out on his collecting round. In a poignant personal poem she speaks of this 'life long dread of parting', an intense yearning for Henry, an intense insecurity : 'Ah, do not be so sweet !/For if you only go across the street/The moment is a year . . ./An instant fled – and life so swiftly gone,/And you so very dear' (*PSJ*, p. 97). With a solicitude resembling George Meredith's, Henry left love notes around the rooms for her to find when he was out, leaving them on the chair, the bed or the piano-table. In these early years of their marriage they were the kind of lovers who were 'at once spiritual, passionate and childless', as she said in *The Golden Arrow*. And again, in the same novel, written at a time when they came nearest to being 'one soul' with each other, Mary is voicing her personal anguish in commentaries on Deborah's agonised love for Stephen : 'Parting – even for a night – was a thing unthinkable to her; herein she paid the lover's penalty, for the very thought of absence from him set her shaking' (p. 281). As desperately as Deborah needed Stephen, Mary needed Henry, not knowing 'how soon' they may be 'wrenched apart'. Always this abyss yawned in front of her, pitching her to the edge of grief in the very moment of ecstasy. She expresses this acutely sad perspective again and again in *The Golden Arrow* : 'For such love as this comes unseen

and passes unknown, like the doom of pain and the impulse of
spring . . . and the hands that reach for it can hold nothing else.'

While the Rose Cottage period was probably one of greater
security and harmony in her relationship with Henry than any
she was to experience subsequently, it was because of this bliss –
'the golden sunlight of our peace' – that she felt all the more
keenly the threat of obliterating cloud. She knew that like a
beautiful, fragile glass, all could be suddenly shattered, could
'shiver and fall inwards'. She sensed her future 'doom of pain'.
And already the intimate peace and understanding of their relationship during those years in their first Shropshire home – a
return to the idyllic and Eden-like existence of her childhood –
was to be disrupted : another ejection for Mary from 'the hills of
heaven'.

The difficulties of wartime living finally forced them, with considerable regret, to resign the tenancy of Rose Cottage. The landlord, Mr Parry, was sorry to see 'the Webbs' go, for though they
had taken more interest in the garden than the house itself, not
being 'house-proud', nevertheless, from his point of view they
were good tenants, 'respectable' and (he said) 'very interesting',
both being writers – Mary 'rather delicate, sweet natured', Henry
'good-looking and very gentlemanly'.

Reluctantly they moved, early in 1916, to cheaper and smaller
accommodation they had found during their walks : one of two
joint cottages situated remotely on Nills Hill at the beginning of
the Stiperstones range. Here the rent was only £13 a year. There
was a small garden in which Mary could grow vegetables and
flowers for their own use and for market, but it was more difficult
to get to Shrewsbury as they were even deeper into the countryside in this isolated spot only accessible by a rough narrow track
which forded a stream. The windows of the cottage faced directly
on to mysterious Pontesford Hill across 'a lone green valley'. At
'The Nills'[7] Mary was the neighbour of the Morris family whose
friendship she soon gained as they understood her gentle, intense
nature, her sense of humour and the sensitivity underlying her
'poor but proud' exterior. The Morris family, in fact, became
devoted to her and she never lost touch with them, even later
when living in London. They are a prime example of the endur-

---

[7] Mary spelt this 'The Knills'; another 'local' spelling she used was Bow-
mere for Bomere.

ing friendships she made with Shropshire country people, and of the lasting affection she could inspire in those who really knew her closely.

In spite of the move to The Nills, their financial position worsened rapidly and Henry was forced into the idea of returning to full-time teaching. The Nills, however, was very remote and sometimes, in winter, inaccessible – there was no possibility of teaching somewhere in the area and returning to the cottage each day.

Henry applied and was accepted for a post at The King's School, Chester. He was to commence on 8 April 1916 as assistant master teaching English, Latin and History. They would live in Chester with Alice Meredith and Olive during the week, returning to The Nills for the holidays and at weekends whenever possible. To Mary this meant, sadly, another exile from Shropshire, yet not so drastic as that at Weston-super-Mare (Chester only fifty miles and a short train journey from Shrewsbury). The prospect of living with her mother again was somewhat daunting and Mary was determined that they would return to The Nills at every opportunity. Without this guarantee of an anchorage in Shropshire, she could not have contemplated the move.

Arriving at Chester, the busy county capital and important military base of Western Command, they were confronted on every side by visible evidence of a war which already had caused the worst carnage in history. Temporarily, Mary's hibernation in the beauty of nature had ended and, to use her own words in *The Golden Arrow*, there was 'a vast of strangeness afore her'.

8

Chester, The Nills – and

Gone to Earth

1916–1917

> Ah, my soul is afraid,
> Homesick, estranged.
> I long for my palace of jade
> And the forest I ranged.
> (*CPAP*, p. 118)

Alice Meredith had returned to Chester to live at Hough Green where she had lived before marriage, little more than a mile from the city and the sandstone Cathedral. She bought No. 76, a tall, white, roomy house.

Chester, even more than Shrewsbury, showed an altered, grim aspect during the war years. Always having a strong military tradition, the city was now a hive of activity with soldiers everywhere coming and going from the headquarters of Cheshire regiments at The Castle (very near Hough Green), and in the heart of the city. Here, too, were centres of the British and Belgian Red Cross, busy with the care of wounded soldiers arriving from the Somme and with frequent fund-raising events. Hospital trains carrying the wounded came in at the General Station, maimed, injured and gassed soldiers taken from there to nearby hospitals. Many of these soldiers, in various stages of recuperation, were seen around the streets where newsboys at corners and in the famous City Rows shouted the latest news of war.

The rich, historical interest of Chester (Deva) which dates from the Romans, in normal times would have attracted Mary, but in 1916 unfortunately was obscured for her by the ever-present gloom and horror brought by war. Although the old, timbered black-and-white buildings, the two miles of ancient sandstone town walls, the coiling river, were reminiscent of Shrewsbury, at the same time this likeness intensified her yearning to return home. She became increasingly unhappy with Henry out all day teaching; and to live again in close proximity to her mother soon proved to be a mistake. Temperamentally they had always had an abrasive effect on each other and this had increased since Mary had run her own household, developed her individual way of living and routines, or, to be more accurate, her lack of routines. It was, in fact, Mary's disregard of the clock and haphazardness in household matters which especially irritated Alice who lived by the rule of time and a stiff scaffolding of strictly adhered-to habit. She had visited Mary only rarely since her marriage as neither of them could tolerate for long such a divergence of priorities. Once, when staying with Mary at Rose Cottage, Alice – accustomed to taking meals at regular hours – wondered whether Mary had forgotten lunch entirely, as there was no sign of any preparations at mid-day. Completely absorbed in what she was doing, Mary's response to the lunch query – 'When the luggage train goes down I generally begin to think about it' – was indicative of the minor significance she attached to meals as well as to timekeeping.

Neither could Mary tolerate easily her mother's apparent lack of concern about her sons at the Western Front. Reports were coming of the holocaust; newspapers daily listed the dead, wounded and missing. Alice's comments such as 'Oh, they're all right – they're in the trenches', revealed an appalling ignorance of the conditions and dangers of the war, and were characteristic of her tight self-centredness. On the other hand, Alice probably reacted against Mary's acute anxiety for her brothers to whom she was writing so frequently. A personal poem, 'The Lad Out There', which Mary sent to Kenneth – 'my brave lad tramping through the mire' – reveals something of her pity and concern: 'Let him in his long watching know/That I too count the minutes slow ...'[1]

Kenneth had joined the Canadian Ambulance Unit and was at the front line, Douglas was proving that excellence as a soldier which eventually won him the Military Cross, while young Mervyn who had joined up from Keble College, Oxford, was 'in

---

[1] *PSJ*, p. 90. Mary also sent the poem to her brothers Douglas and Mervyn. Kenneth received his copy of the poem in a letter three days after his arrival in Flanders.

the trenches' and later in the war only just escaped death when part of his jaw was shot away.

Further tension between Mary and Alice was generated by their opposing views of religion: Alice and Olive, orthodox to the bone, were deeply committed in Church of England affairs, in particular those of Chester Cathedral; Mary, sharply critical, at this period, of the established Church and dogma, did not conceal either her attitude or her pantheistic outlook, now reinforced by Henry's influence.

Finding no sympathetic atmosphere at Hough Green, and distressed by the war, Mary experienced an increasing weight of depression which she expressed in her introspective poem, 'An Estray', written at Chester during the summer of 1916:

> How did I come so low,
> Wandering here
> Under clouds of wrath and woe
> With a heart full of fear?
>
> How did I chance to roam
> Into the night,
> Away from my delicate home
> Of colour and light?
>
> Out of a land serene,
> Airy and lone,
> I strayed to the sadness terrene,
> To a people of stone.
> (*CPAP*, p. 118)

The final verse of this poem, 'Ah my soul is afraid . . .' (which heads this chapter), indicates the fundamental reason for Mary's depression: 'homesick, estranged', she was longing for the Shropshire countryside, her 'palace of jade', 'the forest' she 'ranged'. Scarcely could she bear now to be separated from this landscape which, since her return from Weston, had become more than ever essential to her existence. Her immersion in nature there had intensified to such a degree that she felt one with it in every fibre of her being, spiritual and physical, responding ardently with the total self to a further deepening of her mysticism which had gained vital renewed illumination through love. Perhaps she herself had not realised, when agreeing to live at Chester, the extent to which the 'colour and light' of her life were bound up in Shropshire.

Her depression and nervous fear were aggravated by the war-conscious atmosphere of the Cheshire capital, clothed in a dark mantle. There was the actual environmental darkness, government orders for 'darkening of windows' between sunset and sunrise because of German air raids, causing complete black-out, house-holders being fined if a chink of light showed. This darkness, more noticeable and ominous in the city than in the countryside, was particularly oppressive to Mary, especially since the glow of lamps in windows was, for her, emblematic of love. Significantly she had written in her poem to Kenneth: 'Now nights are dark and mornings dim . . . I . . ./light the lamp of love for him.' In *The Golden Arrow*, she had used the red glow of lamps as a symbolic motif associated with the loving John Arden; and taking this image which was to recur in her work, back to its biographical source, the guiding or 'kindly light' which had illumined her youth was metaphorically that of her father – literally too, since George Meredith carried a lantern, going each night to feed the dogs and poultry, or crossing fields to check on his cattle.

So much at Chester reflected the pitiless war, the tragic waste of young life: military concentration, soldiers wounded or yet to be wounded, Red Cross fêtes, events such as the visit of Lloyd George to the Munitions Factory, sad reports in every issue of the *Chester Chronicle* of deaths of Cheshire soldiers. And at The King's School the chief interest of many of the boys whom Henry taught was the newly formed Cadet Corps.

During that dreary, drizzly, sunless summer, the weekdays at Chester would have been intolerable for Mary without her return on Fridays to Shropshire. Only there could she work at the novel she had been preparing since completion of *The Golden Arrow*. The remoteness of The Nills, the soothing presence of Pontesford Hill, the timelessness of the ranges helped to bring her renewal at the deepest springs of being, and spontaneously with this renewal, fresh creative impulse. Henry understood the necessity to return, yet was deeply concerned about her recurring depression. In a fragment of poem she speaks directly to him: 'I give you laughing names, dear, for I see/Tears like a sea stand up before the sun/And the whole world grown dark with tragedy/ And life cut off before the laugh is done.' (*CPAP*, p. 116)

Even Henry's calm 'distancing' philosophy could not console. For Mary, with the foreground an insensate, slaughterous war, millions of young men dying in the mud, perspective was lost in a mist of pity. Her compassion becoming active welled up into creative release, and the weekends at The Nills were spent in an intensity of verbal outpouring. She wrote *Gone to Earth* with urgent speed, working at it day and night. The Morris family, who welcomed her return to the cottage each weekend, were fascinated to see her sitting among a mound of papers, reeling off page after page, oblivious of everything except her writing – Mrs Morris and her daughter helped to pick up the pages which had fallen to the floor, and then placed them in order.[2] Working far into the night by the light of a paraffin lamp or candles, Mary hardly slept at all when held in the rush of words. The urgency with which she wrote is felt in the tone of the novel, reflected in the relentless inevitability of the tragedy. An almost Aeschylean sense of oncoming doom pervades from opening paragraphs to last as this tragedy is developed to its conclusion.

Gone to Earth is the passionate expression of Mary's revolt against suffering. Pity is its *primum mobile*, a wild pity which has dispensed with hope. Although 'local' in setting and detail, this poignant country story cannot be dissociated from the vast suffering, spiritual as well as physical and mental, inflicted by the war. It is a novel most intimately related to the tragic times in which it was written, having an underlying significance and meaning beyond the immediate context of life in a remote rural district of Shropshire. As John Buchan pointed out (in his 1928 Introduction), *Gone to Earth* 'is partly allegory'. But in this second wartime novel, Mary Webb is less preoccupied in allegorising her personal experience than the experience of mankind as she sees it. This intensely pessimistic interpretation of life and human destiny, directly influenced by the dark pain-filled climate of wartime, is projected through the story of the ill-fated central character, Hazel Woodus, young, fey, innocent, a true child of nature who is appalled at the suffering of any creature, however small, who is desired by two men – hunted sexually by one, revered spiritually by the other – and who is herself doomed to die the victim of cruelty. In this tragedy of a country girl, Mary Webb is expressing

---

[2] For this information I am indebted to Mrs Key of Pontesbury (daughter of Mrs Morris).

her own insights into the universal human condition, illustrating her view of a callous world where primitive savagery lurks within civilised man unleashing the worst evil – cruelty – and perpetuating the age-old ritualistic betrayal and slaughter of the innocent, the weak, the defenceless.

Drawing an essential distinction between 'world' and 'earth' (nature), Mary Webb is, in effect, underlining the division between material and spiritual which is a recurring, cohesive theme in her work, an aspect of her life-long preoccupation with the question of good and evil. And never had her own need for earth – for nature – been greater than then, appalled and horrified at the pitiless inhumanity of the contemporary 'world' in large-scale war. *Gone to Earth* is the artistic expression of Mary Webb's passionately felt creed – like that of Hazel Woodus, a creed 'of love and pity'. The total statement of the novel is in effect an eloquent protest and plea summed up in a comment of central significance : 'Oh, filthy, heavy-handed, blear-eyed world, when will you wash and be clean?' (p. 188).

Yet although this novel obliquely reflects the anguish caused by the war and is a conscious criticism of civilised society, Church and convention, it is not excessively didactic, but unquestionably an artistic success. While Mary Webb's intention is to stir up the emotions of her readers and to widen awareness, she employs an essentially poetic method, setting up reverberations within the world of her novel, using myth and symbol to invest it with a breadth and depth of significance beyond that of the story itself. *Gone to Earth*, finely wrought, is a unified work of art, a tragedy written with unabated imaginative fire, impelled by urgent compassion – a *tour de force* which was to be greatly admired by discerning contemporaries and later considered by some critics to be her finest achievement, rated even higher than *Precious Bane*.

A bare outline of this tragedy of a Shropshire girl reads as romantic melodrama – as indeed do most of Mary Webb's plots, her strength as a novelist lying not in inventiveness but in her poetic imagination. The tragic protagonist, Hazel Woodus, is virtually the beginning, centre and end of *Gone to Earth*. Her parentage is strange – daughter of a Welsh gipsy woman (who has died leaving her only a book of spells and charms), and Abel, an eccentric bee-keeper, harpist and coffin-maker. Hazel lives with her father, her pet fox cub Foxy, an old rabbit, a blind bird and a one-eyed cat in a hovel 'little larger than a pig-sty', and at eighteen she knows little of the ways of society : rather is she akin to the wild creatures of the woodland, her loveliness and inno-cence attracting Edward Marston, the Non-conformist minister whose chapel is on a nearby hill known as God's Little Mountain. Marston, fascinated by Hazel and feeling that she needs protec-tion, marries her, but with mistaken altruism he denies his own physical passion and does not consummate the marriage. But Hazel's sexual instinct has already been aroused by the brutal fox-hunting squire, Jack Reddin, who pursues her inexorably. Drawn to Marston yet obsessed by Reddin, she undergoes an inner struggle, torn between the conflicting needs of her awaken-ing spiritual self and her awakened sexual self. Ironic coincidences combine to promote her destruction. The magnetic Reddin takes her from Marston making her his mistress; she swings like a pendulum between the two men until eventually her sexual bond with Reddin is insufficient to hold her and, appalled at his callousness to defenceless creatures, she returns to Marston. Finally her glimpse of what life with Marston could be when radiated by a love both spiritual and physical, is tragically to be unfulfilled as she dies attempting to save Foxy from the pursuing hounds.

Such a summary conveys nothing of the imaginative power, the richly concrete presentation, the haunting, evocative quality of this impassioned novel. One can only agree with John Buchan that 'the chief beauty of the book is the picture of Hazel which is done with extraordinary tenderness and subtlety'. Totally one with her surroundings, Hazel is the incarnation of the spirit of the countryside – specifically that corner of hill country in the south-west Shropshire landscape near The Nills where the novel was written, and close to the Long Mynd-Stiperstones setting of *The Golden Arrow*. Like Mary herself, Hazel has been moulded by this countryside – it is of her very essence. And in relation to this it is interesting to quote Mary Webb in a review giving us a rare insight into her ideas on character creation and the art of the novel of country life :

> The hero of a country story must be instinct with the country-side : it is in his very bones. So it must always be in a novel that attempts the interpretation of earth through character. For the dwellers in mountain and forest are under this burden, that they

must unconsciously express those dumb masses and forces that have no other voice than theirs. No novel of the countryside can attain greatness unless it unifies its characters with the earth, half frustrate, half triumphal.   (Moult, p. 280)

Nowhere in her own novels does she demonstrate this more convincingly and effectively than in her portrayal of Hazel Woodus.

Hazel can hardly be imagined separated from her surroundings: 'She had so deep a kinship with the trees, so intuitive a sympathy with leaf and flower, that it seemed as if the blood in her veins was not slow-moving human blood, but volatile sap' (p. 186). Reminiscent of Pearl in Hawthorne's *The Scarlet Letter*, she is a dryad of wood and stream, her voice and song are like that of woodland birds. To Edward she seems the 'spirit of beauty'; there is something inexpressible about her as there is about the landscape to which she belongs. Such is the impression Edward has on first seeing her when she comes with her father to sing at the chapel:

> She sang with passion. The wail of the lost was in her voice . . . 'Poor child!' he thought, 'Is it mystical longing or a sense of sin that cries out in her voice?' It was neither of those things . . . It was the grief of rainy forests and the moan of stormy water; the muffled complaint of driven leaves; the keening – wild and universal – of life for the perishing matter that it inhabits. Hazel expressed things that she knew nothing of, as a blackbird does. For, though she was young and fresh, she had her origin in the old dark heart of earth, full of innumerable agonies, and in that heart she dwelt, and ever would, singing from its gloom as a bird sings in a yew tree. Her being was more full of echoes than the hearts of those that live further from the soil.   (p. 76)

Movement is a life principle for her in a landscape full of inner dynamics. In all aspects she is part of nature, mixed in with the rhythms of her countryside, feeling and enjoying it 'with a passion no words could express'.

Clearly, Hazel is the embodiment of the most ethereal and fey side of Mary Webb herself – as well as her most passionate and earth-loving. While, in *The Golden Arrow*, a great deal of her own attitudes and feelings had gone to the creation of Deborah Arden (more the Mary that the Meredith family knew), in Hazel

Woodus she has depicted her most elemental self – the child of earth – and her own soul's intuitive penetration to the depths of nature. But the character of Hazel Woodus is more than a self-portrait of the author : she is a subtle imaginative creation to which Mary Webb brought vivid substance, pathos, poignant life.

From the first we see Hazel responding to life totally, with unrestrained natural zest. Yet also from the first it is intimated that her grasp of life is as eager and full as it is to be short-lived – we feel that Hazel is a mere pawn of fate, that, for her, life is the bride of death. There are suggestions of this throughout the novel in an allegorical symbolism that alludes to the coming tragedy and adds to the inevitability. Motifs of death recur again and again – for instance Hazel goes to her wedding in a funeral wreath of lilies made by Abel; in the fields she winds a wreath of foxgloves round her head; Reddin waits for her under a black yew tree. Reddin's house, Undern Hall, is itself a symbol of darkness, haunted by its ghostly and ghastly past, pervaded by an atmosphere 'mournful with old pain'. The grounds of Undern, in their sinister beauty reminiscent of Dante's dusky wood, are imbued with as strong a sense of menace as the house itself. Here Andrew Vessons, Reddin's old servant, clips a 'swan' yew tree and shoots birds; here the torture of the hedgehog, the burning of Hazel's bees and the slaughter of rabbits at harvesting prefigure the human sacrifice of Hazel in the ritual frenzy of the hunt. Her 'small coffin' will be made by her own father.

If she is the incarnation of the Shropshire landscape, mirroring its numerous moods, Hazel is also the personification of certain myths and legends of that landscape with which she is totally identified. Mary Webb weaves, with consummate artistry, an interpenetration of myth and reality to culminate in the tragic climax.

In Hazel Woodus, a peasant of the Welsh borders, Mary Webb created a remarkably convincing Celtic primitive. It is interesting to note that Matthew Arnold in *The Study of Celtic Literature* (1867) considered the outstanding Celtic characteristics to be imaginativeness, melancholy and a nature love coming almost more from a sense of nature's mystery than of her beauty. While *Gone to Earth* is the most Celtic of Mary Webb's novels, these characteristics are embodied above all in the mind and personality of Hazel, Celtic in her wild melancholy, her intimate communing with nature, her lilting speech and singing with its echoes of Gaelic lamentations, and her absolute belief in natural magic, legend and superstition. Various myths and legends of her countryside have such a powerful hold on Hazel's mind and imagination that to her they are identical with reality and she feels her own fate inextricably bound up with them : these are the seed-bed of the tragedy – the legends of the Black Huntsman and the death-pack, the lady of Undern Coppy, and, implicitly, the primitive myth of an external soul.

Again as in *The Golden Arrow*, Mary Webb made a conscious selection and elaboration of folk legends and superstitions associated with her landscape, organising around these the imaginative world of her novel, aesthetically shaping the whole before she began the actual writing of the book. Attention has not hitherto been drawn to how finely in *Gone to Earth* the element of myth, superstition and ritual has been assimilated, the extent to which the imaginative organisation depends on it : in looking closely at this aspect we are brought directly to the structural and thematic core of the work. In this novel, folk legends and mythological motifs, some very obvious, others underlying, are of vital significance, integrated and embodied not mechanically and stiffly but as the central informing and cohesive element throughout. An elucidation of the mythopoeic aspect of *Gone to Earth* is crucial to a deeper understanding and appreciation not only of this novel's meaning but of the individual quality of Mary Webb's literary art. Nowhere in her work is Mary Webb's mythic sensibility more in evidence; nowhere does it inform her art more effectively. By exploring the mythopoeic forms taken by her imagination we approach the living heart of the novel and gain insight into the recesses of her mind.

Early in the narrative we hear of the legend of the Black Huntsman. This is a folk-motif common to many European countries in varying forms : hence the ghostly huntsman in the folklore of south-west Shropshire, with tales of Wild Edric, black hounds baying at night, phantom dogs with fiery eyes.[3] In *Gone to Earth* the mythic Black Huntsman is associated with Hunter's

---

[3] The Shropshire legend has it that Wild Edric is seen riding across the Stiperstones with his hounds before a national disaster – in 1914 there were reports from Shropshire countryfolk of his appearance just prior to the outbreak of the war.

Spinney, a wooded hill. Here, so legend has it, 'the Black Huntsman . . . and the death-pack . . . ceased into the hill'. And here
Reddin on his 'tall black horse' stalks his sexual prey, Hazel. The
Black Huntsman rides with the death-pack on stormy nights:
'Harm was for the houses past which it streamed, death for those
that heard it give tongue. This was the legend, and Hazel
believed it implicitly' (p. 23).

Hazel's shuddering dread of this matches her vehement fear
and loathing of the actual hunt. Her fury of pity for the little
foxes, 'fine of nerve', torn apart and 'minced alive', is the expression of Mary Webb's own fierce compassion for hunted creatures,
her abhorrence of bloodsports. Significantly the first edition of
Gone to Earth is prefaced by a quotation – 'Take us the foxes, the
little foxes that spoil the vines' – from the Song of Solomon
which, with the apocalyptic Book of Revelation, was Mary's
favourite part of the Bible. Sub-headings and prefatory quotations
were deliberately selected by Mary Webb as directives in the
reading of her novels, but this particular quotation was omitted
in subsequent editions of *Gone to Earth* (all posthumous as the
novel was not re-printed during her lifetime).

In *Gone to Earth* the figure of Hazel (at once representative
and individual) is symbolic of 'all things hunted and snared and
destroyed', while the hunt and the mythic 'death-pack' are symbolic of universal cruelty. Here Mary Webb is making a wider
statement about the underlying barbarism in society that takes
pleasure in victimising the defenceless, in crucifying others
whether physically or spiritually, in breeding violence – and war.[4]
The 'death-pack' we are told (as well as shown) –

> hunts at all hours, light and dark; it is no pale phantom of
> dreams. It is not made of spirit hounds with fiery eyes – a ghastly
> 'Melody', a grisly 'Music' – but of our fellows, all that have
> strength without pity. Sometimes our kith and kin, our nearest
> intimates, are in the first flight; give a view-halloo as we slip
> hopefully under a covert; are in at the death.　　　(p. 209)

Authorial interpolations such as this, making explicit what is
everywhere implicit, are usually woven in and out of the action

---

[4] Black and scarlet – the colours of the Hunt, the colours of war – recur
as leitmotif.

without being jarringly intrusive or causing unevenness of texture. Mary Webb, although didactic, does not shout over the top of her novel. But in these comments we feel her presence – brooding, passionate, grieved and bewildered.

She sees a world in which death, the reality, is not the nightmare – 'It is mankind's lack of pity, mankind's fatal propensity for torture that is the nightmare'; the horror of the death-pack is 'not the killing . . . so much as the lack of the impulse not to kill'. Such too are Hazel's opinions 'dimly but passionately felt' – throughout she is the vehicle of Mary Webb's convictions.

Again and again these death myths of the Black Huntsman and the pack are woven into the basically realistic fabric of the novel, intensifying the mood and presaging the oncoming tragedy. It is the powerful imprint of this legend on Hazel's conscious and unconscious mind that, combined with the pressures of a cruel humanity (represented by her Aunt, the six righteous men and Mrs Marston as well as the hunt), eventually lead to her death. At the last, myth becomes actuality : to a fear-frenzied Hazel, fleeing with Foxy clutched in her arms, the hunt and hounds are indeed the death-pack itself, and Reddin on his black horse is the incarnation of the Black Huntsman. As Reddin tries to save her by lifting her on to his horse, she sees him only as the Black Huntsman and turning away in terror she falls with Foxy over 'the grey steeps' of the quarry.

Similarly Hazel believes absolutely in the legend of the lady of Undern Coppy (Mary Webb's adaptation of various local folk-tales). To Hazel this legend is, as she tells Edward and a shocked Mrs Marston, 'the bloody truth'. Identifying herself with this girl who died at nineteen, Hazel is sure that she too will 'go young . . . dark and strong in the full of life'.

Another significant but underlying mythological motif in *Gone to Earth* is that of 'the external soul', discussed in *The Golden Bough* (p. 668). Undoubtedly Mary Webb had learned a great deal about myth, ritual and the primitive mind from this fascinating work, a major source book for writers (not least D. H. Lawrence and T. S. Eliot). Frazer, in relating instances of the external soul, stresses that this common folk motif is intrinsic to the highly superstitious primitive mode of thought. It is credible that a solitary creature of the wild such as Hazel Woodus, loving animals passionately (to her they are at least the equal of human beings), has identified herself so closely with her pet fox cub that she unconsciously projects her essential self or soul on the animal. Foxy has virtually become the embodiment of her life principle in a way that recalls the primitive concept of an external soul, the myth and ritual of 'totem animals', in which the death of the creature implies the death of the owner.

This primitive motif is as implicit in *Gone to Earth* as it is in D. H. Lawrence's story 'The Fox' (1922). Hazel's obsessive concern for Foxy's life, and her acute dread of the hunt, stem from deeper emotional and psychological roots than merely anxiety for her pet's safety. Superstition-ridden, she is also fear-ridden and her identification with Foxy brings her to her tragic destiny. The climax is a fusion of those mythological motifs which underlie the narrative development from beginning to end. Myth comes alive in the ritual of the hunt : in frenzied pursuit of Foxy, Reddin and the hunt are in frenzied pursuit of Hazel. The 'death-pack' has 'found', led by the Black Huntsman – Hazel dies a ritual death becoming the sacrificial victim.

The full significance of Foxy's part in *Gone to Earth* has not been recognised hitherto. It is intimated from the very beginning of the narrative that their destinies are bound up together, and Hazel indicates her total identification when she chides the pet cub for wandering : 'If you'm alost, I'm alost', a view she re-iterates passionately to Mrs Marston (who loathes foxes as 'vermin').

Throughout the novel there is a deliberate insistence on points of resemblance between Hazel and Foxy. It is primarily fear for Foxy's safety that leads Hazel to marry Edward Marston. The two are separated only when Hazel deserts the parsonage to live with Reddin, leaving Foxy in Edward's keeping; while she is following the desires of her physical self, her soul or spiritual self remains with Edward (significantly she refers to both the fox and Edward as 'my soul'). Life has not allowed Hazel to develop self and soul in the heart of nature : at first wanting neither Reddin nor Marston, she soon becomes a divided being; part of her tragedy is that her 'body and soul had been put in opposition by belonging to different men' (p. 267). There is to be no love marriage of spirit and flesh in *Gone to Earth*.

Finally, there is the climactic fusion and fulfilment of the myths when Hazel and Foxy fall together – and the hunting cry 'Gone to earth' that rouses 'the shivering echoes' has, like the novel as a whole, several levels of meaning: earth, the fox's covert; earth the final refuge into which all lapse at death; earth the womb of beauty and wholeness to which Hazel and Foxy, two wild creatures of earth, have returned leaving, it seems, the whole world cringing in fear beneath those 'shivering echoes'.

Mary Webb, in this powerful and moving climax, infuses not only fear but an immense pity which encompasses all (hunter and hunted). Her novel is a cry for meaning, expressive both of the tragic spirit of the age in which it was written and the pathos of mankind in all ages. On closing the book we are stunned by that magnificent climax which strikes us in the profoundest areas of our consciousness, calling up in us 'the shivering echoes'.

Gone to Earth is a mythic narrative of timeless and placeless validity, of universal relevance. Timeless, yet essentially of its own time: the mythological motifs in this novel are reflective both of the widespread mood of that time of catastrophe and death, and of Mary Webb's own dark depression and fear. The myth of the Black Huntsman and the death-pack is far more than merely appropriate: it is of archetypal significance and particularly so in that period of bloody war and upheaval, being a manifestation in folklore of the archetypal image of Wotan, god of war, storm and frenzy. Its centrality in *Gone to Earth* is remarkable, for such mythic imagery while arising from the troubled depths of Mary Webb's mind also reached down to the deepest levels of contemporary consciousness.[5] Here is seen the close relation between her individual psyche and the collective psyche. Hazel Woodus, brought to her tragic end like all the countless victims of violence, is herself a mythic symbol. She is a battleground between conflicting passions and powers, the dark myth so deeply engraven on her unconscious mind that it needs very little external pressure to become activated and completely possess her conscious thought. And so too the novel as a whole resonates with Mary Webb's own agonised involvement in this myth.

In this remarkable though flawed novel, one of the chief weaknesses is that the stalking of Hazel by Reddin in the earlier chapters is too contrived, verging on grotesque melodrama. But

[5] C. G. Jung in *Essays on Contemporary Events* (London, 1947), explains the activation and significance of the mythic motifs of Wotan in the European mind at the time of the First World War.

nevertheless, evident everywhere is the technical advance on *The Golden Arrow:* the narrative moves with assurance from start to finish; there is overall a more developed insight into behaviour, a stronger grasp of human motivation; less commentary and more dramatisation through action and dialogue. Again the natural background is used to promote the unity of the novel: evocative descriptive passages are always relevant to the action and to the state of mind of the characters, also emphasising the uncanny mood of that border landscape, conveying a sense of the isolation, loneliness and timelessness of the Shropshire countryside.[6] As in all Mary Webb's novels, it is not merely the external details (always so sharply perceived) but the 'spirit of place', the formless and unchanging essence of Shropshire which above all else is unerringly captured and brought out.

Gone to Earth undoubtedly merits a more detailed textual study than it has hitherto received or can be given here. Apart from the mythic element, other aspects of this novel deserve attention. The characterisation, as John Buchan points out, is 'on the same high level as the drama'. Although *Gone to Earth* is not structured on opposites to the extent that *The Golden Arrow* is, nevertheless the sharply defined contrast between the two major characters Jack Reddin and Edward Marston, is fundamental to plot and theme: both characters have a vivid individuality that takes them beyond bare thematic function as representatives of opposing physical and spiritual values (a polar balancing in relation to Hazel that gives the flavour of a Morality).

Each of the lesser characters is a triumph of portrayal: Edward's mother, Mrs Marston, 'the old sleepy lady' (said by the Meredith family to have been based on Mrs Lyons), utterly conventional, blandly passive, absurdly matriarchal yet not without her moments of true pathos; Andrew Vessons, the gnarled, cynical servant at Undern, Machiavellian, woman-hating, dour and cantankerous; Hazel's father, Abel Woodus, master of the harp and bee-lore, coarse, satirical, unfeeling, living for his 'music', a self-absorbed gifted artist who 'had dark places in his soul' and for whom 'all his means of livelihood were joys'. These

---

[6] Shropshire was said to be 'the star' in the film of *Gone to Earth* made in the 1950s, with Jennifer Jones as Hazel Woodus. Lordshill and its chapel, in the Stiperstones, was the location of 'God's Little Mountain'.

characters are drawn with a Dickensian zest and liveliness of detail, with incisive wit and understanding. On closing the book we are left with vivid pictures fixed in our memory: Mrs Marston looking at Hazel over her spectacles, 'her eyes . . . like half moons peering over full moons'; old Vessons, 'knowing of eye as a blackbird, straw in mouth, the poison of asps on his tongue'; Abel, harping 'madly, till the little shanty throbbed with the sound of the wires'.

Throughout the narrative, touches of lambent humour relieve the tension yet heighten the pathos of the oncoming tragedy. Here Mary Webb's view of a tragic universe unmistakeably recalls that of Hardy. However, with her this is not to be a consistent attitude or philosophy but only a stage or phase in her development, the war having crystallised her pessimism.

Writing in the tradition of rural and regional novel that reaches back to Sir Walter Scott, Mary Webb, following Hardy, was projecting her interpretation of life in terms of passionate, dramatic tales set in her own intimately known country region. Undoubtedly in using the novel as a poetic medium for stories expressing her deeply felt vision, Mary Webb owed a great deal to her reading of Hardy – whose influence is seen above all in her treatment of nature and her use of folk-lore and rural superstition. Obviously to compare Mary Webb with Hardy is not to class her with him, but a comparison can certainly be made between *Gone to Earth* and *Tess of the D'Urbervilles* without disparagement to the former: in each the central theme is the betrayal of innocence and Mary Webb, as Hardy with Tess, makes both the innocence and the fall of Hazel equally convincing, thereby sustaining tragic intensity. In this novel Mary Webb comes close to a spiritual despondency similar to Hardy's. She has swung back to that state bordering on despair which she had known after her father's death – again experiencing 'the Alps of the soul . . . the fierce, God-tormented mountain, where only the stars are our company, and the flare of them kills the heart' (*CPAP*, p. 53). In the early years of her marriage with Henry, love had renewed the optimistic pantheism expressed in *The Golden Arrow*, but this, in her next novel, is replaced by a pessimistic pantheism reflecting her inner regression and doubt.

Pessimistic pantheism may seem a paradoxical term but it

appropriately describes Mary Webb's response to life and to nature at this period. Nowhere does she reach a deeper pessimism than in *Gone to Earth*. A profound scepticism colours her attitude as she questions the ultimate source of life :

> All man's desires – predatory, fugitive, or merely negative – wander away into those dark halls, and are heard no more . . . Is there One who listens? . . . Our heavy burden is that we cannot know. For all our tears and prayers and weary dreaming, we cannot know.
> (p. 91)

Mary Webb, held in the grip of dark uncertainty, has replaced hope by pity: bewildered by a world in which cruelty is triumphant, she cannot gauge the 'vague, unknown power' she feels present in nature and the universe; she is sure only that it is not a personal God.

This is a pantheism from which the Christian element is now completely expunged; no trace is left of the 'deep, pantheistic Christianity' of John Arden. Christ is now seen to be just 'the love-martyr of Galilee' – in the words of a disillusioned Edward Marston who has experienced the breaking of prayer in his hands, 'not God, but only a brave, loving heart hunted to death' (p. 305). And Hazel's anguished outcry against the crucifixion – ' "Not for me ! . . . There shall none die along of me, much less be tormented . . . Blood makes things raddled not white; and if so be any's got to die, I'll die for myself" ' – is that of Mary Webb herself, passionately rejecting the Redemption, repelled at the idea of expiation of sin through another's sacrificial agony and death.

But nothing stood between Mary Webb's own essence and that of nature – her personal temple of refuge and healing to which she consciously turned, retreating in this time of war, with an urgent need : here, 'if anywhere', was 'the cradled God'. In *Gone to Earth* Hazel's response to nature, at times a 'mythical exaltation', reflects Mary Webb's own unity of being in union with earth.

Here, in her despair, her acute pity and revolt against suffering, Mary Webb 'The Apostle and Poet of Pity' has been likened by French critics to the nineteenth-century poet Alfred de Vigny who also abhorred bloodsports and was preoccupied with the question of good and evil.[7]

In *Gone to Earth* Mary Webb's pity is turned into image, her emotion distilled into art. The total imaginative effect of the novel is powerful; everything coalesces in an authentic and intensely individual world.

If she has certain affinities with Vigny and Hardy, she can also be linked with D. H. Lawrence and other sensitive creative artists of her time who, like her, were expressing in their work something of the spiritual plight and outlook of the age and of a society devastated by that 'scarlet' war with its incalculable repercussions at every level of life. No work of literary art was more expressive than *Gone to Earth* of the tragic spirit of those war years when multitudes, slaughtered, were indeed 'gone to earth' – but the contemporary relevance of this novel, its symbolic significance, were lost to critics and readers attuned to direct reflection of aspects of war and to rhetorically patriotic statement.

Mary's dedication of *Gone to Earth* 'To Him Whose Presence Is Home' reflects her utter need for Henry – he was all to her and only with him did she experience, as she had with her father, 'the loving comprehension that meant home'. Her other deepest need – to live permanently in Shropshire – now became a craving, the desperation of which increased with every week spent in Chester. She was finding it an almost unbearable strain to return to Hough Green after weekends at The Nills, this inner struggle bringing in its wake wretched fatigue and overwroughtness. A certain natural exhaustion resulted from her creative outpourings each weekend, but this she could have coped with in Shropshire.

In exile, exhaustion further tightened the dead hand of depression, the feelings of dread which gripped her on coming back to the Cheshire city. During weekdays there, she had neither her countryside nor Henry, who was fully occupied at The King's School : this, together with the distressing irritations that occurred between herself and Alice, resulted in a serious deterioration in

---

[7] Marcelle Magdinier, 'Mary Webb – Apôtre et Poète de la Pitié', *Etudes de Théologie, Philosophie et d'Histoire*, 20 December 1937, pp. 752–64. Mary's poem 'Adam' (*Mary Webb: Collected Prose and Poems*) written in 1919, reveals her later struggle to reconcile herself to cruelty as 'The Lord of Love'.

her nervous condition. Not for the first time, nor the last, Mary had come to 'the sadness terrene', having lost her 'land serene/airy and lone'.

Fortunately Henry was fully aware of the immediate reasons for her depression, for her 'heart full of fear'; he was aware too, that her acute oppression of spirit might bring on another attack of the illness which had wrought such physical devastation after her father's death. It was, therefore, 'for reasons of his wife's health', as The King's School Year Book reports, that Henry resigned his post in the same term as he had commenced it, and sought an appointment in Shropshire. For both of them, it was an enormous relief when he was appointed to teach Classics and English at The Priory School, Shrewsbury, starting in the autumn term.

The last days at Chester dragged out for Mary in the dull June and July of 1916. War news continued to be full of horror. The drowning of Lord Kitchener on *The Hampshire*, which shocked the whole country, was marked by memorial services and by flags at half-mast. Worst of all, the offensive on the Somme, although a success, involved appalling loss of life. During Henry's final week at The King's School, intense emotion was generated in the city by the arrival of more than three hundred injured brought from Southampton by hospital train to Chester Station where a huge crowd gathered to welcome them.

Mary was profoundly thankful when Henry, prize-giving ceremony over on 27 July, came to the end of his term at The King's School and she of her painful exile from Shropshire. They returned to The Nills for the remainder of the summer.

Immediately before their departure from Chester, occurred an event of major importance to Mary – the publication of *The Golden Arrow* (July 1916), which marked the beginning of her public career as an author. Reviews, eagerly awaited, came later when Mary and Henry were back permanently in Shropshire, and though this first novel did not secure a great deal of attention in the weeklies and monthlies, the reviews it did receive were encouraging.

The *TLS* reviewer (8 September 1916) found it 'a remarkable novel' in which 'some of the scenes are handled with an intensity which not many novelists of the day could rival'. Apart from a few reservations about the chief characters – 'rather etherealised poetic figures' – the review was favourable, almost enthusiastic, especially when discussing the novel's 'leading characteristic . . . concentration on "atmosphere" ' :

> Sunshine, mist, storm sweeping over or enveloping the hills, colour the human drama and even guide its course.

The reviewer went on to suggest that 'if the author were a painter she would belong to the class of landscapists who are inspired rather by a passion for nature than by a passion for art'. It would be interesting to know Mary's reaction to such a comment. Yet, doubtless she appreciated this critic's praise of her treatment of nature :

> She is determined to make you feel what she feels, and her poignant sense of colour, sound and meaning in nature often gives a new vividness to the reader's own perception.

Pertinent comments, applicable to all her novels.

She was to become increasingly sensitive to the opinion of reviewers and public. Her own response to the reception of her novels is an important factor, one of the external pressures to which she reacted, her life and art so intimately interfused. Mary's vision and convictions were inseparable from the art in which she embodied them; she was determined not to be deflected by shallow, imperceptive criticism, and to follow only her own fervent purpose. Yet sensitivity to reviewers' comments – particularly sarcastic or negative – caused her sharp disappointment and distress which, when combined with continued public apathy, wore on her spirit and eventually helped to undermine her always precarious health.

But in 1916, she was still at the beginning, and it was too soon then to know how successful *The Golden Arrow* would or would not be with the reading public. Mary with characteristic generous joy gave away to friends the first copies which arrived from the publisher. Among the first to receive one, signed by 'the author', was the Morris family. Subsequently, Tom Morris was so gripped by the story that he missed a day's work – and wages – in the reading of it. Not all Mary's country friends, however, were able to appreciate her writings : some never saw her books, others could not understand them, while many of the cottagers she visited were not even aware that she had written any. It was a sad day in the Morris household when she left The Nills, but Tom Morris gladly helped in the removals, using his pony and cart.

On 14 September, Henry took up his post as Master of Forms V and VI at The Priory School, necessitating another move nearer to Shrewsbury. While this meant giving up The Nills, it also gave them the opportunity to choose another home and Mary's delighted reaction was to find somewhere on Lyth Hill where she had wanted to live ever since her Maesbrook days. There they would be in the countryside yet sufficiently near to Shrewsbury for Henry to be able to travel each day to and fro.

They found a couple of rooms to rent in one of the cottages on the lower part of Lyth Hill, for there were very few houses on the top plateau which was, at that period, still densely wooded. Soon a further plan was evolved: to build a small house of their own on Lyth Hill itself. Mary was overjoyed and determined to bring the scheme to fruition, though in wartime money and materials were scarce. Henry, recalling this later, commented: 'By juggling that now seems marvellous to me, we raised the money.' Mary asked her mother for £100 advance from the Scott funds, with which they bought a rough stretch of field – a clearing on the plateau – quite near the Little Wood. Her enthusiasm was unbounded and she forged ahead, drawing out plans for a small bungalow, designing two rooms, a scullery and a verandah outside the front door where she would sit at her writing. For reasons of seclusion the red-brick, red-tiled bungalow was to be set well back in the small field. It only remained to arrange a mortgage, no easy task during the war. £250 was obtained from a bank and building began late in 1916.

Meanwhile, they continued to live in furnished rooms nearby, Mary working at the last revision of *Gone to Earth* while Henry was out teaching in Shrewsbury. Each afternoon she hurried to meet him down the rutted road to Bayston Hill Village, taking a flask of milk for him to drink before their long uphill walk. The novel, finally ready, was sent to Constable in the early days of 1917, when work on the bungalow was proceeding in the cold, snowy weather. It was to be called 'Spring Cottage', for several reasons: not only was the bungalow completed that spring, but this too was her favourite season – 'the strange, heart-lifting season' in which her heart was 'set'. And at this time of renewed exaltation and mystical ardour, she revised her early essays retitling them *The Spring of Joy,* knowing the immense significance of the spring of joy, both meaning and message of so much in her life and art.

   She had emerged again into 'colour and light' after spiritual regression, her consciousness purged and heightened. It was an experience of growth through pain, the pain a dearth of joy, an absence of illumination: her understanding of this process is clear in 'Joy', a poem depicting the unrelenting journey of her 'weeping soul' through darkness in quest of the spring of joy, the vital source which could only be found after planting 'some little rosy things' – the seeds of love – in 'pain's dark forest'. This poem is a symbolic expression of the mystic's 'dark night of the soul', reminiscent of the writings of the great mystics, especially St John of the Cross in his 'Stanzas of the Soul'. And she suggests the radiance of renewed illumination in the poem's climax:

> . . . And there, at the edge of the forest, gleamed and shone
> A little rocky, rose-encircled spring,
> So fair, so, fresh, its music made us sing.
> And One
> (Oh, marvel!) held a cup for us, and said –
> 'I knew that dark way led
> Straight here. Come, stand in the sun
> And share with me.'
> Then my soul knelt, and I,
> Among the white and glistening flowers around it,
> And drank the vital water with ecstasy –
> So glad because through grief and joy we found it,
> The spring of joy!

(51, pp. 26–7)

9

Lyth Hill – and

The House in Dormer Forest

1917–1921

When autumn winds are on the hill
    And darkly rides the wasting moon,
I creep within your arms, and still
    Am safe in the golden heart of June.
             'Autumn' (*PSJ*, p. 98)

For the mystic . . . time does not exist . . . When
man is self-poised, he awakes from the hallucina-
tions of time and law, and stealing out into the
silence of his own being hears a voice sound beyond
mortality, telling him that place and time are but
bubbles . . . that he is, even now, one with the
immense freedom in which these bubbles float.
             (*HDF*, pp. 32–3)

'To live on Lyth Hill and to live in a house of my own' – these
'lovely impossible things I long for' (Mary wrote to a friend) had
now become realities. At thirty-six, with two novels published,
and living with Henry permanently in her 'hills of heaven',
Mary's future seemed bright with prospects of literary success,
harmonious creative life. Yet she had only ten years left, less than
three of which would be spent entirely on Lyth Hill . . . 'and in
short measures, life may perfect be' (Ben Jonson).

Out on the wooded hill for hour upon hour, she was writing,
watching, listening. Nothing escaped her notice – each changing
aspect of the surrounding hills and vast plain, the flight of
curlews, movements of insects in their aisles of grass, the
individual scents of trees, details of bud and blossom, stamen and
corolla.

Often in the Little Wood she passed almost the entire day in meditation, so completely one with her surroundings that birds would alight on her as she sat motionless. Wood-pigeons especially, reiterating their low, deep sound 'sadly, intermittently', fluttered from branch to branch. Wheeling above, they floated down and settled on her so she seemed 'like a slim tree bent with bloom'. These she thought of as her doves, later the source of imagery in 'Colomen':

> On arms and shoulders doves alight,
> Multiple-tinted, like a bright
> Tapestry that time has faded.
> Softly purple, lilac-shaded,
> The lady standeth like a tree
> Bent down with blossom...
>
> (*PSJ*, pp. 118–23)

Not yet the anguished personal situation she was to symbolise in this poem: hers was still 'the tall, round, sunny cote' (her relationship with Henry), not yet the 'ruined cote' in which she would slowly die.

During those early months at Spring Cottage they worked together, creating the first real home of their own, digging and laying out the garden. Her favourite violets, sweet peas and Mary lilies (described by Henry as 'sacredly luminous at darkest night') were first essentials; saplings of poplar, laburnum, lilac, chestnut were planted, and there was already a hedge of hawthorn which would grow high and be 'white-over' each June.

For the heavy work Mary employed the former shepherd, David Barrett. Their nearest neighbour, whose well Mary shared (at that date there was no piped water supply at Lyth Hill), was Mrs Thorne, with whom 'warmship' grew.

In her new home, small and cramped compared with the houses of her upbringing, Mary joyfully arranged their sparse furniture including her treasured grandfather clock bought cheaply at an auction. Unfortunately the clock was too tall for the low ceilings of Spring Cottage and Mary promptly decided that the bottom should be sawn off, an operation which greatly amused Henry who subsequently wrote a poem, 'Mary's Grandfather Clock'.[1] How far he had abandoned his own literary

---

[1] *The English Review*, vol. 29, 1919, pt. 2, pp. 103–4.

aspirations at this date is not known – but he completed his epic poem about Gilgamesh, accepted by Macmillan in 1917.

On the other hand, Mary's literary career advanced with the publication of *Gone to Earth* in September – a minor success, gaining the attention of critics and securing for her an admiring if small following among established writers and discerning publishers.

Some of the influential reviews were disappointing: the *Spectator* superficial and inaccurate, the *Morning Post* scathing ('the effect of the whole performance . . . preposterous . . . the drama of its personages a sort of Morality' . . . 'of course the blessed word spirituality will be invoked in praise of *Gone to Earth*'). Others were more favourable: in the *Athenaeum* the novel was described as 'a notable work of fiction', and in the *Daily News* Robert Lynd commented: 'Miss Mary Webb is unquestionably a poet. One cannot read the first page of her new novel *Gone to Earth* without realising this. She has written a book rich at once in beauty and excitement . . . We believe in her human beings as symbols . . . rather than as men and women.' Lynd did, however, caution her 'not to strain her gifts'. The *TLS* reviewer criticised her for 'some exaggerated feeling' but recognised that here was a novel 'full of symbolism' and the author's chief concern was 'the problem of suffering, bodily, mental and spiritual'. Gerald Gould in the *New Statesman* (29 September 1917) dealt at length with 'this unsatisfactory but remarkable novel' deciding that it was 'a noble failure . . . a strange mixture of good and bad'. While he thought the theme 'too ambitious', he realised it was 'impossible for the author of *Gone to Earth* to choose a smaller and easier theme . . . That is the dilemma . . . The large thought transcends the expression'. Nevertheless Gould was impressed, praising aspects of her style and technique, 'the passionate beauty' of the book, and concluding, with Robert Lynd, that 'it is as a poet Mary Webb must be judged. Her narrative is strange, fantastic, symbolical'. Gould saw that *Gone to Earth* was 'conceived in a mood of poetry and mysticism'. He was, in fact, the first critic to recognise and discuss her mysticism and his comments are of central relevance:

Miss Mary Webb is a mystic, with that genuine mysticism which feels the essential oneness of the world, and neither cares nor is able to dissociate the seen from the unseen. It is not that to her, as in the definitely religious mystic, things are the symbols and revelations of a worshipped God. She asserts our ignorance of ultimate purposes with that dogmatism that is not less common among agnostics than 'believers'. But none the less the physical world (inanimate as well as animate) *lives* for her with a passionate intensity.

Another encouraging review was Rebecca West's, declaring unequivocally 'Mary Webb is a genius'. Furthermore she proclaimed *Gone to Earth* 'novel of the year' in a symposium of the year's novels for a leading newspaper. Delighted and grateful for such fearless championing, Mary wrote a letter of thanks to Miss West, beginning a friendship by letter which she was to take up in person when living in London.

Among publishers, Sir Ernest Hodder Williams was one of the first to admire 'Mrs Mary Webb'. When dining with the Buchans he told them : 'I know of a woman who writes admirable books but people don't read them much, though she gets good reviews. Her name is Mary Webb . . . She writes about the country beautifully and with intimate knowledge of it. Do read *Gone to Earth* and see if you like it.'[2] Susan Buchan related later how she obtained the novel next day, and was so caught by its 'beauty of phrase and exquisite perception of nature' that she wrote an appreciative letter to Mary, care of her publisher. *Gone to Earth* had, she said, 'opened a new door . . . and told me that magic had not departed from the world'. Mary wrote back enthusiastically, sending the Buchans a copy of *The Golden Arrow*. So began another friendship. The Buchans thought her work 'impregnated with poetry' and recognised that she was deeply read in seventeenth-century literature, noting especially the influence of Sir Thomas Browne.

But, like *The Golden Arrow*, the new novel did not sell. This undoubtedly owed something to the fact that (as John Buchan said), it 'was published in the dark days of 1917'. To the general public and the superficial reader such a novel was out of tune with the wartime mood; yet for Buchan and others *Gone to Earth*, redolent of the English countryside, evoked a strong

[2] Susan, Lady Tweedsmuir, *A Winter Bouquet*, pp. 110–15.

emotional response 'at a time when everything that concerned the soil of England seemed precious'.

Though this novel was not a popular success, the reviews, on the whole, were encouraging to Mary and did not, of course, escape the notice of the publishers. The advance in her reputation is indicated by the fact that several firms competed for the rights in her next novel. She employed a literary agent to negotiate for her as she prepared what was to be *The House in Dormer Forest*. And she now had a growing reputation in America since the publication of her two novels by E. P. Dutton. Good reviews in American journals (*Independent* noted her as 'a realist, romanticist and idealist' combined; *Dial* pointed out a similarity to Thomas Hardy) brought her the attention of American publishers, three of whom – Dutton, Doubleday and George H. Doran – wanted her third novel. After much negotiation *The House in Dormer Forest* was secured by Doran, Mary receiving £300 advance on royalties and an agreement for a further £300 for its successor. The generosity of this advance, a high figure in those days, gives some indication of her standing. On receiving the cheque, Mary promptly (and typically) began to spend the money, paying off their own debts and delightedly buying bicycles and gifts for Mrs Thorne's sons and other children at Lyth Hill.

Meanwhile she had another personal satisfaction : her essays were in print at last. *The Spring of Joy: A* Little Book of Healing, was published by J. M. Dent on 4 October 1917. It received a few brief, lukewarm reviews (the *TLS* acknowledging it as 'a nature book of good-class'). While her essays could now reach those in need of 'healing', they created little or no stir among critics.

In the same month Henry's Babylonian verse epic, *The Everlasting Quest,* made its appearance. His dedication, in turn, was to Mary in a poem suggestive of his 'unflinching' perspectives. Henry's concept of love, 'the flowering thorn', a commingling of joy and pain, echoes Mary's use of the same motif in *The Golden Arrow.* For Henry, love is also an interplay of tension, a 'passionate war'. Of the passion, he had experience in full measure in his relationship with Mary.

In *The Everlasting Quest* Henry's choice of theme as well as the individual interpretation he brings to it, are revelatory of his cast of mind, his philosophic orientation, a certain cool, incalculable remoteness. He speaks in the Introduction of 'the gnawing desire for distances' and makes Gilgamesh the symbolical embodiment of man's unappeased restlessness, hunger for the absolute and unending search for truth. The heroic adventures, based on the Chaldean Twelve Tablets (*c.* 2000 B.C.), are an expression of archetypal quest, Gilgamesh going through earth to heaven and back again to earth seeking what neither holds.

Then teaching full-time at the Priory School and no longer able to spend his days writing and translating, Henry no doubt appreciated the critical comment his book received, especially an enthusiastic review by Robert Lynd in the *Daily News*.

Like the Brownings, Henry and Mary derived mutual pleasure from their literary interchange, turning 'the evening hours to one warm flame', thoughts and ideas overlapping, intertwining. And in relation to this, it is interesting to note that in both *The Everlasting Quest* and *Gone to Earth* (on which they had been working simultaneously), elements of myth and ritual are fundamental.

Yet ironically, during this period of harmony, living a rich inner life, developing intellectually, Mary was moving nearer to the 'wounding sore' predicted in *The Golden Arrow*. And it was her literary work which led to this path of eventual heartbreak, the 'agony of loss' that always haunted her in dark forebodings. In one of the love poems to Henry, her plea is an acknowledgment of her own weakness:

> Ah, do not be so dear!
> The heavy-handed world, if it should hear
> And watch us jealously,
> Would steal upon our love's secure retreat
> And rob our treasury.
> Let us be wise, then; do not be too sweet,
> Too dear, too kind to me!
>
> (*PSJ*, p. 97)

While 'the heavy-handed world' had not yet broken in to disrupt their 'nest of love', Mary was always acutely aware of its threat and of the sad process of change within relationships. So Henry was the focal point of both the ecstasy and the terror intrinsic to her vision of life and love. How long would he be able to sustain his patience or equilibrium at the centre of such intense adoration, such pathetic dread? Under this burden of love would he ever falter in his understanding and loyalty? And if he did, how would Mary, so insecure, fraught with fear and lacking in self-confidence, cope with the situation, or even with those unpredictable external circumstances and stresses that inevitably occur – bringing change in their wake?

Feeling keenly Henry's absence during the day, Mary treasured ever more anxiously the moments together beside 'the evening fire' and the weekends when they walked the lanes and hills, and gardened together as of old. If – as frequently happened – the hours without him became an abyss flinging up phantasmal anxieties and doubts, she tried to allay these by setting out to meet him, walking down the long, rutted path to Bayston Hill Village where his bus came in and where she posted letters and bought paraffin. People who were children of the village at that time have vivid memories of her – dark hair, strange brooding eyes, deeply preoccupied with her thoughts as she went by, a small, slight figure carelessly dressed in long muddy skirts and dresses, often unbuttoned down the back.

Although her Eden could never fully be regained and she was constantly aware, as she said in *Gone to Earth*, of living in 'the moated present, that turreted heaven whose defences so soon fall', none the less this period was one of relative happiness and vigour such as she was never to know again. Living in her own home with Henry in the very 'heart of enchantment', from dawn to dusk, season by season looking out over that inspirational view of wide plain and blue encircling hills, her creative zest and joyous receptivity to life were unbounded, and this is reflected in the novel she was writing – *The House in Dormer Forest*. Works of art essentially absorb the spirit, the vitality of the artist: as we have seen, *Gone to Earth* is pervaded by the anguished dread and gloom Mary experienced during the Chester phase, and similarly *The House in Dormer Forest* is imbued with her vibrant mood at the time of composition, her verve and imaginative energy. Brimming with life, it is both the most humorous and the most populated of her novels. While her first two are not lacking in humour, in this, her third, a rich ironic wit is at work throughout, sustained, energetic: again she writes from the conventional viewpoint of omniscient author, her own humorous irony itself one of the materials of the novel.

It must be kept in mind also in a reading of *The House in Dormer Forest* that Mary was preparing and writing this book at the close of the Great War and in the immediate post-war period. After the armistice had been signed in that little forest clearing at Compiègne, soldiers flocked home and events swept forward in the return to peace. The first flush of joy and release of tension felt throughout the country was swiftly followed by a mood of reaction, a trenchant questioning of the validity of those traditional codes and values on which society was based. Radically the social climate had changed since 1914. Gone irrevocably was the old order, disintegrated by the war with its aftermath of disillusionment and critical scrutiny.

Writers and artists, reflecting in their work these attitudes, were examining contemporary society and the prevalent spiritual aridity. In conscious revolt they were challenging established ideas, inherited values and standards – and probing a solution. Mary Webb must be seen in direct and significant relation to her contemporaries, to writers such as D. H. Lawrence, Aldous Huxley and E. M. Forster who were exploring in their fiction aspects of the human predicament. In *The House in Dormer Forest* she is more than ever concerned with the life and problems of modern man and in demonstrating what she sees to be essential truths both of experience and of possibility. Her characteristic response was to embody both the problems and the answers in a work of imaginative literature in which the characters act out her insights and intuitions. She is taking a step further the criticism of civilised society, Church and convention everywhere evident in *Gone to Earth* and implicit in the primitivism of that novel. But in *Gone to Earth*, written during the devastation of war, she had no constructive anwers to offer – only an impassioned plea, a great cry of pity for mankind and the wistful thought of a race to come 'in the far future' when 'we shall have outgrown our egoism' and attained 'philosophic detachment and emotional sympathy'. In *The House in Dormer Forest* she is preoccupied not only in diagnosing but in giving an answer, showing a way. Embedded in this novel is her intended creative solution for the individual (and thus for the whole), projected in narrative terms and through the interaction of characters with each other, characters with place.

Dormer Old House as much as any of its inhabitants is a protagonist taking a major part in the action. 'Patched and enlarged by successive generations' of the Darke family, it is a foreboding place of potent personality, having 'something of a malignant air'. Situated in Dormer Forest, close to a brook at the bottom of the valley, frequently mist-swathed, its oppressive Gothic atmosphere recalls that of Poe's House of Usher. Most of the Darke family accept and uphold without questioning the 'spider's web of rules, legends and customs' with which 'the house was overspread'; the narrative deals with those at Dormer who do not accept, who refuse to conform. The family house – 'with all . . . its thunderous "thou shalt nots" ' – reacting on the family characteristics is inimical to the development of the individual, to the 'awakening of the soul'.

The action begins with the return of Jasper Darke the rebellious elder son, a disgrace 'by Dormer standards', expelled from Theological College for 'the sin of denying his Maker' and refusing to accept dogma. The family range against him: his father, gruff, insensitive Solomon Darke; Rachel, his cold, unsparing mother; malicious Grandmother Velindre; jealous, impetuous brother Peter – these reinforced in their antagonism by the hypocritical curate, Ernest Swyndle, who comes to live at Dormer, wooing and marrying Ruby, materialistic younger daughter of the Darkes. Only Amber, Jasper's elder sister, is sympathetic, understanding his 'passionate love of truth,' his struggle for self-hood. She sees the danger to Jasper of Catherine Velindre who determines to ensnare him by her loveliness and bring him back to orthodoxy. Book One, 'The House', ends with Jasper captivated by the scheming Catherine but utterly wretched, unable to 'invent a God' to please her and placate his family who exclude him even from the 'humanities' of Christmas. Anguished, he calls aloud for his friend Michael Hallowes, a lecturer, who also has left the theological college 'because he disagreed with the Head'.

In Book Two, 'The Forest', the arrival of Hallowes at Dormer is climactic. A man of burning integrity and awareness, 'strong, sane, cognisant of the world', he counterbalances 'the weight of shadows' at Dormer to precipitate Jasper's liberation. Catherine Velindre in her turn is captivated by Michael who rejects her as she has rejected Jasper. The suffering of Jasper is prefigured

by that of earth-mystic Enoch Gale, Dormer's 'oddman', who
loses his love Marigold (a maid-servant at Dormer) to Peter
Darke. Jasper, flinging himself in Dormer brook, is assumed to
be drowned, but Michael has rescued him and subsequently
brings both Jasper and Amber (whom he marries) out of the
soul-stunting atmosphere of Dormer. Peter Darke also leaves,
having defied his parents by marrying Marigold who bears his
child. Finally Dormer Old House, set on fire by the archaic,
fanatical grandmother, meets the fall predicted by Enoch.

Human interaction is to the fore in this, the most complex of
Mary Webb's novels. The cross-threads of relationships are
woven with considerable skill and ingenuity, and with lively use
of human contrast. On the other hand, there is not as much
interplay as in the previous novels between characters and landscape since the action is largely centred within the house; and
here we find that Mary Webb's observation of human nature is
as close and acute as her observation of nature itself. Nothing
escapes her vigilant eye: miniaturist in her wealth of detail, she is
imaginative and subtle in her use of it. *The House in Dormer
Forest* well bears out the view expressed by Ernest Baker in *The
History of the English Novel* that the works of George Eliot and
Mrs Gaskell contributed much to Mary Webb's formation as a
novelist.

In taking this penetrating look at an ancestral country house
and its inhabitants, Mary Webb is exploring aspects of human
loneliness. She is concerned primarily to demonstrate the ways in
which society with its codes and creeds can stifle and destroy the
individual trying to find his own reality. She is preoccupied
with 'herd instinct', 'predatory collectivism' and the isolation of
the individual who, like Jasper Darke, has a 'passionate love of
truth' which slices away 'the safe things' of conformity and leaves
him 'shivering in the cold air of individual effort'. As Jasper says,
'I want myself'; and in a flash of insight he knows the real reason
behind his family's hostility towards him in his rebellion against
'the idiotic hotch-potch of the churches' – he realises 'You're not
angry with me because I don't believe in God but because I'm
different from you'. The Darkes' attitude is 'You are not as we,
so we crush you' (p. 42). Jasper sees this clearly, aware that 'those
at Dormer now, those at Dormer in the past' had always made

'springes for the souls of people like himself' – 'Because his soul was alive and would fly they wished to cage it. Because it sang its own song they wanted to kill it' (p. 176). Jasper Darke reminds us of Rupert Birkin in Lawrence's *Women in Love* (also published in 1920), in his refusal to compromise, his passionate rejection of negative archaism.

The House in Dormer Forest, central in Mary Webb's canon, is her most significant work although overshadowed by the success of *Precious Bane*. And it is undoubtedly her most modern novel, the one most likely to appeal to readers today. In the major theme of the individual's striving towards wholeness, towards spiritual re-birth, an awakening and shaping of the essential self; in her preoccupation with the unconscious; in her concern with problems of 'being' or 'non-being', what is reality, what unreality, Mary Webb is unquestionably a modern writer, though transitional, as she uses the traditional methods of prose narrative and does not invent new fictional techniques. *The House in Dormer Forest* has technical faults and failures, but Mary Webb, in dramatising Jasper Darke's struggle for 'self-hood', and in making this part of her larger vision of modern man's spiritual and psychological problems, creates a dimension in her work which should affect the view we take of her contribution to the twentieth-century novel. This significant aspect of her work has been overlooked – her rôle, as Charles Sanders has pointed out, 'in diagnosing "the modern temper" '. Mary Webb's novels are undoubtedly 'essays in the life of the spirit', as H. R. L. Sheppard emphasises in his 1928 Introduction to *The House in Dormer Forest*, but as Professor Sanders maintains, 'they are essays of the peculiarly "modern" spirit, rendered universal through traditional symbolism and allegory'.

Again she organises symbol and metaphor in the interests of her main theme. Features of the setting are major symbols, consciously elaborated (and sometimes, as in her earlier work, overinsisted): these are devices of structure as well as vehicles of meaning. Setting, structure and symbol synthesise in this work of high visual and imaginative power. Mary Webb is creating here a coherent symbolic world, again, as in *The Golden Arrow* and *Gone to Earth*, self-contained and uniquely her own. The lesser symbols, repeated images and motifs (usually details of nature) point in the same direction as the major symbols and are binding, unifying. An elucidation of these leads directly into the primary theme.

The setting is all-important, taking us at once to a deeper level of meaning. It is put before us in the opening chapter with a vividness and significance reminiscent of Thomas Hardy's presentation of Egdon Heath at the beginning of *The Return of the Native*, and (as in Hardy's novel) we do not meet any of the human characters until the second chapter. Here is the opening description :

> Dormer Old House stood amid the remnants of primeval woodland that curtained the hills. These rose steeply on all sides of the house, which lay low by the water in the valley. This was called Oolert's Dingle, and there were plenty of owls to justify the name. On a moonlit night, passing, high up, from side to side of the cuplike valley, they looked like breeze-blown feathers. Higher still, on the very rim of the cup, the far-travelled winds shouted across to one another, all winter, news of the world. When the bats slipped from their purlieus in the cobwebby outbuildings and climbed towards this rim, they had to ascend step after grey step of the windless air, and only attained their ambition after long flying.
>
> From these heights, in fine weather, the house and its gardens lay open to view, small but clear, beside the white thread that was Dormer brook. (p. 15)

A rich, concrete evocation, typical of many in this novel. The obvious major allegorical symbols – house, forest, brook, predators – are presented at the start; and also the implicit symbols – circle and water – which carry the deeper thematic significance and meaning, and which, variously embodied, recur as leitmotif throughout the novel.

The effectiveness of the first chapter is, however, weakened by an excess of didactic statement. The exhortation beneath the title, 'Let the sleeping soul awake', is a directive in the reading of the novel, and further strong authorial directives are given in the opening pages. Mary Webb, making clear her intention at the beginning, gives explicit signposts to the ideas she goes on to dramatise. The narrative does not really start until the second chapter when she progresses from didacticism to art.

The 'cuplike valley' contains the House, the Forest, the Brook, the Four Waters, the Beast Walk and Grotto. Above, at the highest point of the Forest near the 'rim of the cup', is the Shepherd's Hut occupied by Michael Hallowes. Those at Dormer who 'dare to be free' come up eventually from the valley to attain the 'rim of the cup'. Of the main characters only Michael Hallowes is fully free and whole. Significantly he does not appear until Book Two, 'The Forest'. And then, 'learning to look after sheep', he leads both Amber and Jasper Darke out of Dormer (like John Arden, a human 'Flockmaster').

This 'cuplike valley' is a circular theatre where most of the action takes place (recalling the Greek theatre) peopled by 'rank on rank' of the 'watching trees'. An understanding of the importance of the circle in this novel's design is necessary in order to penetrate to the visionary core of the work. That Mary Webb was fully aware of the symbolical significance of the circle is already made clear in her earlier work, *The Spring of Joy*, particularly in the fine essay 'The Beauty of Form'. The circle is, she wrote,

> a symbol of things men feel but cannot understand; so Merlin 'made the round table in tokening of the roundness of the world'; so Vaughan saw eternity 'like a great Ring' . . . a circle, however small, is immutable, holds infinity; because of this, and because of the implied centre, it is the most perfect symbol of Divinity.
>
> (*PSJ*, p. 189)

And it is the symbol of wholeness, whether infinite or finite, of the absolute or the self.[3] How far the many variations of this symbol, occurring throughout *The House in Dormer Forest*, were consciously wrought, how far unconsciously, we cannot be sure. But it would seem that in the passages Mary wrote out of an inspired and sustained lyrical flow (especially the descriptions of Amber's mystical apprehension in the Upper Woods and Birds' Orchard), these symbols rose intuitively and uncontrived from the centre of her own experience.

---

[3] The circle is a traditional symbol of the ultimate mystery. Hermes Trismegistus echoed earlier philosophers when he defined God as 'an infinite sphere whose centre is everywhere, whose circumference is nowhere'. The central theme of *The House in Dormer Forest* is the development of the individual soul, the attainment of totality (wholeness), and this has been 'symbolised by the circle or sphere from time immemorial. "In Neo-Platonic philosophy, the soul has definite affinities with the sphere" . . .' Jolande Jacobi quoting Jung in *The Psychology of C. G. Jung*, p. 6.

While Dormer Old House, seat of the Darkes (names allegorically appropriate), infested with rodents and death-watch beetle, is
representative of society (particularly the archaic and predatory
aspects), the Forest, in contrast, symbolises the abiding presence
of nature, external and indifferent to the fate of short-lived man,
but from which he can draw spiritual succour and strength.
Though the Forest is 'austerely aloof', this is a freedom where
man's spirit, his awakening soul, can develop ('indifference is not
hampering as interference is'). Here are the pristine Upper Woods
and the Birds' Orchard. The 'sleeping house' shackles the spirit,
but those that 'feel within them the stir of a growing soul . . . fly
from the house of man to the forest' – this, the entwined stories of
the younger Darkes variously demonstrate.

The Beast Walk is a remarkably powerful and original allegorical symbol of the unconscious. This nightmarish avenue of
trees at the rear of Dormer – 'grotesque' like the house and added
to by each 'regnant Darke' – consists of 'strange beasts and birds
cut out of gigantic yew trees . . . it was as if each ancestor had
breathed such ferocities as were in his soul into his especial
creation'.[4] The Beast Walk may well have been suggested by 'the
Beast' in the Book of Revelation and in her awareness of the
implications of 'the Beast' Mary Webb anticipates another
woman mystic, Simone Weil. The allegory is obvious, the evocation vivid. If ruled by 'mass-mind' and 'herd instinct', man may
revert to the beast in carrying out and upholding the structures,
sociological and religious, which he has created and inherited
('when man is herded he remembers the savage'). The Beast Walk
symbolises this dark aspect of the unconscious mind (both personal
and collective), a storehouse of instinctive drives and repressions,
sordid and selfish desires. Appropriately the Dormer Beasts are
made of yews, cemetery trees, 'owls of the tree-world', witnesses
of death. This is forceful imagery with a profundity of symbolic
meaning. Above all, the Beast Walk is of central significance in
the story of Jasper, a tortured, Hamlet-like figure.

At its top end the Beast Walk is dominated by the grotto which
'built of grey stone and flat as a tortoise, might have been a

---

[4] Topiary was popular in country house gardens at that date. In the
grounds of Kynnersley Hall, adjoining Leighton Lodge, the lawns were
bordered by old yews in the shape of animals. Mary would certainly have
known of these.

sacrificial altar'. If the beasts, wind-blown, seem 'like creatures silently reaching out for a victim', it is at the grotto that the 'victims' are tortured in their crises: here the tormented Enoch is tempted to murder as Peter and Marigold make a 'magical house' of sex; here the sly Catherine ruthlessly imposes her 'sentence' on Jasper, and here also he is cruelly disillusioned and humiliated, as she herself is when Michael spurns her advances.

Jasper is a figure of ironic as well as tragic significance. In delineating his inner development (and that of Amber), offsetting this against the archaism of the older Darkes, Mary Webb is exploring the question of being or non-being, related intrinsically to her view of reality. Jasper's problem of spiritual loneliness and his struggle to become an individual in the fullest sense, are of central relevance to the predicament of modern man, and particularly of modern youth. His spiritual crisis and search express that of the age.

His name (like the other Darke children, he is called after a precious stone), again suggests the Book of Revelation, specifically the 'Vision of the New Jerusalem' ('The first foundation was Jasper').[5] We see a developed Jasper in the individuated Michael Hallowes who, discussing society at the Darke dinner table, declares: 'You can't co-ordinate individuals until you have individuals to co-ordinate.'[6] Jasper's development is temporarily halted by his infatuation with Catherine Velindre whom he put 'into the empty nich in his spiritual life'. It is a painful stage (suffering again an index of sensibility, of inner growth). Eventually his insight sharpens and 'slipping into a hypnotic dream', staring into Dormer brook, he sees the people of Dormer (including Catherine) passing in the water as they really are – their unreality (similar to the juxtaposition of realities in Amber's visionary dream at Ruby's wedding dance). Jasper's spiritual yearning is an agony of dark night, 'a neuralgia of the soul'. He is 'homesick for God and could not find Him'. He must plumb the 'opaque and fathomless pool lying within his own being . . .'.

Jasper's descent into the water, his 'drowning' is, like the storm

[5] Revelations 21 : 18, 19. 'And the building of the wall of it was of jasper, and the city was pure gold, like unto clear glass'.

[6] This statement is reminiscent of Jung's: 'Only the accumulation of individual changes will produce a collective solution'.

drowning in *The Tempest*,[7] concerned with the transformation from one state of being to another. His soul 'seemed to be globed in water, like a tiny insect in a rain-drop'. At Dormer he is thought to be dead (this precipitating Amber's dark night of the soul, a spiritual regression intrinsic to the progress of her mystical consciousness). Having undergone a re-birth, the re-made Jasper reappears to shock Dormer which has gone into enthusiastic mourning.

The four main characters of *The House in Dormer Forest* – Amber, the love-mystic, Jasper, the spiritual seeker, Enoch, the earth-mystic, Michael the individuated, self-poised lover – represent a quaternity, demonstrating each in their individual way the human potentiality of wholeness. Mary Webb is here giving direction to the spiritual impulse which is in us all. It is an everlasting quest, as old as human thought, the tenuous yearning of mankind in search of meaning. And at another – and humorous – level in this important novel, Mary Webb expresses this in ironic metaphor as the quest for gold (suggestive of the hermetic alchemists).

All her previous reading in mystical literature, to which she was attracted because of her own mysticism, was a preparation for the writing of this novel. And at this period she read deeply in the expository works of Evelyn Underhill[8] (finding much that was part of her personal experience), also the work of William James on psychology and religion, especially *The Varieties of Religious Experience* in which James makes his celebrated definition of the 'four marks' of a mystic.

But though deeply read in mystical literature, Mary's spiritual insights are her own. Similarly she had an innate understanding of the psyche, and was drawn to the 'new' study of psychology. Her reading certainly included Freud, but Mary was by temperamental affinity and intuitive grasp very much a Jungian, whether or not she had read the writings of Carl G. Jung, few of which were available in translation at this date. There are many Jungian parallels in her work (arrived at intuitively), particularly in *The House in Dormer Forest*. In the symbolism of this, her central

[7] In *The Tempest*, the metamorphosis is summed up in Ariel's song:
Nothing of him that doth fade,
But doth suffer a sea-change
Into something rich and strange.
[8] Later, when living in London, Mary met Evelyn Underhill at a gathering held by their mutual friend, May Sinclair.

achievement, Mary Webb expresses both the process of re-birth to wholeness (which Jung calls 'individuation') and also, repeatedly and variously, the unconscious (personal and collective) – as in the work of many mystical poets – by images rising spontaneously as symbolical utterance of what is deeply known and can never be adequately or exhaustively told. Already, in *Gone to Earth*, as we have seen, she reveals her awareness of the influence of the subconscious and the significance of myth, reminding us of our collective inheritance :

> . . . we are all as full of echoes as a rocky wood – echoes of the past, reflex echoes of the future, and echoes of the soil . . . The echoes are in us of great voices long gone hence, the unknown cries of huge beasts on the mountains; the sullen aims of creatures in the slime; the love-call of the bittern . . . the ceremonial that passes yearly in the emerald temples of bud and calyx – we have walked those temples; we are the sacrifice on those altars. And the future floats on the current of our blood like a secret argosy.
>
> (*GTE*, pp. 76–7)

So in *The House in Dormer Forest* the love-mystic Amber Darke attempts to explain to her sister Ruby 'what she knew, how she knew it' :

> 'It's something deep down,' she said, 'far down, like a pool in a mountain hollow. I look down; I see things pass there, faces looking up, hands beckoning. It's as if the things other people have felt come and lean over me. And I see them, far down and faint –'
>
> (p. 110)

Repeatedly in her articles and reviews Mary Webb reveals her preoccupation with 'the well of the subconscious' which she defines (in a *Spectator* piece) as that 'which includes individual memory, race memory, deductions drawn from them, and something else as yet unnamed' (*CPAP*, p. 72).

Mary took longer writing this novel than the two preceding ones. Again the gestation was lengthy as she carefully thought out structure and design, discussing the theme and details with Henry. But once actual composition had begun, she wrote inspirationally, sometimes in prolonged day-and-night sessions, nothing stopping her until she had exhausted her flow. Interruptions were resented, and even a request from her agent, asking that part of the book should be sent to Hodder and Stoughton, was viewed in this light: 'I must think it over', she replied. 'If there is anything in my books it lies a great deal in the cumulative effect and this, in a few chapters, is not apparent. Also, I am just in the middle of a "rush" – ideas coming too fast for the pen, and if I have to stop and tidy up for the typist it will be a bother.' In between these creative spells she renewed herself in nature, roaming her hillside and meadows, going at dawn and dusk to the Little Wood (her equivalent of Amber's Birds' Orchard) where, thinking deeply about her novel, she would sit watching and listening, listening.

Not only in the Little Wood, but also at Bomere Pool near Condover, not far from Lyth Hill, she spent days in deep contemplation, having walked there in the early mornings across dew-fresh fields and farms. Like Thoreau at Walden, Mary at Bomere watched the great stretch of water at all times of the day and in all seasons, in 'glass-clear' and 'sad-coloured' weather. Very deep, reputedly bottomless, this gleaming mere set in steep, wooded banks is a strange, lonely place of 'unbreathing quiet'. Farm labourers passing by on the woodland path on their way to work would see Mary sitting very still among the trees close to the water, and she would be there in the same place on their return in the evening. Here it was so silent she could hear 'fish rising out in the middle, and the water lapping against the stiff leaves of the bulrushes'.[9]

The mere in summer is ringed by water-lilies, by the tall rushes 'with their long trembling shadows', and by great trees extending branches and 'sending down their coloured shadows . . . so that the tree-tops almost met in the middle'. She watched there in spring when it seemed like 'a blue mist in a yellow mist of birch-tops'; in summer when the dragon-flies struggled free from their shrouds, the water 'thick and troubled' in the 'breaking of the mere'; and she watched in winter when it was 'cruddled with ice' till near the deep centre, 'the lily leaves frozen under' and the stark trees 'mounded up with snow'.

From Mary's close watching at Bomere Pool and the smaller Shomere tucked in the woods nearby, she derived the inspiration and much of the detail for Sarn Mere in *Precious Bane*, written a few years later. Yet as a creative artist, she invariably selected

[9] All these quotations are from *Precious Bane*.

her descriptive details for the thematic and symbolic significance they could yield, never merely copying an actual geographical location (see Appendix). Sarn Mere, like other settings in her novels, is a compound of several places (including Ellesmere and Colemere in North Shropshire), and of various selected features of these fused and transfigured by her imagination.

Uncovering an artist's source material does not explain his art, but it can contribute to our interpretation of it. During the hours of meditation at Bomere, the timeless moments of wholeness, Mary experienced a deepening of her mysticism, an inward extension. This is reflected in *The House in Dormer Forest* both in the primary theme of the novel and in the individual progress of Amber and Jasper Darke (a development confirmed later in *Precious Bane*). But implicitly Amber's progress is a mystical one whereas Jasper's is a psychological development in the struggle to find himself.

Amber is a water image of Mary herself, and particularly the younger Mary as she was in her Maesbrook days of affluent, middle-class family life in an old country house with a brook flowing through wooded grounds . . . 'something of a mystic, though not exactly a religious mystic, nor that wilder, sadder creature, an earth-mystic'. And Amber, like Mary, loves 'maternally, protectively, perceptively' – her insight is lovesight. Laughter too (her 'irrepressible humour') is fundamental to Amber's response to life. But intensity takes its toll. As Mary had learned, a high price is paid physically : 'perceptiveness and emotional beauty, even the gift of humour must be paid for to the last drop of vitality . . . This is often so with minds of peculiar strength or tenderness . . . The soul is impregnable so the body breaks.' Amber with her plain looks and sallow complexion, 'in growing nearer to the spiritual ideal hinted by her own face in childhood, had lost the physical expression of it' – for her, as for Mary, a painful irony. But nevertheless Amber Darke's lover, like Mary Meredith's, comes to her under the trees and sees her inner radiance – she is no longer 'the honeyed flower that no bee visits'.

Mary's attitude to nature is clearly revealed in this novel, both in the descriptions of Amber's daily communing and in the occasional fervent, overt comment : 'the love of nature is a passion for those in whom it once lodges. It can never be quenched. It cannot change. It is a furious, burning physical greed, as well as a state of mystical exaltation' (p. 277). To this theme she would return again and again in review articles written during the Twenties: 'nature passion . . . spiritual, exotic . . . can be so intense and all-pervasive as to take the place of sex love, and so dynamic as to devastate the life into which it comes'. There was a post-war vogue for 'Nature' and of this she wrote scathingly: 'It is a surprisingly small company, that of the true children of earth, in a world where everybody talks of "love of nature", everybody writes "nature books", everybody is "fond of the country". If you are a child of earth you are not 'fond" but impassioned, devastated, recreated by these things . . . It is not an easy way.' While she yearns to grasp 'the innate mystery of the world', there is nothing sentimental in Mary's attitude to nature ('not a kind mother').[10]

Through her major female characters, Mary is revelatory of her own attitudes and responses and the development of her mysticism. Amber, as a mystic, experiences dark night as well as rapture. Her 'ideas of God were vague and shadowy. The moment she tried to materialise them they vanished'; but in nature she apprehends a higher reality, the spirit of life, immanent yet transcendent – and ever elusive: 'It passed in the wood as sunlight passes, or the wind goes by . . . Yet in the wood it never nested, never came homing to the spangled meadow. For it possesses itself forever in a vitality withheld, immutable. It was this that drew Amber . . .' Her mystical experience in the Upper Woods and Birds' Orchard is that of Mary herself in the Little Wood, 'listening not with the ear but with the soul'.

The descriptive passages in which Mary Webb strives to convey what is certainly her own mystical apprehension and exaltation, are very highly charged (as George Sampson put it – 'intensity of feeling and intensity of expression reaching almost beyond the scope of prose'[11]). Her impulse is to share her journeying into

---

[10] *CPAP*, pp. 51–2, 55. Her attitude can be summed up in the title of one of her *Spectator* contributions, 'Sense and Sensibility out of Doors', in which she says: 'It is as unwise to be sentimental towards Nature as it would be to sonnetize in her presence the rosy lips of a cannibal queen'. And elsewhere she stresses: 'The great thing to remember is that Nature is utterly different from, utterly careless of, man, and that there lies its primal fascination'. *ibid*, pp. 79, 71.

[11] *Concise Cambridge History of English Literature*, pp. 975–6.

spiritual landscapes – this is creative desire serving her vision of wholeness, and in its expression she synthesizes spiritual genius and literary talent.

Mary Webb's nature symbolism is in the tradition of the finest mystical writing. There is a cumulative, almost overwhelming effect in the allusiveness of these passages in which the symbolism is partly conscious art, partly unconscious : she is writing here as a bird sings, from the springs of being – imagery rises from her spiritual reservoir, symbols break through spontaneously from a deeper level. But looked at from another angle – that of novelistic art and technique – this writing may seem excessive, too ardent and lyrically high-pitched. From this viewpoint, some critics (seeing melodrama and extravagance but not mysticism in her work) have regarded such passages as 'purple prose' or have attributed this defect, the 'overcolouring' of her style, to an imagination fevered by the effects of her disease. (She was, however, in remarkably good health at the time when she wrote this novel and *The Golden Arrow*.)

There is no space here to make the close textual study *The House in Dormer Forest* merits and would richly repay (particularly the visionary and ironic meaning). While the tempo of the narrative is slower than in the two previous novels, and it is less gripping than these, it is also richer, fuller, more convincing, not so tightly woven and schematic. A complex, if flawed work, it swings between comedy and prophecy. There is the comic world of social behaviour, as observed by Mary Webb's sympathetic but sharply penetrating eye (investing the novel with a humanising sense of fun, spiced with satiric wit); and there is the poetic world of symbolism and allusion : both are vital to the embedding of her theme and vision, her counterpointing of realities.

One of the strengths of Mary Webb's writing undoubtedly is this blending of the prose truth of observation with the poetic truth of suggestion and evocation; and one of the main weaknesses is a tendency to didacticism. Both are manifest in *The House in Dormer Forest*. In this novel she is often overt in her message, at times allowing the doctrine, rather than the drama demonstrating it, to occupy her attention. This didacticism sprang from the urgency of her desire to give the 'blear-eyed world' a new vision of life, following the disaster of the Great War. Critical of society but compassionate, her impulse was to help the fragmented, divided world, those who suffer and also those who, like the people in Amber's waking dream at the Dormer wedding dance, are held spinning in a tiny vortex, caught in a tight cone or prison ruled by conformity, instinctive behaviour, rootless intellectualism, prejudice. Such a compound of love, pity and insight resulted (as with Amber), in this 'perpetual chafing of the wistful mind for things not in Dormer'. In her later work, however, Mary was bringing her didacticism under control. Reaching her prime as a literary artist by the time she wrote *Armour wherein he Trusted*, unfortunately to be her last (and unfinished) work, she knew that 'if a thing is too near us, so that we cannot get the measure of it proper, and if it is too dear, so that no word is bright enow, then it is best to tell of some other thing, and in telling of that we shall tell of the dearest thing, though in roundabout fashion, for at such a time we stamp the image of our one thought on everything' (*AWHT*, p. 75). And this strange fragment shows how great a novelist she might have become.

Sensitive readers will look beyond the obvious faults and surface level, to grasp the inner meaning of *The House in Dormer Forest* – to be evaluated as both a visionary work and a compassionate, humorous novel. Here Mary Webb was asking the right questions and the answer she provides is one of increasing relevance, as modern man is still in search of a soul.

The House in Dormer Forest, in its symbolism, its directives to wholeness, is a literary mandala which can be read, contemplated, and then re-read, extending our insight and making us more aware of the meaning of our lives.

And ironically, soon after writing the novel, her own wholeness was put to the test – a progress to tragedy relentlessly gathering pace, 'the scene . . . laid for tragedy – not necessarily overt tragedy but a drama of the spirit, more devastating, more searing'. And it was the critical reception of this book which helped to precipitate her 'drama of the spirit'.

*

Negotiating the rights of *The House in Dormer Forest*, Mary's agent, Mr Dakers, acted for her, though, as her letters reveal, she was more than capable of directing terms herself : 'I wish to have the book published before the end of June. Provided Cassell's will do this and guarantee to push it and to begin advertising at once I will consent to let them have the option on the next two . . .

Please put in the agreement that subsequent books must be read in a month and published in four months from receipt. That in all cases I have a choice of the format of the book (wrapper, colour etc). That no book is published at less than 7/6. That if one is refused I need not offer another. Will Cassell's give me the reading work?' This was Mary at her most brisk and businesslike. Anxious now for success with the public, she wanted a publisher who would 'push' her novel. Hodder and Stoughton were interested in it, Sir Ernest (whose appreciation was for good literature rather than the trend of public taste) asking to see a part. Mary's reply was cautious and throws light on her creative method – she was reluctant to stop working at her book in the middle of an inspirational 'rush' (see above, p. 193) but would 'think it over'. She stressed to Dakers: 'I quite definitely don't want to be committed to Hodder & S. in any way. I want to know what terms he thinks of. Having heard those perhaps I'll send some of the book and see whether they go up or down.'

Eventually Hutchinson secured the rights. Mary was pleased with the generous advance of £200 but experienced some irritation during the proof stage and wrote impatiently (11 May, 1920):

> Spring Cottage,
> Lyth Hill,
> Shrewsbury.

Dear Mr Dakers,
I have today received and returned corrected the first batch of proofs. When are the sketches and proofs of the wrapper coming? There have been no notices or advertisements that I have seen. Neither have the press cutting agency sent me a thing. I wanted them back as far as March. Miss Hickling has seen the photos and I will send Hutchinson as many as they would like. Will you ask them? I have sent one to *The Bookman*. If you are there at any time soon would you mind just asking to see it. It was the same I sent you. I have now got proof that inclosures are taken out of my letters and others substituted, so I want to make sure. Would you kindly post these? If there is anything Hutchinsons would like with regard to notes about my work I shall be pleased to send them.
Many thanks for your help regarding letters.
> Yours sincerely,
> Mary Webb.

Her extreme sensitivity and insecurity led her neurotically to suspect the integrity of those who handled her affairs. She herself was extraordinarily prompt where her literary work was concerned. With immense energy and enthusiasm she would read, correct, return proofs on the day she received them – and expected a similar alacrity in her publishers. She was quick to express annoyance, but also her appreciation and gratitude. To Dakers she sent a parcel of home-grown goods (a typical gesture), and hoping 'the things will travel well', she told him: 'The honey is from a neighbour's under the hill, made in the real old straw skeps such as Virgil knew. We meant to send some of our own, but haven't taken any so far this year. But all the other things are our own produce.' Her hive, given to her by Kenneth in 1919 just before his return to Canada, was kept on the lawn at the left of Spring Cottage: 'There I lie in warm content/And listen to the velvet bees/Watching their dark blue shadows fall/Along the half-transparent wall' (*PSJ*, p. 30).

The 'neighbour's under the hill' where the old skeps fascinated her was Westley Farm down to which she walked (going across the meadows) for eggs and butter, often arriving with her long skirts 'sobbin' wet'. Sometimes young Muriel Cullis (granddaughter of Mr Barrett) fetched milk for her after school, carrying it in an old white can with a handle which Mary would place at the back door. The child did not always see Mary, only the can; and if 'Mrs Webb' did appear at the door it was to give a sweet or an apple, shyly, quietly. Her manner never varied and although to a child of twelve she seemed rather severe and 'old-fashioned' in appearance with her dark bun, serious expression, large intense eyes, and wearing always long drab skirts and laced boots, yet the girl felt and remembered her great gentleness, her timidity.

Mary was often seen watching intently from her garden as Muriel and other children of the hill were taken to the little chapel, trailing along behind Mr Barrett. She had a need to watch children at this period, hovering bird-like near her hedge, taking sidelong glances at the small picnickers who came regularly to Lyth Hill with their mothers on fine weekends and holidays. One group in particular used to have milk left for them under a large tree on the grassy part of the plateau near Spring Cottage. Mary, seeing the milk, would wait for them to arrive and look at them longingly as they played, listening to their shouts and cries spilling into the clear air, sweet, strident, sporadic as birdsong. For she yearned to have a child, a yearning which became increasingly intense as hope for fulfilment was extinguished. Again it was ironical that she who had been 'mother and sister combined', who so tenderly and maternally loved children, never had one of her own.

Sadly she confided to friends such as Caradoc Evans how much she wanted a baby, how she would have liked 'several'. In a most effective poem, highly charged with personal pathos, she expresses her wistfulness on seeing 'The Neighbour's Children' :

> They run to meet me, clinging to my dress,
> The neighbour's children. With a wild unrest
> And sobbings of a strange, fierce tenderness,
> I snatch them to my breast.
> But *my* baby, ah ! *my* baby
> Weepeth – weepeth
> In the far loneliness of nonentity,
> And holds his little spirit hands to me
> Crying 'Mother !' and nearer creepeth;
> Beats on my heart's lit window anxiously,
> Shivering and sobbing, 'Mother, let me in !'

Never can the desperate yearning and frustration of childless women have been expressed with such point and lyrical power. The poem continues with the voice of her unborn child calling to her, and ends with an evocative and characteristic image of the spirit-child like 'a moon-awakened bird' :

> Then, shadowy, wild and wan,
> A little face peers in,
> Except in dreams unknown even to me,
> And like a summer cloud is gone.
> It is the neighbour's children, playing near,
> With voices ringing clear.
> But far in twilight, like a moon-awakened bird,
> Was that another, fainter laugh I heard?
>
> (*PSJ*, p. 74)

With unthinking cruelty, people caused her further suffering – some who did not know or understand her loving heart but thought her odd in manner and appearance, deliberately kept their children away from her, warning them not to talk to 'queer Mrs Webb'.

It is not surprising that in the novel she was working on at this period (*The House in Dormer Forest*) Mary expresses more than once, and with a degree of passion, her view of motherhood, in comments reflecting her own childless state. She offsets the aridity of Rachel Darke, cold, antiseptic, fanatical, 'lovelessly producing four children', by the tenderness of Amber Darke, love-mystic, spinster – and thereby underlines that 'the gift' of motherhood 'does not go inalienably with the production of offspring, and it is sometimes found in strange places – in the eyes of spinsters or invalids, in the smile of some whom the world despises' (p. 136). A heartfelt subjectivity here. Mary's 'genius for loving', like Amber Darke's, was a maternal extension ('Love had a way of flaring up like a beacon, changing the world and consuming even herself').

In the poorer parts of Shrewsbury were many undernourished waifs to whom Mary was a shy 'fairy godmother' – she bought them complete outfits of clothing as well as food, and could not bear to see 'a little child begging', as her poem of that title indicates ('from the dark your hungry eyes/Behold the cook-shop's paradise').

Spring Cottage was now visited regularly by tramps and beggars who always went away provided with produce and money. On one occasion, wrung with pity for a poor man who knocked at her door, Mary asked him 'Is there anything I can do really to help you?' Told that he had 'a young daughter ready for service but without respectable clothes in which to leave home', Mary (as she related to a friend afterwards) 'got him to give me his name and address and promised to write to him'. Her letter asked him to bring his daughter to Shrewsbury. She took the girl to a large draper's shop buying her two outfits 'for service', a leather case, note-paper, envelopes and a pen (this attention to small necessities characterised Mary who, as Hilda Addison said, had 'charming thought for little comforts').

Similarly she offered to equip for service the eldest daughter of the postman Mr Mold, whose family she often visited in Bayston Hill village. Mrs Mold, a proud, practical woman although poor, may have appreciated 'Mrs Webb's offer', but firmly refused it.

At Christmas each year she gave a present to every child at

Lyth Hill. Her giving was now compulsive and on a lavish scale. She supplied whatever gifts the child requested – dolls, engines, bicycles, regardless of the hardship or trouble this often entailed for herself. One year a girl asked for a piano. And sure enough, a piano arrived.

'Ladysmock' – so she was named by 'the neighbour's children' when showing them the frail mauve lady's smock and other wild flowers on the hill. Ladysmock's Christmas gift – or 'Mrs Webb's present', as the parents preferred to call it – was eagerly anticipated but was also inadvertently the cause of considerable friction and jealousies in the cottages. For these were simple people, many of them ill-educated, most of them poor: the arrival of Mrs Webb's presents constituted a very big event, especially when she went to live in London and the exciting parcels came by post. In early autumn Mary's list would have been taken round by one of Mrs Thorne's sons, and next to each name was a blank space for the required gift to be written down. Some of the cottagers were too proud to ask for presents and left the spaces blank beside their children's names, while others put down expensive items, knowing that their children were sure to receive them. This caused some tensions in the district and disappointments too, for often enough when the choice was left to Mary she chose presents which were totally inappropriate or were considered to be inadequate and these were then unfavourably compared with those received by others. Many of her gifts were torn up or given away in disgust.

To the Molds she sent, one year, a large roll of pink voile out of which Mrs Mold made three dresses for her girls: a more successful gift than the three hats in London fashion boxes which arrived on another occasion, unfortunately all the same size and in the latest cloche style, unsuitable for village wear even if they had fitted. Mary, not having practical experience in these matters, did not take sizes into consideration, or the rapid growth of children, and occasionally she sent baby garments, socks and bootees for children grown to school age.

Some of the Shropshire cottagers in the Lyth Hill district resented Mary's kindness, and she experienced the silent hostility of those who regarded her as 'different' from themselves, peculiar, 'a lady' of higher class and background, unable, so they thought, ever really to understand how they lived, how they struggled. Suspicious of her, they despised her charity. Yet Mary, in giving presents to their children was expressing love; it was her way of communicating, sprung from her own need but showing at the same time that 'someone cares'. As indeed she cared passionately for mankind, seeing people as children 'wailing and beating on a dark, vast door'.

It is tempting to speculate at this point how far Mary's life and outlook might have differed had there been children of their marriage – how far, for instance, motherhood and a more rounded family life would have influenced her literary work or her relationship with Henry. As it was, childless and in her late thirties, her extraordinary love energy was channelled into a burning creative impulse, an intensification of inner life, and an increasingly obsessive focus on Henry (all the more concentrated because of her mysticism, as this unitive state – dispersed in the multiplicity of daily living – heightened her need for a unitive human relationship). Lover, husband, father, son – Henry was all in one to Mary and she centred on him her 'accumulated stores of love'. But intrinsic to this intense union was a dangerously intense emotional dependence. So the hours when Henry was away teaching often wore on her, and she was wracked by exaggerated anxieties, obsessive fears – fears for his safety and the safety of their love. In April 1919, Henry gave up his post at the Priory School. Suffering from recurring back trouble, he had been teaching part-time since the previous September ('ill health preventing Mr Webb from working in the afternoon' – the Staff Register reveals). Mary, deeply relieved to have him home, cared nothing about the loss of salary – she had soaring hopes of her literary success at this time, and a growing need to thrust ahead.

This increasing personal urgency prompted Mary to ask editors of journals such as the *English Review* to give her 'some reviewing'. Several editors agreed to keep her in mind and a few were sufficiently interested to want to meet her. Literary ambition was leading her inevitably to London.

An appointment with Austin Harrison, editor of the *English Review*, brought her on a short visit to the capital and to his offices in Garrick Street. Though she did not secure any book reviewing, Harrison encouraged her to submit work and introduced her to Adrian Bury, a critic, who was subsequently one of her valued literary friends. Bury related later how Mary had brought 'into the dull and mechanical routine of a journalist's office a breath of the Welsh hills'. She told Bury how much she was 'heartened by the applause of discriminating critics', this compensating for public apathy. 'Despite her frail appearance and timid approach, she managed to convey the impression that she was determined to succeed in her ideal whether or not she achieved material success.' It was apparent too how this intense sense of purpose and tenacity were merged and muted in the very wistfulness of her desire for success.

Bury appreciated her 'ready sense of humour' and her impersonation ('if she was in the mood') of 'some of her characters, speaking their dialect without hesitation or embarrassment'. Such close knowledge of country people, he realised, was gained not at the wicket gate but at the hearthside. Her nature was 'essentially tender', but she could also be fierce : 'she hated any kind of cruelty so passionately that I have seen her face pale with anger at some story of brutality or intolerance. Nor could she abide the least hypocrisy either in religion or social life.' Though she poked fun at the Swyndles of life, and was as furious as Hazel at the callous cruelty of those like Reddin, yet beneath her satire and her anger coursed an unfailing sense of pity which encompassed, as Amber's did, even malevolent fanatics such as Grandmother Velindre.

Her writings, which moved him by 'their deep mystical spirit and lucidity of expression', were those of a creative mystic impelled to give literary form to her spiritual insight; she 'was not obscure like many mystics', but had 'a wonderful power of presenting the subtlest truths in the clearest language, either in writing or conversation'. Bury's valuable first-hand impression of Mary Webb re-affirms those of others who knew her well : her voice was 'singularly sad but sweet'; she was 'small of stature' with 'attractive features', 'shy and somewhat nervous in manner' and 'intuitive' to a degree he had never experienced in any other person. She 'could almost divine what one was thinking, and it was this gift that gave her access to the hearts and minds of men and women of all classes'. A view which confirms those of Edwin Pugh ('She could divine your inner self, read your secret thoughts . . . It was well nigh impossible to deceive her') and Kenneth Meredith ('She took everything in and seemed to know what you were thinking, those large eyes sizing you up'). While this high degree of intuition and penetration enabled Mary, as she put it, 'to grasp the essential', it also made her rather uncanny, disturbing (some people regarded her with suspicion).

And such insight prompted her to seemingly impetuous, arbitrary (and often extraordinary) actions. As she pointed out in *The House in Dormer Forest* (pp. 51–2): 'The mystic, whatever received opinion may say, is always practical. He arrives at his ideas more quickly than others, reaching the centre while they grope in a circle.' And as Henry had learned, it was both useless and inadvisable to obstruct her. He knew the strength of mind and will through which, for example, Mary was able to make long walks of twenty or thirty miles across the Shropshire hills, fragile though she looked and was, or to spend exhausting days of continuous writing and meditation, scarcely pausing to sleep or rest, working far into the night and still not 'a stranger to the dawn'.

An incident during the early summer of 1920 illustrates this. The Buchans had recently moved into their Oxfordshire manor-house, Elsfield, and were holding a garden fête to raise funds for the heating of the church. In a letter to Mary, Susan Buchan made incidental mention of the fête and Mary, in replying, enquired about the date. What followed is related by Lady Tweedsmuir in *A Winter Bouquet*: 'I had rushed into the house to fetch something, and on emerging to regain my post at a stall of fancy odds and ends, I saw standing there a small and eager-looking woman, neatly but rather shabbily dressed . . . To my amazement she said: "I am Mary Webb, and I have come from Shrewsbury to help you".' Mary had made a train journey to Oxford, then had walked the five miles out to Elsfield. To the Buchans it seemed extraordinary that she should have 'come all the way with so much difficulty and expense, to help us with a trivial little village festival'. But Mary 'was quite unconcerned and helped magnificently, seeming to have an intuitive power of knowing what the country women wished to purchase when they came to the stall'. Afterwards Mary went with John Buchan into his library where 'they had a long talk together'. For Susan Buchan, Mary's unexpected presence at the fête 'gave the whole day a lift', making that 'small occasion' memorable. And she hoped that for Mary the meeting with John Buchan had 'made up a little for the fatigues of the day'. There can be no doubt that it did.

Exceedingly active physically and mentally at this time, Mary was increasingly caught up with her writing, eager to make the most of her few important contacts in the literary world. She had, for instance, kept up a regular correspondence with Caradoc Evans and it was during this phase of fairly prolific output that she approached him about her poetry as she was hoping to have a collection in print. Caradoc Evans knew publishers – she wrote asking if he would speak on her behalf.

Evans mentioned her collection to Andrew Melrose. This publisher then read *The Golden Arrow* and was so impressed that he offered to publish the poems he had not even seen. But there was to be no royalty advance and Melrose wanted the first option on her next three novels. Mary promptly declined the offer. As Evans pointed out, 'she had nothing to do with any publisher who did not pay her well in advance of royalties'. And he recalled that at this date Mary was needing money 'to finance the publication of an anthology another person was compiling for a learned firm of publishers'. This person was Henry, and the book his anthology of translated verse. They were both to be disappointed. Mary, however, continued to send her poems to periodicals, occasionally having them placed, never ceasing to hope that one day her greatly desired collection would appear, and never ceasing to write. And of course, that longed-for-collection eventually was published – but, ironically, not until after her death.

On one occasion Mary declared to Caradoc Evans that she 'thought more of her verse than her novels': always she saw herself as primarily a poet and wistfully desired recognition. She worked carefully at her poems, and extant drafts show her revising hand, her alternatives and variations. Discussing with Evans the differences in her composition of prose and poetry, she told him: 'You have no idea how hard I work over a poem.' As Walter de la Mare said of her poetry, it is 'at its best when it *seems* most spontaneous' – the apparent spontaneity only apparent. She had a sure command of form and in her choice of the exact epithet, the evocative word, strove for intimate relation between perception and feeling. In most of her mature poems such as 'The Land Within', 'The Ancient Gods', 'Presences', 'To a Blackbird Singing in London', 'Goodbye to Morning' she achieves successfully a fusion of strong emotion, close observation, precise expression. And evident everywhere in her poetry from first to last is her intense involvement with nature which she expresses with characteristic clarity and candour. Quotation of selected lines is inadequate – her quality as a poet can best be illustrated by considering a complete and typical short poem, 'Sunset':

> Dull is the sun as an old lanthorn guttering,
> And wild the valleys where the coughing sheep,
> With wool torn by the brambles, climb and leap.
> Here on the hill-top the old wind is uttering
> His ancient, weary, unassuaged complaints,
> Baying among the rocks that rise like tombs;
> Shouting aloud the wild and secret dooms
> Of all things living, while the evening faints
> Amid the torn white flocks of cloud that fly
> In panic all across the western sky.
>
> (51, p. 49)

Evident here is what Coleridge called 'the shaping spirit of Imagination': she infuses into this generalised pastoral description a mythic quality, charging her ending with personifications to intimate the mysterious and inevitable dark fate of 'all things living'. As Wilfred Gibson said, reviewing her posthumous collection, 'her gift was something more exquisite, more searching than acute observation'. Again and again in her poems, she expresses her intuition of an ultimate reality just beyond grasp, ever eluding, like Francis Thompson's 'half-glimpsed turrets'. Even the least accomplished of her poems rings with a pure simplicity and mystical love (similar to that in the Sufi poets), conveying her response to the soul of creation and her celebration of nature.

A reflective, personal accent is also strong throughout her work. In her finest poems, in which her individual voice is unmistakable, there is often a note of urgency and pathos; and in some pieces her passionate nature is in evidence – 'Eros', 'The Wood Witch', 'Thunderbolts', 'A Farewell' and the love poems to Henry bear out the opinion of W. Eugene Davis that 'instead of regarding Mary Webb as a lady Housman, perhaps it is time to view her as a female Lawrence'.

Her union with Shropshire, her intense relationship with its countryside, is the main informing element in her poetry as much as in her prose. But as a Shropshire poet so evocative of her county, Mary Webb has stood too long in the shadow of A. E. Housman whose *A Shropshire Lad* (1896) gained increasing popularity during the Great War. More effectively than Housman she expresses the essence of Shropshire, its spirit and mood – which indeed is her own. For Mary 'The Spirit of Earth' is also the spirit of Shropshire, and constantly it calls to her :

> Love me – and I will give into your hands
> The rare, enamelled jewels of my lands,
> Flowers red and blue,
> Tender with air and dew.
>
> From far green armouries of pools and meres
> I'll reach for you my lucent sheaves of spears –
> The singing falls,
> Where the lone ousel calls.
>
> When, like a passing light upon the sea,
> Your wood-bird soul shall clap her wings and flee,
> She shall but nest
> More closely in my breast.
>
> (*PSJ*, p. 41)

She does not need to employ place-names to create this atmosphere and sense of place. While she rarely mentions specific places, there is nothing vague or indefinite in her artistic portrayal of Shropshire : it is her special alchemy to convey in both poetry and prose the timeless, formless essence of her county, to suggest an unchanging meaning and a sense behind her closely observed exterior picture.

Mary Webb's poetry is indeed, as Walter de la Mare remarked, 'more than usually her very self's'. In particular that interfusion of joy and pain, a quintessential mingling of love and suffering, sounds again and again in her work. It is hoped that some indication of her individual voice will have been given by the inclusion throughout this study of poems and parts of poems seen in the context of her life; and that, at the same time, this will have demonstrated the extent to which her poems are poems of experience.

This aspect of her achievement has been overlooked. Her output was not quantitatively small, and qualitatively was finer than that of a number of the better-known minor Georgians. Yet she has been almost totally forgotten as a poet. Her poetry and novels stand in intimate relation but neglect has shrouded her work in general: she was not placed with other women poets of distinction of whom there had been merely a few – Elizabeth Barrett Browning, Emily Brontë, Christina Rossetti, Emily Dickinson, Alice Meynell, Charlotte Mew. Another reason for this undoubtedly is that the posthumous collection did not adequately represent her achievement. *Poems and the Spring of Joy* (1928) was brought out hurriedly as a volume in the Collected Works to meet the sudden public demand. But it is an uneven collection, containing too many early and weaker poems and does not do justice to Mary Webb as the mature poet she was becoming in her forties.[12]

These, however, are the perspectives of literary history.

Mary's passionate feeling for poetry and deeply considered ideas about it are found in 'The Core of Poetry', published in the *English Review* (February, 1920) – the first of her critical articles to be published, one of her few statements about her understanding of her art. Written during the preparation of *The House in Dormer Forest*, in both article and novel there is a similar preoccupation with the influence of the 'subconscious'. 'The Core of Poetry' (*CPAP*, pp. 37–8), belonging to this period of advance in her literary and intellectual development, was probably an offspin of her novel in much the same way as some of the essays of D. H. Lawrence were overspills from his prose fiction.

Mary puts forward here her very definite views of what poetry is, its source and significance. She begins: 'Poetry is the subconscious self breaking from its prison of silence and finding its way through the mazes of the written word. Very often it frees itself from the tyranny of the word, expressing itself, not through the thing said, nor even through the idea, but through a rhythm, a cadence, or a chiming of sounds.' She believes with Pater that 'our best work is out of the unconscious' and it is because of her insight into her own creative experience that she can speak of 'the being that dwells far within the poet's deepest self . . . quickened

---

[12] A new collection by the present author — *Mary Webb: Selected Poems* (with an introductory essay) — consists of a selection from *Poems and the Spring of Joy*; from *Fifty-One Poems* (a group found later among her papers and arranged for publication by Henry B. L. Webb); and from a private collection. See also my Introduction to *Mary Webb: Collected Prose and Poems*.

to some latent memory'. True poetry, for her, is that which 'breaks forth', that in which 'the subconscious, with low inward-sounding whisper arrests us'. She asks: 'What is this mysterious thing that inhabits the depths of man, glimmering there like an underwater town, sounding from the recesses of being like a plucked harpstring of a mermaid beneath the waves?' This 'core of poetry', as she knew, defies precise definition. Yet she attempts elucidation:

> It has an affinity with the intellect, but it is not the intellect – it is swifter and more unerring in its ways. It holds communion also with the emotions, but it is greater than the whole sum of them. It is akin also to the animal world, so that the poet of genius is more in tune with the bee than he is with the poet of talent.

In a statement that recalls T. S. Eliot's idea of the 'dark embryo' she says of such poetry: 'The harpstring has sounded: a human soul has come forth to us, bringing out of the depths something strange, deific.' So a poem is to be tested by whether it emanates from the deeper self, and 'by this standard almost the whole of contemporary poetry either shrivels or is revealed as prose'.

'The Core of Poetry' leaves no doubt about Mary Webb's pre-occupation with the unconscious, evident in *The House in Dormer Forest* and explicit in future review articles. It is her conviction that 'if we could get at the subconscious self of the whole race we should reach a revelation such as there has never yet been'. Maintaining that it is 'through poetry' that this can be achieved, she is echoing the statements of Arnold and Hardy about the significance of poetry for mankind:

> It was because Shakespeare had so great a share of subconsciousness that he was able to express the deepest instincts of the race and something that, lying beneath them, seems to be the nearest we have yet come to a revelation of God. It is through poetry that we shall come nearer to it (*CPAP*, p. 38).

After the publication of 'The Core of Poetry', Mary seemed on the threshold of an important advance in her literary reputation, awaiting the concurrent publication in Britain and America of her third novel and hoping this time for a wave of acclaim and popularity which would make up for the apathetic public response to her first two works. The months prior to the publication of *The House in Dormer Forest* (July, 1920), were a time of contentment and anticipation, spent among her 'green haunts' on Lyth Hill where she knew intimately, like the 'Populus Tremula' of her essay, 'the green sunrise, the voice of the plovers wailing for summer, cries from the farm, the sea-sound in the wood, the infinite faint murmur of the plain' (*PSJ*, p. 225). And one of the most memorable happenings of that golden summer was the visit of the Buchans to Lyth Hill. They were motoring to Scotland with their two elder children, taking a route through Shrewsbury. Susan Buchan's account of this second meeting gives a valuable, indeed a unique impression of Mary in those surroundings with which she was essentially integral.

It was 'one of those August days when all the countryside is wrapped in a kind of slumbrous peace'. After their bumpy ascent up the unmade road to the top of the hill, the Buchans' chauffeur, anxious about the car, drove cautiously along the rough track of the plateau as they looked out to Wenlock Edge 'soft and ochre-coloured on the near horizon'. Mary, eagerly anticipating their arrival, stood waiting with Henry, 'her greeting . . . at once shy and enthusiastic, his shy and quietly welcoming'.

During the afternoon, 'leaving the two men to talk to each other', Mary, Susan Buchan and the children 'wandered away into a little wood on the side of the hill'. This was Mary's Little Wood.

'The afternoon had grown warmer,' Susan Buchan recalls, 'and the trees were so motionless that the wood was like a piece of tapestry, except for the insects who kept up a loud monotonous buzzing.' The Little Wood wove its sure enchantment. Receptive to this, Susan Buchan observed that Mary 'missed nothing of the scene around us – not a glitter of sunlight on a leaf or the movement of light on the hills opposite us escaped her'.

During the 'very good tea' she had provided, Mary herself ate only bread and butter, and Henry, by way of explanation, remarked that 'Mary would live on bread and butter entirely' – a sad comment on her diet, as years of undernourishment certainly contributed to her early death.

'I remember Mary Webb's bird-like glances at myself and the children and John, and how these darting glances took in each detail of our faces and clothes.' Susan Buchan, like others who knew her, stresses this 'bird-like' quality, her way of 'sizing you up' with a sidelong glance. That evening Mary urged the Buchans to dine with them at a country hotel built of Shropshire's deep red velvety sandstone'. Susan Buchan recalls the warmth and charm of the occasion, Mary's 'sudden fierce statements about people and things and her equally sudden charming gentleness and kindness'.

After this, the friendship continued 'mostly by correspondence', and Mary sent 'each of her books as they came out' to the Buchans who were among the first to discern the finer elements of her writing and provide valued encouragement.

*

Soon after the completion of *The House in Dormer Forest* Mary was planning her next work, *Seven for a Secret*. When discussing the new novel with Henry, they decided to combine a short holiday with an exploration of the area of countryside Mary had chosen as her setting: the south-west borderland around Clun, and immediately across this border into Radnorshire. Mary was drawn to this heavily forested region where Shropshire blends into Wales, and no doubt the fact of her Welsh ancestry, the pronounced Celtic vein in her nature, accounts a great deal for the attraction this part of the borderland held for her with its distinctive atmosphere and beauty.

While *Gone to Earth* is infused throughout with a strong Celtic element, *Seven for a Secret* is patently the most Welsh of her novels. On one occasion she told Caradoc Evans 'of course, all my characters are Welsh'. The truth of her comment is certainly borne out in the characters of *Seven for a Secret*. She began developing her ideas about these characters while absorbing totally the curious, powerful atmosphere of the Border during her holiday with Henry in the early summer of 1920.

The minimum of luggage in their pony cart, they set off on a route through the Hope Valley to Clun, staying each night at country inns. The Clun area, with its high moorland and dense woods was especially fascinating: this she chose as the central setting of her novel, re-titling it Dysgwlfas-on-the-Wild-Moors; here the chief characters of her story inhabit isolated farms and inns. South from Clun she and Henry travelled into Radnorshire, stopping at the old town of Knighton, centre of markets and ponyfairs, 'the town on Offa's Dyke', to be called 'Weeping Cross' in the novel. From here they went a short distance further into Wales before turning back for the return home.

It had been a shared experience, again a oneness in the beauty of the landscape, recalling the days at Rose Cottage and The Nills, and their long walks across the hill country. But neither of them knew then that this was to be the last summer they would spend entirely in Shropshire – and entirely together.

On 12 July *The House in Dormer Forest* was published by Hutchinson. Her hopes were high that with this book she would secure the attention of the post-war reading public. As St John Adcock commented later of her wartime novels, those 'like so many good books published during the Great War, though they were well enough received by many critics . . . were engulfed and soon lost in the more momentous distractions of that inauspicious period'. This she herself realised, and was not yet unduly dismayed that the sales of *The Golden Arrow* and *Gone to Earth* had not run into thousands in either case. But now she was hoping that her third novel would be enthusiastically received and would fulfil the predictions of those who believed in her ultimate success.

It was not to be so. When the reviews appeared she was utterly disappointed and disheartened. *The House in Dormer Forest* was given attention in only a few of the influential journals and then comment varied from adverse to lukewarm. Worse than this, the reviewers apparently did not see the novel's deeper meaning, the implications of its symbolism, its intended significance for contemporary society.

The *TLS* reviewer for example (23 July, 1920) not only failed to see beyond the narrative level, but found no humour: the world she creates here is 'a very gloomy place' and the result of 'so much unrelieved intensity is to produce not only gloom but monotony'; furthermore 'her people become flat images of certain mental states, not rounded human forms'. And in the *Athenaeum* (6 August, 1920) the reviewer thought the ending of the novel 'utterly incredible'.

There was a more appreciative review in the *Bookman* (September, 1920) – 'this grim and powerful story which awakens memories of Charlotte Brontë and Thomas Hardy' . . . the characters 'differentiated and portrayed with remarkable skill'.

The reviewer saw rightly that while 'there is much of gloom in the story and a little of tragedy', there is also 'an all-pervading humour. The descriptions of the house and of people are touched in with a very agreeable wit.' Encouragingly the reviewer concluded, 'the writing is of a quality not only to indicate promise but to excite interest in the author's previous works with which the reader, like ourselves, may be unacquainted'. Yet here again there were no indications of awareness of the novel's vital theme, no response to those insights and perspectives around which she had structured all and which she considered to be so important for the individual and for society.

Like William Blake, she felt the urgent desire to 'cleanse the doors of perception'. When her vision of reality embodied in this novel with its symbolised truths was not understood, her disappointment was acute. In spite of the invocation under the title, 'Let the sleeping soul awake', and her ardent directives at various points of the narrative, her deeper level of meaning was missed. She was so distressed by the reviews that she became ill, and during the early autumn of 1920 suffered the first serious attack of Graves' Disease since before her marriage. To be heard yet not heard is the most devastating denial the world can inflict on a visionary writer. 'Sing your own song': she had sung, but it seemed that no one had heard; she felt stifled and this affected her more than the physical and nervous exhaustion which always followed her intense periods of composition.

The illness receded after a while, but Mary's depression continued. She became thinner and more despondent. As her mystical experience had deepened so had her literary ambition – there is no paradox in this, since as a creative mystic she felt a fierce necessity to transmit her inner landscapes, to reveal an unimagined reality to the world. Not that the myopic critical reception of *The House in Dormer Forest* would deflect or deter her. But now she had only her own fervent conviction to support her, and although her sense of purpose was not destroyed, she was, for the time, extremely dispirited and depressed.

Mary's doctor suggested a change of environment to rouse her from this melancholic lassitude, and Henry, taking up the suggestion, was convinced that London would provide the necessary stimulus. Her literary career would be promoted if she could live in the capital, meet those writers and critics with whom she was corresponding and attend literary functions with her contemporaries. And he was sure that progress in her career would bring improvement in her health.

He, too, felt the need for a change, to rise to a challenge, and was attracted by the idea of teaching at one of the most progressive schools in the country – the King Alfred School at Golders Green (co-educational, following Pestalozzi and Froebel methods). He applied for the post of Assistant Master for Senior English and Latin and was immensely enthusiastic on being appointed, explaining the new venture to Mary with eloquent arguments. She agreed. To go to London seemed the inevitable path towards which all had been tending.

To what extent did she feel misgivings and fears about such an extreme move, she who so often was 'unquiet in heart', prey to 'chill presentiment'?

> The evening smoke ascends again
> Out of the sapphire-circled plain,
> And to the oatfield, pale as wax,
> A black swift hurtles like an axe ...
> *(PSJ,* p. 59)

A characteristic intimation of impending dark fate. If she did feel unease, then her decision to go was the more courageous, made in the realisation that she would be leaving behind virtually part of herself: the hills, her cottage, the Little Wood and all the 'green charm'. But it was her sense of purpose that took her forward, life and art inseparably interwoven. Desperately she needed to gain a hearing. Perhaps Henry was right: she would have a greater chance of succeeding at the centre of the literary world rather than in the remote countryside of the Welsh Borders. Added to which she knew Henry was restless and needing new opportunity.

Again, as when they planned the move to Chester, Mary was determined that this would be only a term-time absence from Shropshire. Her permanent home must, and always would be, Spring Cottage: here they would return at weekends, coming by train from London to Shrewsbury; here they would spend every holiday.

Mrs Thorne agreed to look after Spring Cottage for them while they were away. Henry readily complied, knowing that for the sake of Mary's happiness this was the only course : Lyth Hill was to her as Grasmere to Wordsworth, the moors at Haworth to Emily Brontë.

They spent the Christmas of 1920 at Chester with Alice Meredith and Olive, after which Mary prepared for London. It was to be a fatal step.

PART FOUR

THE SADNESS TERRENE

1921–1927

You took the rare blue from my cloudy sky;
You shot the one bird in my silent wood;
You took my rose – one rose alone had I.
You have not known. You have not understood.
Mary Webb, from 'To the World'

10

Bayswater – and *Seven for a Secret*

1921–1923

> Within some hearts the conflict cannot cease :
> They are the sick world's factories of peace.
>
> (*CPAP*, p. 127)

Henry's appointment at The King Alfred School began in the spring term, 1921. It is not difficult to imagine Mary's feelings leaving Spring Cottage as the wicket gate swung behind her and she took a last look at the plain and mountains when setting off by taxi for Shrewsbury station.

At first they lived in a furnished flat at 117 Adelaide Road, Hampstead, where Henry was quite near his school. But this was only temporary accommodation, and within a few months they had transferred to a Bayswater flat at 46B Leinster Square. Her health improved. Yet she felt claustrophobia, the closed-in effect of the tall stuccoed blocks of Bayswater only slightly alleviated by the knowledge that Kensington Gardens was nearby. Here she was able to continue her early morning walks, hear the birdsong that never ceased to thrill her. Reviewing a book by Gilbert Coleridge for the *Spectator* a short time later, she comments :

> He is one of the few Londoners who know the fascination of Kensington Gardens in the early morning, when, beneath the soft murmur of the tree-tops, companioned by the water-birds, bewitched by the deep voices of the wood-pigeons, one is no more in London, but in some charmed fragment of elfin wood-land which has floated up, intact and secret, out of a remote world, whither it will return at the milkman's plaintive cry.
>
> (*CPAP*, p. 75)

Such was her own heightened appreciation of London greenery.

During those first months she made herself known personally to writers and critics, sought work as a book reviewer and joined a

few of the most important literary groups, the P.E.N. club (introduced by Austin Harrison of the *English Review*), the Tomorrow
Club and the Bookman Circle, coming into contact with most of
the established writers of her day. Among those who befriended
her were May Sinclair, Robert and Sylvia Lynd, Mrs C. A.
Nicholson and Martin Armstrong.

Mary's was an eager, yet shy and painfully self-conscious, extension into London literary life. A pathos surrounds those first
hopeful ventures, as so many of her dreams of success and friendship were to be unrealised, some acute disappointments were
ahead. She was now mixing in a world the sophisticated callousness of which she was unable to gauge or protect herself against.
Highly intuitive and incisive of insight though she was, her
inexperience, her optimistic faith in people and the extreme
vulnerability of her sensitive nature left her ill-equipped to cope
with rebuffs, wounding remarks, broken promises.

One friendship which did not disappoint, and which grew, in
fact, to a firm and fruitful relationship, was that with Caradoc
Evans. His book *My People* had been published in the same year
as *The Golden Arrow*, and the two had been compared by a
Times Literary Supplement reviewer. Their friendship had begun
by correspondence after Caradoc's own enthusiastic review of *The
Golden Arrow*. Forthright and volatile, strong in his likes and dis-
likes, Caradoc was attracted by Mary's sincerity as well as by her
understanding of the Welsh. He thought she was going to be
'truly great' and told her so, admiring her writing immensely – 'It
was like finding a diamond.' Mary, on her part, enjoyed
Caradoc's unstinted recognition and praise, and confided to him
her hopes – and also some of her anxieties.

Their first meeting was 'at eleven o'clock on a morning' outside the Garrick Club and the *English Review* offices. Caradoc
was apparently more than a little surprised by her appearance,
expecting to meet a woman whose looks matched her 'pretty as
dewdrops' handwriting :

> A spindly, earthy little woman came to meet me . . . Her feet
> were biggish, her fingers were thin and trembly and long and
> like a sewing woman's . . . her eyes were brilliant, bulging . . .

Mary told him in her 'deep husky voice' that two leading critics, namely Arthur St John Adcock, acting editor of the *Bookman,* and Robert Lynd, the distinguished essayist and literary editor of the *News Chronicle,* had promised her some reviewing. St John Adcock was to fulfil his promise and the Lynds too promoted her: Sylvia Lynd who worked for Cassells, tried to get her some 'reading', while Robert Lynd assisted with introductions and advice. As Caradoc Evans said, these important men helped Mary 'not for the reason that she looked pathetic or pestered them for work, but for the reason that they saw in her a great artist'.

They met fairly frequently, Mary responding to Caradoc's lively Celtic humour and his constant encouragement (' "You're the greatest living woman novelist . . . going to be as famous as George Eliot" '). Caradoc's own controversial work attracted much attention in the press. Something of a forerunner of Dylan Thomas, he expressed himself boldly and with energetic originality.

He wrote of Mary:

> She was smiling. There was always a smile on her face. God spread it there to cover up the trouble in her heart . . . Sometimes we sat in the Embankment Gardens, sometimes we strolled round and about Fleet Street, sometimes we drank tea (mine very strong, hers very weak and without milk or sugar) in a teashop. Mary mostly spoke about her work and loved to listen to my praise of it, my honest praise. Persons as characters did not interest her, and when I brought Shropshire into our talk she quickly changed the subject. Once she dropped her handkerchief and I picked it up; and her eyes told me I had done a most unusual thing for her.

Mary evidently brought out Caradoc's sense of gallantry. She trusted him sufficiently to confide in him when feeling slighted and hurt, Caradoc restoring her by his brisk commonsense and wit, and also protecting her at literary gatherings ('self-adoration parties') from the 'underhand sayings' of certain 'third-rate women novelists' who were, he maintained, 'spit-venoms'. He admired Mary's bravery on these occasions, for she always arrived late and drew everyone's gaze as she entered, 'a filmy material' hiding her goitre, 'a subdued frock' hanging on 'her stoopy shoulders'. Fearing that Mary would hear the slighting remarks of the 'spit-venoms', Caradoc 'in a loud and Welshy voice' would say: ' "I like your dress Mary. Paris?" "Isn't it pretty? It took me three days to make" '.

Caradoc was sympathetic when Mary told him of her disappointment over the low sales of her first two novels which, at that date, had not exceeded two thousand copies. It seemed that they would soon be out of print altogether and Mary felt desperately anxious as 'she knew her greatness'. Caradoc knew it too: ' "Mary Webb Shropshire . . . you'll be the English novelist when you're dead." She put a cold hand on mine and shivered.' A prophecy ironically to be fulfilled – and sooner than either of them knew.

Edwin Pugh, novelist and 'very competent critic', also met Mary during her first year in London, becoming her staunch champion and close friend. Then reviewing for the *Bookman*, Pugh had been one of the brilliant young novelists of the 1890s and had a specialist's knowledge of Charles Dickens.[1] A Londoner of Welsh descent, he had, in common with Mary and Caradoc Evans, a lively sense of humour, strong sympathy and equally strong detestation of any kind of falsity. *The Golden Arrow* had impressed him unforgettably and as each of her other books came out he became convinced of her genius.

They were introduced at the Bookman Circle, and afterwards he called on her at Leinster Square, offering to show her some of the places in London she particularly wanted to see. Quick to perceive Mary's sensitivity to suffering, he refused to show her the slums, persuading her against going in terms to which he knew she would respond, telling her 'that London was a world in embryo, as foreign and remote from the most assiduous observer as her own countryside and people would be to me. She understood that, and never again broached that subject.'[2] So they reached an understanding! Pugh did however 'show her some things she had never seen but longed to see', and during their excursions she was 'avid of excitement, experience, new sensations. She had the curiosity of a cat.' He was fascinated by this aspect of her, her 'clear all-seeing eyes of a child', her voice 'softly

---

[1] Pugh wrote two Dickens studies: *The Apostle of the People*, 1908, and an exhaustive account of *The Dickens Originals*, 1912. His *City of the World*, dealing with London life, was said to be one of the best of its kind.

[2] Edwin Pugh, 'Mary Webb', *The Bookman*, April 1923, pp. 7–8; July 1928, pp. 193–6.

musical as the piping of a bird'. He admired too her 'genuinely modest spirit' which was 'so essentially a part of her strong shy personality, the grace and charm of her gentle ways and simple manners'.

Mary was indeed appalled when on coming to London she was brought to a fuller realisation of the effects and aftermath of the Great War so much more evident in the capital than in the Shropshire countryside. She had arrived at a time of general depression, the post-war slump accelerating, the numbers of un-employed increasing daily. Men stood around the streets in aim-less groups, beggars everywhere, at street corners, down the Underground passages, hundreds of maimed and injured ex-servicemen among them.

London in 1921 was dismal, heartrending. Like Rilke, torn by the suffering he saw in post-war Europe, Mary was moved by anguished pity. She could not refuse any plea for help, and gave from her already slender resources with passionate recklessness. Her sensitive spirit became consumed with a sense of guilt that she spent the war years hibernating, as she said, 'in the beauty of Nature'. At literary gatherings this sense of guilt increased when she heard of the contribution other writers had made to the war. Not only the men who had survived and returned to resume their literary careers, but also the women who had given up writing to participate actively.

She expressed this later in urgent tones in a letter to G. Wrenn Howard, Cape's partner (28 July, 1924):

> I wanted to say when I was in the office (having heard that you were in the army in the war) that I knew I didn't deserve as much success as May Sinclair and so many other women who gave up their writing and helped. Because I didn't.
>
> It was all so heartrending that I just hibernated in the beauty of Nature. And so, when I came to London and realised it all, I said to myself that I should have to tell any soldier I met.

She did not merely 'tell': she gave extravagantly in a hopeless gesture of mingled pity, grief, guilt, anxiety, an overwhelming urge to console and heal. So began a downward course into a tangle of personal debt and stress from which she never emerged.

After coming to London, part of the intensity of her desire for public success hinged on her desperate need for money – 'big sales' would bring the means to alleviate the suffering she saw all around her, at every turn of the streets. Royalties, loans, payment for review articles were rapidly expended in this way. She flung herself unsparingly into literary work, pursuing any offers of reviewing or reading for publishers. Heedless of her health and needs as she had always been, this self-neglect now increased with her sense of purpose, precipitating the tragic decline. Those who did not understand her motivation interpreted her actions as erratic, even somewhat unbalanced.

Mary's creative work continued to reflect her passionate pity. Several of the short stories written between 1921 and 1927 express actual experiences. 'Palm', a brief character sketch, is one of the best of these, depicting the plight of an old palmseller Mary met in Leinster ('Tower-of-Babel') Square. The sketch reveals Mary's active compassion. When the palm-seller told her about her daughter of the 'gold hair and little taking ways', who was expecting an illegitimate child and had no money for a lying-in shift, Mary gave the palm-seller 'a bundle of linen' and she departed 'leaving many blessings', among them the words 'and may no child ever look darkly upon you!' – painfully apt. The palm turned Mary's thoughts to home :

> Her palm stands up against the pale wall, softly budded in pale silver. Spring is in it. Light lingers on it. Looking at the slender boughs, one sees again in Tower-of-Babel Square the weary woman lifting up her voice in the sweet twilight of early spring, to speak her daughter's confession and magnificat. And one is reminded of long brown country roads, and of voices, penetrating, obstinate and melodious, of the clover-breathing kine lowing after their young.
> (*AWHT*, pp 197–8)

The depressing effect of London upon her was always to intensify when the year turned to spring. As the buds and leaves grew in the city parks so her longing for Shropshire increased. She was missing those 'dark April dawns' and 'sweet twilights' at Lyth Hill. A keen nostalgia overtook her when a parcel arrived from Mrs Thorne containing a box of spring flowers from her own garden :

> I did not think the violets came so soon,
> Yet here are five, and all my room is sweet;

And here's an aconite – a golden moon
Shining where all her raying leaflets meet.
(PSJ, p. 80)

She yearned to be once more in the 'inviolable places' partaking of her 'sacrament'.

With great joy she returned to Lyth Hill for the Easter holiday of 1921. Again tending her garden, weeding, digging, 'setting' potatoes and other vegetables, looking down to the plain 'multiple-tinted, magical, still', hearing the silvery fluting notes of birds, knowing again each sharp or subtle smell and scent, she experienced continually the 'undernote of ecstasy'. Much of the day – especially dawn and twilight – was spent in the Little Wood, her rapture there an 'intolerable sweetness'.

On returning to London, both she and Henry felt renewed. Yet for the first time she was having serious difficulties in creative flow as she worked at *Seven for a Secret* – this was possibly due to the unsettling influence of those early months in London and the moves from one residence to another. But most of all it was the sharp separation from her landscape, from the quiet lovely hill, the 'earthy mysteries', and the garden where it was her habit to sit writing or typing no matter the weather. She was deeply distressed when her writing did not come in the usual inspirational 'rushes'. Fragmentation of time and energy was not good for her; London seemed 'sullen'. Even the sky pressed in. They returned to Lyth Hill for the Whitsun holiday, and when it was over Henry came back to London alone, leaving her to stay on at Spring Cottage. Here perhaps she would be able to work at her novel as she had *The House in Dormer Forest* (written entirely on Lyth Hill).

Yet this was not a satisfactory solution. The June countryside was overwhelmingly beautiful, but Mary was torn. This was now her tragic dilemma: in London she longed intolerably for Shropshire; in Shropshire she longed intolerably for Henry. She was not used to separation, neither could she bear it. Always she had dreaded his absence. On occasions when he used to visit his mother at Weston-super-Mare (where she was not invited), Mary sometimes felt impelled to follow by train. She would be seen walking up and down the street outside the house: not that she would be asked in, but she did need desperately to be near him. Her insecurity, which always threatened to break her, that fear of cruel, unpredictable fate, was a very real pressure which Henry, on the whole, handled with patient care. He knew her genius, had helped it to blossom, understood perhaps that the acute agony was an essential part, intrinsic to her exquisite sensibilities. Now there seemed little more that he could do. His work was in London, and there he had to be. The conflict was Mary's.

Her poem 'Absence' written in June 1921, is pervaded by yearning, impregnated with the atmosphere of Lyth Hill. There she walked without him on 'the clear bright grass', looking down to the pastures 'gossamer green', hearing 'the sounds of hay-making' filling the air, the 'fugitive voices' of the haymakers rising from the still plain. This seemed truly a 'land of rest' far removed from the squalid depressing sights of London – here 'no hands tremble and no eyes weep' – except her own, for she was craving for Henry, remembering the shared joy of previous Junes when the thorn was 'white over'. She could find neither rest nor ecstasy:

> I care not for day, while linnet and swallow,
> That have no sorrow, possess the sky;
> I care not for night, when the dark blue hollow
> Is full of stars for the white owl's eye.
>
> Sad is the rose-red flower of the dawn,
> And the smell of the hay in the tender dew;
> I hear no sheep, nor birds on the lawn,
> Because of my own voice, calling you.
>
> (*51*, pp. 42–3)

Henry travelled back to Lyth Hill at weekends, but as the weeks passed the strain of the situation was intolerable. Mary, utterly lonely, could not bear the days and even more the nights, without him. If he could not come to her at the weekend she suffered paroxysms of fear, fear of all kinds, especially that he was ill, that he no longer loved her . . . Eventually she packed the manuscript she was struggling to write and returned to London. Back in the city she longed for Lyth Hill, her *hiraeth* evident in a descriptive poem 'On the Wild Hill', written at Bayswater, in which she recalls the curlews drifting through the summer air 'like tawny leaves', their 'icy' voices 'Discovering some chill pre-sentiment/Like a fugitive soul that grieves'. These lines have a sensually arresting, spiritually haunting quality which becomes increasingly characteristic of her writing during the final years. She knew 'the fugitive soul that grieves', for this was her innermost self, long familiar with 'chill presentiment'.

The return to Spring Cottage with Henry for the summer holiday of 1921 brought a temporary joyful relief. At last she was able to gather renewed creative impulse and spontaneity after walks deep into the hill country and days spent in the leafy quiet of the Little Wood. Again the soothing green world, promising blue of hills, the timeless inviolable contours of her landscape. No longer distressed by partings from Henry, and free of the 'old homesickness vast and dumb' which wore on her spirit in London, she could again give prolonged concentration to *Seven for a Secret*. Exploring the locations of her story in the Clun Forest area, at one with the atmosphere of the border countryside, she was garnering a wealth of fresh perceptions with which to invest her descriptive passages.

The novel was completed, the typescript prepared for her publishers (again Hutchinson); and early in 1922, with that characteristic blend of courage and timidity, she requested Thomas Hardy's permission to dedicate this book to him (in her opinion, the greatest living novelist). Enormously she valued his letter praising her work; exhilaration and delight ring in the words with which she prefaced *Seven for a Secret*: 'To the Illustrious Name of Thomas Hardy whose Acceptance of this Dedication has Made Me so Happy.' She was invited later to his Dorset home, Max Gate, but the meeting never came about as illness and depression – 'dark weather' – overtook her. Hardy too was a sick man by then and was to die shortly after Mary – at eighty-eight having almost doubled her life span. It is interesting to note that Hardy had once tried, as Mary did, a period of London life in the hope of promoting his literary career, and for him also this had proved an unhappy phase ending with severe illness. In 1880, the year before Mary was born, he had left London and moved back to his own countryside.

In *Seven for a Secret* we find another variation on a major theme that recurs throughout Mary Webb's work from first novel to last: the antithesis between sacred and profane love. Again in a story of human passion, sacrifice and redemption, this obsessional theme is embedded and her concept of love illustrated – a deeply held conviction intrinsic to her vision of life. The love that ennobles and enriches human relationships is again shown to be primarily, fundamentally, of spiritual quality: without this spiritual union with the other's soul or essential inner being, physical passion (merely the satisfying of sexual urge) is not love, cannot bring lasting harmony, and tragic experience often ensues. For Mary, as we have seen, her view of the nature of human love and passion was an *idée fixe* central to both her life and art.

Gillian Lovekin, the central character of *Seven for a Secret*, is demonstrating the author's concept of love when she is involved in a struggle (as were Jasper Darke, Hazel Woodus and Stephen Southernwood) between the higher and lower in her nature, a struggle that brings suffering to herself and others. The only daughter of Isiah, a rich farmer at Dysgwlfas-on-the-Wild-Moors, Gillian is magnetic, strong-willed, utterly selfish, determined to get everything out of life rather than give to it: insensitive to the steadfast but silent spiritual love of Robert Rideout, her father's cowman-shepherd, she is lured by the sexual attraction of wealthy Ralph Elmer, who seduces her. Realising at last that she loves Rideout, but too late to avoid marriage with the wrong man, she leaves the farm to live unhappily at 'The Mermaid's Rest' with Elmer and his strange entourage, the weird evil Fringal and mute gipsy housekeeper Rwth (to whom Elmer is already secretly married). Ultimately, as a result of Robert Rideout's patient love, and at the cost of Rwth's life (Elmer murders her), Gillian emerges from the tangle of lust and sin to higher being and new life in union with Robert. The relationships of Gillian, on the one hand with Ralph Elmer and on the other with Robert Rideout, form the hub of the book's meaning.[3]

Seven for a Secret is as much the story of the passionate poet Rideout (loved by the dumb, doomed Rwth) as it is of the self-centred Gillian. Rideout endures anguish, Rwth dies and Gillian, redeemed by love, does not escape unscathed. As in all Mary Webb's novels, suffering is the index of inner development, of the progression of her characters to fuller vision and deeper insight.

Together with the major theme of the nature of love, this

[3] Looked at another way *Seven for a Secret* is something of a *bildungsroman*, the unheroic heroine being educated by experience, her adventures transforming her from a selfish adventuress into a chastened lover eager to make the most of her second chance with Rideout.

associated theme of the significance of suffering is, as we have seen, of central importance in Mary Webb's reading of human experience: as leading preoccupations of her fictional art such themes have binding, cohesive power. In *Seven for a Secret*, however, in contrast to the other novels, they are themes pursued on one level only. This novel in fact marks a departure or a falling away from Mary Webb's usually finely wrought work: again in the tradition of moral fable, it is slight, lacking the density and fullness of implication hitherto so characteristic of her writing; unlike its three predecessors, each richly meaningful novels written in highly charged prose, *Seven for a Secret* does not extend in the symbolic level. However, it was not Mary Webb's intention on this occasion to write another work such as *Gone to Earth* or *The House in Dormer Forest*, poetic, allusive, resonant with multiple suggestiveness, requiring sustained vigour of imagination. To this type of novel she was to return splendidly and successfully in *Precious Bane*.

Seven for a Secret, though thematically linked, stands separately in the body of Mary Webb's work and can be regarded as an attempt on her part to write a different kind of novel, blending satire, fantasy and fable. But this book was prepared and written at a difficult period for her – during exhaustion and illness following publication of *The House in Dormer Forest*, the move to London, the effort of adjustment to new surroundings. A literary friend, who had personal knowledge of Mary and her circumstances during the composition of *Seven for a Secret*, emphasised that it was written during a period of 'lowered creative vitality'. At this stage of her literary career she had not yet recovered from the blow to her hopes that the critical reception of *The House in Dormer Forest* constituted. Dismayed at the general lack of understanding of this work, she had deliberately written *Seven for a Secret* in a lighter vein, had set out to tell a fabulous tale (although still embedding central concerns) creating her characters as Robert Lynd noted, 'in a high fervour of the romantic spirit'. And such a novel with its vivid surface presentation and interwoven elements of love, mystery and murder would perhaps have wider popular appeal. Subtitled 'A Love Story', it seems to be almost a parody of her own previous work.

In his Introduction to *Seven for a Secret* (Collected Works, 1928), Robert Lynd described this novel as a fable told 'with

vehement good faith', written 'in a vein of noble and appropriate
exaggeration', the characters 'a little too fabulous' – Fringal and
Rwth, for instance, are grotesques after the fashion of Hugo.
Directives for reading the novel as a fable are provided from the
outset with the prefatory Old Rhyme and the opening description: 'On a certain cold winter evening, in the country that lies
between the dimpled lands of England and the gaunt purple
steeps of Wales – half in Faery and half out of it – the old farmhouse that stood in the midst of the folds and billows of
Dysgwlfas-on-the-Wild-Moors glowed with a deep gem-like lustre
in its vast setting of grey and violet.' This tone is maintained until
the close when all the loose ends are neatly, if hastily, tied, the
reader's questions answered, and the moral all too summarily
rounded off.

Again using the omniscient mode of narration, Mary Webb
views her characters with mild affection, gentle amusement – no
doubt her conscious artistic intention, but the characters are over-
distanced and this creates cumulatively a sense of unreality. The
world of the novel loses solidity and human depth, lacks a sense
of the vitality of life. One feels a detachment in the narration
(at times even a tiredness). We do not experience intimate involvement with her characters, their lives and affairs never seem part
of a complex pattern of life – as one reviewer said, they 'seem too
far away to make us grieve or shiver'. This novel, half-fantasy,
half-parable, has a somewhat abstract, remote quality. Occasionally an authorial comment takes us too far out of her fictional
scene. The total effect of the book is unconvincing – the elements
of fantasy and realism do not cohere; the 'uncommon' and the
'ordinary' (to use Hardy's terms) are harnessed uneasily and
unsatisfactorily in this, the least aesthetically satisfying of the
Mary Webb novels. If by her imaginative energy she still compels
us to 'suspend disbelief', there are parts of *Seven for a Secret*
(especially the last third of the book) where she only just succeeds
in this.

Yet we feel, nevertheless, that, as one reviewer commented, 'the
author loves her art': this novel does not entirely lack (particularly in the early chapters) that feeling of joy in composition, an
inspirational zest usually so sustained in her work. Although
Seven for a Secret contains some of her worst writing, it also
contains some of her finest and most arresting: while the closing

chapter, for example, is clumsy and makeshift (as several reviewers were to point out), the opening chapter is one of her best.

And even in its least successful parts there are flashes of poetry, brilliant nature drawing, an abundance of sharp sense-impressions. 'Mrs Webb,' in the words of a critic, 'cannot entirely withhold beauty from anything she does.' Among the most memorable descriptions are those of the farm at Dysgwlfas, a 'quiet place, drenched in old silence'; of the 'large mysterious expanses' of the moors which 'at sunset . . . darkened like a frown'; of 'the sharp young moon' that 'sidled up over the dark eastern shoulder of the moor'. The passage in which Gillian and Elmer come to Weeping Cross 'over the lovely levels, the steep descents of the moor' is typical of the many evocative descriptions in the novel:

> They came through the green places and the brown; they traversed the near and attained the far purple distance, and it melted before them and became the near. Then they saw a long way off, in a veil of rain, the small shining steeple, the low shining roofs – red and brown and blue – the clustered trees, half in leaf, the nestling ricks, the apple-green fields of Weeping Cross.
>
> (p. 220)

Again the overall view, the effect of far distance, the all-seeing eye coming to focus like a zoom lens on a specific scene, this giving a Hardy-like sense of man's smallness, and of the inconsequential pigmy affairs of the protagonists in the immediate context of lonely hills and sweeping moorland and in the ever-widening context of an unknowable cosmos.

A shared feature of Mary Webb's novels is, of course, the always superb evocation of the Shropshire countryside in all its contrasting aspects and the way in which the characters are revealed in relation to this environment. In this book the relationships of the characters are developed in the vast wild landscape of high moors where the seasons roll on magnificently indifferent to human passions and aspirations, where 'the everlasting whisper of the moor . . . changed into a roar but never died, and . . . was, even at its quietest, like the lisp of one destined to become a conqueror'. There is a pervading sense of the onward sweep of the natural cycle, its beauty, terror and mystery; of dark elemental forces both within man and without in the ancient untamed places – a concentration of which in the 'Unket Place', 'a long narrow cover of stunted larches and birches' known as the 'Gyland', culminates in the murder of Rwth. Robert Rideout's explanation to Gillian of why the 'Gyland' is foreboding, is that of an intuitive countryman :

> 'It's like as if there were places where the Lord o'Darkness comes borsting through, and they bear the mark before and after. Like as if good's thin there – only a croust – and he can come through easy. All the while afore it, the place bodes it. All the while after, it minds it. So it's different from other places for ever and ever.'
>
> (p. 74)

Here we find a synthesis of Mary Webb's preoccupations with folklore, superstition and the problem of evil. She understood, and demonstrated in her novels, how a combination of these, their interaction in the human mind, can weave invisible cross-threads of fate to create a tragic nemesis.

But in her novels, as we have seen, Mary Webb also reveals as strong a sense of comedy as of tragedy, and in *Seven for a Secret* again she creates with humorous relish a group of secondary characters – accident-prone, garrulous Jonathan Makepeace, grim Aunt Fanteague, insipid faded Emily, the strange toothless Fringal – these joining Sarah Jowell, Andrew Vessons, Mrs Marston, Patty Arden and other successfully realised minor characters who contribute so much to the vivid actuality of life in her novels. It is primarily by means of these lesser figures that she gives the sense of contact with a real world.

The major figures of *Seven for a Secret* (apart from Robert Rideout) are more stereotyped: Rideout is the most fully delineated and individualised of the four, and in his portrayal Mary Webb gives further evidence of her ability to create convincing male characters. Like Stephen Southernwood and Jasper Darke, Rideout is young, attractive, full of dynamic potential yet lonely in spirit; but he is also more mature than they are, richer in understanding, acute in his intuitions, aware of his own awareness. A cowman-shepherd, he is close to the earth and responds with a poet's soul to his moorland environment. In Robert Rideout we find a typical 'border mixture' – he is essentially a mingling of Welsh and Salopian and like Mary herself has the Celtic poetic imagination combined with Saxon tenacity. One of the most convincingly drawn aspects of Robert is his innate compulsion to write 'penillions' (poems) and his persistence in learning technique (journeying across the Border for tuition from Gruffyd, an old Welsh bard). Robert's struggle for lyrical expression is well done : Mary Webb is rather ingenious in showing the development of his 'penillions' and in shaping them so that they seem truly to have sprung from his desire to mingle his soul with the moor and with the soul of Gillian. We feel that Robert has indeed written them, and not the author.

It would, of course, be easy to interpret the central characters of *Seven for a Secret* as a fourfold projection of aspects of Mary's personality : Gillian, the embodiment of her thirst for personal success and immortal fame, her strong will and drive; Robert her self-giving love, her poetic imagination unifying with the beauty of earth; Ralph, her sensuality and sexual urge; Rwth, her intense maternal love focused adoringly on one person yet ever extending, madonna-like but impeded from normal human communication by physical disability.

However, such a line of exploration in this particular novel with its overtones of fantasy and deliberately 'larger than life' flavour could be a misleading exercise, for while Mary undoubtedly did draw on self-knowledge in creating these characters, it would be presumption to regard them as anything more than either conscious (perhaps ironic) inflations of parts of her own immensely complex nature, or what Robert Liddell refers to in his *Treatise on the Novel* as 'portraits of potential selves'. It is, however, generally accepted that in creating heroines who in one way or another lack physical beauty – Gillian with her facial blemish ('the scar which seamed one side of her forehead and gave that profile an intent, relentless look'), Amber Darke plain and sallow, Prudence Sarn marred by a hare-lip – Mary is symbolising her own disfigurement, her sense of physical inferiority.

But in contrast to Amber and Prudence, Gillian Lovekin has nothing of the mystic in her, and the scar which adds to her 'relentless' look yet does not spoil her attractiveness, is emblematic of her flawed character : by this she knows herself to be 'a child of sin' and behaves accordingly, pursuing her ruthless, egoistic path, playing 'the Devil's May-games' with the affections of her aunt's suitor, Mr Gentle (who dies as a result), with Robert, and, to her cost, with Ralph. Gillian, in this contest between light and the powers of darkness, finally comes through. But 'the secret', of course, is never told :

> Is there more? Out in the early summer morning, listening to the silence, you know that there is more . . . Every sigh of the mystic, every new word of science is fraught with it. Yet its haunts are further away than time or space or consciousness . . . It may be that death reveals it. Certainly life cannot . . .

The sense of the 'secret that's never been told', the inescapable mystery, runs throughout Mary Webb's work : she conveys in all her novels the beauty shrouding that secret, the mystery wherein it moves.

Seven for a Secret, published 27 October 1922, gained wider, more lengthy critical attention than any of her previous novels. The reviews, while containing the usual mixed comments, were on the whole far more favourable than those of *The House in Dormer Forest*.

Perhaps the most perceptive review was that in the *Spectator* (11 November 1922), by Martin Armstrong. Its heading, 'The Heart of the Country', epitomises what he regards as the book's chief success: 'On laying down *Seven for a Secret* our first impression is that we have penetrated deeply and intimately into the country . . . Of her characters, too, we feel that they have grown out of the country of which the author is so passionately aware – are, as it were, materializations of the wild places from which she can so seldom turn her attention." This review gives recognition of Mary Webb's 'acute sensibility' but points out the novel's failure 'on its psychological side' which 'is not always sufficient to its theme'. The concluding comments are interesting :

> Mrs Webb has not, we believe, yet given us her best book. . . . If we have appeared over-critical it is because we have felt it due to Mrs Webb to judge her by high standards.

Gerald Gould in the *Saturday Review* (2 December, 1922), admired in Mary Webb's work 'that rare and exquisite gift – a naturally beautiful style : words seem to run to do her bidding . . . passages . . . which have the thrill of poetry. She can write about nature without being unnatural.' But he saw serious defects in

Seven for a Secret (its 'hackneyed plot, its lack of spontaneity') –
in his opinion a novel which while 'melodious and charming, yet
cannot rank with, or near, *Gone to Earth*'.

Raymond Mortimer in the *New Statesman* (27 January, 1923),
while admitting that he did not like 'country life as opposed to
country house life', allowed that 'it becomes apparent even to my
immensely inexpert eye that Mrs Webb knows the country intimately and describes it honestly'. Although she gives a 'comfortable' view of rustic life when compared with Zola, she writes 'just
as candidly' and 'if her picture is brighter it is because she is
herself a countrywoman, and country sensibilities are different,
though not necessarily more obtuse'.

Mary could not have been dissatisfied with these reviews or
with American critical response when the novel was published
there by Doran's (June 1923), especially as reviewers were now
accepting her as a poetic novelist, notable for her style and evocation of nature. Although *Seven for a Secret* was to be no more
successful with the public than *The House in Dormer Forest*, it
did contribute considerably to the growth of her reputation
among reviewers and in London literary circles.

Martin Armstrong, then literary editor of the *Spectator*, was
convinced that her finest achievement was still to come. He
helped to expand her literary activity by securing for her, late in
1922, regular reviewing for the *Spectator*. She was engaged to
review natural histories, novels of country life and children's
nature books. Confident in her knowledge of nature, he gave her
the expert's task of reviewing books by distinguished authorities
such as Henri Fabre. She contributed approximately one review
each month between December 1922 and June 1925 (*CPAP*,
pp. 71–92).

In spite of the restrictions of this form of writing, regarded as
'bread and butter' work, Mary brought to it both integrity and
penetration. As St John Adcock who dealt with her *Bookman*
contributions, commented : 'She did a good deal of reviewing,
was an acute and discerning critic, and wrote her reviews with all
the care and grace of fancy and beauty of phrase she put into her
novels.'

Mary certainly took the opportunity criticism afforded to bring
in and expound her own ideas. In her reviews, as in those of
Edward Thomas, the lyricist emerges and sometimes takes over;

she often expresses herself rather than the book under review. Frequently she deals directly with deeper questions such as the nature of soul and of mind, intuition and instinct – in fact thoughts which, as she says in one review, delve 'to the heart of creation'. These interesting digressions have only the thinnest connection with the books she is purporting to discuss – even children's nature books gave her pretext enough to put forward philosophic insights. Her central interests and concerns never varied and she projected her vision of life into all she wrote. So her total output forms a cohesive whole and her *Spectator* reviews stand in significant relation to the main body of her work.

Her engagement to write for this long-established journal was certainly a sign of her growing reputation, and following, as it did, the publication of *Seven for a Secret*, brought her the attention of a wider public. She began by contributing a short essay 'Roots' in the issue of 4 November 1922, and her first review, 'Birds, Beasts and Trees', appeared on 2 December.

Henry was genuinely pleased to see the progress Mary was making, fulfilling something of their expectations that her success would be promoted by living in the capital. He was delighted that her circle of friends was widening, especially when she was invited to Walter de la Mare's Sunday gatherings at Anerley. To Mary this was both a compliment and an honour. She had for long been enchanted by de la Mare's poetry, admiring his nature imagery and his ability to capture the wonder of childhood. The poem 'To a Poet in April' is Mary's tribute to him : 'You speak my joy in silver words/I thought none knew so well, but birds.'

To be given at last some recognition of her poetry was greatly stimulating. Walter de la Mare liked her poems sufficiently to include three ('Green Rain', 'The Water Ousel' and 'Market Day') in his anthology *Come Hither* (1923). This vastly encouraged her. And her poems were appearing in various periodicals, for instance 'An Old Woman', 'The Vagrant', 'When the Thorn Blows' and 'Viroconium' in the *English Review*, 'The Lost Orchard' and 'Praise' in the *Sunday Pictorial*, and 'Green Rain' in the *Spectator*.

Yet hers was a cruel destiny – she was never to have the literary success she strove for so intensely, never to have the gratification of seeing her collection in print or knowing that Walter de la Mare himself would write the Introduction. But perhaps she did

gather during those Sunday meetings at de la Mare's home something of the high regard for her work which he was to express in
that well-known introductory essay.

De la Mare's personal impression of Mary's 'gentle yet ardent'
company reaffirms the word pictures given by others, and adds
another vivid glimpse :

> She brought her own quietness into a room . . . bird-like,
> demure. She loved to listen to others talking quite as much as to
> talk herself, but her own talk had an extraordinary eagerness and
> vivacity. Then her nervousness was no more, and she shared her
> own intense interest and her own happiness.

During one of their literary conversations, de la Mare propounded
to Mary a conundrum : 'What is it that best sellers and geniuses
sometimes have in common which holds the imagination of the
everyday reader?' Mary hazarded in reply – 'Humanity'. As she
said, recalling this in a review article, 'You never find a cold book
becoming popular . . . the ordinary person cannot bear frigidity'.

Mary's London friends were mainly those distinguished men of
letters generous enough to acknowledge that her literary ability
was of a high order. Women writers whom she met tended to be
patronising and superficially friendly. They engaged her in conversation at literary functions but then made adverse criticism or
indulged in paltry analysis (Virginia Woolf and Vita Sackville
West particularly). There were a few exceptions.

Soon after her arrival in London, Mary sought the friendship
of Rebecca West.[4] They had continued to correspond after Miss
West's acclamation of *Gone to Earth* and Mary was eager to
develop a personal relationship. Intellectual, vigorous and lovely,
Rebecca West was one of the first women to be successful in the
male province of journalism. Designated 'the wittiest woman in
London', she was already well-known as novelist and critic. Since
Mary valued Miss West's high opinion of her writing, doubtless
she was immensely encouraged and stimulated during the early
days of their friendship. Miss West, on her part, although some
twelve years younger, had more experience of the world, and
sympathised when hearing from Mary of the seriousness of her

[4] The following account is from Dame Rebecca West's personal recollections as told to the author.

literary effort and her mounting disappointment at public apathy. She admired Mary's determined intentions to succeed, finding this particularly courageous in view of her disease which, at this date, was threatening to take hold again.

Only too well Miss West knew the suffering and severity of Graves' Disease since her own mother was in the grip of it and was then reaching an advanced stage of deterioration. Having this unfortunate experience of the physical havoc wrought by Graves' Disease and its complications, Miss West was concerned for Mary whose self-neglect was obvious. She seemed consumed by her mental energy, her overdriven impulses, her burning pity, impelled on by a relentless interior clockwork that gave no pause. As the months passed, Mary was becoming thinner, increasingly nervous and highly strung, the effects of the disease more pronounced. As Miss West knew, there was now some treatment available for Graves' Disease, but this was only likely to be successful if given in the early stages. Mary refused anyway to have medical attention, usually resenting fiercely any suggestions that she needed it, always driven on by her irreducible will. Eventually it became unbearable for Miss West to observe in Mary signs of this distressing condition from which her mother was then dying – so unbearable that she felt unable to develop a closer friendship. Sometimes when Mary phoned to arrange a meeting, Miss West, not wanting to see her, would make the excuse that she would 'be out' : but uncannily, persistently, Mary whom (as others found) it was 'well nigh impossible to deceive', would turn up on the doorstep just the same. When Miss West left for a lecture tour of America, they continued to correspond, genuinely admiring each other's achievement.

Lady Cynthia Asquith was another who befriended Mary during the first years in London, her love of the countryside attracting her to the novels. Her literary interests were strong, and since 1918 she had been Private Secretary to Sir James Barrie (who lived not far from Mary at Bayswater and was himself very enthusiastic about her writing). At dinner conversations as the guest of Lady Asquith, Mary talked of her work and her hopes. Lady Asquith invited her to social functions where she met celebrities and leading writers of the day. 'I am going to a ball, tomorrow, fancy dress, at the Hyde Park Hotel,' Mary wrote to Mrs Thorne. 'Seemingly, there are to be Ambassadors, Consuls and such people as thick as blackberries. Next day, there is to be a dinner, at which Princess Louise and the French Ambassador will be present.'

At the same time Mary was running into serious financial difficulty. The post-war rise in prices, the cost of keeping Spring Cottage and a London flat, the accumulation of old debts with new ones, were all, of course, important contributory factors. In addition, her £100 allowance was now effectively worth far less, while Henry's salary at the King Alfred School was exceptionally low.

The major reason for Mary's shortage of money was her lavish generosity to the London poor. She was giving almost all she possessed, and was then in distress to meet the needs of herself and Henry. In desperation, and without telling him, she turned to her influential friends, hoping they might help. At first they did. Lady Asquith acted very promptly, probably feeling that Mary needed support of every kind. A letter of Mary's to Mrs Thorne in November 1921 reveals a great deal:

> Lady Asquith rang me up last week to ask me to lunch and to say that somebody very much wanted to know if a hundred pounds would be any use to me! So I accepted it as a loan, as we were very short while waiting for the American money. She said the only thing was that I mustn't ask his name. And she said that he was so well off he wouldn't know he'd spent anything at all.

Neither the unknown benefactor – thought to be a well-established writer – nor Lady Asquith herself had then any inkling of Mary's plans for the £100. Immediately she provided her brother with 'another good cheque'. Henry, of course, was not neglected: Mary, always anxious about his health, informed Mrs Thorne that he was 'a lot better' and that she had bought him 'a mackintosh with a woollen lining to take out in warm weather, so he is ever so cosy and there is no weight in it'. But this was a minimal expense. Most of the loan was spent in an effort 'to save a consumptive boy and his family by sending them to the sea' – Mary's prime objective on delightedly receiving the money. She had befriended the family who were living in sordid conditions, greatly pitying their plight, both child and mother ill, the father out of work. Mary eagerly supplied their train fares, board and lodging for a fortnight, and food parcels, expending time, energy and money in arranging the whole thing. Her letter to Mrs Thorne continues :

> They couldn't go as they had no money. So now I can pay their fares and rooms for a fortnight and food till they can get work. It will save the boy, living at the sea, and also, I think, the mother who looks very ill. It has been their one longing, to get away from their one room in a back street. So now they'll be able to sit out by the sea and get strong, and she will be able to sell her knitted things, which are just what people want at the sea.

Unfortunately for Mary, the needy were not always appreciative of her efforts and preyed upon her kindness. This particular family wrote complaining letters and asked for more money which, needless to say, Mary gave. Eventually they sold the things she had provided and returned to a London slum. Such ingratitude did not have the effect of hardening Mary's heart. Rather the reverse : it increased her pity but also a gnawing feeling of futility. As Hilda Addison has said, 'unselfishness on Mary's scale is a very expensive virtue'. Certainly it was difficult for those around her to understand it, especially those who, feeling sorry for her pathetic state – financial worry, fragile health, lack of material success – gave her substantial 'loans' which she so rapidly dissipated. She dissipated their patience too.

How far was Henry exasperated by Mary's compulsive giving? That the 'loans' were an embarrassment to him when he heard about them cannot be doubted. He had watched her great sympathy for the poor and afflicted develop over the years into this uncontrollable compassion. Yet he of all people, nearest to Mary, could best understand her desperate need to extend to others, to be one of 'the sick world's factories of peace'. He knew how tenderly, fiercely she desired to give balm. His attitude was one of unusual tolerance and patience : appreciative of this, Mary loved him all the more passionately. Their area of mutual understanding was, in fact, far wider and deeper than outside observers realised. At least this was so for the greater part of their married life.

In the early years of their relationship they had greatly admired in each other that splendid will for the simple life as lovers of Nature, focusing on inner experience and development, maintaining a dauntless disregard for the temporal, material values of the world. Yet their individual development during fifteen years of marriage brought them on increasingly divergent paths. Mary never deviated from that active philosophy of existence which had gradually crystallised within her even before she met Henry. Rather did her vision of life intensify and its active expression stretch to the limits. For at its core her view of human existence arose from her innate mystical temperament and the acuteness of her pity and her passion. As she progressed in an ever-deepening mysticism by the unswerving tendency of her nature, so in resultant degree was her behaviour and outlook affected. After experience of mystical unity, on her 'return' to the everyday world with its multiplicity and stress, Mary's desire, like that of all true mystics, was (using Dame Julian's words) 'to be naughted of all things that are made' – and more than this, to give a practical extension of love as an answer to the pain and misery of humanity. Mary saw love and suffering entwined at the heart of human experience. To assuage, to give, was her way of coming to the centre of realities. Henry understood something of this, and allowing for her exceptional nature and talents, he accepted what to others seemed extremes and extravagances verging on madness.

Mary never desired for herself more than the bare necessities. Apart from a sentimental attachment to certain objects – her grandfather clock, Henry's 'fount-pen', her mother's ring, a gun-metal watch from Kenneth, the silver teapot given by her father – her most valued possessions were her books, and of these she had relatively few, not more than thirty and nearly all presents from relatives and friends.[5] Their home was frugal and she made her own clothes – in old-fashioned styles which became more out-dated as the 'gay' Twenties advanced. This disregard of self was reflected in her appearance: blouses, skirts and gowns 'once-turned', darned, invariably dark or a shade of her favourite purple, relieved by flimsy scarves or enormous untidy bows of fly-away material around her throat.

Yet she made sure that Henry never looked shabby. As his colleagues have recalled, while he was not richly dressed, neither

[5] *News Chronicle*, 28 April 1938; and Elkin Matthews. Her small library of 'shabby wellworn volumes . . . her daily companions', heavily annotated and marked, included Everyman editions, Chaucer, Milton, George Herbert, Sir Thomas Browne, two volumes of Browning, a work by Spinoza, Gilbert White's *Natural History of Selborne*, novels by Jane Austen, three books of legends.

was he the reverse. This was in keeping with the intense attention of which he was the focus. Staff of the King Alfred School at that date clearly remember how Mary would arrive there breathless having hurried down over the heath with Henry's mackintosh if rain threatened; and how she would telephone him during the day on any slight pretext, trying desperately to keep in touch.

Mary, however, was an easy target for criticism, for ridicule. Villagers, for instance, practical countrywomen who did not understand anything of the relationship of Mary and Henry, liked to gossip about her odd appearance and ways, her 'neglect' of her husband – 'busy at her books' . . . 'she never bothered to feed him' . . . 'didn't look after him properly' . . . 'never darned his socks'. And in London she was criticised in more sophisticated terms, with a subtle, polite abuse from certain quarters and a definite hostility from others (Henry's family, especially his mother and his sister Ethel Shelley, continued to dislike her).

But Henry too was unambitious in the worldly sense. He preferred, when not teaching, to go about in very old clothing, relaxed in comfortable corduroys and well-worn jackets, particularly during evenings by the fire reading, writing or conversing with his usual ready wit (a slightly satirical sense of humour) and relishing rounds of his favourite 'bread and cheese'. Content with a very low salary at the King Alfred School, he would never dream of asking for a higher rate – he had accepted the post knowing that the rewards would be in terms of satisfaction and fulfilment, not money.

It must also be remembered when considering Henry's reaction to Mary's wild generosity and their financial chaos, that he had always willingly left the management of household affairs entirely in her hands – and with it the financial worrying. It was she who paid the rent, settled the bills, arranged to pay off debts little by little. Yet faced by the straitened circumstances of life in post-war London, Henry's tolerance was slowly being eroded – the situation exacerbated by the additional financial strain of the upkeep of two homes.

Fundamentally though, it was not financial stress or similar factors that made their paths diverge. While Mary, constantly insecure, over-anxious, easily cast down, prey to suspicions, was difficult to live with, Henry was patient, as he knew so intimately her sad-sweet nature, her acute sensitivity and the agony which was intrinsic to her love; he was aware how keenly and gratefully she appreciated what he called 'the peace of being understood' – for her a 'rare peace'. It was rather that his own development was leading him, especially in his thirties, away from his early ideals and aspirations, and eventually – in London – away from Mary.

Their relationship had been an exceptionally close one : in 'the nest of love' they had only each other, sharing their thoughts and feelings, working in harmony, gardening, writing, walking, watching together 'the splendid seasons'. While they lived at Lyth Hill there was no serious threat of disintegration in this pattern – no threat from within, although Mary constantly dreaded that outer force from 'the world' which might 'break in' and 'rob our treasury'. But on coming to London they came to grips with 'the heavy-handed world' and soon their relationship was subjected to pressures which severely strained it and tested its durability.

Henry's love of nature and of solitude professed in *The Silences of the Moon*, had always been intellectually based and was not an essential part of his emotional and creative life as it was of Mary's. In London he did not pine for the Shropshire countryside and their former way of life as Mary did. On the contrary, he became increasingly caught up in a socially oriented existence, desiring now a broader, more stimulating and sophisticated milieu. While Mary was satisfied with his company alone, he was needing to expand into a circle of his own. He began to feel cramped in his marriage; their closeness was having a claustrophobic effect.

There were several factors aggravating this situation, one of which was that Bayswater was not very convenient for his school on the fringes of Hampstead Heath. And wishing to take part in school affairs during evenings, Henry felt inhibited knowing how worried and fraught Mary became if he stayed out too long.[6]

For the first time in his career, Henry was truly enthusiastic about school life and activities, enjoying and sustaining a wholehearted commitment. K.A.S. suited him very well. There were less than a hundred pupils when he joined the school and the

---

[6] The entire staff was animated by a spirit of enthusiasm for K.A.S. educational aims and took part in committees dealing with special matters such as 'propaganda' (promotion of the ideas of the Society) and finance, as well as being actively concerned in close liaison with parents.

small numbers facilitated the progress of studies on a teacher-pupil, one-to-one relationship. This method was the ideal one for Henry who preferred to be tutor rather than class teacher, excelling at 'drawing out' his pupils. Kind and patient, he soon established himself as a favourite with girls and boys alike. His fashionable moustache added to his physical appeal, and he projected a lively, up-with-the-minute personality to which the children readily responded. The staff too formed a high opinion of him, as charming, cultured, exceptionally modest about his own abilities, reserved concerning his personal life. That special, rather boyish brightness which Mary loved so dearly, his infectious laughter and brilliant smile won all hearts at K.A.S.

Mary's sense of threat intensified as she felt that Henry's need for her was diminishing. Much of the strain on their relationship was caused by her acute insecurity, the feeling of dread that she would lose him : life for her was lived on a keen knife edge – 'like taking a pauper's penny and throwing it to and agen o'er a pond'. She was only too well aware of the strain on Henry of coping with her intensities; she saw clearly how patient he had been. But perhaps he would tire of this and want a more normal, fuller life in the world's accepted everyday way? Her level of reality, as she lived it to her cost, was certainly not the everyday plane. Again the vicious circle of insecurity, the sharp fear of losing Henry, that he would weary of her, seek the bright company of some golden-haired girl.

The rift between them was developing, although it had not yet reached the stage of crisis. Their next move was made in an effort to ease the strain – they decided early in 1923 to leave 'Tower-of-Babel Square' and live at Hampstead.

Hampstead – and *Precious Bane*

1923–1926

> . . . how all things grow estranged
> 'Magic' (*51*, p. 50)

> Sing on, dear bird! Bring the old rapturous pain,
> In this great town, where I no welcome find.
> Show me the murmuring forest in your mind,
> And April's fragile cups, brimful of rain.
> O sing me far away, that I may hear
> The voice of grass, and, weeping, may be blind
> To slights and lies and friends that prove unkind.
> Sing till my soul dissolves into a tear,
> Glimmering within a chaliced daffodil.
> So, when the stately sun with burning breath
> Absorbs my being, I'll dream that he is Death,
> Great Death, the undisdainful. By his will
> No more unlovely, haunting all things fair,
> I'll seek some kinder life in the golden air.
> 'To a Blackbird Singing in London' (*PSJ*, p. 84)

'Transplanting to London did not suit her' – Henry's retrospective comment was a gross understatement. The truth of it, however, must have been increasingly evident to him from 1921 onwards. This London period was, in fact, disastrous for her health and personal life.

The move from Bayswater to Hampstead did seem, at first, to offer a brighter prospect. Mary liked the more leafy surroundings and atmosphere of the district and Henry of course was now very near his school. She could eagerly await his early arrival home each evening, or go down through the trees to meet him as she used to do at Lyth Hill. And possibly she would find solace, when missing Shropshire, in the high sprawling heath, that natural observatory for sky and woodland.

They rented a diminutive terraced cottage in The Grove, one of the narrow streets lined by lime trees near the top of the hill, very close to the heath. At 5 The Grove, there were two tiny rooms downstairs, two bedrooms above, and a basement below where a fire could be lit in a large hearth to heat the whole cottage. Outside, the smallest imaginable strip of garden was dominated by a lime tree, and here the blackbird of her poem sang, evoking for her a 'murmuring forest' and the yearning for 'some kinder life in the golden air'. In this brief little garden she could again grow flowers which would sweeten her room. She planted lilies, sweet peas and violets, three of her favourites. But she did not know then that, after caring for these in their growth as tenderly as if they were children, after the joy of sitting outdoors among their scented presences as she typed her manuscripts, she would look down from the small upstairs window early one morning, shocked to find her garden bare and bereft. Thieves were to come in the night, not once but on several occasions, heartlessly taking every flower and bud; these would then be sold at street corners or door to door – a mean and particularly cruel blow to one who so passionately loved flowers and people as Mary did. The garden thefts sharply upset and depressed her, such disappointments becoming harder to bear as the state of her health and nerves was crumbling.

In 1923 however, the move to 5 Grove Cottages still held promise of a more settled and happy period: Mary's literary career was unquestionably benefiting from the contacts made in London and she was beginning work on the novel which was to be regarded as her masterpiece.

One of the assets of living at Hampstead was its literary atmosphere. Here Mary was in close proximity to famous contemporaries such as Galsworthy, only a few yards away at Admiral's Walk. Their own cottage had been occupied fairly recently by Catherine Carswell who was visited there by D. H. Lawrence. And it pleased Mary to know that Edwin Pugh and his wife Laura were near neighbours. Pugh, then a dapper little man in his late forties, had become one of Mary's most fervent admirers and drew attention to her novels in an enthusiastic article. It was the first critical article on her in a literary journal, and appeared in the *Bookman* 'Gallery'. Pugh began courageously: 'To pass from the work of the average modern novelist to the work of Mary Webb is like stepping out of a stuffy room into the fresh air.' Then followed a whole-hearted acclamation of her genius. Mary could be excused for thinking naively that 'her name was now made', since Pugh had proclaimed: 'Mary Webb is one of the greatest of English novelists in this genre.'

Early in 1923 he sent her a copy for approval before it came out in the April issue. He related later her reaction: 'She went half crazy over it. "That anyone should write about me – Me! – like that!" she cried brokenly. "It doesn't seem real. I feel I must have dreamt it." '

His assessment was based on the four published novels:

> She has the full dower of poet and seer: wit and wisdom, humour and fancy, the twin senses of tragedy and comedy.

In 1923 her most successful novel, *Precious Bane,* was still to be written. Admiring her 'clear-sightedness and poise', Pugh saw too that 'there never was an author in closer kinship with nature'. He understood how intensely she lived in 'The Land Within' – as she herself called it – even when physically present in London, her mind and spirit tending always to Shropshire: 'She still lives in Shropshire and has her being in her beautiful dreams – as one likes to think of our immigrant birds away from England.'

During 1923–4 Edwin Pugh was a frequent visitor at the Webbs' cottage and came to know Mary fairly intimately. Though he had refused to take her to the London slums, he was pleased to show her 'some of the less-known beauties of Hampstead Heath'. They went for walks over the sand-pits beyond the Spaniards Road and Mary was 'amazed, delighted. She had never dreamt that so wild and picturesque a piece of countryside could be found so near to London'. Pugh gives a memorable description of Mary on one of these walks:

> . . . flitting like a blue moth hither and thither among the trees and undergrowth, calling to me and bidding me to share her exultation. We came upon a tree which seemed to me an unusual sort of tree. I asked her, 'What tree was that?' She rounded

astonished eyes at me. 'Surely, Ned,' she exclaimed, 'you know a
wild cherry when you see one.' I confessed that I knew little of
the lore of the countryside. And I think for a minute or two she
was not only surprised but even a little disdainful of my
ignorance.   (*The Bookman,* July 1928, pp. 193–6)

She admired Pugh nevertheless and always spoke of him as 'a tall
man', even though he was very much the reverse. This was typical
of her insight into the inner self, her penetration through the
'outward aspect'. Once when Pugh pointed out to her that he
was 'a little man' she turned her 'large questioning eyes' on him.
Pugh described occasions at her cottage when –

> a visitor would drift in; and then, if he were her sort of man
> (as she used to say) she would talk. She talked well, but not much.
> She seemed to prefer to listen. She was so modest, retiring, so
> unsure of herself that she seemed half afraid to express herself
> freely . . . except when she was alone with what she called a dear
> acquaintance, and then she would be at once gravely earnest,
> almost impassioned, when she was not venting her inborn gifts of
> inimitable wit and humour.

Pugh, most certainly a 'dear acquaintance', introduced Mary to
the Dickens Fellowship, of which he was a leading member. She
was elected to the Fellowship in 1924, and Pugh accompanied
her to the annual Dickens Ball at Caxton Hall. She went charm-
ingly dressed as Madeline from *Nicholas Nickleby*, in a gown she
had made. It was just before Christmas and she had photos taken
in the period gown and bonnet, subsequently sending some as
Christmas cards, one going to Minoni 'with my love, Gagga'. One
wonders what Minoni thought on seeing this, as it reveals how
frail and thin Mary had become; her expression too is sad and
intent, showing something of the strain of financial and other
personal difficulties which were intensifying at this time.

The Dickens Ball, however, was a pleasurable occasion. She
liked to mingle with literary celebrities and keep up these contacts, even though to do so was a struggle financially. Her delight
at having been made a member of the Fellowship is expressed in
letters to friends. And in January 1925 her short poem of tribute
to Charles Dickens appeared in *The Dickensian*. Edwin Pugh was
one of the first critics to recognise the humour in Mary's work
and to liken it to that of Dickens: 'the humour that springs

from creation of character.' Pugh counted her among 'the few real humorists of the twentieth century'. As Hilda Addison pointed out, she had 'a vivid power of unfolding humour and pathos together' and this often 'took shape in some peasant character'. In her amused and tender understanding of rustics, in her crisp delineation of them, and her warm intimate laughter with them, Mary Webb surpasses the gloomy Hardy. She saw much comedy in life, this reflected in her work, an undercurrent which often bubbles obviously to the surface when joy is present, and becomes, when tinged with pain, a deeper ironic wit.

On one occasion Edwin Pugh was impelled to speak of her *extempore* at an important literary gathering of which 'the star' was another woman novelist who had, as Pugh put it, 'done excellent work and reaped her full reward in praise and pence'. Mary was there with Pugh and Laura, the hall packed. Sitting on the floor, Pugh (as he related later) heard 'speaker after speaker not only beslaver the star of the evening but almost every other popular woman novelist'. Spontaneously, he scrambled to his feet and told the surprised audience that 'though the women novelists who had been cited were all worthy of respect, there was a far greater novelist than any of them, and her name was Mary Webb'. This 'extraordinary performance' by Ned caused Mary to weep on Laura's shoulder. Fortunately, in her emotion she did not notice 'the few tepid sentences of that faint praise that spells damnation' which followed his 'outburst'. She was overcome to hear such acclaim at a time when she was plummeting into an increasingly bitter despair of ever gaining public recognition and serious critical attention.

Her unrewarded struggle for success was regretted by others too. St John Adcock, writing after her death, discussed that 'something of greatness' in her novels, her 'uncanny understanding' and 'a beauty of style that none of her contemporaries surpassed'. He spoke of the unfortunate situation during her life when reviewers, giving her no special attention, grudgingly acknowledged on the whole that her books were very good, but showed no enthusiasm about them. Adcock maintained that this was lamented by the 'discriminating' of whom there were more than has been thought, for 'such work as hers could not fail of appreciation'. But the confirmation of such evaluation had to wait until the chorus of approval that followed Baldwin's praise, and that came too late for Mary herself. As Adcock said, Pugh had been 'very much a voice crying in the wilderness'. He did not stop after his public 'performance', but 'courageously and persistently . . . proclaimed her genius in reviews for the *Bookman*'.

Among her American admirers, Ellery Sedgwick (editor of the *Atlantic Monthly*) recognised the 'delicate individuality' of her work, 'the perception and complete fidelity which underlay each page'. Visiting her at Hampstead in 1923, he was impressed by her courage and determination : 'Something about her compelled a sympathy that went deeper than awareness of her once-turned gown and her mended gloves, each with a tiny hole inside the thumb. These spoke her poverty and not her will.' In the 'toy parlour' of the 'tiny house' they talked 'of true success and what it might mean' and Mary spoke about 'the inspiration of places, of Wenlock Edge and the dear delights of Shropshire'. Clearly, 'London was a desert to her'.

Leaving behind these 'wastes' of the metropolis, Mary returned with Henry to Spring Cottage for the summer of 1923. Her letters written from there to literary people in London reveal her joy at being back on Lyth Hill. In August she wrote to St John Adcock: 'They are harvesting in the plain today and from here to the blue ring of hills there is mile upon mile of golden light on golden fields' . . . 'Last night . . . it was so beatific that I thought we had come to heaven unbeknown to ourselves.' And in a typical postscript to another letter to St John Adcock, she adds that she is sending some flowers for his daughter and wishes that she 'could also include the birdsong – so loud and sweet morning and evening'.

Renewing her immersion in the familiar countryside, she spent many hours of that summer at Bomere Pool, gathering inspiration and detail for the novel which was to be regarded as the peak of her literary achievement – *Precious Bane*.

She had been contemplating and preparing this novel for a long time, as usual carefully planning the setting, plot and characters. At Lyth Hill, spiritually renewed, a ferment of composition possessed her once more. She took three months to write *Precious Bane*, and according to her family she made a draft of the last chapter first – an indication of how thoroughly she had worked out the whole book, if not on paper, certainly in her mind. And we feel from the novel's opening sentence – 'It was at a love-spinning that I saw Kester first' – that the entire story has been held within her, awaiting only the onrush of creative energy. As Hilda Addison commented (pp. 76–7):

> The book opens with one of those simple sentences which haunt the mind until the curiosity thus aroused has been satisfied . . . It strikes a note which never fails throughout; it opens with a beauty which is justified to the last sentence. That is one of the most remarkable things about *Precious Bane*. Many excellent novels have their flats and shallows, but here Mary Webb consistently soared at the same height. The book might have been written at one sitting, so perfectly has she captured a mood. Before inspiration had time to fold its wings she has told her swiftly moving story.

Although begun at Lyth Hill, it was written mainly during the autumn of 1923 at Hampstead where, again isolated from her countryside, she drew on her inner vision, recreating with great richness and clarity of descriptive detail the life and countryside of the Shropshire meres. One feels that the lyrical intensity of this novel set at 'Sarn Mere' has sprung directly from the inspiration of those hours she spent contemplating in the uncanny stillness of Bomere itself, at one with its brooding atmosphere and haunting loveliness. The book seems indeed to have been written there instead of, remarkably, in a city environment under London skies. Stanley Baldwin was to say of this in his 1928 Introduction:

> Her sensibility is so acute and her power over words so sure and swift that one who reads some passages in Whitehall has almost the physical sense of being in Shropshire cornfields.

Separation from her landscape resulted, as it had done at Weston-super-Mare, in bringing concentrated inner focus: her 'land within' was a distillation of Shropshire, all that it had given her in quickening of the senses, in shaping of her spirit, in nurturing of mystical love; a country of the soul and the imagination vitally real with its own intense reality.

Set in nineteenth-century Shropshire in the decade of Waterloo, *Precious Bane* is narrated by Prudence Sarn who, as a 'very old woman and a tired woman, with a task to do before she says good night to this world', looks back, telling her own story woven with the tragic story of her brother Gideon. The title – taken from Milton's *Paradise Lost* (I. 690–2 : 'Let none admire/That riches grow in Hell; that soyle may best/Deserve the pretious bane') – held a personal significance for Mary Webb, and is appropriate to the stories of both Prudence and Gideon Sarn. Prudence's bane is her disfigurement – a 'hare-shotten lip' – the affliction which brings her to a mystical 'blessedness she might otherwise never have found' (this clearly a reflection of her creator's own experience); Gideon's bane is gold – his lust for wealth and ruthless determination to acquire it by means of the potential (and actual) gold of corn.

Generations of Sarns – sullen, dark, said to 'have the lightning in their blood' – have farmed at the mere, an eerie place where people are afraid to go after dusk because of the 'frittening', and where the 'thin sound of bells' comes over the water, seemingly echo bells from the old church at the far end of the mere or ghost bells from the village drowned 'beneath the furthest deeps'. When Father Sarn dies of a stroke in a fit of anger, Gideon, at seventeen, takes over the farm, becoming his father's 'Sin Eater' at the funeral in return for his mother's promise of undisputed possession of the land. Tall and powerful, with cold grey eyes 'like the mere in winter', Gideon seems older than his years, 'set' in his mind and ways, a 'driver'. Ambitious for power and position, his obsessive aim is to make 'a mort of money' out of Sarn by working the land, then to sell it and buy a fine house in Lullingford. He makes Prue pledge herself to a life of unquestioning, unremitting toil on the farm – her reward, when his goal is achieved, will be the purchase of a cure for her hare-lip (then thought to be the sign of a witch). Because she wishes to have, one day, a husband and 'a babe in a cot of rushes' and 'be queen' in her own skep, Prue agrees to do all that he asks. But when she takes a vow to him on the Book, she feels a sense of foreboding 'as if Sarn Mere was flowing right over us'. Part of Gideon's plan is that Prue should learn to read, write and keep accounts, taking lessons from Beguildy, the local wizard : she is 'joyfully willing' as this is 'like a big window opening'.

Gideon spares neither himself nor anyone else in his drive for wealth. After a few years of hard work and thrift, his rick yards are filled with corn; he falls in love with his childhood friend, the blonde Jancis, daughter of Beguildy. They are betrothed, and at the love-spinning[1] Prue meets, and loves at once, 'a man to die for' – the Weaver, Kester Woodseaves, who discerns her beauty of spirit. The love of Kester for Prue is 'the one maister-thread of pure gold' in this tapestry of dark and light. Gideon comes to his hour of choice when Jancis is to be sent away by Beguildy to be hired as a dairymaid at the Hiring Fair: she too is sacrificed to Gideon's ambition as, giving her 'the nay-word', he puts off marrying her because she and 'the babies' would be more mouths to feed. His greed grows, and encouraged by the Corn Laws he turns more and more land over to corn. Meanwhile Prue reveals her love for Kester by saving his life at the bull-baiting (when he takes on the savage dogs to put a stop to 'the cruelty').

When Jancis breaks her apprenticeship and flees back to Gideon, he agrees to marry her a week after the harvest if it is a good one. It seems as though his fortune is made as the rich golden grain is gathered in: contented at last, he awaits the valuer. But not waiting for the wedding, he takes Jancis to bed – and all is lost in a single night when the ricks are fired by her enraged father, Beguildy. The harvest is consumed in the flames and with it 'the very stuff of Gideon's soul'. After this, his nature hardens beyond reach – hating Jancis (' "Like father like child" ') he totally rejects her, and in the dark winter months that follow, he poisons his ageing mother because she can no longer work for her keep. Finally, when Jancis returns with their baby, Gideon spurns them both, wanting 'neither the one nor the other'. Jancis drowns herself and the baby in the mere. From then on, Gideon is haunted by the ghost of his mother and even more by the ghosts of Jancis and her child until he commits suicide, following them into the mere. The next day is the yearly fair at Sarn – Prue, after a night of 'grief and fear' decides to leave the farm and take the flocks and herds to be sold at the fair. The superstitious local people, led by Prue's enemies, blame her for the deaths at Sarn, accusing her of evil eye and witchcraft (' "Three times a murderess! . . . Suffer not a witch to live!" '). The crowd seizes Prue and ties her in a ducking stool – half-drowned, she is rescued at the last moment by Kester who carries her away on his saddle and kisses her 'full on the mouth'.

---

[1] The 'love-spinning' was a custom which died out as the nineteenth century advanced. In that period of domestic industry, the neighbours of a bride-to-be would gather at her home and do a day's spinning for 'love'.

A summary brings out only the sensational, melodramatic lines of the plot, but cannot convey the densely wrought texture of this novel or the power and poetry of the vision which informs it. *Precious Bane* is a strange blend of romantic allegory and personal testament; and it is remarkable not so much for what Mary Webb says, but for the way in which she says it.

Again merging reality and unreality, she creates a half-real, half-fantasy world uniquely her own, peopled by figures as like as they are unlike those of the world we know. Her narrative power is as unflagging as in her first two novels, but this – her last completed work – is richer, more complex. Once again she presents those themes, variously embodied in her novels, which give coherence to her imaginative world – universal themes, the significance of suffering, the struggle between spiritual and material values, love and lust, the givers and the takers. Of all her works, *Precious Bane* is most readily comprehensible as a poetic parable. Looked at from another standpoint it is a rather bizarre, historical novel, but certainly far more than just a 'Georgian brew' or period piece. Mary Webb had learned much from Thomas Hardy in her use of a regional past : she took great care in the preparatory research, aiming to incorporate accurate historical detail yet achieve a sense of rural timelessness.

Written when she was reaching her artistic maturity, *Precious Bane* is Mary Webb's most technically perfect novel. She was well suited by the first person narrative form and employed it with unerring sureness of touch, surmounting the considerable technical difficulties of this method. The story unfolds at the same time as the mind of an individual is revealed – a country mind, highly susceptible to superstitition, augury, sign and symbol. There is one centre of consciousness controlling, ordering, unifying the whole : the informing consciousness, the innately poetic sensibility of the narrator Prudence Sarn – that of Mary herself. So Mary's personality and spirit, mirrored in Prudence, permeate the book : the unity of the work radiates from the central figure and from the richly evoked sense of the Shropshire world in which she moves. The filtering of everything through this single, ardent consciousness gives the novel a curious, sustained intensity.

The plot is linear, but Mary Webb makes subtle use of the independence of consciousness from chronological sequence as in telling her story the mind of Prudence Sarn moves back and forth in time, merging past and present experience. Her technique has remarkable fluidity. She achieves depth and penetration by the stylistic device of 'telescoping' from carefully chosen contact points of association and recollection. This gives us some of the most memorable parts of the novel : for instance, the early scene in the kitchen at Sarn, 'all dim like a cave, and the red fire burning still and watchful', a retrospect to when Gideon was seven and Prudence five, Father Sarn in a temper with them (bringing in the first indirect reference to Prudence's hare-lip); or after Gideon's drowning when Prue thinks 'a year back' to the last fair at Sarn when Gideon and Jancis took part in the Wake games (a description which imparts true pathos).

In *Precious Bane* Mary Webb is less overtly didactic than in her previous novels, as her opinions are presented as those of the narrator who indulges in homely moralising and philosophising now and then. Thoughts expressed by Prue are clearly Mary's own : 'When folk grumble about this and that and be not happy, it is not the fault of creation, that is like a vast mere full of good, but it is the fault of their bucket's smallness' (p. 255). 'Times I wonder if heaven will be thus, a long gazing on a face you canna tire of, but must ever have one more glimpse' (p. 169). Such aphoristic remarks do not occur obtrusively as interpolations, but unfold within Prue's story, often as musing afterthoughts or digressions in the telling of her tale. In recounting, for example, the erotic, sensual episode of 'Raising Venus', Prue describes how she self-sacrificingly substitutes for Jancis and is 'crucified in nakedness', hanging by ropes 'in the rosy light' of Beguildy's room – this leading her to consider the question of flesh and spirit.

Further illumination of Mary's attitude to life at this time is given by the yearning undertone in the narration and a sense of the joys and troubles of life intermingled, the tragic note relieved by flashes of humour (usually in descriptions lit by effective similes, such as that depicting the rooks 'sitting each in his tree like Parson in pulpit'). It is essentially a romantic and emotional vision which colours all : as Baldwin rightly said, 'emotional force . . . glows in these pages'. And this (off-putting to some readers) is true of the entire work of Mary Webb – to use Frank Swinnerton's words when commenting on 'the richness' of

Precious Bane, 'her books are all charged with feeling and under-standing of an uncommon order'.[2]

In *Precious Bane*, the interaction between human and land-scape is handled more subtly than in the earlier books. The fusion of the inner world of the individual sensibility and the outer physical world, is now almost imperceptible, giving a greater unity to the novel. Sarn Mere is the essence of Gideon's character as well as the stage for his tragedy. Mary Webb here has mastered her tendency to overdo the use of suggestive atmosphere, to manipulate details of the natural scene as chorus to the action. We have a sense of the shifting seasons moving on beyond the world of the protagonists, passive as well as active in the events. And nowhere in her work does she surpass the descriptive passages threaded throughout this novel which, it is generally agreed, are peculiarly, hauntingly evocative: this, in which she describes the 'discouragement' at Sarn, is typical of many:

> It may be the water lapping, year in and year out – everywhere you look and listen, water; or the big trees waiting and consider-ing on your right hand and on your left; or the unbreathing quiet of the place, as if it was created but an hour gone, and not created for us. (p. 18)

Her symbolism is now more delicate and covert. Here is a passage of central importance:

> So the mere was three times ringed about, as if it had been three times put in a spell. First there was the ring of oaks and larches, willows, ollern trees and beeches, solemn and strong, to keep the world out. Then there was the ring of rushes, sighing thinly, brittle and sparse, but enough, with their long, trembling shadows, to keep the spells in.
> Then there was the ring of lilies . . . (p. 216)

Throughout the novels, her artistic portrayal of her countryside is the product of her spiritual experience. And in *Precious Bane*, the development in her treatment of nature corresponds to a develop-ment in her mysticism – this already discernible in *The House in Dormer Forest*. As she indicated in that novel, she had reached

[2] *The Georgian Literary Scene*, pp. 246–8.

a richer, 'self-poised' mysticism : the 'more vital, the more awake' the human mind, 'the more it must turn inwards. For within, deep in the tenebrous recesses of sub-consciousness, man hopes to find God. Not in churches, not in his fellows, not in nature will he find God until he has seen all these things mirrored in that opaque and fathomless pool, lying within his own being, of which, as yet, we know nothing' (*HDF*, p. 117).

In *Precious Bane* this deepening and extension of her mysticism is clearly reflected in the inward experience of Prudence Sarn who has a vibrant affinity with her surroundings but not the ecstatic communing with nature, the 'mystical exaltation' of Hazel Woodus and Amber Darke. In her last completed novel Mary has gone beyond the pantheistic mysticism which permeates the earlier works and is no longer striving to express her mysticism through descriptions of nature : these are the more effective because her perceptions and similes are as arresting as ever but she is not now straining after her effects. Such is the unique spiritual quality of her art that her own experience of illumination is mirrored in her writing like moonlight on water.

In *Precious Bane* she shows us not only the latest phase of her own spiritual development but also her early bruising : the shock of realising physical inferiority and rejection when eager for life and reaching out to it. So the withdrawal into herself of the young, keenly sensitive Prue who, hurt by the realisation that because of her marred appearance she is cruelly set apart, retreats to the attic 'close under the thatch' where apples and pears are stored and where she first experiences pure mystical intuition :

> There came to me, I cannot tell whence, a most powerful sweetness . . . It was not religious, like the goodness of a text heard at a preaching. It was beyond that. It was as if some creature made all of light had come on a sudden from a great way off, and nestled in my bosom. On all things there came a fair lovely look, as if a different air stood over them. It is a look that seems ready to come sometimes on those gleamy mornings, after rain . . .
>
> For there was nought in it of churches nor of folks, praying nor praising, sinning nor repenting . . . And it was as wilful in its coming and going as a breeze over the standing corn.
>
> (pp. 70–3)

Prue's spiritual sense is awakened :[3] she has found, as Mary had, 'the core of sweetness in much bitter'. The mystic, as Mary said in *The House in Dormer Forest*, steals 'out into the silence of his own being' beyond space and time, and is 'one with the immense freedom' – so the inner world of Prue is rich with spiritual awareness and fruition, symbolised by the apple-filled attic which, to her, is 'parlour and church both'. Such mysticism burns within like an enclosed light. Her first experience of this 'visitation', Prue tells us, 'changed my life' : she is able to reconcile herself to her physical disfigurement, thinking 'how all this blessedness of the attic came through me being curst' (the value that inheres in suffering is another meaning of the title, *Precious Bane*). The visionary aspect blends with the humanly warm, giving this work timeless value and relevance. As Margaret Lawrence maintained, in her interesting study of women writers, *The School of Femininity*, 'Mary Webb is the greatest of the women mystics writing in English'.

Precious Bane is projected more fully and directly than any of the preceding novels from the centre of Mary Webb's experience. Prudence Sarn, possessed of her creator's mysticism and intense emotionalism, has also her deep need for unitive experience in human relationship. With a desire grounded in humility, Prudence longs for a lover, a 'Master' to whom she will surrender her total being – and she finds such a man in the Weaver, Kester Woodseaves. In her mystical unitive state, Prue's spiritual love has no religious focus; but in her love relationship with Kester, she unconsciously blends her image of a lover with Christ's image. Kester, seen through Prue's eyes, is a Christ-like figure – 'the very marrow of Him that loved the world so dear !' At the bull-baiting he fulfils Prue's vision of him when he takes the place of the bull which is to be set on, prepared to sacrifice himself in his solitary crusade against cruelty (and subsequently suffering persecution by Grimble, Huglet and others). There are several parallels and allusions to the crucifixion in this central episode in which Kester sheds his blood.

Kester Woodseaves is, like Michael Hallowes in the previous novel, another variation on the symbolic 'Flockmaster' figures of *The Golden Arrow* – John Arden and the redeemed Stephen

---

[3] The medieval religious meaning of the name Prudens is 'one endowed with the capacity of perceiving divine truth'.

Southernwood. Mary Webb's own passionate archetypal projection, still possessing her mind and imagination, is clearly reflected here – her obsessive love, first for her father and then for Henry. Kester (as the Meredith family have affirmed) is based on Henry, and the novel is dedicated 'to my dear H.B.L.W.'. Like Henry, Kester has 'a kind of arrowy look' and 'a voice that made its own summer'. Prue, admiring his 'silent power', is caught in his spell, but she is dominated by two opposing male figures – the dark negative force of Gideon as well as the light positive power of Kester (these, in Jungian terms, being 'animus' projections). While Gideon's materialistic ambition leads to destruction, Kester's ambition is purely creative – to learn 'the coloured weaving' (weaving is symbolic of the creative Eros, making meaningful connections).

In the character of Kester, Mary Webb was attempting – as with Michael Hallowes – to embody a higher reality and, in so doing, to demonstrate the human potentiality of inner wholeness. Both Kester and Michael are integrated personalities, balanced in their totality, having, as a result, considerable vitality and charisma; both are keenly perceptive (Kester sees Prue's loveliness of inner self, as Michael has the shining soul of Amber Darke); and both transcend their environment. These characters lack, however, the human complexity and substance of their early counterparts, John Arden and Stephen Southernwood, and in considering this we arrive at a central problem in Mary Webb's literary art: at this stage of her artistic development, she was striving to create characters representative of a higher, extended consciousness, expressive of her vision of wholeness, but she had not yet succeeded in investing these with true human presence – they do not seem to act out of a complete existence. Hence the criticism that these figures are not convincing portrayals, do not 'develop', are little more than abstractions or stereotype. Yet Mary Webb had considerable ability in character creation, manifest in her acutely observed and vivified lesser characters. Had she lived longer, she may well have surmounted this difficulty (as her unfinished novel indicates), and successfully combined in her central figures both the embodiment of a valid higher reality and full, vivid presence as real people. In a letter to Jonathan Cape (Easter Monday, 1924), answering his criticism of certain phrases in *Precious Bane* (and explaining that such 'defects' came 'of my being absorbed in telling the tale'), she made an interesting comment about Kester which gives us one of the few insights we have into her own thoughts about her work – and refers in particular to this artistic struggle in portraying a character who was conceived more in the spirit of the twentieth century than that of the historical period in which the novel is set :

> The chief thing that worries me is that Kester is not sufficiently subdued to the canvas. I mean that as he can't be submerged in the atmosphere like the others, he sometimes climbs out of it altogether . . . Partly it is because he can't talk much. It is not in his character. Therefore the few things he says should be perfect, and as they can't be perfect in the archaic way of the rest, it is difficult to do them properly. But the present breathing space will help me, I think.

In this novel, Mary Webb perfected her unique literary style – a poetic style, of 'exceptional flexibility', as Frank Swinnerton said; in fact the critics are in agreement that in this respect at least, *Precious Bane* is a remarkable book. The fusion of Shropshire dialect and natural speech with evocative descriptive prose is perfect for the expression of Prudence Sarn's (and Mary's) reflective mind and emotional sensibility, innately disposed to see allegorical meaning.

The language, lyrical but artificial, has echoes of various moulding influences – the Bible, works of seventeenth-century prose writers and the medieval mystics, especially Dame Julian of Norwich. Prudence Sarn's quaint phrases, the spice of humour in her observations, the simplicity of her wisdom, are strongly reminiscent of Dame Julian : but on the whole this is due less to direct imitation than to affinity of personality, as that particular blend of warm homeliness and mysticism, simplicity and depth, gravity and joy is as characteristic of Mary (and her 'mommet' Prudence) as it is of the anchoress.

Again and again there are passages imbued with a peculiarly Biblical atmosphere – Prudence's description of Sarn fields under corn is typical :

> There would be warmship that wrapped you round, and the queenly gift of the scent of corn. What other scent is like it? There is so much in it, beyond other sweets. There is summer in it, and frost. There is water in it, and the heart of the flint which

the corn has taken up into its hollow stalks. There is bread in it, and life for man and beast. (p. 253)

While in each of the novels this tone, an echo of the rhythms of the Bible (and the use of aptly chosen texts usually for humorous or ironic effect) recur more or less, it is most apparent in *Precious Bane*.

An important feature of Mary Webb's style is her lyrical handling of dialect. Fascinated from an early age by the talk of of Shropshire country folk, Mary had, like Synge with the Aran islanders, lived among her people and grown to know intimately at their hearthsides how they lived, thought and spoke. With so keen an ear for the substance, rhythms and intrinsic beauty of country speech, she was able skilfully and with innate poetry to blend the local idiom with her own prose (as Synge did with Gaelicised English). Hers was an expert's knowledge of the Shropshire dialect through which she came in direct touch with the peasant mind and spirit – and to a continuity with the past. She wrote in a review: 'How these words and phrases chime and murmur! . . . The geography of words is a fascinating study. One finds that in mountain country a word in daily use on one side of a range will be non-existent on the other. Even in the plains words will fade away suddenly like the fringes of a rain-storm'.

But the artist in Mary Webb was uppermost – though she loved the rich, apple-like quality of the words in dialect she was aware, like Thomas Hardy, of the danger of excessive localism, and only occasionally employed purely dialect words, achieving her effect more subtly by idiomatic suggestion, the use here and there of a well-placed local word or turn of phrase giving widespread flavour. And the meaning of these vivid words or expressions can always be 'caught' through the context. When Hazel Woodus tells us 'the sun's undering' and Prue Sarn calls herself Kester's 'poor, daggly angel' or describes how under the elms 'it was all dimmery with summer leaves', we know what they mean. Many of the local words and turns of phrase which she incorporated are not exclusive to Shropshire and the Welsh border but are modifications of those in use elsewhere: in *Precious Bane* such country speech is particularly appropriate, adding to the authenticity of a narrative told by a countrywoman, helping to create the feeling that this story really has come out of

Prudence Sarn. With sureness of touch, Mary Webb sustains from beginning to end the natural flow and rich country flavour of her narrator's speech, yet this is charged through and through with poetry. Prue's descriptions have a rare lucidity and simplicity – before the close of the first chapter, in which she sets the scene at Sarn, we are captured; her words are as arresting as birdsong:

> Well, it is all gone over now, the trouble and the struggling. It be quiet weather now, like a still evening with the snow all down, and a green sky, and lambs calling . . . I call to mind the thick, blotting woods of Sarn, and the crying of the mere when the ice was on it . . . There was but little sky to see there, saving that which was reflected in the mere; but the sky that is in the mere is not the proper heavens. You see it in a glass darkly, and the long shadows of rushes go thin and sharp across the sliding stars, and even the sun and moon might be put out down there, for, times, the moon would get lost in lily leaves, and, times, a heron might stand before the sun. (pp. 20–1)

Passages like this, occurring on almost every page, haunt the memory and compel re-reading.

In the dialogue as well, Mary Webb carefully conventionalises dialect speech, again using purely dialect words sparingly, but conveying the spirit of peasant talk by employing pronunciation spellings, elided or modified common words and local expressions ('in good sadness', 'comic-struck', 'in very poor case'). This rustic speech, mainly of the lesser characters, is found throughout the novels, but most extensively in *Precious Bane*. And it is primarily by means of dialogue that the minor characters are so effectively realised, the ease, naturalness and differentiation in their speech adding to the sense of vital and varied human presence.

In *Precious Bane*, as in each of the preceding novels, there is a group of memorable secondary figures, again lively portrayals given considerable individual variation, but not obtrusive. Little Mother Sarn – with her 'married all over look', her hands like 'a mole's little hands, lifted up to God when it be trapped', her 'grievous smile' and 'very plaintive voice' crying over and over, 'Could I help it if the hare crossed my path? Could I help it?' – is brilliantly suggested. Wizard Beguildy is vividly drawn: we see him in his part-cave Stone House at the edge of Plash Mere, planning with artistry (helped by mead) his spells and charms, strangely smiling his 'very slow, stealing smile, that came like a ripple on the water, and stayed a long while', or beating on a row of flints making 'small and flinty music' – a sign, so Prue tells us, 'that his patience was over'. A 'preached-against man', rancorous, there is in 'his fiery mind' a bizarre mixture of philosophy and skulduggery. Much of Beguildy's 'wizardry' provides comic relief (Mary Webb often using her minor characters as Shakespeare and Scott did, to lighten the serious or tragic tone). Beguildy is another variation of a type of fiercely individualistic, harsh old countryman of the Shropshire borders that Mary Webb understood and depicted so well: less convincing perhaps than Abel Woodus and Andrew Vessons in *Gone to Earth*, he has more human reality than the hell-fire preacher Eli Huntbatch in *The Golden Arrow* or the fantastic Fringal in *Seven for a Secret*. The host of rustic figures in *Precious Bane* adds richly to Mary Webb's gallery of country characters – while some, such as Sexton's Sammy, Grimble, Moll and Sukey, or Huglet are little more than sharp caricatures, others such as Tivvy, Missis Beguildy and Felena are deftly touched in.

In *The Concise Cambridge History of English Literature*, George Sampson notes that 'the presentation of rural superstition and its cruelties in *Precious Bane* is intensely individual and penetrating'. Mary Webb, as we have seen, made her own thorough researches into folklore, and in the Foreword to this novel acknowledged the authors of *Shropshire Folk Lore* 'for the verification of various customs which I had otherwise only known by hearsay'. More than once in articles and reviews she speaks directly of her fascination with traditional beliefs and customs: 'Though we continually emerge from the past into better things, yet there are many ideas of humanity expressed in books or in folklore which are immortal, shining out like lamps beyond their dark century' (*CPAP*, p. 39). She knew from a life lived in the West Shropshire border hills and valleys, the extent to which folklore and superstition penetrated the everyday existence of countrydwellers, influencing the unconscious as well as the conscious mind – and this even more so in the days to which she reached back in *Precious Bane*, a time when superstition was rife and often closely interknit with religion in such isolated rural areas.

Drawing on her great fund of knowledge, she wove almost

two hundred instances of lore, legend, custom and superstition into the fabric of *Precious Bane*, some obscure, others well-known – not only traditional Shropshire folklore but also universal motifs. Among the most important are the superstitions about a hare-lip and witchcraft, the custom of sin-eating, the telling of the bees and the telling of the rooks (after a death), the night burial with mourners carrying sprigs of rosemary, the love-spinning, and the legends of the Seven Whistlers (a death warning by mysterious birds), the drowned village, Wild Edric, the bogeys of the mere, 'the roaring bull o' Bagbury' and the ghostly chariots. Mary Webb used folklore and superstition partly to heighten the local flavour and authenticity (together with traditional farming customs such as the Love Carriage and Harvest Home), but mainly to establish and support the mood of impending tragedy which permeates the entire book. Portents of disaster are introduced from the first chapter onwards when we hear of the 'discouragement' at Sarn.

Yet, as a reviewer said when praising the 'suffusive beauty' of *Precious Bane*, 'one can only clamour against a too much richness of lore and season'.[4] Too many customs and superstitions are brought in; and though most of them are incorporated with skill so that they are never meaningless embellishments, occasionally their inclusion is rather contrived. Folk beliefs and practices, and mythological motifs are assimilated more finely and successfully in *Gone to Earth*. But two of the superstitions integrated in *Precious Bane* – namely those associated with a harelip and the custom of sin-eating – are of fundamental importance to almost every aspect of the novel. And again, as in *Gone to Earth*, these dominant mythic forms taken by Mary's imagination give us insight into the darker crevasses of her mind, revealing her deepest preoccupations and anxieties.

Throughout the novel the oblique references to Prudence Sarn's bane – her harelip – are particularly well done. As Prue grows to young womanhood, she becomes aware of the suspicion in which she is regarded by others, of the tales spreading 'in the lonely farms' that she is cursed and has the devil's mark, that she assumes the form of a hare at midnight and is a witch. In Prudence's bewildered sensitivity, in her increasing hurt at being set apart

---

[4] Austin Clarke in *Nation and the Athenaeum*, 2 August 1924.

by her fellow creatures and thought of as odd, evil, a witch, we see Mary's own extreme vulnerability, especially as her thyroid condition was now worsening, her goitre growing : even in Shropshire she was shunned, viewed with suspicion, and remembered years later for her 'peculiarities' (untidy clothes, 'odd eyes', solitary ways) rather than for her achievements. The hurts and slights felt keenly by Prue are Mary's own experience of 'the critical, sly stare' (as she expressed it in the poem 'Safe'), even to the querying of her sanity. So Prue says wryly, when telling us how Mrs Beguildy doubted her ability to learn : 'She always thought, in common with many people, that if there was anything wrong with a person's outward seeming, there must be summat wrong with their mind as well' (p. 65).

While much of the strength of *Precious Bane* lies in how intimately and effectively Mary has embodied her own personality and thoughts in Prudence Sarn, one of the main weaknesses of the novel is that ultimately it fails to convince and satisfy because of the weak, almost fairy-tale 'happy ending'. Mary's need to provide such an ending – when Prue finds her 'bit of Paradise' with her 'dear acquaintance', the perfect Kester – evidently overcame her finer artistic sense. In her imagination Mary was reshaping the world close to her heart's yearning. As in her personal life she constructed, at tragic cost, an earthly Eden with her 'dear H.B.L.W.' as the central figure. This was the dream woven into her life, the personal myth which – if she could not transcend it – held the power to destroy her. The unstained hero Kester, an idealised Henry, could remain faultless in Mary's created world, half-fantasy, half-romance, but could the human Henry, in the imperfect world of actuality, sustain the rôle of an idealised Kester?

The superstitious custom of sin-eating was also selected in the interests of one of her main, and obsessional, themes – the problem of evil, its nature and part in human life, its relation to good. In considering this aspect of *Precious Bane*, we find another important key to Mary's personal tragedy.

The strange custom of sin-eating, which had long since died out on the Welsh border, appealed strongly to her imagination and dramatic sense : it is integrated skilfully and effectively in the dark story of Gideon. When Father Sarn dies 'in his wrath, with all his sins upon him', Mother Sarn at the funeral calls for a Sin

Eater. Such men, as Prue explains, would for a fee 'take the bread and wine handed to them across the coffin', eat, drink and take on the dead man's sins. Sin Eaters were thought to be cursed, irretrievably lost, but Gideon has no belief in the superstition. For motives of material gain, in return for his mother's promise of 'the farm and all', Gideon 'standing up tall in the high black hat, with a gleaming pale face', becomes his father's Sin Eater, declaring over the coffin : ' "*I give easement and rest now to thee, dear man. Come not down the lanes nor in our meadows. And for thy peace I pawn my own soul. Amen.*" ' And as Prue says, Gideon utters these words 'like somebody warning off a trespasser' (pp. 42–4).

The sin-eating deepens the dark atmosphere and forecasts Gideon's impending doom. Auguries of his fate occur throughout the novel, but he has no true tragic stature, unlike Hazel Woodus in *Gone to Earth* : though Prue speaks of Beguildy as 'the villain in our story', the real villain is Gideon who is ruthlessly ambitious, a materialist, a seducer, a murderer. But Prue underestimates and excuses too readily her brother's power for evil. In telling her story, she repeats Kester's optimistic philosophy that if you think of sin rightly 'it just wunna there' – he thinks of evil as mere absence of good (*privato boni*). Prue's fatalistic thoughts throw light on Mary's own attitude at this time; explaining her pity for Beguildy, Prue sees both evil and good as part of God's design :

> We are His mommets that made us . . . The play is of His making. So the evil mommets do His will as well as the good, since they act the part set for them. How would it be if the play came to the hour when the villainous man must do evilly, and see! he is on his knee-bones at his prayers. Then the play would be in very poor case. There was a mommet once called Judas, and if he had started away from his set part in fear, we should none of us have been saved. Which is all a strange mystery, and so we must leave it. (pp. 181–2)

And there too Mary left it, apparently unable to effect a resolution of the problem first postulated in *The Golden Arrow*, unable to hold on to and develop the insight implied at the close of that novel and in both this title and the title 'Precious Bane'. She could not ultimately accept evil and suffering as part of the

13. Facsimile of Stanley Baldwin's letter to Mary Webb, 14 January 1927

14. Facsimile of Mary Webb's reply to Stanley Baldwin

mysterious unity in the universe to which she responded and surrendered herself totally. And so she regressed in the path to her own wholeness. Mary's failure to come to terms with her realisation of evil in human nature, to integrate this into her conscious acceptance of human duality, dark and light, the innate potential for both in the individual, caused her in her last completed novel to sweep the 'evil mommets' from her play, leaving the 'good mommets', as in traditional morality, to survive for their 'happy ending' – and leaving the novel itself 'in very poor case'.

Sprung from 'the opaque and fathomless pool' of her unconscious, *Precious Bane* seems seen 'in a glass darkly'. Sarn Mere symbolises the dark unconscious in which Gideon drowns and from which Prudence, at the last, turns away. It is Prudence's failure to come to grips with the negative and evil side of Gideon that partly helps to bring about the tragedies. At the close, the novel loses power and conviction; and Mary in her personal life was soon to be lost in her own dark regions. Had she been able to provide a different ending for *Precious Bane*, she herself may well have surmounted her personal difficulties and found many another 'task to do' before saying 'goodnight to this world'.

Precious Bane, with its strange story, its compelling tone, its unusual and poetic literary style, undoubtedly will remain the favourite Mary Webb book for many readers, but the neglected novel *The House in Dormer Forest*, which marked a turning point in her literary career and personal life, is her most meaningful work in which she came nearest to creating an enduring symbol of wholeness.

*

As *Seven for a Secret*, like its three predecessors, had sold little more than a thousand copies, Mary experienced difficulty in securing a satisfactory agreement with publishers for *Precious Bane*. Martin Armstrong suggested she should try the new firm of Jonathan Cape (a partnership between Jonathan Cape and G. Wrenn Howard established in 1921). Cape was always ready to secure a possible best seller: calculating business man though he was, he had intuitions and acted upon them. He was immediately interested in *Precious Bane*, partly because it was Mary's fifth novel – and he had intuitions about fifth novels. As Michael Howard tells us in his history of the publishing house: 'For

Jonathan, a fifth novel held an almost mystical significance. He believed that it established firmly an author's reputation or made the breakthrough to success if the beginnings had been slow.'[5] Mary's novel was secured by Cape for £100 advance on royalties – a lesser sum than for any of her previous books.

Her relationships with publishers were usually difficult – neither was this to be easy. She tended to harass the office by letters and telephone calls, anxious about delays in proofs, impatiently expecting prompt replies to her queries. In general, the rather cool, objective attitude of the commercial side of 'the world of letters' was something which, when she came up against it, often caused her disappointment.

One problem with publishers was of her own making and arose from her inability to correct her work in typescript, necessitating a reliance on the proof stage. This fault was one to which she readily admitted. For instance, after Jonathan Cape's criticism of certain discrepancies in the typescript of *Precious Bane*, Mary replied (Easter Monday, 1924), 'I shall see these defects in the proofs', and explained, 'If I had read the typescript again it would have been useless as I have become, as it were, dull to type, from doing it so continuously I suppose. In the print the errors will fly at me in a second.'

Yet to alter proofs was, and is, an enormously costly procedure as Mary certainly knew, assuring her publisher that she realised that 'if I make too many corrections in the proof I must pay for them'. But she regretted very much that Cape's were not providing galley proofs: 'I do *wish* I could have galley proofs,' she wrote. 'They are always my strength and stay. But anyway I can do no more to the typescript.'

When *Precious Bane* came out a few months later and Mary was sent 'two early copies', she was delighted and thought the production 'beautifully done', complimenting the firm on 'the whole format of the book', adding with characteristic candour, 'I am sorry that I couldn't have the arabesques I chose on the wrapper', but concluding with equally characteristic generosity, 'Still, it is very nice'. Mary's 'very nice' was always heartfelt.

There were, however, a few minor disappointments from her point of view. She had wanted the titles of two books 'in prepara-

[5] *Jonathan Cape: Publisher,* p. 98.

tion' at the front of *Precious Bane*. These were left out though
Mary had written back that she 'thought it might be a good thing
to insert them'. One of these books may have been her collection
of poems, and the other most probably the novel she was then
preparing, entitled 'A Strong Man Armed' (this she subsequently
changed to *Armour wherein he Trusted* after hearing of an
American novel of the same title). Mary was also disappointed
that her address was omitted after the Foreword and requested
G. Wrenn Howard (29 June, 1924) to 'please instruct them to
put it in again'. She went on: 'It is quite usual to insert it and
I have reasons for wishing it to be in.' Whatever her reasons were,
it was probably then too late. In a postscript to the same letter she
made another request: 'If you *could* make publishing day 9 July
it would be very nice. Like all countrywomen I am superstitious
about Fridays.'

The first reviews seemed to augur well for the success of
Precious Bane. L. P. Hartley, in the *Spectator* (2 August, 1924)
wrote enthusiastically: 'It is Biblical in style, lyrical in mood.'
Hartley pointed out that features such as 'unassimilated fragments
of folklore; curious customs culled from diverse centuries; pro-
verbs and wise saws made unfamiliar by local words; attractive
tit-bits from the antiquary's store' are usually found in this type
of novel, but in *Precious Bane* 'how transfigured, how reanimated,
how refreshed! Mrs Webb makes them an aid, not a bar to the
development of her theme.' Hartley went on to praise, in particular, her handling of the love scenes, 'the excellence' of which
'alone would make *Precious Bane* a memorable book'. These
scenes, in his opinion, 'have a Meredithian quality in that they
kindle anticipation and recollection. . .'

We are given a glimpse of Mary's reaction to this review in a
letter to Jonathan Cape (25 September, 1924):

> The *Spectator* review was good, didn't you think? Only Mr
> Hartley appeared to think that all the Latin I construe is *amo*,
> I love. But then, I have never had the pleasure of meeting the
> reviewer, or he would know that this is not the case.

In the same letter she thanked Cape for sending her 'the notices
of Edwin Pugh's astonishing review' – referring here to the
unequivocally enthusiastic review in the September *Bookman* in

which Pugh, praising her 'rich performance' in *Precious Bane*, made laudatory statements about her art as a whole :

> She is equipped at every point with all the talents that go to the the making of masterpieces . . . she has a style of exquisite beauty which yet has both force and restraint, simplicity and subtlety . . . she can moreover tell a story and so intrigue you with its sense of inevitableness that it seems more real than reality.

Once again he proclaimed with conviction :

> She has, in short, genius. And though she has not yet come fully into her own, the day is surely not far off when she will be acclaimed . . .[6]

A month previously Mary had been delighted when *Precious Bane* was chosen as 'The Book of the Week' by T. P. O'Connor, who gave it lengthy attention in *T.P.'s and Cassell's Weekly* (2 August, 1924) under the heading 'The Hunger for the Land'. How deeply gratifying to her this must have been. Not only was she given front-page publicity, with her photograph on the cover, but in the two-page review article, T.P. commented : 'Mrs Webb is already known as one of the most brilliant among the younger generation of novelists – every new volume of hers is eagerly expected and favourably, sometimes even enthusiastically received . . .' *Precious Bane*, he said, is a novel that 'gains in strength from the admirable artlessness with which it is told'.

Another good notice was Austin Clarke's in *Nation and the Athenaeum* (2 August, 1924): 'Mary Webb's rich idiom and rhythm cannot be overpraised.'

Not all the important reviews were as favourable as these, and while praising aspects of the novel had some serious reservations. The *Times Literary Supplement* reviewer (17 July 1924) thought the tragedy of Gideon 'classic in its outlines', the drama 'well arranged and convincing'. But this reviewer found the chief obstacle to a full acceptance of the novel, 'not so much that it is written in a highly poeticised Shropshire dialect, but that

---

[6] The only thing which Edwin Pugh did not like about *Precious Bane* was its title. But Mary had received reassurance from other literary friends about this : May Sinclair, for instance, who had said some 'perfectly delightful' things about the book, and Rebecca West who 'expressed approval of the title'. (Letters of Mary Webb to Jonathan Cape.)

it is supposed to be narrated by an ill-educated country woman who found time to keep a diary during a life of hard work on a farm'.

In making this obtuse comment the reviewer revealed ignorance of the details of the narrative and the subtlety of the characterisation of Prudence Sarn. It was conceded, however, that 'those who accept the figment that Prue had a cultivated mind and a power of expressing it in words as well as a noble spirit will find here a good story'.

Another influential review undoubtedly disappointing to Mary was that by John Franklin in the *New Statesman* (30 August 1924). Here *Precious Bane* was ambivalently assessed as a respectable failure. Franklin, while allowing that her work 'has a serious charm that must appeal to many', concluded that 'somehow all is wrong; it is *simplesse*, not simplicity'. Yet he recognised that 'her observation is organised in relation to a conviction about good and evil and is offered as the direct product of love for what she observes', and he described the novel as 'a conceit in the old sense of the word, a fabric all laced with folklore and dialect, suggesting a sampler stitched through long summer evenings in the bay-window of a remote farmhouse'. Mary Webb succeeded in keeping 'the spirit' taut, 'the keynote single', the facts 'harmonised on a scheme'.

After the completion of *Precious Bane*, Mary had not immediately pressed on with her next novel. There were several reasons for this, not least her exhaustion after the creation of a work of literary art to which she had given all that she had of essential being, an exhaustion similar to that experienced by other 'inspirational' writers (such as Virginia Woolf and Katherine Mansfield) following intense creative outpouring. And her depression and nervousness undoubtedly were aggravated by the serious financial distress in which she found herself throughout this time. This pressure created another – her frantic efforts to obtain money quickly by placing short pieces, stories and articles. In addition to these stresses, she was struggling during the summer of 1924 to recover from a deep personal sadness.

At the end of April she had been summoned to Chester: her mother was dead. At Llandudno for 'a change', Alice Meredith had suffered a seizure from which she never recovered. Kenneth (now returned from Canada), hurried to Llandudno and arranged for her body to be brought back to Chester for burial. Sadly the Meredith brothers and sisters gathered at Hough Green, and on 2 May 1924, four days before her seventy-second birthday, Alice was buried in a leafy corner of the cemetery, near the river bank, her grave marked by a red sandstone cross.

Distressed by her mother's death, Mary felt unsettled during the months that followed. Although their relationship had not been close, the bond of affection between them had grown stronger of late. In Mary's poem, 'To Mother', written at Hough Green during Christmas 1920, she reveals an aspect of Alice well understood by George Meredith : that behind the tight, brusque reserve was hidden a sentimentality and need. Spending this Christmas with her mother before leaving to live in London, Mary stood 'within the doorway' of Alice's room, and was moved to see how she had 'set out' in the candlelight all the 'little treasures' given to her years ago by her children : 'Here was the robin, very round and bright/Painted by one of us with fingers small . . .'

In the poem Mary describes (wishing to preserve) this scene that had touched her deeply. And in *Precious Bane* she worked something of the pathos of the ageing Alice Meredith into Mother Sarn. To Prudence the old lady seems 'so little and so lost', child-like, her hands 'like the little praying paws of a trapped mole'. The maternal, protective love which Prue has for her aged mother derives from Mary's own unfailing pity : we hear Mary's voice in Prue's heartfelt cry : 'Poor Mother! Oh my poor Mother! Shall we meet you in the other world, dear soul, and atone to you for our heedlessness?'

The loss of her mother renewed for Mary sorrowful memories of her father's death and burial some fifteen years previously, also severing another link with that period of her golden relationship with him and close family life at The Grange, The Woodlands, Maesbrook. Often she re-lived in her innermost self those days of oneness with her father, of shared response to nature's beauty and mystery – the early Eden of inner totality she had lost, and for which she was homesick all her life.

At Hampstead the writing of reviews of natural history books for the *Spectator* took her back not only to the 'dear delights of Shropshire', her 'delicate home of colour and light', Lyth Hill and 'the enchanted plain', but also to her own blissful childhood and

adolescence. She begins one review, 'When the Pie was Opened'
(1 December 1923) with a very significant passage :

> When the parcel of review books came, the birds did indeed
> begin to sing. Before, one had just been a dull, grown-up person
> in a room in London, wondering if the sun was going to get
> through the fog. Came Carter Paterson, Santa Claus of daily life,
> with twelve Nature books for children, and the sun *did* come out.
> Not only that. Also, the London sky folded itself up neatly,
> selvedge to selvedge, and put itself away in a drawer with the
> grown-up feeling and winter. A vast blue heaven, where larks
> hung like Christmas-tree angels, arched above, and a small child
> wandered in the standing hay-grass of a long-suffering father . . .
>
> (*CPAP*, p. 80)

Describing in detail this ecstatic 'vision' of nature as she – the
'small child' – sees it, she gives us a glimpse of herself totally
receptive, totally immersed in a world of the senses, responding to
an almost overwhelming profusion of scents and sounds, of bird
and insect life in a Shropshire field. Significantly again, she closes
the description with a reference to her father and the security she
had known in her childhood world :

> The night-jar's spinning wheel had been busy a long while
> when – hark! it is the father's bed-time call. Through long
> shadows and moony gleams the child runs home, secure in the faith
> that 'tomorrow will be as to-day, and much more abundant'.

Apologising humorously for 'the enormity of such disquisitions',
Mary went on to review, at last, the dozen nature books. But her
delightful digression is revelatory of her mind and attitude.
Clearly 'the old homesickness vast and dumb', as she expressed it
in a poem, was a yearning for the past as well as for Shropshire
. . . 'far, far away it seems, and long ago'.

Personal grief brought depression, fatigue, and it was to be
almost a year before Mary returned to major literary effort. *T.P.'s
and Cassell's Weekly* (20 December 1924) reported : 'Mary Webb
. . . is weary of novels for the moment and is devoting her energies
to the art of the short story.' Few, reading this, could have known
the dire actuality behind it, or that in concentrating on short

stories and articles, Mary was making a desperate effort to bring in some money as she and Henry were in extreme financial need.

Since moving to 5 Grove Cottages in 1923 they had been contending with mounting debts. The cottage was unfurnished so they had to buy what was virtually a second home, as well as providing for ever-recurring expenses of rent and heating. Immediate cash was needed too for rail fares to Shropshire as the urgency of Mary's need to return was increasing rather than diminishing the longer she lived in London. When it came to a choice between food or a rail ticket to Shrewsbury (as it frequently did), Mary starved. On one occasion an advance of £5 from Jonathan Cape enabled her and Henry to return 'by excursion'. It was the Whit holiday of 1924, and her deep joy at being home is evident in the tone of her letter to Cape :

> We came here by excursion and by living ascetically are managing very nicely and having a good holiday. I have been earthing-up the potatoes we put in at Easter and though the garden is otherwise a wilderness, yet it is lovely with purple iris and heavy-blossomed laburnum . . . Excuse this hasty scrawl. Hands very earthy and the world outside the window very alluring.

Gratefully she added : 'Thank you again, so much, for the loan of the five pounds.'

She also expressed her appreciation when sending Jonathan Cape two short pieces for the firm's journal *Now and Then* : 'The Crockman' and the first part of an interesting paper, 'Glimpses of Old Shropshire', written for a Caradoc and Severn Valley Field Club meeting in March 1923 ('Mrs Webb greatly regretted that she could not be present herself to read the paper'). Subsequently published in the Field Club *Transactions* and the *Shrewsbury Chronicle*, the two carefully researched essays which comprise her paper are vivid re-creations of historical Shropshire (*CPAP*). The first of these, 'A Dream of Uriconium' (which Mary sent to Cape) is a memorable evocation of the Roman city at Wroxeter. Mary was deeply interested in the excavations of the site, abandoned in 1914, recommenced in 1923, and the effective poem 'Viroconium' was also written at this time. Significantly her last two novels are both set in the Shropshire of earlier times, imaginative penetrations born of her intuitive understanding and feeling for the past of her

county. 'Glimpses of Old Shropshire' thus indicates the direction
her work would take in what was to be the final phase.

Among other lesser-known pieces Mary wrote during these years
(*CPAP*) are two short stories accepted by Lady Cynthia Asquith
for anthologies she was compiling: the bizarre 'Mr Tallent's
Ghost' (*The Ghost Book,* September 1926), and an enchanting,
witty fable 'The Cuckoo Clock' (*Sails of Gold,* October 1927).
Both show a more accomplished command of the art of the short
story than the ten rather weak stories published later in the posthumous collected edition of her work. Two others must be mentioned briefly: 'The Sword', a sophisticated, typical 'Twenties' tale
of a returned soldier and the tragedy of his post-war love affair;
and 'The Chinese Lion', a longer story, again on the theme of love
and destiny (*CPAP*). Neither of these was published during her
life, but Henry, after her death, found them among her papers,
and arranged for their publication at a later date. These little-
known works of Mary Webb together with reviews, articles,
poems, indicate the intensity of her literary effort towards the end
of her life: a fairly prolific output in spite of failing health and
personal difficulties.

She was trying immensely hard throughout the years in London
to gain the attention of the reading public and to earn some
money to pay off increasingly pressing debts. She tried in every
direction. When Ellery Sedgwick was about to return to America,
she left a packet of a dozen stories at his hotel with a message:
would he read them on the voyage and tell her whether the
American market offered hope? Sedgwick's comment that 'not
through excellence alone can words be minted into dollars' was
to be tragically true until the very last in her case. However he
did his best for her and subsequently one story, 'The Prize', was
published in *Atlantic Monthly* (April 1924).

Her desperate financial situation and the inhibiting circumstances in which she had to write are revealed in her letters to
Jonathan Cape. This correspondence gives a vivid picture of her
difficulties:

> I do so hope the book 'will go' as we are struggling to pay off
> a load of debt, and it makes one feel like an ant under a landslip.
> I shall never do my best work till I've paid every penny. Hence
> my anxiety.   (28 July, 1924)

. . . I promised four people money this week – owing to two of them for some time. In fact I have already sent two of the cheques, post-dated. I have only five pounds to provide all food and other housekeeping necessities till October. So you will see that it is rather urgent. (6 August, 1924)

As negotiations with the American branch of Macmillan brought renewed hope of a contract and U.S.A. publication of *Precious Bane*, Mary asked Jonathan Cape for £30 advance on 'a part of the sum' she was expecting to get from Macmillan. Cape wrote back at once saying that he could not do this and reminded her of the £5 loan which she had not yet paid back. Her reply by return (8 August 1924) rings with indignation and disappointment:

> Spring Cottage,
> Lyth Hill,
> Shrewsbury.

Dear Mr Cape,
I was very much surprised at the tone of your letter for (1) I thought you had a kindly feeling for my work and me (2) I thought I had made it clear that I couldn't pay back the five pounds till I got my American money, and that meanwhile I wished you to add it to my advance which is therefore £105. And (3) I gave you the 'Crockman' and offered you the article in the Severn Valley Field Club paper also, and neither you nor Mr Howard have even acknowledged it. You say my American publication is doubtful, but in my letter I told you I had been asked to send the MS. to Macmillan. We seem rather at cross purposes. However I will continue to fend for myself as to American rights.

> Yours sincerely,
> Mary Webb
> (Mrs. H. B. L. Webb)

It is significant that in her letters to her publishers she used this second form of signature whenever she felt insecure, slighted or dealt with unfairly.

By the end of September 1924 she was back in Hampstead with no money at all, virtually starving and distressed by a summons for debt. Accepting the fact that no further advances would be forthcoming from Jonathan Cape, she pleaded with him to give her work reading manuscripts (30 September 1924):

We are terribly hard up on account of my getting so much less advanced for this book, and we are still paying instalments on furniture and gas fires etc. I have paid away what my trustee sent me from my father and mother – not very much – and now today a summons has come for my husband for an old Shrewsbury bill which I have been paying off bit by bit . . . When Macmillan's £50 comes it will have to go to pay off an overdraft. So you see I am very much in need of work, for as I pay cash for food these sudden bills mean that I starve. My husband has his chief meals out (at school), but I don't. I had hoped to get work for Cassells but it fell through.

The contract with Macmillan fell through too, and her financial plight dragged on throughout the autumn and winter of 1924, into 1925 and 1926, the year of national emergency and the General Strike. This prolonged period of worry and undernourishment, when she existed on little more than 'bread and scrape and tea', undoubtedly had a drastic effect on her health, precipitating the fatal decline. Her own reckless generosity was bringing tragic personal repercussions. To St John Adcock she wrote asking for work and lamenting that she must write begging letters because she and Henry had 'no money at all just now'. But unable to say 'the nay-word', she would give whatever money she had to the down-and-outs who tapped at her door. A friend related how she might have twenty pounds in the morning (payment for literary work) and less than a pound left by the evening. For a pathetic ex-soldier who had been gassed in the war, she bought a bicycle, then a pedlar's kit costing five pounds, and finally she helped to set him up with a small shop. So her own debts rose and she was distressed by the demands of both creditors and beggars.

The pressure of serious financial worry sometimes caused her to behave erratically, in a manner which seemed strange, occasionally even aggressive. After her mother's funeral, for instance, she rushed away from the house in Hough Green, upset by Kenneth's proposal for the division of Alice's jewellery and personal possessions. Although Mrs Meredith had died a fairly rich woman, she had arranged in her will for almost her entire wealth to be put in a fund for Olive her only unmarried daughter, while her jewellery and other personal items were to be distributed between the three daughters in equal shares. Mary, as eldest daughter, expected to be given the first choice. She felt that her rights had been swept aside. Distressed, she ran from the house intending to catch the next train to London. Kenneth hurried after her and persuaded her to come back. She explained that she did not want the jewellery for herself, as her sisters did, but would sell it because she badly needed the money, being overcome with worry, ill with anxiety over debts.

Her first two novels had gone out of print; it seemed that her last two would meet the same fate, and very little was coming in from *Precious Bane*. In desperation she was pressing Cape's, feeling that royalties must surely be accumulating. Yet less than fifteen hundred copies of this novel had been sold by the end of the first year after publication and it had not earned even three-quarters of the £100 advance on royalties. Mary's sense of grievance was intensifying at this continued lack of tangible reward, especially since *Precious Bane* had been well received by the critics. But Jonathan Cape told her that though the novel 'has had some very good reviews and we will certainly do all we can to find a public for it, unfortunately the sales never measure up to what the reviews lead us to hope for. For a book to be very successful it is invariably caused by a chapter of happy accidents.'

It was an immense irony that the 'chapter of happy accidents' did come, but only after (and partly as a result of) her death, *Precious Bane* becoming one of the best-selling novels of the next decade, more than three quarters of a million copies sold.

However, in 1925, though Jonathan Cape still had faith in its ultimate success and there were those associated with him (notably Edward Garnett and the young Hamish Hamilton) who firmly believed that Mary Webb's novels would become popular eventually, he would not be pushed by her into advancing further sums of money or issuing a cheap edition of *The Golden Arrow*. He told her

Later, when your work is selling round about 5 or 6000 copies or more, the question of re-issuing your earlier work in a uniform edition, possibly at 3 and 6d., could be considered. To bring out *The Golden Arrow* at the present time would most certainly mean that we should not sell anything like sufficient to make it profitable.

This was a bitter disappointment to Mary who was already having to fend for herself in the matter of American publication of *Precious Bane* – this involving effort, frustration and the dissipation of her diminishing energies. A dispiriting process which continued until 1926 when a contract was signed at last with E. P. Dutton of New York – and this as a result of Mary's own unswerving determination.

Her life during this London period had become increasingly focused in literary purpose. Unsure of herself though she was in some ways, none the less, as a creative mystic with a vision of unity, of wholeness, she was convinced of the importance of her work. Immense energy and drive she still had – this partly the overactivity caused by her disease – but her physical strength was now beginning to fail fatally as the thyroid trouble was making it difficult for her to rest either mentally or physically, even when fatigued. She was becoming even thinner, more worn-looking, desperately restless at night when she would work or brood into the early hours, the intensity of her literary effort and inner life leaving her exhausted, prone to recurring giddiness and head pains. And she was aware of her physical deterioration, painfully conscious that her eyes were protruding more noticeably, that her goitre had grown larger.

The artist Ethelbert White, her immediate neighbour at Grove Cottages, was amazed at what he described as the 'striking fluctuations' in her appearance. Frequently he saw her in the tiny garden adjoining his, either sitting typing or tending the flowers – and often watering his as well as her own. Impressed by her gentle manner, White was shocked to see her sometimes so utterly ravaged physically. She could look twenty years older in a day. Then he would be equally surprised at her marvellous recoveries: after not being seen for a while, she would emerge restored, her whole aspect transformed, looking younger again and radiant. These fluctuations came about as a result of her illness and the fervid creativity which undoubtedly engendered further physical suffering. But her intense inner life, while it strained her physically, also brought her to the deepest springs of creative vitality.

Certainly *Precious Bane* is informed by a sustained lyrical energy which also flows into the reviews, short stories and poems that she wrote at this date – a period of concentrated literary activity. She was trying to attend as many literary gatherings as possible, although ill-health and shortage of money impeded her. Often she was seen hurrying from her cottage (her brother tells us – 'Mary always ran rather than walked') and wearing her dark, unfashionable clothes with the large fly-away scarves and bows that hid her goitre, she would hasten downhill to take the Hampstead tube to central London. Her membership of the Bookman Circle was fruitful : there she met friends such as May Sinclair, the Lynds and Mrs C. A. Nicholson, enjoyed lectures by established writers and poets (including de la Mare), and occasionally took part in discussions.

Burdened with self-consciousness, she was sure only of her ideas and purposes. Geraint Goodwin observed that she had no realisation of her own 'capacity for inspiring deep and lasting affection among the small circle which really knew her'.[7] He saw that she was 'frightened, timid, with the timidity of some wild and delicate thing of the woods', that she 'had none of that self-assertive swagger which a modern world demands'. In the circles in which she moved, 'she felt her only recommendation was her work and was painfully grateful for friendship'.

Frank Swinnerton, that sharp observer of the Georgian scene, wrote a description of Mary at a literary gathering which is well worth quoting :

> This woman had no happiness in city life; she loved hills and gardens. I saw her only once, when she made a little speech, composed and modest, about some subject which had been debated by others with a good deal of futility. She stood very straight, a slight figure, with a serious face and rather protrusive eyes; and she spoke well and without nervousness. It was clear that she knew her mind and would hold it in spite of any other opinion.

And to Ellery Sedgwick, her guest at a P.E.N. Club dinner, it seemed that she had 'something of just pride, of distrust of the world's opinion, of confidence in her own purposes', though it was obvious that 'she felt her own way barred before her'. To Sedgwick she spoke of 'the dumbness of criticism and of that inert resistance which the crowd feels towards the quiet reflection of small things'. Immersed in a way of life as literary as it was

[7] Geraint Goodwin, *The Everyman*, 2 May 1929, pp. 14–15.

mystical, her art was, above all else, an expression of her mysticism. For her, as she told Sedgwick, literature was vital, of central importance: she could never look upon it as 'the herbaceous border of life's garden'. Needing desperately both money and encouragement, very little of either was forthcoming. During these last years she was often on the verge of despair about public indifference to her work and confided this in letters to friends. Even in Shropshire there was a singular disinterest in her novels. But she had long been aware that 'in the world of art and letters . . . the artist must elbow and push, and . . . if he did not often stop his honeyed utterance to shout his wares, he would not be heard at all' (*GTE*, p. 75).

Occasionally in her writing she expressed disillusionment or spoke out forcefully:

> Today the craft of letters has been turned into a strictly commercial transaction, and books are manufactured with the prompt, neat aplomb of a pot of factory jam. Those must have been great days when it was a hall-mark of nobility to have written a book; when nobody wrote except for the love of it; when no mediocre work was turned out. Greater days still when it meant martyrdom to have written a book; when the whole life and soul of a man went into it, freighting it with such beauty and wonder that it would defy the centuries. Have we lost the art of distillation by which the spirit was rendered to an essence and preserved in an indestructible form?

This was her own experience, to have put her 'whole life and soul' into her writing, and she is expressing here her conscious artistic purpose: to distil the spiritual and with this essence to freight her work with 'beauty and wonder'.

Immensely grateful for appreciation, candid and childlike in her thirst for more, she would occasionally invite critics who had given her good reviews to 5 Grove Cottages, when they would talk about her work. Geraint Goodwin, another Welsh border writer, was one such critic. After her death, he said of her:

> . . . self-questioning and introspective as every creative artist must be, there were times when she could not escape the fact that the public steadily and resolutely avoided her, and we can well see her wondering whether, after all, the friends, the critics were all wrong and the public . . . she had not written for the public

it is true – the well of her inspiration to the last remained clear and unmuddied by the demands of popular appeal.

It was difficult for Mary, amid effort and hardship, to realise that she was indeed making progress, albeit slowly, for her reputation was growing steadily and not only among the discriminating. *Precious Bane* was gradually making that 'breakthrough to success'; her articles, reviews and short stories were helping to make her name known. It was a definite step forward when she was asked to write for the *Bookman* (commencing in 1925) – this as a result of St John Adcock's regard, as he had nothing but the highest praise for her talent as a novelist. She contributed fairly lengthy reviews of novels by Helen Prothero Lewis, E. L. Grant Watson, André Maurois, Martin Armstrong, Osbert Sitwell, May Sinclair and others, and wrote perceptive critical articles on Fanny Burney and Jane Austen (*CPAP*).

This association with the *Bookman* brought her the friendship of St John Adcock and his daughter Almey. Drawn by St John Adcock's sympathetic manner, Mary applied for work as his assistant, and was disappointed when the post was not available. However she frequently sought his advice about literary matters and came to him with her personal worries. He described her as she was near the end of her life :

> in appearance . . . a small fragile person with large anxious eyes. Her manner fluctuated between shyness and a sort of hesitant self-confidence; she was very highly-strung, worried terribly about trifles and was so sensitive that she was often deeply wounded by wholly imaginary slights, and would come and complain to you of these with a childishly desperate seriousness at which it was at times impossible to refrain from laughing, and as soon as you began to laugh she would see the absurdity of her agitation over such a trifle, and laugh at herself, and the trouble was over.

At the period when St John Adcock knew her – the last, tragic phase when she was struggling against failing health, depression, financial worries and, worst of all, disastrous insecurity in her relationship with Henry – she felt keenly any slights, real or imaginary though these may have been. And there were more real ones than St John Adcock knew of. She was subjected to uncharitable criticism, even mockery, by people who totally misunderstood her or who pitied Henry. Much of her distress

arose from the slow process of deterioration in their marriage . . .
'Ah, bitter grief – / Remembering the hills of heaven / And
yesterday!'

Mary sensed that she was becoming less and less essential to
Henry, that there was someone else of central importance in his
life, perhaps a golden-haired Jancis or Lily. She watched and
brooded, and Henry knew by the look in her large eyes that she
was gripped by deep dread. He had ceased teasing her out of
this, as he used to do earlier in their marriage – the mutual spirit
of banter and humour between them had failed. No longer in
love with her, he was less inclined to meet her needs, lift her out
of her wretchedness, help her to help herself – just as he had
given up trying to persuade her to nourish herself properly, rest
when necessary. If he wanted to stay behind after school hours
he did so. Interested in school dramatics, he undertook the
building of an open air theatre consisting of circular tiers in the
Greek style. He spent hours digging and laying rows of stones
for the theatre, in spite of Mary's objections and her concern
about his back, his health.

She grieved that he was increasingly unwilling to return to
Lyth Hill for weekends and holidays. He had lived for years a
country life in deference to her wishes (at first, when in love, a
romantic idyll); now, finding a congenial sphere of his own in
London, pulled by outer forces and his own needs, he went back
less frequently to Spring Cottage.[8] But he never tried to prevent
Mary from returning, and he continued to encourage her in her
literary work, knowing that if only success would come it could
do so much to give her life new purpose and fulfilment . . . one
of the many 'if onlys', warp and weft on the loom of tragedy.

And when he did come to Lyth Hill, divisive tensions rose
between them. The growing friction did not go unnoticed by
people of the hill. There was, for instance, a disagreement about
the hawthorn hedge. Henry asked Mr Barrett, who was building
a rockery for them, to cut the hedge which had grown very high.
Mary rushed out and passionately countermanded the order,

---

[8] She returned alone for the Whitsun holiday, 1925, when planning her
next novel in which she extended westward from the Shropshire borders into
Powys, and back in time to the middle ages. It was reported in *T.P.'s and
Cassell's Weekly*, 6 June 1925: 'Mary Webb has returned from Shropshire and Radnorshire where she had been seeking inspiration for a new
novel' (p. 200).

whereupon Henry again told Barrett to go ahead. Confronted by
deadlock, the white-bearded Barrett tossed the stones out of his
wheelbarrow and stormed off, never to return.

A twelve-year-old girl from Bayston Hill Village called at
Spring Cottage one Saturday afternoon selling tickets for a Girl
Guides raffle. Mary spoke to her kindly but nervously tore off
three counterfoils instead of two. Asked to step inside while Mary
found the money, the girl felt at once a tense atmosphere. 'Mr
Webb was sitting at a table near the window overlooking the
front garden, with his back to the drab room. He behaved in an
unusual manner, as he remained motionless, looking out, and
neither spoke nor even turned to glance at us as we talked near
the fireplace. It struck me as very odd . . . I was pleased when
Mrs Webb bought the three tickets, but I can still remember
my relief when I had thanked her and could escape from the
room.'

On another occasion after a clash, Henry had gone out in a
temper. Mary, terrified that he had left her, hurried to Mrs
Thorne whose husband and sons helped her to look for him all
over the wooded hill. Later Henry returned, having merely gone
off for a long walk on his own.

In London the pressures were even more intolerable as other
relationships too disappointed and wounded her, any small
failure or betrayal now harder to bear ('slights and lies and
friends that prove unkind'). She was prone to exaggerated
anxieties and suspicions, magnifying incidents out of proportion,
the ache of loneliness intensifying as Henry's love, understanding
and support were gradually withdrawn – she wondered why? who
was taking him from her? Painfully shy, she had wanted no
social contact with his associates and colleagues (apart from
Ethel Wicksteed – the Headmaster's wife, a vigorous woman,
interested in geology, archaeology and the countryside – who
tried to befriend her); and she antagonised the staff by her
repeated phone calls asking for him, her seeming aggression (once
desperately demanding his cheque), her persistence in enquiring
where he was. Those associated with Henry thought her 'difficult',
'ridiculous', 'impossible'. But there were very few who knew her
at all closely. A literary friend said, 'She lived in her own mind
rather than in the world which she viewed with timidity marked
by a rather pathetic defiance . . . She was naturally shy and

nervous, yet in matters of business and her rights she was surprisingly firm-minded.'[9]

And so at this period 'the sweet, keen trouble of living' became increasingly more keen than sweet . . . 'Far beyond, far beyond, / Deeper than the glassy pond, / My shivering spirit sits and weeps / And never sleeps.' She had come to the ultimate test of her own wholeness, and this, in a curious, inverted way, almost self-precipitated. In *The Golden Arrow*, she had shown how Deborah unknowingly propelled Stephen away by her frantic fear, the pressure of a love freighted with suffering, 'a doom of pain'. Perhaps in her striving towards wholeness there was an unconscious will for her fear to be fulfilled – if so, the ordeal of total aloneness was at hand. There were times when she wished for death, 'Great Death, the undisdainful', as she wrote at Hampstead in her blackbird poem. And in such a frame of mind she wrote 'Safe' :

> Under a blossoming tree
> Let me lie down,
> With one blackbird to sing to me
> In the evenings brown.
> Safe from the world's long importunity –
> The endless talk, the critical, sly stare,
> The trifling social days – and unaware
> Of all the bitter thoughts they have of me,
> Low in the grass, deep in the daisies,
> I shall sleep sound, safe from their blames and praises.
>
> (*PSJ*, p. 71)

Misunderstandings and the disloyalty she sensed in Henry intensified her acute *hiraeth* for Shropshire, making her later London days a protracted torture. Added to this was the misery of seeing suffering and hardship among the post-war poor and knowing how ineffective were her own efforts to assuage. She still gave wildly when she had money but there was now a curious fatality in her giving – the hopelessness of 'patching', as she called it, affected her deeply, leaving her with a wretched sense of futility. All these disillusionments, including the low sales of her books, chafed on her spirit.

When this became unbearable she would pack a small bag with the minimum of clothing and her books and papers, and catch the next train to Shrewsbury. Then Henry felt relief from her

[9] *Today*, 27 April 1928.

ever-anxious watching, her intensity of grievous love. And often
she came back just as suddenly, unable to be away from him for
long. These comings and goings became more arbitrary and
erratic as time went on : she was like a migratory bird, impelled
from one point of destination to another, magnetically pulled
back and forth, attuned to auguries, to deep unease.

How long would her frail health hold out under these tensions,
the keener stress still to come? Already her physical decline,
brought on by the long period of strain and undernourishment,
was gathering pace in 1925. She was excessively nervous, sleepless,
debilitated. The severe headaches and giddiness became worse :
one day at the Hampstead cottage she fainted and fell against
the settee, injuring her knee. She did not know – and neither did
Henry – that pernicious anaemia was developing. And this blood
disease, incurable at that date, virtually meant death within a
fairly short period, a few years at the most. While pernicious
anaemia was diminishing her strength, the Graves' Disease
reached a more advanced stage, toxics from her deteriorating
thyroid gland gradually poisoning her whole body. The end was
now inevitable : toxaemia, collapse of the heart and nervous
system.

Chill presentiments gripped her, sounding an inward warning
of the precariousness of her hold on life, heightening still further,
and with intolerable clarity, the beauty of the physical world.
The feeling of impending separation from that beauty imbues
her later poems with a yearning undertone and urgency, a
haunting sense of departure :

> Let fall your golden showers, laburnum tree !
> Break the grey casket of your buds for me –
> Soon I shall go where never gold is seen,
> And who will be with you as I have been?

> Quick with your silver notes, O silver bird !
> Wistful, I listen for the song I heard
> Many a day, but soon shall hear no more,
> For summoning winds are out along the shore.
>
> *(PSJ*, p. 66)

These lines from 'Farewell to Beauty' are among her best
known. In 'The Birds will Sing' there is again this wistfulness, an
emotional immediacy arising from her intimations of death. The

reflective poem, 'The Land Within', one of the last that she wrote, is also one of her finest and most remarkable, a sad depiction of her inner world, memories, desires; again she uses nature as her metaphor, transmuting the outer landscape to inner, the imagery derived from long contemplation at Bomere Pool. She begins with her present winter state :

> This is a land of forests, and of meres
> Stirless and deep, replenished with my tears.
> Here the pine harps, and many voices moan
> Within the cedar, crying, 'Lone! Alone!'
> Sharp on green heaven the green ice peaks arise
> Through the deep snows of thawless purities.
> Ten thousand stars are drowned within the lake,
> Beneath grey ice . . .
>
> *(PSJ,* pp. 114–5)

And looking back – 'In dreams, my soul! in dreams' – she sees the lost summer . . .

> And somewhere in the lake's confused reflections,
> Remote and fair as childhood's recollections,
> Smothered in wavering lilac leaves, and blurred
> With bloom, the shadow of a gable stirred
> With every tide, and a twisted chimney flowered
> In pale blue smoke, that in the water towered
> Downward. And through those deeps, pillared and aisled,
> Came a brown woodman, and a boy who smiled,
> Running towards the shifting wicket-gate,
> And waved an under-water hand, to spy
> One leaning from the casement – that was I.

On Henry – both her 'brown woodman' and her 'boy who smiled' – she had projected, to her cost, a perilous emotional centralisation. The final section of the poem indicates how far she had travelled into disillusion :

> Where was that cottage with its lilac trees,
> Its windows wide, its garden drowsed with bees?
> Where stood the echoing glade whence the faggot came
> To turn the evening hours to one warm flame?
> And that brown woodman, where and whence was he –
> That woodman, with the eyes that dazzled me
> Far more than rosy fire or golden gleams
> Of April? O, in dreams, my soul! in dreams.

It is with relief that we learn of any brightness in her life at this time. One event (recalling her girlhood pleasure in improvising entertainments and tableaux for children), was a theatre outing with Edwin Pugh in September 1925 to the first matinée performance of *Taffy* at the Royalty Theatre. This gripping, witty play by Caradoc Evans had a riotous first night, almost as stormy as that of Synge's *Playboy*. Evans' vehement criticism of the Welsh had roused their anger, an irate contingent disrupting the performance with a demonstration and loud singing of the Welsh National Anthem.

Edwin Pugh has described how totally Mary was absorbed, how hugely she enjoyed the entire afternoon : 'She sat so enrapt, enthralled, throughout the performance.' Pugh was near the truth when he said, 'I imagined she was living in her childhood once more', for Mary had retained, in spite of all, her childlike receptivity and capacity for wonder, her girlish spontaneity of reaction. She sighed when the performance was over : 'How I would like to see behind the scenes' – so they went backstage to talk to Evans and the principal actors. Entranced by this glimpse behind scenes, Mary 'drew a deep breath as she stood among the ugly pulleys and general clutter'. Pugh relates how 'presently she wandered away from us on to the stage. She went slowly as far as the footlights, and there she paused to peer into the dim auditorium. At last she returned laggingly to us, as one walking in her sleep, and her face was transfigured . . .'

Mary may well have been inspired in those moments to thoughts of creating a play of her own. It was possibly after this that she bought a manual on play-writing. After her death, this manual, together with her other books, was disposed of by Henry, sold by a Mayfair dealer in 1938. The manual, sold for £15, was described as 'so heavily annotated that it was considered to be proof of her intention of writing a play'.[10]

Pugh told of her preoccupied silence on leaving the Royalty Theatre that afternoon :

> She said nothing for a while. She maintained an impenetrable silence . . . until I took her somewhere for tea, and then she broke into raptures about her peep behind the scenes.

[10] *News Chronicle*, 28 April 1938.

12

The Last Years and –
Armour wherein he Trusted
1926–1927

... And as I was with Nesta in the litel grey garden
I knew well that the hours were glass, bright glass,
to crackle inward when God pleased.

(AWHT, p. 99)

There was a lady small and thin
(Oh, grave! Why did you let her in?)
Her voice was sad as a dove's, her feet
Went softly through the yellow wheat ...
'Colomen' *(PSJ*, p. 118)

In the final phase she went down in an agonising struggle against increasing odds: the devastating emotional and mental distress of a break-up in her personal life and, bound up with this, irreparably broken health.

During 1926 her relationship with Henry disintegrated. In her 'New Year's Day' poem 'To H.B.L.W.' she wrote tenderly, gratefully, of his 'patient love' which had radiated her 'cold and grey' life, making it like 'a wood blessed by one dove'. On New Year's Eve, as on many other nights, lying awake, restless, she had watched him sleeping: 'I lean across your pillow all night long/ To see you, when through the first cloudy rift / The light comes fair and new' (*51*, p. 44).

Later that year she was to write another poem, 'To the World', a powerful and sorrowful indictment of a world which, in taking Henry from her, took the 'rare blue' from her 'cloudy sky', shot her 'one bird', snatched her rose – 'one rose alone had I' – this she had feared from the outset of their relationship, an 'agony of loss' predicted in poems such as 'Isolde' and 'Today', the crucifixion of love pre-figured in her first novel by the ordeal of Deborah, devastated when Stephen deserts her.

Yet in the earlier part of 1926, though physically weak, she was still preoccupied with literary work, writing now with less idea (or hope) of breaking through to public success but with the assurance of a mature artistic command and the knowledge that she was achieving, as one London publisher said, 'a reputation that lived among the elect'.

The first months of the year were spent working at her new novel, set in the reign of William Rufus. *Armour wherein he Trusted* reveals her innate sense of history, expressed earlier in 'Viroconium', in 'Glimpses of Old Shropshire' and *Precious Bane*. However, *Precious Bane* did not require such a complete reach of the imagination into the distant past as *Armour wherein he Trusted*, for early nineteenth-century Shropshire was not greatly removed from early twentieth, although the details which make the difference were thoroughly researched and manifest in adept touches. Yet here and there, in *Precious Bane*, these details stand out a little obtrusively, whereas in *Armour* all is perfectly knitted into the texture.

The medieval atmosphere is subtly conveyed in this last work, those 'memoried glances' of the past becoming a muted scene of grey-green and silver. It is as if a veil has been penetrated and she takes us through: we experience another kind of reality, the substance of things and times now insubstantial. We become part of a gossamer tapestry. And the fragility of the thread by which she was clinging to physical and creative life can be felt as it weaves this tapestry. The delicate colours and tones threaten at any moment to be misted over, the painting on the web to be dashed into nothingness.

Mary's wistfulness for the beauty of earth was never greater than now when she felt her physical life fading – this she allegorises in the story of Sir Gilbert's struggle to renounce the world and especially to leave his Nesta who symbolises the earthly love and loveliness that beckon and haunt, that cause an almost intolerable ache of yearning when unattainable, that can give ecstasy, or wound bitterly when withdrawn.

In a story of human passion and suffering, she is again embedding a theme of universal significance: the age-old struggle between physical and spiritual realities, the contest of body and spirit. This wrestling between earthly and mystical love, one of the recurrent themes that give Mary Webb's work coherence, is more sharply drawn in *Armour wherein he Trusted* than in any of the preceding novels except perhaps *Gone to Earth;* and closely related to it is another of her central concerns, the striving of the individual to create an individual self, to find his own soul, this inevitably by way of 'pain's deep forest'.

However, in commenting on her last novel, it must be kept in mind that as we have it, so did Mary leave it at her death – unrevised and less than half completed. Yet it is clear from this fragment that following her usual method, she had first worked out the story and characterisation thoroughly in her mind and had completed her research before commencing to write.[1] It is indicated in the early pages that Sir Gilbert of Polrebec will live to old age and become the 'Holy and Pious Abbot of Strata Florida', his wife Nesta dying before him; we are shown how Sir Gilbert, having first fulfilled his desire for mortal love by marrying Nesta, can no longer resist the intimations of Christ which haunt him and so, yielding to the urgings of mystical love, he leaves wife, parents and castle to join Peter the Hermit in the First Crusade; and we learn, before the fragment breaks off, that he is gone for seven years during which Nesta, the 'Flower of the West', is courted by many men and especially by Sir Gilbert's rival, Jorwerth, the King's Escheator.

In setting this story, with its theme of contest between spiritual and physical awareness, in the Middle Ages, Mary selected a particularly appropriate period since the concept of opposition between spirit and flesh, and the related questions of good and evil, salvation and damnation were especially prominent in the medieval consciousness. As Martin Armstrong said, 'the theme, the period and the antique style' are 'carefully and skilfully adopted' and give 'ample scope to the sharp, visual quality which is one of her most delightful gifts'.

---

1 She researched carefully in both local history and period background in order to conjure the spirit and atmosphere of the late 11th century. Topographically the Polrebec country is her own landscape (see Appendix 1 – the demesne of Sir Gilbert includes 'Lyth and Condor and Hundeslit – that some call Stapleton . . .' Sir Gilbert's father is Lord of Stretton-in-the-Dale. Polrebec is Castle Pulverbatch (near the Long Mynd), now a high grassy mound, from which viewpoint vast tracts of the Shropshire landscapes can be encompassed.

When, after her death, the fragment was published with ten of her short stories in the Collected Edition of 1928–9, most of the critics agreed with Martin Armstrong's comments in his Introduction to the volume. But speculation on the novel's success had it been finished, is futile. As the *Times Literary Supplement* reviewer remarked (31 January 1929), 'picking holes in these fragments is a thankless task. They will be welcomed, to quote Mr Armstrong again, "for the sake of those qualities which make her novels the vivid things they are".' And as *The Times* critic (28 January 1929) put it, 'Lovers of her work . . . will welcome these last crumbs which have all the flavour of her best loaves'.

Most of the reviewers drew attention to Mary's unusual style in *Armour wherein he Trusted* ('delicately wrought', 'a certain stiff charm', 'artificial', but 'fresh and vigorous'). It is a development from her style in *Precious Bane*, composed of poetic, dialect and archaic elements, again passionate yet pithy, informed by freshness of feeling, pointedness of thought and a lyricism that rings from the soul. She shows in this highly individual style the influence of her reading in the English medieval mystics, particularly Dame Julian of Norwich – and above all in the descriptions of Sir Gilbert's 'visitations'.

And in writing this final novel, Mary was writing for herself, writing essentially what (and how) she wanted, with not the slightest concession to popularity. Stylistically adventurous, she comes close to technical inventiveness in *Armour wherein he Trusted*. Here, as in *Precious Bane,* she uses first person narrative form, giving further proof of her mastery of this difficult technique by which she conveys a curiously beautiful and radiant intimacy, taking us as completely into the mind of Gilbert de Polrebec as she did into that of Prudence Sarn, and now remarkably subtle and convincing in projecting a male rather than a female character. The personality of the narrator is a unifying factor as all is viewed from one centre of consciousness – and the voice of the narrator is that of Mary herself acting out her own insights.

Although Mary Webb is not a technical innovator in the way that Dorothy Richardson, James Joyce and Virginia Woolf are, she was developing in this last phase a technique of extraordinary fluidity, enabling her to move back and forward in time with subtlety and ease, weaving together retrospection and anticipation, introspection and action. It is a narrative technique which in its intimacy is utterly persuasive, involving the reader at once in the mood and atmosphere of the story, permitting an unusual inwardness and depth, the suspension of chronological time, and exploration of an individual mind and sensibility.

Gilbert's voice is her own when he expresses the concept of time as an eternal now:

> Yet, if we think right, there is no *Now* or *Then*, no wall of glass or of water, no hour shut away, but all, whether sad or merry, spent in Eternity, there lapsing, there renewed.   (p. 76)

In the words of Almey St John Adcock, reviewing *Armour wherein he Trusted* in the *Bookman* (March, 1929): 'Mary Webb had an imagination that broke down barriers; barriers of the spirit and barriers of time.'

The same critic saw that in 'the conflict between Gilbert de Polrebec's spiritual self and his earthly love for Nesta . . . the two forces of her own character – as discovered in her earlier work – were curiously blended', namely 'a keen consciousness of physical life mingling with and merging into spiritual ecstasy'. Unfinished though it is, this novel is both the most sensuous and the most mystical of her works. It is also remarkable for Sir Gilbert's portrait of Nesta – surely one of the strangest and most intriguing of Mary Webb's characters. Sir Gilbert, at the beginning of the story, riding through 'the springing April forest' near Powis Castle, finds Nesta Llanvihangel ('Lady Powis's new waiting woman out of Wales'), within 'a thicket of Christ thorn' in 'a small bower' like 'a witchen house'. A fey creature, 'very fair', but 'not altogether of mortal clay', she is 'of Merlin's line', and although she assures Sir Gilbert that she is 'no Ill Person', she is associated with witchcraft and magic, and her background is shrouded in mystery and fantasy. To Jorwerth, the Escheator, she states her mysterious lineage:

> 'I come from the Cymru, sir . . . and my home is in the waste; and my lineage is elf-lineage, and for our sign, it is a churn-owl with a kingly crown upon his head.'
> . . . 'Where, then, is this waste situate?' asked the Escheator . . .

'Sir,' she made answer, 'it lies betwixt Salop and Radnor. It lies also between life and death. It is betwixt and between all things.'

(p. 47)

Nesta comes from the Castle of Tochswilla, in this land of 'Betwixt and Between' – it is not in 'Doom Book', and the ground, 'very unket', is 'faery copyhold' which cannot be measured: 'times it will widen to eternity and yet again it will shrink to a knife-edge'. Aptly she speaks in paradoxes since she herself is a paradox. She has simplicity, a child-like innocence and pathos, yet 'at times, like the licking of a litel flame, would come a touch of craft, like a lizard in the crevices'. And like Hazel Woodus, Nesta seems ill-omened, an inevitability of doom surrounds her. In Nesta's disloyalty to Gilbert while he is away fulfilling his mystical and spiritual calling (intimated near the end of the fragment), and in Gilbert's (implied) struggle to accept the situation, we see Mary's sublimation of her deepest personal problem and glimpse her attempt to come to grips with it.

Clearly she intended Nesta to be a figure of major symbolic significance and an allegorical contest was to be waged for her soul between the powers of light and darkness, this paralleling Sir Gilbert's struggle with spiritual and earthly love.

In these first sections of *Armour wherein he Trusted,* threads of religion, magic and romance are closely interwoven. There is a characteristic use of superstition and augury, and an integration of legend (both Arthurian and local) – always an important element in Mary Webb's work. But it has been said that in this novel there is not the concrete presentation of the Shropshire countryside that usually characterises her writing. Martin Armstrong, among others, noted a serious limiting of 'the rich and profound sense of the country which gives to all her other books their unforgettable atmosphere.' Yet those who know the 'Polrebec country' well, will probably agree that Mary has captured here the very essence of that landscape: the feeling of great age and lonely stillness in those quiet green hills, a sense of ingathering and mystical restraint which is indeed the tone which pervades her novel, especially in the visual descriptions of the Polrebec demesne and castle set high on its 'round pyatt' – 'so small a castle hid away between mountain and woodland in the great silence of those places'.

Again Mary creates and takes us into her unique world, a world unified within itself, 'half in Faery and half out of it'. Gilbert's 'litel grey garden' at Polrebec, for instance, is felt to be both in and out of that particular time and place:

> It clung like a nest, this my garden, to the grey wall of our castle, and it was grey itself with the quiet greyness of doves. The lavender was all spiked over like a castle guarded by halberd-men, and the maiden pink held up fresh buds, the grey-leaved rose bloomed white beneath the heavy dews. There were no citizens of the litel grey garden save Nesta and I, the grey-brown bees and the portly grey pigeons walking in the sun, like abbots ... For certain hours of the day the sun played on us, basking with the bees and the green slipping lizards. And for part of the day the blue, solemn shadow of Cotardicote mountain covered it like an interdict. (pp. 99–100)

There can be no doubt that Mary Webb, reaching her prime as a literary artist, was producing in this successor to *Precious Bane* what would have been, had she lived to complete it, another major work of high imaginative order. Tragically, however, it was to be, as the *New York Times* critic expressed it, the 'last leavings' of a 'fine talent'.

We must turn now from the novel itself back to her life and specifically to those months of 1926 when her personal tragedy was intensifying.

In London literary circles increasing interest was being shown in her new novel as a result of *Precious Bane,* and she had secured a publisher without the slightest difficulty. Holden's in 1925 readily signed an agreement, the terms of which Mary outlined with her usual firmness and which included the publication of *The Golden Arrow* (July 1925) in Holden's Lyceum Library edition. By her determined efforts she had brought her first novel back into print. That Holden's had granted exceptionally liberal terms for the new novel of which they had seen nothing, was a sign of her growing prestige. Increasingly too, she was mentioned in literary journals, and was contributing fairly regularly to leading periodicals.

Both T. P. O'Connor and his assistant editor, Caradoc Evans, invited her to submit articles to *T.P.'s and Cassell's Weekly,* and in April 1926 two were published within a fortnight and were given front page publicity. Her centenary article on Mrs Craik (3 April) was followed on 17 April by 'The Poetry of The Prayer Book' (*CPAP*, pp. 43-6). Here, discussing 'the poetry of common prayers', Mary repeats a view which she had expressed elsewhere that 'all religions are like a lonely arab in the desert'. She maintains that whatever our personal belief or non-belief about God

> The important thing is that here we are, very small and blind and weak . . . bound for an unglimpsed country, and our hearts 'burn within us', and we weep like lost children . . . These ancient prayers help us to be articulate. They express our own souls for us. The best of them express not only one nation, one age, but all.

In such prayers we come 'in direct touch with the deepest life of the race' : these

> have grown upwards from below, not downwards from the educated . . . have grown gradually, as folk-music does, and legend, and public opinion as to right and wrong.

Appraising 'the poetic beauty of the Liturgy', she states succinctly :

> although Cranmer was the goldsmith who wrought the Liturgy – with others – yet the metal had been accumulating for centuries.

The value of the Prayer Book, for her, resides in this aspect of it as 'the folklore of the soul'.

Mary's highly nervous and uncertain frame of mind at the time of writing this article is revealed by Caradoc Evans in his commemorative essay. He relates how, dissatisfied with her work, she 'came on the telephone every half hour to change words and phrases' and even after the article had gone to print she phoned the printer wanting to make alterations until she was told that it had 'gone to bed'. Phoning Evans again in the hope of deferring the printing, she heard that it was too late, and a cheque of ten guineas had been passed. Immediately she asked Evans for a higher payment although she knew this was hardly possible. Fortunately they understood each other and with good humour he accepted her apology.

Again she was in a desperate situation financially and this

undoubtedly was undermining still further her spirit and health. The need to seek immediate returns from articles and reviewing was a pressure taking time, tapping off the creative energy which, she felt, ought to be devoted to her novel. But even small amounts of money from this kind of work could help to eke out their tiny resources. At times she had barely enough cash to buy food. There is a note of bitterness in her reply to Mrs C. A. Nicholson's letter expressing concern about her ill-health and enquiring whether she was having medical treatment. Mary wrote :

> When I have succeeded in getting paid fairly by the British public for my work, I shall naturally have the best treatment I can get. But not till then. Also, it is less treatment that I want than ordinary good food and a suitable amount of rest and exercise. I have this week existed on bread and scrape and tea. If I give up going to the few things I do go to, I get out of touch with everybody.

Such a concept of 'being paid fairly by the British public' was symptomatic of her increasing sense of frustration, grievance and disillusionment. Knowing that *Precious Bane* was selling better than any of her previous novels, she harassed Cape's with distraught pleas for money, either telephoning or going in person to 30 Bedford Square in the hope of receiving a cheque. Her behaviour seemed erratic, annoyingly pressing to the publishers, who knew that even if money was advanced to her she would probably give it away at once to the first pathetic beggar. And financial stress was now adding to the emotional strain between herself and Henry.

He had been invited to tutor, after school hours, one of his former K.A.S. pupils who wanted to gain University entrance – a brilliantly clever girl in her late teens, keenly interested in languages and literature. He had not lost touch with this girl and her parents after she left K.A.S., as like many other families associated with the schools, the Wilsons had kept up their interest and connection with it. And Kathleen was, as he once said of her in a report, 'one of those for whom English Literature is written'. He enjoyed tutoring at her home with its comfortable, cultured atmosphere; there he was made very welcome and became a friend of her parents who were impressed by his intellect and charm and invited him for meals. Kathleen, together with most of his pupils, had adored Henry from the time he first came to K.A.S., and he, on his part, was now captivated, stimulated by her youthful affection and enthusiasm.[2]

Henry, increasingly caught up in his relationship with Kathleen, saw no reason why he should curtail an arrangement which he found pleasant (and flattering) and which also brought in some extra income. He spent more and more time with Kathleen, taking walks on the heath and visiting her at home. There were evenings when Mary sat alone, tormentedly watching the clock while Henry dined with the Wilsons, not returning for the meals she had prepared for him. On one occasion her control snapped and she arrived at the Wilsons' door with the joint she had cooked, telling the startled servant to 'take this to Mr. Webb – it's a pity to waste it, and it's of no use to me !'

Resenting Mary's questioning of his movements, Henry felt oppressed and hostile towards her. But to Mary it was obvious that, as she had predicted in 'Isolde', 'busy stranger, eager friend / Break in and – never knowing – steal our all'. Henry preferred now to be elsewhere than in her company, and whereas previously he had patiently explained his activities and reassured her, now he was no longer prepared to either explain himself or allay her acute anxiety. They lost real communication as the friction between them increased. For Mary this was an intolerable agony : she had found for so long with Henry what she had lost at her father's death, that rare and precious peace of utter understanding. Now, as this was disrupted, her distress was extreme : it seemed that Henry had closed his heart and mind to her and this was like the chill grip of death . . . 'yet, in truth, we did not measure the deepness of our peace until it was shattered like a bowl of fine glass'. Painful personal experience is behind these words from her last novel with its tone of indrawn sorrow.

Mary's distress and the effects of her disease were interacting disastrously. Nervously overwrought, she seemed trapped in a tragic vortex, anguish undermining both her spiritual and her physical health. It was a drawn-out process of deterioration both

[2] Later, almost two years after Mary's death, Henry B. L. Webb and Kathleen Wilson married. They lived for a while at 5, Grove Cottages before moving to a house in Golders Green. There were two children of the marriage.

15. Henry Bertram Law Webb
(1924)

16. Mary Webb as Madeline at the
Dickens Ball (1924)

17. Mary Webb in her last years

in her physical condition and in her relationship with Henry. A gradual but inexorable distintegration.

Yet there were still to be patches of light in the gathering shadows, still some minor triumphs before the end.

Notification came that on 11 February 1926, she had been awarded the Prix Femina for *Precious Bane*. Established in 1918, this was a coveted literary prize, decided on by a committee appointed to discover 'the best imaginative work in prose or verse descriptive of English life by an author who has not gained sufficient recognition'. It was announced in *The Times* that the Femina Vie Heureuse Committee had voted the 1924–5 prize to Mary Webb for *Precious Bane*.[3] Her excitement and elation at this award and the flood of congratulations which followed, can readily be imagined. It was a tremendous *succès d'estime*. Her firm admirers in the literary and publishing world were delighted that at last some long-deserved recognition had come to her, and a number of critics affirmed the Prix Femina to be 'an honour to which the book was pre-eminently entitled'.

The prize was to be presented at the Institut Français on 6 July. With mingled nervousness and exhilaration Mary prepared for the presentation, looking thin and frail in her heliotrope gown adorned by a belt on which she had embroidered the fleur-de-lys 'as a compliment', she said, 'to the French'. Around her throat was a matching scarf-bow, carefully placed to conceal her goitre which had recently become so enlarged.

Henry accompanied her, pleased at her success, and with them was her brother Douglas, newly returned from the East: as St John Adcock noticed, 'half her happiness was in having them to share it with her'.

The gathering of distinguished writers and journalists at the Institut, presided over by Violet Hunt, included a number of Mary's personal friends, Edwin Pugh and Rebecca West among them. Sir Edmund Gosse gave an address on 'Literary friendship between France and England', and Mary was then introduced to the audience by Sylvia Lynd. It is a pity there is no record of the speeches that followed, made by Mary herself, St John Adcock, Beatrice Harraden and Rebecca West, among others.[4]

---

3 *The Times*, 12 February 1926, Telegrams In Brief, p. 11.
4 *The Bookman*, August 1926, p. 253.

St John Adcock, recalling the presentation, was sure that Mary's 'undisguised pride and delight in the occasion were unalloyed . . . by any thought of how much good work she had to do before this honour fell to her'. She probably thought, as others did, that she was about to come into her own. The relative success of *Precious Bane* augured well for her future, and it was announced later that a French translation of the novel was planned by the Femina Vie Heureuse Committee. The publicity was good for sales : it seemed that the reading public was at last responding and *Precious Bane* went into a fourth impression. Meanwhile, in America, it had been published by Dutton on 19 April and received excellent reviews, praised for its 'rare vitality' (*New York Times*), 'Hardyesque sense of doom' and 'pictorial vividness' (*New York Herald Tribune*), 'sweeping inevitability' (*New York World*), its style 'rich and strong', the whole work 'full of colour' and 'keenly attuned to the darker rhythms of country life' (*Boston Transcript*). One reviewer (*Springfield Republican*) designated it 'a book in a thousand . . . throbbing with life, vitality and truth'.

But ironically, as her literary career was taking a turn for the better, her personal life was plunging more deeply and irretrievably into chaos.

Looking forward to spending the summer at Lyth Hill with Henry, Mary was shocked when he suggested that Kathleen Wilson should come to Spring Cottage for a short holiday. He wanted to show Kathleen the Shropshire countryside – apparently oblivious of the effect this visit would have on Mary. Kathleen came, and Henry took her on picnics to the places he and Mary knew so well, to Pontesford Hill, the Long Mynd, the Devil's Chair and other favourite walks.

Mary was gripped by fear, her insecurity which partly stemmed from deep feelings of physical inferiority, intensifying as she compared herself – greying, goitred and middle-aged – with this young and golden girl. And Henry, formerly so sensitive to Mary's needs and attuned to her suffering, was uncaring about the extent to which his new and developing relationship would torture Mary, putting her on a rack of doubt and suspicion. Fascinated by Kathleen, he was apparently unable either to curb the relationship or cope with the havoc it was causing.

After Kathleen's return to London, Mary could not remain

silent about her brooding suspicions, the fears gnawing at her constantly. In losing Henry, she would lose all – but while it was unbearable for her to think of this, it was also unbearable for Henry, faced by her anguished questioning and no longer sure about his own deepest needs. The tension between them strained to cracking point during those August days at Lyth Hill. One afternoon, returning from a solitary walk, Mary found Spring Cottage empty and Henry gone. There was no note of farewell. Frantically she ran down to the village from where she took a taxi to Shrewsbury station. At the barrier, a ticket collector answered her enquiry and detailed description of Henry, confirming that he had caught the train for London a short while previously.

Mary's distress was so acute that she could not bring herself to return to Lyth Hill: clinging to a wild, remote hope that Henry would come back on the early morning train, she sat the entire night in the station waiting room.

When Henry was not on the train, and it became starkly clear to her that he was not returning, she took a taxi as far as Bayston Hill where she pleaded with friends to let her have a spare room for the night. Dreading the lonely darkness at Spring Cottage, she knew that, unable to sleep, she would be haunted by the thought that her worst wears were fulfilled, Henry irrecoverably gone. Like Deborah Arden she had come to her 'longest night.'

Her request for a room was rejected by villagers who probably did not understand her desperation and were suspicious of her lost, wild-eyed look. This must have seemed another blow from a critical, unfeeling world: she walked slowly back up Lyth Hill in the grip of terror, anguish, grief which overwhelmed her during the days and weeks that followed. There was no one to whom she could turn.

The situation worsened when Henry sought the advice of his Headmaster and friend, Joseph Wicksteed. Mary's extreme agitation is clear in an agonised letter to St John Adcock (26 September), expressing her fear that Wicksteed was advising that she and Henry should separate. Apparently she had received a letter from Wicksteed to this effect. Not knowing what to do, she asked Adcock's help, urgently stressing that it was a situation she could not bear, and which, she said, 'will end in my death'. That she should make such an appeal for help to the editor of the *Bookman* is a measure of her desperation – and her solitariness. Frantic with anxiety, she was totally alone, having no child to claim her care and concern, divert her thoughts – or prove that the marriage had been consummated.

Acting on Adcock's suggestion, she came to Hampstead and, after the initial tense discussions, was relieved to find that Henry was not intending a separation. Perhaps he sensed that she did not have long to live. It was decided that she should stay, and as she gradually picked up again the threads of her London life, the situation relaxed somewhat, though Henry remained detached and pursued his own course, spending as little time as possible at the cottage. His love for her was temporarily overlaid by bitter memories of the recent strife between them, and distanced by the fresh, vivid impact of Kathleen. Literally too, Mary watched him walk into the distance each day as she continued her habit of watching him from the gate when he set off for work. She would watch until he was out of sight, but now he walked resolutely on and never looked back to give that answering wave.

There were other worries too, contributing, at this time, to Mary's overwrought nervousness and insecurity. An unexpected pressure came from the landlord of 5 The Grove, who informed her in the autumn of 1926 that he was thinking of selling the cottage. To Mary this news was extremely unsettling – she did not have the resources, physical or otherwise, to cope with another move, apart from the even more unnerving thought of what effect this might have on Henry. In the present strained state of their relationship, Mary feared that Henry would not tolerate yet another troublesome search for a flat or cottage, further upheaval, expenditure, mounting debt: again there loomed the worst fear of all, her 'lifelong dread' that he might leave her. These deep personal concerns tearing her – and loathing the thought of strangers coming to look in her 'nest' – she wrote anxiously (3 November 1926):

Dear Mr Stephens,
    I enclose cheque for the rent. I hope you are not still thinking of selling this house? It would be so very disturbing to feel that you would be wanting people to come and look at it. In any case I should have to have a few days notice every time anyone wanted

to come, and I hope very much you are not thinking of it. I can send you the Christmas rent about the 18th of December. I mention this in case the earlier date will be convenient to you.

Yours sincerely,
Mary Webb.

Pressures such as this caused further physical and nervous deterioration as the advancing Graves' Disease and pernicious anaemia were fatally weakening her entire system. She had lived on her reserves to the point of exhaustion: always undernourished, even the small amounts of food she ate were of little use to her now since Graves' Disease, drastically affecting her metabolism, involved serious gastric difficulties. She was only forty-five, but in a hopeless state of slow, relentless decline. With increasing frequency she suffered attacks of vertigo and severe head pain; her mind was excessively active, allowing her frail body no rest. Sleepless yet fatigued, deplorably weary, thin and brittle-boned, she was prone to long periods of depression during which, unable to write, she plunged into deeper despair, feeling she had failed in everything. To friends in Shropshire she wrote desperately that her heart was breaking, that there was now 'little left to live for'.

It is good to know that in this time of long darkness some praise and encouragement came to her from a most unexpected quarter.

In January 1927, a letter arrived from 10 Downing Street, bearing the Prime Minister's crest. Baldwin had read *Precious Bane* during the Christmas vacation and was so deeply impressed that he wrote a letter of appreciation:

Dear Mrs Webb,

I hope you will not think it an impertinence on my part if I tell you with what keen delight I have read 'Precious Bane'.

My people lived in Shropshire for centuries before they migrated to Worcestershire, and I spent my earliest years in Bewdley which is on the border. In your book I seem to hear again the speech and turns of phrase which surrounded me in the nursery. I think it is a really first-class piece of work and I have not enjoyed a book so much for years.

It was given to me by one of my secretaries and I read it at Christmas within sight of the Clee Hills, at home.

.Thank you a thousand times for it.

Believe me to remain
Sincerely yours,
Stanley Baldwin

Baldwin, one of the most literate of Prime Ministers, was among many discerning readers who considered *Precious Bane* to be 'a really first-class piece of work'. His letter was one of a number that Mary received from the famous and established admiring her novel, especially after its success in winning the Prix Femina. H. R. L. Sheppard sent a letter telling Mary that he had read nothing more inspiring in modern literature : he was convinced of her genius.

It was directly due to Hamish Hamilton, a fervent admirer of her writing, that *Precious Bane* had come to Baldwin's attention. Hamilton, a young apprentice publisher at Cape's when the novel was published, had become devoted to Mary Webb's work – an enthusiasm shared by Edward Garnett, Cape's reader. After leaving the firm, Hamish Hamilton continued to meet Garnett, and late in 1926 invited him and Tom Jones, then Deputy-Secretary to the Cabinet, to dine at the Bath Club. During the evening, Hamilton and Garnett enthusiastically discussed *Precious Bane,* describing the Shropshire setting to Tom Jones who remarked that such a novel 'would interest the P.M.'. Promptly following this up, Hamish Hamilton sent a copy of the book to Tom Jones, asking him to give it to Baldwin, which, of course, Jones did.

At a future date, hearing from Hamilton of his part in bringing the novel to his notice, Baldwin exclaimed, 'My dear boy, I owe you a debt of gratitude !' He had been so impressed after reading it at Christmas 1926, regarding it as 'one of the best of its kind' that he 'inquired about the author' from two of his literary friends, Sir James Barrie and John Buchan. Both expressed to Baldwin their high opinion of Mary Webb : 'one of about the three best living writers of English today but no one buys her books.' And subsequently he wrote telling her of the 'keen delight' with which he had read *Precious Bane.*

Mary's appreciation of Baldwin's letter and the encouragement it undoubtedly gave her at the time, are evident in her reply dated 25 January:

Dear Mr Baldwin,
Thank you very much indeed for your most kind letter which I received last Tuesday. That the man with least leisure, I suppose, of anybody in the British Empire, should spare time to write me a letter with his own hand about my book, has delighted and touched me very much. That one notably versed in the classics should find my style pleasant is a feather in my cap. That a personality of so much breadth and vigour should find my ideas worth reading, is perhaps, best of all.

I shall have great pleasure in asking your acceptance of the book I am now writing, which is about the Welsh Marches just after the Norman Conquest, when Bewdley, as I expect you know, was a famous City of Refuge for people fleeing from the depredations of the Lords Marchers. I hope it will be published this spring. It is nice that you read *Precious Bane* within sight of those enchanted hills.

Please accept a little bunch of violets for your writing-table. I am sending them tomorrow.
    Yours sincerely,
      Mary Webb,   Mrs. H. B. L. Webb.

She added, with a characteristic touch of grave humour, 'I am very much obliged to your Secretary'. It was equally characteristic of her to send a small bunch of her favourite flowers. And it is significant that she was gratified most of all that Baldwin had found her 'ideas . . . worth reading'.[5]

However, it was a desperate hope that the new novel would be 'published this spring'. Still far from completed, she had added little to it of late, neither did she in the early months of 1927. Aware of time and strength ebbing, she sensed death near as she struggled to write. The note of farewell that sounds with poignant wistfulness in her last poems also permeates the tone and atmosphere of this novel which, she was feeling increasingly

---

[5] St John Adcock related that Mary called on him with the news of the Prime Minister's letter, and he suggested that she should obtain Baldwin's permission to print the letter in an advertisement. Mary, 'being highly nervous and possessing no professional instinct . . . was horrified at the suggestion. Mr Baldwin might not like it. He might take offence at such a request. She could not think of such a thing'. (Moult, p. 259)

certain, would never be finished. There is a muted urgency even in the opening paragraphs and underlying the entire fragment a sense of the impending end of physical life. Her yearning for the beauty of the physical world, sharpened by premonition of death, is expressed through the words of her narrator, Sir Gilbert of Polrebec:

> spring drawing near, with great gatherings of starling in the reeds, evenings, and rosaries of buds in the ellum trees, it has come to me in a dream that I must hasten with my story, that I may finish it . . . (p. 38)

This season which always caused her soul to hurt 'with too much bliss' was experienced for the last time, not now with transcendent joy but ineffable sadness:

> All is so fair, I never saw the leafless thorn so snowy-white outside our monastery wall. I never heard the merle and the mavis cry and whistle so sweetly, nor smelt such freshness of life in the wild gales. (p. 38)

Mary knew – and Sir Gilbert knew listening to the call of God – that there was now less than a year left:

> 'Look long on the apple-blow, for you will not see it agen. Listen well to the mavis, for come a year I shall have invited thee to my house. And leaning from heaven's wall you will see the white thorn shining deep down, like snow in summer, and you will hear the mavis sing so faint and far away that you must fill up the glats in the song from memory.' (pp. 38–9)

When Sir Gilbert reveals his awareness that 'come another Easter morning' he 'shall be away' – and this before any have read his book – it is a prophecy of Mary's own fate and that of her novel.

In this final phase her personal identification with birds becomes her means of symbolising death's approach, release of the aspiring spirit and hope of continued spiritual presence in nature. Birds in flight symbolise her own spirit as well as the spirit of earth and air. As her poems reveal again and again, she longs for her 'wood-bird soul' to be absorbed more closely into 'the spirit of earth'. As in 'The Wood':

... Like a bird, with wings
Dusky and silent, I would flit through spring's
Wistful, immaculate colours; through the dream
And hush of summer; down the rush and gleam
Of autumn; and when winter, with a moan,
Swept through the freezing wood aloof, alone,
Prisoning the pine needles in shining, hollow
Cases of ice, yet the brown bird would follow.
Light as a last year's leaf I'd flutter by,
With the sad noise of finches in July.

(PSJ, pp. 51–2)

– an exquisite desire for her spirit to be forever at Lyth Hill and in the Little Wood in shadow form, as shadow bird.

For Mary doves are symbols of grief rather than peace: they signify a deep, secret sadness iterated in their low, long-drawn sound: 'Like the autumn dove that grieves, / Darkly hid in dove-like leaves, / So I moan within a woe / None may know.' During that last summer the wood-pigeons in the Little Wood, 'with feathers of rose and snow', again settled on her. And, totally desolate, she wrote the strange, narrative poem, 'Colomen', product of her tortured imagination, a fantasy on her broken relationship with Henry:

When all her thronging pigeons cooed
Around, with outspread arms she stood.
She seemed a pale and slender tree,
Bent with snow and not with bloom –
Bent lower towards the tomb.

(PSJ, pp. 118–23)

In this poem, found later by Henry among her papers, the theme of entwined love and death is developed. Mary uses dove imagery to express her indrawn anguish, doves now symbolising not only personal grief but death itself.

Recalling Coleridge's 'mystery' poems, 'Colomen' tells with sorrowful urgency of a wandering portrait painter and his lady of the doves, of their love in the 'sunny cote', of treachery when he is taken from her, and of her self-inflicted death. There is much in this tragic poem not merely wrought but wrung from her own sad experience:

All day, beside the memoried cote
She lay so still they thought her dead,
Her doves, that wheeled above her head.
But in her eyes a wild, remote,
Inhuman sorrow slumberèd . . .
She dragged her leaden limbs across
The grey lawns, to hear the sound
That turned a sword within her wound
And made her agony of loss
So keen that if she held her breath
She almost heard the feet of death.

The doves with their 'heartbroken, sweet/Clamour of some eerie thing' presage the tragedy :

She would be free of the distress
That men call joy, the littleness
That men call life – as birds are free.

So beside her portrait the 'lady pale and thin' hangs herself, as Fidelia Thatcher (in the short story 'Blessed are the Meek') hung herself after seeing the young swallows fly into 'the soft, dove-coloured evening'.

Armour wherein he Trusted has the same dove-greyness as 'Colomen', but the note of interior misery so strong in this poem is muted in the novel into a pervasive sense of resignation. Her 'agony of loss' is diffused in the feeling of imminent loss of life itself.

It was with mingled pain and weariness of spirit that Mary returned to Lyth Hill for the summer of 1927. She and Henry had become increasingly shut off from one another : a barrier had grown between them more painful and terrible to her than even physical separation; and in this situation, their continued physical proximity heightened the suffering. There was only one place to go where perhaps she could find again, as she had always been able to in the past, that inner calm 'where no winds stir'. Here, at Lyth Hill, she could remember 'the dear, the good' in Henry, recall this at a distance instead of 'beseeching for it childishly' as she said in the personal poem 'A Farewell'. But here too there would be no escape : 'Yet will the breathless moments when you smiled/Looking upon me, haunt me'.

Perhaps, had her health not been irretrievably broken, her work would have saved her, as she had been writing superbly and knew it : this, and the deep peace of the woods and hills of Shropshire, her mystical union with her countryside – a relationship which would never fail, disillusion or wound her. Yet how far into pain she had come since the days when she had written with joyous optimism her 'little book of healing'. Could nature heal such anguish as hers? Perhaps, given time, but time, for her, was running out. 'Life's severe detention' was to hold her for only a short while longer.

Mary spent most of that last summer at Lyth Hill, and it was spent alone. She returned there for the Whitsun holiday, and Mrs Thorne who, as usual, had aired Spring Cottage and filled it with flowers from the garden, noticed at once how desperately thin and frail she had become. Soon it was apparent to everyone who saw Mary that she was indeed very seriously ill. If she walked now, it was slowly and not far; mostly she took a chair and sat out, either in the garden or on the plateau immediately in front of her gate from where she could contemplate the 'meadows dear and low' in the changing light and the distant rim of her 'shaken, pansied hills . . .'

Often she was seen leaning at the wicket gate or at the Keepers' gate of the Little Wood to which she had managed to walk. Yet although she had little physical strength left, she still had mental energy; she was still writing, working spasmodically. If her creative vitality was ebbing, this is not apparent in what was her last review, a critique of Edith Wharton for the *Bookman* (September, 1927). Always quick to see ironic meaning, Mary's sense of irony remained keen to the end. She entitled the article 'Irony and Mrs Wharton', and the opening paragraph could apply to herself :

Ironic genius is rare, though plenty of us have observed the generous helpings of irony, with or without tragedy, which fate lades out to us. Nobody, one supposes, ever felt it as the Greeks did – a beautiful race in a lovely summer land, yet obsessed by this dark vision. But after all, who is afraid of a dead leaf in winter? Only in the rose gardens of summer is it a threat. So the people of richest vitality and fullest experience are usually those whom irony haunts. *(CPAP, pp. 69–70)*

And she was well aware of the irony of this in her own life. Often an applied irony is at work in her novels (particularly *The House in Dormer Forest*) – an aspect of her writing which arose from her intense vision and demanded considerable control of language, imagination, idea and design. That this control was still hers in the summer of 1927, even though her hold on physical life was failing drastically, is proved by her final review, incredibly poised, crisp and trenchant from the pen of a dying woman. The haunting irony now was that as she was reaching her artistic maturity, about to fulfil her full potential as a novelist and on the verge of establishing her reputation, she was to be cheated by crumbling health and a premature death.

In this last article, discussing Edith Wharton's *Twilight Sleep*, Mary's critical statements give us insight into her views on the art of the novel. Foremost among her requirements are 'exquisite touches of nature' and intimate relationship of character to setting; and she places emphasis on 'solid pathos', 'sudden, swift-hidden drama silently shattering a life'. Significantly *Twilight Sleep* fails for her because 'there is no inevitability, there is nothing of the sense of helpless humanity struggling in a net set for it before time was'. Inevitability there is in her own novels, above all in *Gone to Earth* and *Precious Bane*, while *Armour wherin he Trusted* is pervaded by a powerful sense of impending fate towards which all is tending as the fragment fades.

She had long sensed the inevitability of her own tragic end and was now facing it at a time of personal devastation. Out of bitter experience, she expressed that sad reality : 'After all, who is afraid of a dead leaf in winter?'

Alone at Lyth Hill that summer, Mary had neither the strength nor the will to look after herself. Not that she ever had cared much about her own welfare. Living a fervid inner life, she bothered little about such things as regular meals, wet feet or skirts 'sobbin' wet', soaked half-way up her legs where she had gone through the long grass in the early morning. Her brother Kenneth never forgot an occasion at the annual Shrewsbury Show one wet Edwardian summer when, during a torrential downpour, everyone flocked under a large marquee. Outside, the band bravely played on under the bandstand and one solitary figure in a black-and-white summer dress was seen sitting outside listening to the music, enrapt and oblivious to the rain. It was

Mary, drenched to the skin. This was typical of her complete disregard for her bodily welfare, especially when her mind and feelings were preoccupied.

Self-neglect was now accelerating her physical decline: unutterably lonely and sad because of the breakdown in her relationship with Henry, she slept little, and her appetite, always small, was now negligible. Mrs Thorne did her best to encourage her to eat and look after herself, but Mary seemed beyond caring. She knew that Henry was not actually leaving her, as she had feared, but – equally hard to bear – he had retreated into a remote interior depth where she could no longer reach him.

Early in their marriage she had written a poem to Henry about her death ('Winter'), beginning 'If I should be the first to go away' and expressing the hope that 'gathered safe within your voice, your eyes/Your dear protecting smile, I shall not know/When the black frost sets in, the dark wind cries'. This was not how it was to be: fully aware of the desolation, she was facing the 'black frost' alone.

Illness had sapped her spiritual strength, her ability to plumb the 'opaque and fathomless pool' within her own being – and she was lost in her own dark regions. This was the core of her tragedy, the personal trauma now inextricably bound up with her physical and nervous condition, one influencing the other, emotional stress and strain contributing crucially to the complete break-up of her fragile health. As Hilda Addison explained, writing less than four years after Mary's death:

> . . . there were wounds and sorrows which Nature could not heal. The foundations of her mental, spiritual and emotional life were crumbling about her, yet the common-sense road to reestablishing them – medical attention, rest and peace of mind – she flatly refused to allow herself. Hence she grew steadily worse.

Yet during those final weeks at Lyth Hill, she may have found, if only in fleeting returns of her lost wholeness and balance, the peace of acceptance. This is perhaps indicated in her intimate poem, 'Summer Remembered', in which, looking back to the beginning of her relationship with Henry, she is grateful still, 'hearing the golden words that once were spoken/And so are spoken now' (*51*, pp. 36–7).

Her countryside was enfolding her once more as the days of that last sad summer drew on. Extremely weak, she leaned at the wicket gate or sat outside it on the open hillside near the plateau's edge, her eyes and soul drinking in the loveliness from which she would soon be separated. From early morning until dusk all the summer long, hour upon hour, she looked out over the plain with its 'blue ring of hills', gazing longingly, renewing, although not ecstatically now, her spiritual oneness with nature. There can scarcely have been a more poignant personal farewell to life than that in her poem, 'Goodbye To Morning' :

> I will say good-bye to morning, with her eyes
> Of gold, her shell-pale robe and crocus-crown.
> Once her green veils enmeshed me, following down
> The dewy hills of heaven : with young surprise
> The daisies eyed me, and the pointed leaves
> Came swiftly in green fire to meet the sun :
> The elves from every hollow, one by one,
> Laughed shrilly. But the wind of evening grieves
> In the changing wood. Like people sad and old,
> The white-lashed daisies sleep, and on my sight
> Looms my new sombre comrade, ancient night.
> His eyes dream dark on death; all stark and cold
> His fingers, and on his wild forehead gleams
> My morning wreath of withered and frozen dreams.
>
> (*PSJ*, p. 68)

She decided eventually to return to Hampstead and to Henry whose new term had already begun. Locking Spring Cottage for what was to be the last time, she gave the keys to Mrs Thorne; and the village taxi-driver (one of the Barrett family, who knew her well) took her in his cab to Shrewsbury station. Leaving Lyth Hill, on the road to Shrewsbury, he was aware of a deep sadness and strangeness in her attitude : she was unnaturally silent and withdrawn, sunk in thought. Then, on arrival at the station she became distressed, finding that she had left her money behind at Spring Cottage. The young man paid her train fare and later, when refunded by Mrs Thorne from the forgotten purse, he told her about Mary's strange, preoccupied silence throughout the drive from Lyth Hill, and said he sensed that she was feeling she would never return.

She had gone to London hoping to heal her relationship with

Henry, but it was a forlorn hope as she was to find that his cold attitude towards her had not changed. Frail and exhausted by the journey, she entered the Hampstead cottage clutching her small case which contained a few letters and all she had written of the new novel.

This manuscript of *Armour wherein he Trusted* is, in fact, the only manuscript of her novels which is extant: a cheap notebook and odd-sized sheets of paper (and scattered between the pages cuttings taken from magazines, including a colour print of four bees, life-size). Her handwriting reveals her haste, the sense of urgency as if she knew that time was against her, that this was a race against death. Her 'fast-flow' pen, running out of ink, is discarded, the writing continuing almost indecipherably in faint pencil, and then again in pen. Years later, Henry told a Mayfair book dealer, Elkin Matthews, to whom he sold the manuscript and the books in Mary's small library: 'All the other manuscripts were burnt. They took up too much room in the tiny cottage, and, besides, they made a splendid fire which lasted a long time.'[6] The truth of it was that Henry and Mary had been in such dire straits financially that the papers were used for fuel. Yet his remark has ironic overtones for there was to be metaphorically another 'splendid fire' – the blaze of her literary fame, at its height in the Thirties.

And the manuscript of *Armour wherein he Trusted* only just survived: there are 'marks of fire on the whole MS.' and 'the beginnings of a tear across the notebook' – the visible signs of Mary's distraught attempt to destroy the book. During September 1927, ill, weak, desperately unhappy, she despaired of ever writing any more of the novel; one evening, overwrought and depressed, she tried to tear up the manuscript but did not have sufficient strength to rip it across, so hurled it on to the fire. Then, greatly distressed, she rushed from the room and telephoned St John Adcock in whom she had recently confided her troubles.

Adcock related later that she began by telling him how unwell she had been, but then interrupted herself: 'I have destroyed all I had done of the new novel.' To his surprised 'Good Lord, what-

---

[6] *News Chronicle*, 28 April 1938. 'Mary Webb's Pathetic Little Library Sold. Shabby Volumes Now Rare Pieces'. Some of the books were Everyman editions, and fetched up to £35 a volume.

ever made you do that?' there was no immediate answer as she was weeping : Adcock had 'seldom heard anything more piteous than the subdued, broken sound of her crying at the other end of the line'. When she spoke again it was in a stricken voice and 'she blamed herself miserably' but said she had 'felt so dissatisfied, felt she could not finish it and would never write any more so, on a sudden impulse, had torn it and put it on the fire'. She did not know then that Henry had retrieved the scorched papers from the flames. Adcock recalled that 'by degrees she quieted down' and as their conversation ended she assured him that she could recall the novel 'nearly all word for word and would at once set about rewriting it'. It must have been with thankful relief that she found it saved.

That September, unable to write, she sat sewing clothes for a doll intended as one of her Ladysmock Christmas gifts for the children at Lyth Hill. In spite of her personal trouble and illness, Mary had not forgotten the children – the usual list had been made and she had begun to gather together presents for a festival she would never live to see. Henry, after her death, was to have the sad task of taking her last gifts to the cottagers, including the doll in its nearly completed outfit, together with a small cot for which she had made an eiderdown and pillow (this for one of the daughters of Mrs Cullis). During these final weeks of her life, the shortening September days, she had tried to work at the presents, sitting alone at her flower-filled window in the tiny cottage at Hampstead, so ethereally pale and fragile that she seemed indeed to belong to the flowers, as Geraint Goodwin said of her – a 'wraith' that 'at any moment might vanish'.

Rapidly she was losing her hold on life. Vertigo, extreme weakness, severe head pains were dire effects of the pernicious anaemia which was killing her. With Henry a stranger to her, she had lost all incentive to make meals, keep warm. Mrs Wicksteed called at the cottage one afternoon and found her on the floor, a small exhausted heap in front of the cold grate with its dead ashes. Then a fall down the staircase, although not serious, shook her fragile frame so severely that she became even weaker.

Previously she had resisted stubbornly and tearfully the advice of friends to have rest and medical attention. This was now heeded, but it was too late : like Emily Brontë, she had allowed herself to sink to a point beyond recovery. She felt that the only person she wanted to be near now was Minoni; it was a pathetic reaching back into the past, into the lost security of days when her father was the stable centre of her world. And so it was arranged that she should go to a nursing home in Sussex near where Minoni lived at West Hill, St Leonard's-on-Sea.

Mary was too weak and frail to make the journey alone. This was obvious to anyone who saw her, though she still had will enough to resist offers of help, insisting that she could manage on her own. Henry, of course, would not be accompanying her : he had retreated even further behind his enigmatic mask although he knew now that her illness was fatal. His immersion in the life of K.A.S., a genuine enthusiasm, was also something of a therapeutic absorption, in view of his personal difficulties. He too had suffered, but he was careful to conceal his feelings, and certainly to his colleagues and friends he showed only his usual charming, calm exterior. Undoubtedly he was greatly relieved when Mary finally arranged to go to St Leonard's, although he did not realise as she was carried to the taxi that it was already too late, that she was, in fact, dying.

Mrs Wicksteed insisted on going with her, in spite of Mary's protestations. She was convinced that the effort of the journey would prove too great for Mary's small remaining strength and she would collapse on the train. As the taxi drew away from 5 Grove Cottages, Mary waved goodbye to Henry and smiled at him. It was the last time he saw her conscious.

She seemed more cheerful and alert on the train journey than she had been for many weeks, regaining a little of her vitality and enthusiasm as she anticipated her reunion with Minoni and responded to the stimulation of travel. Mrs Wicksteed noticed how she enjoyed the aroma of tobacco in the compartment, saying it reminded her of her old home. Again the memories of Maesbrook, of Kenneth, of her father; again a feeling of vital life through the senses, those hyper-acute senses through which she had known in fullest, keenest measure a mingling of physical and spiritual ecstasy, senses now dulled and deadened by long struggle, inexorable bodily deterioration.

It was only a brief revival, but during it she very firmly urged Mrs Wicksteed to get off the train at the first of the two stations at St Leonard's, leaving her to meet Minoni alone. Ever sensitive, even at the last, to the feelings of those she held dear, Mary was anxious that Minoni should not be alarmed at seeing her helped from the train. She intended to step out of it alone, wanting to explain to Minoni in her own way and from her own point of view, the state of her health, mind and personal life. This was the old independent spirit. Mrs Wicksteed complied, understanding that to create tension by resisting would only worsen Mary's condition; she knew that Miss Lory would be shocked anyway as soon as she caught sight of the feeble form and deathly pallor.

It was a pathetically brave intention. Spirit proved stronger than body, and before she arrived at the station where Minoni was waiting, Mary had collapsed. A porter carried her from the train and across the platform. She had no strength to stand, nor scarcely enough to speak. In the taxi, she whispered anxiously 'Where are you taking me . . . it isn't an asylum?' Minoni soothed her reassuringly and took her immediately to Quarry Hill Nursing Home.

Her room was at the top of the building. Before they helped her into bed she looked out from the large window to the sea. The Channel waters were shining in a late September sunset, suffused with the lingering beauty of summer's end. She exclaimed at this loveliness, 'I shall get better here'. But the sea, although beautiful, to Mary was also bitter. This view of waves and horizon reminded her of Weston and the early years of marriage, their happiness and close companionship; and it evoked, as it had acutely then, deep insecurity, her present pitiful plight a fulfilment of that powerful intuition of a 'cynic fate' which, stealing steadily upon them, would take Henry from her :

> How stealthy comes the dark and ebbing sea,
> When one, arms empty, calls on vacancy
> And hears the echoes mock on every side. . .

. . . and so, as foretold in 'Isolde', 'the bitter surf is in our eyes'. Turning her face into the pillows, she wept.

Once she had written in a youthful poem, 'No, there is nought but to love and to be'. Love had been life and religion, joy and agony, means and end. Now with less than two weeks left 'to love and to be', Mary gently caressed and kissed the small flowers which were brought to her each day by Minoni – her favourite sweet peas and violets, delicate, fragile. When her brother Douglas, sent for by Minoni, arrived two days before her death, she managed to say very faintly, 'Hello, Duss, are the leaves turning yet?' Minoni told her they would have tea together in the afternoon and she smiled, 'That will be nice', her words only just audible.

Her condition deteriorated rapidly and on the morning of Saturday, 8 October, she was scarcely conscious, not aware even of Minoni's fresh flowers by her bedside. Henry had been sent for. He came, bringing lilies which Mary had planted in her tiny garden at Hampstead. Perhaps he remembered the lines of one of her first love poems to him : 'Gather me lilies in the darkling valleys.' He had indeed set her in 'a love that laughs and a love that grieves'. Now the grief was his, for he arrived too late : Mary had already entered 'the valley of the night'.

At noon, on 8 October, she sank into a coma and by two o'clock she was dead :

> . . . And then the spirit rests no more in this or that carnal thing of petalled delight, but starteth away hastily over the waste waters, like a seamew, plaining for eternity. (*AWHT*, p. 78)

The realisation that all was over caused Henry anguished remorse. In *The Silences of the Moon*, he had written facilely, optimistically of 'the death of my lady', putting his hope in memory : 'for all power lies in memory – does she not act as bearer of messages from the lady's stilled heart?' Now, some sixteen years later, confronted by the stark reality of his lady's 'stilled heart' and by the poignancy of memory, he was, at first, inconsolable. The deterioration of their relationship, Mary's acute and protracted distress, the pathos of her final decline : memory here brought diminishment, misery. Perhaps the impact of his loss was renewed years afterwards when, just before his accidental death in August 1939, he compiled and edited *A Mary Webb Anthology* with the entire heritage of her written work before him, culling the essence of that intensely lyrical literary and spiritual genius which he had fostered, with which he had lived – and suffered. Although his early 'lover's idealism' had been somewhat trampled under his own feet, to have held that 'lover's idealism' at all was much in itself. He had given her a great deal and for long : of this 'patient love' Mary, in her passionate yet tortured understanding, had been fully aware, keen insecurity heightening her gratitude. Tenderly she had expressed it in her 1926 New Year poem to him :

> For, oh ! I love you more than mothers do,
> And should if all your gleaming right were wrong.

She was to be brought home to Shropshire for burial. Henry made the funeral arrangements by telephone, and on Sunday, 9 October, he wrote a few necessary letters. One was to Mrs Thorne :

> 'You have always been such a good friend that I feel I must let you know of my poor Mary's death. She died yesterday, in a nursing home at St Leonard's-on-Sea, of pernicious anaemia. I am glad to say that she suffered very little, and passed away peacefully in her sleep. She had been there about ten days, and she chose the place herself because her old governess lived there, close by, and was able to be with her nearly all day. I was sitting with her that morning.'

The funeral was to be at Shrewsbury cemetery, near Meole Brace, on Wednesday, 12 October at 3 p.m.

It was a fine October afternoon, 'glass clear weather', and she was buried beneath a lime tree in the higher part of the cemetery from where her 'hills of home' can be seen, those 'changeless heights' of Pontesford, the Strettons, the Stiperstones. Around her grave stood Henry, Kenneth, Olive, Douglas and other relatives, the Rev. Bather, Minoni and several friends from Lyth Hill including Mrs Thorne; and there were flowers, flowers brought from her garden and wild flowers from the hill, and dying leaves that fell from the lime.

> In the forest are many voices, and no man riding under the leaves hears the same voice as his companion. For they are diverse as the steep winding paths up into Heaven-Town, to which no man can come by any other way than that his own torch shows him . . . his one only way is by the Christ-thorn gleaming above the chasm.

These opening words of the unfinished novel are an epitome of her life and of the meaning she had wrought from her experience of 'agony-wonder', seeking for and finding 'a core of sweetness in much bitter'.

Epilogue

> A single violet transplant,
>   The strength, the colour and the size,
> (All which before was poore and scant,)
>   Redoubles still, and multiplies.
>   John Donne from 'The Extasie'

The rest belongs to literary history : surely one of the strangest, most ironical stories in its annals. She – who had died prematurely worn out by her long struggle, disappointed by public indifference to her books, some of which were out of print – became within a year of her death a best-selling novelist, her works going into new editions, numerous reprints, and soon bringing a small fortune to Henry B. L. Webb and the publishing firm of Jonathan Cape. But the full irony of Mary Webb's posthumous fame only emerges when seen in relation to the facts of her tragic life.

Her death had gone almost unnoticed by the press. Only two newspapers (not leading ones) and three literary journals mentioned it; and another six months were to pass before many of her friends heard that she had died. At first it seemed that her efforts to establish a literary reputation had, after all, come to nothing as she had feared, that she was indeed among those who waste their sweetness on the desert air.

Caradoc Evans who knew that she had, as he put it, 'gone into the country to die', wrote in *T.P.'s and Cassell's Weekly* (31 December 1927), the sole tribute, regretting that she had 'died unsung' and proclaiming her 'in the first flight of English women novelists . . . the best of the women regional novelists . . . she is as important in the prose of her little kingdom as A. E. Housman is in its poetry.' And St John Adcock in the *Bookman* (December 1927), assessed her as 'a novelist of great and growing ability . . . with more than a touch of genius'. After this – silence. Until 25 April 1928, when Stanley Baldwin, then Prime Minister, acclaimed the novels of Mary Webb before a large, distinguished literary gathering, and thereby was responsible both for the growth of her public reputation, literally overnight, and (yet another irony) for the stunting of her critical reputation among generations of scholars.

The background of Baldwin's famous tribute is as curious as its consequences. Early in 1928 at a celebration for the British Olympic Rowing Team, Baldwin met Hamish Hamilton (who was stroke). Discussing *Precious Bane*, he told Hamilton he was thinking of speaking about the book at the Royal Literary Fund dinner in April, thereupon requesting further information about the author, which Hamilton readily supplied. At this point neither of them knew that Mary Webb was dead. Then on the day before the dinner (24 April), in a chance conversation with John Buchan on the front bench (as the Commons was assembling for Churchill's budget), Baldwin heard of a letter Susan Buchan had just received containing news of Mary Webb's death. Like the Buchans, Baldwin was sorry and surprised to be only then learning of it, this giving him further incentive for his eulogy of the dead and neglected Shropshire novelist. So it was that he tossed a large stone into the literary pond, setting off, after the initial splash, never ending ripples.

At the Mansion House, Baldwin addressed the Royal Literary Fund Society and guests (including Professors G. M. Trevelyan and Arnold Toynbee). He spoke 'as a lover of literature', one to whom books had been his 'principal and most enjoyable food', and as he continued, his at first rather general and amusing speech turned into an enthusiastic commendation of the little-known author of *Precious Bane*.

Telling the somewhat stunned (but attentive) audience of his conviction that hers was work 'of absolutely first-class quality', he quoted the opinions of Barrie and Buchan that Mary Webb was 'one of about the three best writers of English today, but nobody buys her books'. Baldwin expressed amazement that her death had caused no stir, that he had seen no notices in newspapers. Wishing 'to pay a testimony to her' for 'the extreme pleasure' she had given him, he referred briefly to her Celtic ancestry, likening her gifts to those of the novelist George Meredith, and then proceeded to define the appeal her writing held for him. He spoke of 'her love of nature . . . the parent and dominating factor', and of something he found difficult to describe – 'an "atmosphere" . . .

the creation of a beautiful and almost inspired mind, noble, with a very high degree of art.' His concluding statement referred to the Welsh Border Country of Shropshire and Worcestershire : 'In any case speaking for that part of the world which I know and love so well, I am more than satisfied that it should be known to England through Mary Webb, through Housman and *The Shropshire Lad*.' When Baldwin closed, the Archbishop of York proposed the toast 'Literature', to which Professor Trevelyan replied while the name of Mary Webb was still ringing in the minds of the guests. All of which recalls Mary's own words in a poem about a neglected old woman who wanted flowers but was not given any until she was dead : 'This would have pleased her once. She does not care/At all tonight.'

Newspapers the next day, under headings such as 'Neglected Genius', gave prominence to Baldwin's tribute. And on 27 April a belated and rather begrudging obituary of Mary Webb appeared in *The Times*. It began : 'Mrs Mary Webb, the novelist whose work was so highly praised by Mr Baldwin at the Royal Literary Fund dinner on Wednesday night, died last October at the age of 46. It is unfortunately true that her early works were neglected by the public, but there had been signs of a change, and she was probably at her death on the verge of making a great reputation.'

That 'great reputation' soon followed. The public flocked to buy her books, including those out of print, even asking for the uncompleted (and as yet unpublished) novel, *Armour wherein he Trusted*. Hastily written articles, reminiscences and correspondence (much of it romanticised), about this 'woman writer of genius' proliferated both in Britain and America.

Jonathan Cape meanwhile, having heard about Baldwin's intended speech and realising at once what this publicity would do for sales, had lost no time in approaching Mary Webb's former publishers, buying the rights in all her earlier works, planning a Collected Edition with Introductions by well-known figures. He was already negotiating before Baldwin made his speech, and had correctly gauged public reaction. The books that had previously been ignored could hardly be printed quickly enough to meet public demand. G. K. Chesterton, John Buchan, H. R. L. Sheppard, Robert Lynd and Martin Armstrong wrote Introductions to the novels, Walter de la Mare to *Poems and the Spring of Joy*, and Baldwin himself to *Precious Bane*, the sales of which were phenomenal – it was reprinted five times within six months in 1928.[1]

And what of Mary's H.B.L.W.? He stayed on for a time at the Hampstead cottage, plunged into unexpected wealth and a new rôle as manager of his dead wife's literary estate. In August, 1928 he had written a letter to Mary's brothers and sisters proposing that a deed should be drawn up in which he would relinquish Mary's one sixth reversionary interest in the £4,000 put in trust for Olive and keep the net estate to which he was entitled as her widower, together with the copyrights in her books.[2] He considered 'the value of the copyrights' to be 'problematical', and explained 'the exact position concerning Gladys' books', including the publishers' advances still to be paid off. Assuring the Merediths that 'there is obviously nothing of a goldmine in Gladys' copyrights', he added, 'the management of her literary estate has become my chief interest in life recently and it would be a satisfaction to me to feel that I had quite a free hand in dealing with it'. But the 'goldmine' did materialise beyond all expectations and continued to accrue as the books sold steadily throughout the Thirties. Already by December 1929, Henry was sufficiently well off to be able to retire permanently from teaching and devote himself to his own literary work, translating poetry and writing historical novels which were published under his pseudonym, John Clayton: and this certainly Mary would have wished for him with all her heart.

[1] *Precious Bane* continued to be a best-seller for many years. The following précis of its printing history will give some indication of the book's success. First published by Jonathan Cape Ltd 1924. Reprinted 1924, 1925, 1926, 1928. Travellers Library edition 1927: reprinted April, May, July, August, September 1928. Collected Edition 1928 (with Introduction by Stanley Baldwin): reprinted November, December 1928; March, July, September, December 1929; April, December 1930, 1931, 1934, 1935; April, November 1936, 1939. Florin Books 1932: reprinted May, August, September 1932; January, August, October 1933, 1934; January, June 1935, 1936; March, November 1937, 1938, 1939, 1941. Illustrated Edition 1937: reprinted 1938, 1939, 1940; February, November 1941, 1942 . . . 1964. Sarn Edition 1937: reprinted 1938, 1939, 1941, 1942, 1943, 1944, 1945 (twice), 1946, 1948, 1949, 1954, 1956, 1957. Four Square Paperback 1958. In a *Sunday Times* survey of memorable literature, readers voted for *Precious Bane* to be added to the list of 100 books (1961). It won by a 'short head' from George Orwell's *1984*.

[2] Mary had died without leaving a will. Her estate was valued at £936.14s. 11d. When Henry died, twelve years later, his estate was valued at £35,804.15s.7d. He left a six-page will (made 8 February, 1938).

In September 1929, Henry married Kathleen Wilson bringing
her to live at 5 Grove Cottages – he was then almost forty-four
and twenty-three years older than his former pupil (who graduated
with a first-class honours in Italian). Spring Cottage, leased since
Mary's death, was sold and they bought a house in Wellgarth
Road, Golders Green, in which Henry had a cork-lined study
specially built. He died at the age of fifty-three soon after com-
pleting his personal selection of Mary's work – *A Mary Webb
Anthology*. On 19 August 1939, having travelled alone the previous day from Weston-super-Mare to Wastwater in the Lake
District, he fell to his death from the pinnacle of Scawfell. His
unrecognisable body was brought down the 3,000 feet from Deep
Ghyll on a stretcher carried by shepherds. With that agonising
dread Deborah had feared such a fate for Stephen . . . and Mary
acutely for Henry.

Subsequently Kathleen, left with two young children, inherited
the literary estates of both Henry and Mary. In 1943 she married
Jonathan Cape (by whom she had one son, Timothy), and after
the war Jonathan purchased from her the Mary Webb copyrights.
By a strange coincidence Kathleen died – as Mary had – of
incurable disease at the early age of forty-six.

The immense popularity of Mary Webb's books spread during
the Thirties to countries abroad. Her novels were translated into
at least fifteen languages and were highly regarded especially in
France and Germany where her work was given perceptive
critical appraisal in articles and theses,[3] while in America a
literary shrine was made at the North Texas State College.
Undoubtedly her remarkable popularity in Britain during the late
Twenties and the Thirties was due partly to the Georgians' pre-
dilection for 'Nature' and the country novel, a reaction from the
upheaval and horror of the Great War, reflected also in the
prevalent sense of nostalgia for the pre-war period in which many
of them had been born and brought up. Mary Webb's novels,
once attention had been drawn to them, had such a wide appeal

[3] In France she was thought to be 'une grande artiste' by critics such as
André Bellesort and Gabriel Marcel. She was compared with the Brontës
and George Eliot, and her novels, translated into French by Jacques de
Lacratelle and Marie Carnaveggia, were widely popular. In the German
universities of Gottingen, Griefswald and Tübingen theses were written concentrating on the importance of folklore and nature in Mary Webb's world
view.

not only because of their deeply rural atmosphere and evocations of the countryside, but also because of their Edwardian and late Victorian settings.

It was perhaps the intensity of this vogue, verging on cult, which caused it to be incorrectly assumed that Mary Webb's novels were the sole and direct target of Stella Gibbons' satire *Cold Comfort Farm* (1932), awarded the Prix Femina Vie Heureuse in 1933. It is time that certain misconceptions about this were cleared up.

There had been, in fact, considerable treatment of country life in novels of the early decades of the twentieth century. In the tradition of rural writing, the modern heirs of Gilbert White, Izaak Walton and William Cobbett, were those novelists who, following Scott, George Eliot, Emily Brontë and Thomas Hardy, made the countryside the setting for their work. Thomas Hardy in particular influenced his twentieth-century successors, shaping his rural material to his own purpose, evoking a powerful sense of locality, using the rural and regional novel as a poetic medium for stories expressing his deeply felt, tragic view of life. *Cold Comfort Farm* parodies the most marked characteristics of the 'country life' novel, making zestful mockery of excesses such as the over-working of local, rustic and primitive elements, the use of stock characters and situations, intense emotionalism and overdone nature descriptions. But it would be an injustice to Stella Gibbons to regard *Cold Comfort Farm* as directly based on any single model: composed of many literary ingredients, it has a bearing on many novels including *Wuthering Heights*, the works of Hardy and earlier novels of D. H. Lawrence as well as lesser twentieth-century novels. That it is not a parody of any specific book and certainly not exclusively of Mary Webb's work has been confirmed by Stella Gibbons in correspondence with the present author. *Cold Comfort Farm* was intended to be a parody of the genre of rural novel – a genre of which, at that time, the works of Mary Webb were the most popular, but which included also those of Sheila Kaye Smith, John Cowper Powys and T. F. Powys (all of which Miss Gibbons had in mind).

Be that as it may, *Cold Comfort Farm* dealt a severe blow to the genre: and it effectively damaged Mary Webb's reputation (but not immediately the sales of her books), since it helped to reinforce among academic critics and intellectuals the antipathy towards her work which had set in with Baldwin's praise. While some influential literary figures had swung in behind Baldwin with a belated chorus of approval, others such as Arnold Bennett clearly resented 'the pronouncements of Prime Ministers about imaginative literature',[4] and the young intelligentsia of the day reacted scornfully against what they regarded as a politician's usurping of the functions of literary critic. Dislike of Baldwin, disparagement of his judgment, unwillingness to allow any validity in his comments, necessarily involved dismissal of Mary Webb from serious scholarly attention. And *Cold Comfort Farm* was used not merely to poke fun but to eclipse. Yet this entertaining book was one that Mary Webb, with her own keen sense of humour, probably would have thoroughly appreciated at its level.

But unfortunately, though Mary Webb's novels are more than just rural romances or regional works, the wave of popularity swept over them superficially and while numerous articles were written about her, none made a penetrating evaluation, none succeeded in clarifying the essential nature of her achievement – and so this was neither understood nor established critically. The change in literary tastes during and after the Second World War also went against her, the novel becoming predominantly urban and readers requiring increased sophistication, a drier tone. So the pendulum swung – Mary Webb went 'out of fashion', her public reputation waning rapidly in the post-war decades, her critical reputation still awaiting illuminating interpretations (such as continental writers had made in the early Thirties).

What is the position today, some fifty years after her death? There is a renewal of interest in her work among both general readers and students, and recently Mary Webb Societies have been formed in Britain and America. This follows that familiar pattern in literary achievement – popularity, reaction, revival – if rather delayed in her case. A few perceptive minor critics in the late Twenties and Thirties had foreseen such a revival of Mary Webb's work among future generations more attuned and receptive to her meaning. Geraint Goodwin, who regarded her

---

[4] Arnold Bennett, although antagonised by Baldwin's comments, had previously been sympathetic towards Mary Webb and had admired her writing. In 1923 at the prompting of Ellery Sedgwick, Bennett had given Mary Webb a substantial 'loan'.

as 'one of the most sensitive and best equipped of women writers', saw as early as 1929 that 'the difficulty of rightly assessing the true value of her work is a difficulty that time can repair. The times were and the times still are out of joint for a taste of its full flavour.' And I. Shipton, writing in *The Bookman* (December 1932) about Mary Webb's posthumous popularity and 'the inevitable reaction', affirmed 'we shall doubtless have to wait a little while longer before we are able to assess Mary Webb's work at its true worth'. Frank Swinnerton's appraisal in *The Georgian Literary Scene* (1934) was also significant as he pointed out that her work 'is written upon a plane above that of the conventional novel'. Perhaps the most discerning assessment of her in a literary history is that by George Sampson in *The Concise Cambridge History of English Literature* (1946). Discussing women novelists and the genuine impulse to fiction, Sampson considers Mary Webb 'the most natural woman novelist of later years . . . whose books . . . have poetic and emotional qualities as well as a rich, haunting sense of place that raise her far above the numerous contemporary women writers . . . The talent of Mary Webb was highly original; but she followed the usual patterns of fiction and raises no technical problems. That perhaps is why she missed the "penny plain" public of the suburbs and the "twopence coloured" public of the studios.'

There has always been, and probably always will be, an ambivalence of attitudes towards her – no doubt her work will continue to have its vehement admirers and equally vehement detractors. At times her writing can be luminous, but she has obvious weaknesses and excesses, faults especially prevalent in her earlier novels (such as insufficient dramatisation, a tendency to didacticism and overuse of suggestive atmosphere). Yet it should be remembered that she was still developing as a novelist when her career was cut short. And without the flaws we would not have had the writing. To say that Mary Webb is a great artist, a pure artist, is not to claim that she is a great or major novelist. But it does suggest – and I hope this study has vindicated – that she should at least occupy a more significant place in literature than she has previously been accorded. If the highest achievement in art is to represent the spiritual through the material, few in the modern novel come nearer to this than Mary Webb. As H. P. Marshall said of her in the *Edinburgh Review* (1929): 'I think we do not yet fully realise how much Mary Webb has given to the world . . . We must be careful by what canon we judge [her] . . . she had in her gift an understanding of the spiritual truths of life which we should be unwise to refuse.' This aspect has continued to be overlooked. While P. N. Furbank in *The Pelican Guide to English Literature: The Modern Age*, discussing the twentieth-century best-seller, describes Mary Webb's books as 'the most odd, and perhaps the most interesting' of the 'country novels', he concludes that, though she followed Hardy, her novels are 'shorn of any wider meaning'. I hope, in showing the nature of her imaginative world and the vision which informs it, to have refuted such myopic assertions.

As a novelist of country life, Mary Webb holds a special place, uniquely combining mystical and regional elements. In her work outer and inner landscapes occur as one; and her writing, shot through with poetry and insight, has, at its finest, an irreducible quality. Yet she is an authentic novelist – imaginative rather than inventive, warmly human and concrete, rich in humour, irony, passion and compassion. Scholars are now recognising that she is a peculiarly modern writer. Though not an innovator (she uses traditional narrative procedures and does not extend the boundaries of her art in the technical sense), she writes out of a twentieth-century consciousness, her work informed by deep intuitions of the modern spirit. Professor Charles Sanders has pointed out, in connecting her with literary developments in her period, that she has 'a curious "modern" facet which makes her work truly transitional' Her central concerns – the individual's search for self, inner awakening and growth to re-birth, to wholeness. the importance and influence of the unconscious, the herd instinct and pressure of society on the individual, the spiritual nature of love – are of immediate contemporary relevance. Perhaps the observations of Carl G. Jung in *The Spirit in Man, Art and Literature* (p. 77) will be found to be particularly appropriate in her case :

We have often found that a poet who has gone out of fashion is suddenly rediscovered. This happens when our conscious development has reached a higher level from which the poet can tell us something new. It was always present in his work but was hidden in a symbol, and only a renewal of the spirit of the time permits us to read its meaning. It needed to be looked at with fresher eyes, for the old ones could see in it only what they were accustomed to see.

The time is right for Mary Webb 'to be looked at with fresher eyes', for the long overdue revaluation of her work and her place in English literature. Stripping away the associations of the Thirties, we can, almost half a century later, effect a 'transplant', see her in a clearer perspective, make a more penetrating assessment.

However, in evaluating her we need to set aside the conventional frames of reference, the usual tenets of criticism. She fits into no definite category. But critical attention directed to her imaginative organisation, her assimilation of universal myth and folklore, her treatment of nature and landscape, her symbols, her binding themes, will reveal the unity and coherence of her work, the strength and significance of her intensely individual vision. Her work functions at several levels of meaning; by her visionary quality she conveys truths for her time and those to come; and she beckons us not back to nature but forward to it. In reading her receptively (and allowing for flaws) we gain sharpened perception, extended awareness.

I have attempted to show in this biographical and critical exploration, the intimate interrelation of Mary Webb's life and work, and to reveal the mythic quality and significance of both. This, above all: the quest, attainment and trial of wholeness in an extraordinary individual – artist, lover, mystic. Biography here has, I hope, illumined art, insight into the life deepening our understanding of the work. Mary Webb, as we have seen, was a yea-sayer to life, a life enhancer. She can be placed among those creative mystics whose work she studied, those who so splendidly desired not just to express but to communicate their vision of reality. She was activated by her mysticism and her compassion, love of her countryside and love of humanity with 'its limitless desires, its weak, small hands'. The editor of the *Sufi Quarterly*, devoting a large part of an issue to her in June 1931, wrote an appreciative foreword, expressing a regret 'That even now many students of literature and the mystics do not know Mary Webb', and making a claim that 'she was more than a novelist and poet – she was a great mystic: one of the greatest produced by the

West in modern times.'[5] It is my hope that these pages have presented Mary Webb in a new light and indicated the most fruitful lines of future exploration.

As for Shropshire, Mary Webb not only evoked with remarkable richness and lucidity her border landscape, its changing moods and abiding essence, but as Thomas Hardy with Dorset, Emily Brontë with the Yorkshire moors, she made her native region the setting of literature of timeless validity and universal significance. Her memorial will always be the Shropshire countryside, its enduring hills, meres, fields and flowerset lanes. She totally expressed and never wished to be free of its enchantment.

> As a grey moth passes
> Through October grasses,
> So I come and go,
> Softlier than snow.

[5] The *Sufi Quarterly* was an international philosophical review published at Geneva. Contributors included Richard Wilhelm who collaborated with Carl G. Jung in *The Golden Flower*, a study of Chinese mysticism. In the issue of June 1931, six of Mary Webb's poems and lengthy quotations from her prose were included as well as an appreciation by the Editor and a 'personal impression' by Adrian Bury.

Appendix 1
Mary Webb's Shropshire

All the novels, including *Precious Bane,* are set in the border country of south-west Shropshire. But in her fictional world Mary Webb does not use the real place-names of significant locations and, like Thomas Hardy, she often presents us with a topographical puzzle. Usually she borrows actual place-names and re-applies them to her chosen settings : Weeping Cross, near Shrewsbury, is used for Knighton (SFAS); Slepe, west of the Stiperstones, is used for Ratlinghope on the Long Mynd (GA); Wilderhope, the name of a manor near Wenlock Edge, is used for the Long Mynd (GA); Sarn, near Clun, is used for Sarn Mere (PB); Disgwlfa, a place on the old Bishop's Castle railway, is used for the farm at Dysgwlfas-on-the-Wild Moors sited in the Clun Forest area (SFAS). Sometimes it is not possible to identify a location because it is purely a creation of Mary Webb's imagination, or is drawn from numerous separate features of the landscape intimately known to her. The most important of the composite locations is Sarn Mere (PB) : the topographical source of this has been much debated, some placing it as Ellesmere in north-west Shropshire, others identifying it as Bomere Pool near Condover, south of Shrewsbury; but Mary Webb's descriptions of Sarn derive from her close observation at various meres and pools, including those in the district of Ellesmere – notably Colemere – as well as (and especially) Bomere and Shomere, just as in a similar way, she imaginatively applies to Sarn many legends and superstitions associated with these various meres. Undoubtedly though, the individual atmosphere of Bomere Pool is that of Sarn Mere, and it was here that she found the inspiration for *Precious Bane* (see above, Chapter 9).

Occasionally Mary Webb uses Shropshire place-names for the names of characters in her novels : for instance, Beguildy, a border village in the Clun area, becomes the name of the old wizard in *Precious Bane*; Felindre, another border village, suggests the name of two of the characters in *The House in Dormer Forest* (Catherine and Grandmother Velindre); Vessons and Cantlop near Condover provide the names of other characters. Mary Webb's choice of name, whether of a place or person, is usually descriptive of the quality or characteristic she wishes to convey: e.g. Bitterley, Undern, Dormer, Diafol.

The following list of place-names in the Shropshire of the novels gives the actual locations (in italics). My investigations have taken me deeply into the Mary Webb country, often to places as isolated now as they were in Mary Webb's days, remarkably little change having been wrought there by time and man. Some of my identifications of her settings will possibly be disputed; some sites are well established; and there are others which will always remain an enigma.

Bitterley ... *Habberley* (GA)
Condor ... *Condover* (AWHT)
Cotardicote ... *Cothercott* (AWHT)
Diafol Mountain ... *The Stiperstones* and the *Devil's Chair*
Dormer Forest and Valley ... *Hope Valley* (HDF)
Dysgwlfas-on-the-Wild-Moors ... *Clun Forest area* (SFAS)
God's Little Mountain ... *Lordshill* (GTE)
High Leasowes ... *Leasowes on the Long Mynd* (GA)
Hundeslit ... *Stapleton* (AWHT)
Lostwithin Mines ... *The Bog, Stiperstones* (GA)
Lullingford ... *Ludlow* (PB)
Lyth ... *Lyth Hill* (AWHT)
Mallard's Keep ... *Bishop's Castle* (HDF, SFAS)
Mount Gilbert ... *The Wrekin* (AWHT)
Polrebec ... *Castle Pulverbatch* (AWHT)
Sarn Mere ... composite, especially *Bomere Pool, Shomere Pool, Ellesmere, Colemere* (PB)
Shepwardine ... *Church Stretton* (GA)
Silverton ... *Shrewsbury*
Slepe ... *Ratlinghope* (GA)
The Callow ... *Callow Hill* (GTE)
The Clays ... *Pennerley* (GA)
The Junction ... *Craven Arms* (SFAS)
Undern Hall ... *Wilderhope Manor* (GTE)
Weeping Cross ... *Knighton* (SFAS)
Wilderhope ... *Long Mynd* (GA)

Appendix 2
Comments on Mary Webb by her Contemporaries

Few writers indeed have left behind them so rich a posthumous gift.
Walter de La Mare

Mary Webb is a genius. Rebecca West

Impregnated with poetry . . . No one of our day has a greater power of evoking natural magic . . . Mary Webb need fear no comparison with any writer who has attempted to capture the soul of nature in words and to 'tease us out of thought' by glimpses into our ancient inheritance. John Buchan

Her work is written upon a plane above that of the conventional novel . . . her books are all charged with feeling and understanding of an uncommon order. Frank Swinnerton

One of our best living writers. J. M. Barrie

The light in the stories of the Shropshire Lass is a light not shining on things but through them. G. K. Chesterton

Mary Webb had power; she could create beauty and she is truthful concerning human nature. Arnold Bennett

Mary Webb had that always fascinating quality of genius – imaginative energy. It is a quality so precious that when an author possesses it the waves of criticism beat against his work in vain . . . Her work is alive with the fiery genius of sympathy, pity, and awe . . . It is not too much to say that in her writings fiction becomes a branch of poetry. Robert Lynd

A feeling for the magic of words, a beauty of style that none of her contemporaries surpassed. Arthur St John Adcock

One of the most brilliant among the younger generation of novelists. T. P. O'Connor

She has the full dower of poet and seer : wit and wisdom, humour and fancy, the twin senses of tragedy and comedy, and those attributes of human sympathy and divine compassion which are born only of a full understanding and great love. Edwin Pugh

One of those fortunate writers who became a master craftsman without ever serving an apprenticeship. Martin Armstrong

Mary Webb is a mystic, with that genuine mysticism which feels the essential oneness of the world. Gerald Gould

Select Bibliography

A. UNPUBLISHED SOURCES

I. Manuscripts

1. Letters of Mary Webb to various friends
2. Letters of Mary Webb to her publishers, Jonathan Cape and G. Wrenn Howard, 1924
3. Letters of Mary Webb to her agents, Mr Dakers, 1920, and Mr Curtis Brown, 1921
4. Letters of Henry B. L. Webb to the Merediths, to Mrs Thorne of Lyth Hill, 1927-8 and to Mrs Justine Courson Weaver of Texas, late 1920s and 30s
5. Diaries of Alice Meredith (Sarah Alice Scott), 1875-9
6. Letters of George Edward Meredith
7. Poems and miscellaneous papers of George Edward Meredith
8. The Rev William Bather's sermon at the funeral of George Edward Meredith
9. Wills of Harriett Marian Scott, George Edward Meredith, Sarah Alice Meredith, Henry B. L. Webb
10. Log Books of Holy Trinity Church, Meole Brace, 1900-12
11. Staff Registers, Priory School for Boys, Shrewsbury and The King's School, Chester
12. School Records, The King Alfred School, Golders Green
13. School Report from The Grange, Much Wenlock, by George Edward Meredith of pupil St John Trevor, 1889
14. Kenneth Meredith's recollections of Mary Webb

II. Theses

1. A Bibliography of Mary Webb by M. P. G. Tolfree (University of London Diploma in Librarianship, 1965)
2. 'Mary Webb and Shropshire', Bernard Menneson (Université de Montpellier, Diplomes d' Etudes Superieures Anglais, 1963-64)

B. PRINTED SOURCES

I. Works by Mary Webb

1. Books, with dates of first editions

> *The Golden Arrow* (Constable, 1916)
> *The Spring of Joy* (J. M. Dent, 1917)
> *Gone to Earth* (Constable, 1917)
> *The House in Dormer Forest* (Hutchinson, 1920)
> *Seven for a Secret:* a love story (Hutchinson, 1922)
> *Precious Bane* (Cape, 1924)
> *Armour wherein he Trusted* A novel and some stories (Cape, 1929)
> *Poems and the Spring of Joy* (Cape, 1928)
> *The Chinese Lion* (Rota, 1937)
> *Fifty-One Poems* (Cape, 1946)
> *A Mary Webb Anthology,* edited by Henry B. L. Webb (Cape, 1939)
> *The Essential Mary Webb,* edited by Martin Armstrong (Cape, 1949)
> *Mary Webb: Collected Prose and Poems,* edited with an Introduction by Gladys Mary Coles (Wildings, 1977)
> *Mary Webb: Selected Poems,* edited with an Introduction by Gladys Mary Coles (Headland, 1981, second edition 1987)

2. Stories, Essays, Review Articles

> These are gathered in *Mary Webb: Collected Prose and Poems* (above)
> 'A Cedar-Rose', Tales of Country Life, *Country Life,* 10 July 1909, pp. 47-8
> 'Glimpses of Old Shropshire', *Transactions of the Caradoc and Severn Valley Field Club,* vols. vii and viii (16 March 1923), pp. 87-93
> 'Mr Tallent's Ghost', *The Ghost Book,* ed. Lady Cynthia Asquith (Hutchinson, September 1926), pp. 290-330
> 'The Cuckoo Clock', *Sails of Gold,* ed. Lady Cynthia Asquith (Hutchinson, October 1927), pp. 93-105
> 'The Sword', *The Cornhill Magazine,* April 1934 (vol. 149, no. 892), pp. 401-9
> 'The Core of Poetry', *The English Review,* February 1920, vol. 30, pp. 142-4

The Bookman

'The Soul of Australia', October 1925, pp. 44-5
'Morton Luce', June 1925, pp. 148-50
'Helen Prothero Lewis', November 1925, pp. 111-12
'Contrast', April 1926, p. 52
'Plus Que De L'Esprit', May 1926, pp. 130-1
'The Wing of Psyche', July 1926, p. 214
'Pilgrims of Eternity', August 1926, p. 265
'A Posy of Sweet Flowers', September 1926, pp. 300-1
'Knowest Thou the Land', November 1926, pp. 122-3
'One Coming from Calvary', December 1926, pp. 177-8
'Our Immortal Jane', February 1927, pp. 256-8
'Little Miss Burney', June 1927, pp. 163-4
'Irony and Mrs Wharton', September 1927, p. 303

The Spectator

'Birds, Beasts and Trees', 2 December, 1922
'Our Birds, Their Haunts and Nests', 27 January, 1923
'Birds, Beasts and Flowers', 24 March, 1923
'Wild Life in Many Lands', 11 August, 1923
'Sense and Sensibility Out of Doors', 6 October, 1923
'When the Pie was Opened', 1 December, 1923
'Natural History', 8 December, 1923
'Quite Wild Animals', 22 December, 1923
'The Honey Bee', 9 February, 1924
'Dabbling in the Dew', 21 March, 1925
'The Wayfaring Tree', 27 June, 1925
Reviews of novels : 15 December, 1923, 29 December, 1923, 26 January, 1924, 2 February, 1924

T.P.'s and Cassell's Weekly

'New Year Customs', 27 December, 1924, p. 387
'Hark How the Birds Do Sing', 27 June, 1925, p. 324
'John Halifax Gentleman', 3 April, 1926, p. 844
'The Poetry of the Prayer Book', 17 April, 1926, p. 904

II. WORKS ON MARY WEBB

1. *Books*

Addison: Hilda L. Addison, *Mary Webb: a short study* (London, 1931)
Byford-Jones: W. Byford-Jones, *The Shropshire Haunts of Mary Webb* (Shrewsbury, 1948)
Chappell: W. Reid Cappell, *The Shropshire of Mary Webb* (London, 1930)
Coles: Gladys Mary, *Mary Webb* (Seren Books, Wales, 1990)

Moult: Thomas Moult, *Mary Webb: her life and work* (London, 1932)

Wrenn: Dorothy P. H. Wrenn, *Goodbye to Morning* (Shrewsbury 1964)

2. *Miscellaneous studies, and other works consulted*

Adcock: Arthur St John Adcock, *The Glory that was Grub Street: impressions of contemporary authors* (London, 1928), pp. 321-30

Armstrong: Martin Armstrong, Introduction to *Armour wherein he Trusted:* a novel and some stories, Collected Edition, 1929 and all subsequent editions
Introduction to *The Essential Mary Webb* (London, 1949)

Baker: Ernest A. Baker, *The History of the English Novel* (London, 1936), vol. x, pp. 221-6

Baldwin: Stanley Baldwin, Introduction to *Precious Bane*, Collected Edition, 1928 and all subsequent editions
Speech at The Royal Literary Fund Dinner, *The Times*, Thursday, 26 April 1928, p. 18

Bastide: Roger Bastide, *The Mystical Life* (London, 1934)

Buchan: John Buchan, Introduction to *Gone to Earth*, Collected Edition, 1928, and all subsequent editions

Buchan: Susan Buchan, Lady Tweedsmuir, 'Mary Webb', *A Winter Bouquet* (London, 1954), pp. 110-15

Buchan, *DNB*: Susan Buchan, Lady Tweedsmuir, 'Mary Webb', *Dictionary of National Biography*, 1922-30, pp. 901-2

Burne: Charlotte Burne, *Shropshire Folk Lore* (London, 1883)

Bury: Adrian Bury, 'An Impression of Mary Webb', *The Sufi Quarterly*, vii (Geneva, June, 1931), pp. 11-13; see also Foreword to Mary Webb's Poems, pp. 7-10

Chapman: Grace Chapman: 'Mary Webb', *London Mercury*, xxiii (February, 1931), pp. 364-71

Chesterton: G. K. Chesterton, Introduction to *The Golden Arrow*, Collected Edition, 1928, and all subsequent editions

Cockburn: Claud Cockburn, *Bestseller* (London, 1972), pp. 173-82

Coles: Gladys Mary Coles, 'Mary Webb – as a Book Reviewer', *The Shropshire Magazine*, September 1970, pp. 17-18
'Mary Webb's Roman Shropshire', *Country Quest*, August, 1971, pp. 8-10; 'Child of Spring', May, 1978
'Mary Webb: 50th Anniversary of her death', *The Shropshire Magazine*, December, 1976. 'Mary Webb – Fifty Years On', *The Shropshire Magazine*, October, 1977, p. 21
'The Poetry of Mary Webb', *Poetry Wales*, Autumn 1981, Vol. 17. No. 2, pp. 83-93
Walks with Writers, Mary Webb Walks (Shropshire Books, 1992)

Collard : Lorna Collard, 'Mary Webb', *Contemporary Review*, CXLIII (April, 1933), pp. 455-64

Davis : W. Eugene Davis, 'The Poetry of Mary Webb : an Invitation', *English Literature in Transition*, 1969, pp. 95-101

de Lacratelle : Jacques de Lacratelle, Preface to *La Renarde* (*GTE* traduit par Jacques de Lacratelle et Marie Carnavaggia, Paris, 1947)

Jacques de Lacratelle, Preface to *Sarn* (*PB* traduit par Lacratelle et Madeleine Gueritte, Paris, 1936)

de la Mare : Walter de la Mare : 'Introduction', *Poems and the Spring of Joy*, Collected Edition 1928, and all subsequent editions

Evans : Caradoc Evans, 'Mary Webb', *Colophon*, new series, III (Winter, 1938), pp. 63-6; also in *The Welsh Review*, March, 1944

Gibson, Wilfred Gibson, 'The Poems of Mary Webb', *Bookman* (London), LXXV (February, 1929), pp. 269-70

Hecht : Hans Hecht, 'Der Sundenesser', *Englische Studien*, LXVII (November, 1932), pp. 238-46

Howard : Michael Howard, *Jonathan Cape: Publisher* (London, 1971)

Knapp : Ilse Knapp, *Die Landschaft in Modernen Englischen Frauen-Roman* (University of Tübingen, 1935), 'Mary Webb', pp. 81-94

Kunitz : Stanley J. Kunitz (ed), *Authors Today and Yesterday* (New York, 1936), pp. 331-8

Kunitz and Haycraft : Stanley J. Kunitz and Howard Haycraft (eds), *Twentieth Century Authors* (New York, 1942), p. 1486

Lawrence : Margaret Lawrence, *The School of Femininity* (NewYork, 1936), pp. 331-8

Liddell : Robert Liddell, *A Treatise on the Novel* (London, 1960)

Lynd : Robert Lynd, Introduction to *Seven for a Secret*, Collected Edition, 1928, and all subsequent editions

Magdinier : Marcelle Magdinier, 'Mary Webb : Apôtre et Poète de la Pitié', *Etudes de Theologie, Philosophie et d'Histoire*, CCXXXIII (20 December, 1937), pp. 752-64

Marinoff : Irene Marinoff : 'Die Romane Mary Webbs', *Anglia*, LX (June, 1938), pp. 434-48

Marshall : H. P. Marshall, 'Mary Webb', *Edinburgh Review*, CCXLIX (April, 1929), pp. 315-27

O'Connor : T. P. O'Connor, 'The Hunger for the Land' (Book of the Week : *Precious Bane*), *T.P.'s and Cassell's Weekly*

(2 August, 1924), pp. 487-8

Parsons : Alice Beal Parsons, 'Mary Webb', *Nation,* cxxix
   (7 August, 1929), pp. 145-6

Peake, Gladys E. Peake, 'The Religious Teaching of Mary
   Webb', *Congregational Quarterly* (England and Wales), xi
   (January, 1933), pp. 41-50

Pugh : Edwin Pugh, 'Mary Webb', *Bookman* (London), lxiv
   (April, 1923), pp. 7-8
   'Mary Webb', *Bookman* (London), lxxiv (July, 1928), pp.
   193-6

Reade : A. R. Reade, *Main Currents in Modern Literature*
   (London, 1935), pp. 197-213

Rosati : Salvatore Rosati, 'Letteratura Inglese : George
   Moore – Katherine Mansfield – Mary Webb', *Nuova
   Antologia,* ccciii (October, 1935), pp. 555-7

Sampson : George Sampson, *The Concise Cambridge History
   of English Literature* (Cambridge, 1941), pp. 995-6

Sanders : Charles Sanders, 'Mary Webb : An Introduction',
   English Literature in Transition, ix : 3 (1966), pp. 115-7;
   and 'An Annotated Bibliography', pp. 119-36
   'The Golden Arrow : Mary Webb's "Apocalypse of Love" ',
   English Literature in Transition, x (1967), pp. 1-8
   'Webb's *Precious Bane,* book iii, chapter 2', *The Explicator,*
   xxv No. 2 (October, 1966), p. 10

Schneider : Gertrud Schneider, *Die Verwendung Und Beden-
   tung Der Folklore In Den Romanen Von Mary Webb*
   (University of Gottingen, 1934)

Sedgwick : Ellery Sedgwick (ed), *Atlantic Harvest* (Boston,
   1947), p. 375
   The Happy Profession (Boston, 1946), pp. 192-5

Shepherd : Frank Shepherd, 'Mary Webb, A Modern Ishmail',
   Many Mansions (Leigh, 1960), pp. 20-7

Shepherd : W. Shepherd, 'The Faith and Fiction of Mary
   Webb', *London Quarterly and Holborn Review,* 1949, pp.
   306-11

Sheppard : H. R. L. Sheppard, Introduction to *The House in
   Dormer Forest,* Collected Edition 1928, and all subsequent
   editions.

Sheppard : Oscar H. Sheppard, 'The Essays of Mary Webb',
   Papers of the Manchester Literary Club, vol. 63, 1937, pp.
   17-22

Tiemann : Marianne Tiemann, *Naturbetrachtung Und Wel-
   tanschauung In Den Werken Von Mary Webb* (University of
   Greifswald, 1936)

Webb : Henry B. L. Webb, *The Silences of the Moon* (London, 1911)
The Everlasting Quest (London, 1917)
Welby : T. Earle Welby, 'Mr Pound and Others', *Saturday Review* (London) CXLVI (22 December, 1928), pp. 851-2
Weygandt : Cornelius Weygandt, *A Century of the Novel* (New York, 1925), p. 479
The Time of Yeats (London & New York, 1937) pp. 386-428
Underhill : Evelyn Underhill : *Mysticism* (London, 1911, rev. ed. 1945)

3. *Film and Video*

Gone to Earth, (Powell and Pressburger) GB, 1948, 110m, Technicolor. London Films / David O. Selznick.
Secret Shropshire, (Shropshire Books, 1996, QV Production)

Index

Adcock, Almey St John, 250, 282, 293
Adcock, Arthur St John, 213, 221,
    235, 249, 250, 277, 282, 299, 300,
    301, 302, 305n, 313–14, 321, 334,
    338
Addison, Hilda L., xii, xvi, 10, 27,
    43–4, 48, 80, 104, 107, 116n, 201,
    240, 249, 251, 311, 337
Alice in Wonderland (Carroll), 34
'Arden, Deborah' (*GA*), 17, 46, 78,
    81, 97, 119–28, 130, 134, 135, 142,
    150, 151, 161, 285, 290, 301, 325
'Arden, John' (*GA*), 17, 21, 38, 46,
    47, 66, 78, 81, 89, 119–28, 135,
    157, 170, 258, 259
Armstrong, Martin, 42, 74, 140, 141,
    220, 234, 235, 267, 282, 292, 294,
    323, 334, 336, 338
Arnold, Matthew, 84, 162, 210
Arnold, Thomas, 22
Ashes Valley, 113
Aspects of the Novel (Forster), 144
Asquith, Lady Cynthia, 238–9, 275,
    336
Atlantic Monthly, 250, 275
Austen, Jane, 75n, 241n, 282, 337

Baldwin, Stanley, ix, xi, xii, xxi, 75,
    250, 251, 255, 303–5, 321–3, 327, 338
Barrett, David and family, 69–70, 177,
    199, 283–4, 312
Barrie, Sir James, 238, 304, 322, 334
Bather, Rev. William, 70, 91, 108,
    318, 335
Bayston Hill Village, 174, 182, 201,
    284, 301
Bayswater, xx, ch. 10 *passim*, esp.
    219, 222–6, 238, 243–4; 245
'Beast Walk, the' (*HDF*), 188, 189–90
Bennett, Arnold, 118, 327 and n, 334
Bewdley, 303, 305
Bible (see also MARY WEBB), 10,
    19, 21, 29, 53, 66, 79, 120, 164,
    189, 260–1
'Birds' Orchard' (*HDF*), 99, 188,
    189, 193, 195

'Black Huntsman, the' (*GTE*), 163–5,
    166
Blake, William, 74, 76, 214
Blunt, Elizabeth (godmother of
    MW), 10, 11 and n
Bomere Pool, x (map), 152n, 193–4,
    250–1, 287
Bookman, the, xx, xxi, 59n, 149, 198,
    213, 220, 222 and n, 235, 246–7,
    250, 269, 282, 293, 302, 309, 321,
    328, 337
Boston Transcript, the, 300
Brontë, Charlotte, 125, 213, 263, 325n
Brontë, Emily, xiii, 73, 81, 118–19,
    209, 216, 314, 325n, 326, 331
Brown, Curtis, 335
Browne, Sir Thomas, 72, 131, 179,
    241n
Browning, Elizabeth Barrett, 104,
    181, 209
Browning, Robert, 74, 104, 181, 241n
Brynmelyn Boys' School,
    Weston-super-Mare, 113, 114, 129,
    130
Buchan, John, xx, 118, 127, 158, 168,
    179–80, 205, 211–12, 304, 322, 323,
    334, 338
Buchan, Susan (Lady Tweedsmuir),
    xvi, 179, 205, 211–12, 322, 338
Buildwas Abbey, x (map), 3, 13
Burne, Charlotte, S., 72, 134, 263,
    338
Burney, Fanny, 282, 337
Bury, Adrian, 139, 203, 204, 331n,
    338

Caer Caradoc, x (map), 23
Cambridge University, xix, 74–5, 97,
    98, 99, 132, 147
Cannon, Beatrice (friend of MW), 37
Cape, Jonathan, xvii, 105n, 138, 223,
    259, 267, 268, 269, 270n, 274, 275,
    276, 277, 278, 297, 304, 321, 323,
    324n, 325, 335
Caradoc and Severn Valley Field
    Club, 274, 276

Carding Mill Valley, 113
Carswell, Catherine, 246
Chaucer, 241n
Chester, xx, 11, 114, 153, ch. 8
    passim, esp. 154–7, 171–2; 215, 216,
    271–2, 277–8
Chesterton, G. K., 144, 323, 334, 338
Christian mystics, 101, 116–17, 120,
    191, 260, 292
Church Stretton, x (map), 113, 291n,
    333
Clarke, Austin, 264n, 270
Clayton, John (Henry B. L. Webb), 324
Clun and Clun Forest, x (map), xiii,
    212, 227, 332, 333
Cobbett, William, 326
Cockburn, Claud, 105n, 338
Cold Comfort Farm (Gibbons), xvi,
    326, 327
Colemere, x (map), 194, 332, 333
Coleridge, Gilbert, 219
Coleridge, Samuel Taylor, 207, 307
Come Hither (de la Mare), 236
'Condor' (*AWHT*), 291n, 333
Condover, x (map), 69, 84, 193, 291n,
    332, 333
Constable (publishers), xvii, 146, 336
Cox, David, 21
Craik, Maria, *John Halifax, Gentleman*,
    296, 337
Cross Houses Workhouse, 70–1, 107
Cullis, Muriel, 199
Cullis, Mrs Nellie, xvii, 70, 314

Daily News, the, 178, 181
Dakers, Mr (literary agent for MW),
    197, 198, 199, 335
Dante, 162
'Darke, Amber' (*HDF*), 43, 93, 94,
    99, 100n, 105, 108, 120, 126,
    184–97, 201, 204, 233, 257
'Darke, Jasper' (*HDF*), 82, 86, 93,
    94, 184–6, 188–91, 194, 228, 232
Darwin, Charles, 47, 72, 95, 127
de la Mare, Walter, xiii, 42, 58, 99,
    206, 208, 209, 236–7, 280, 323,
    334, 339
de Vigny, Alfred, 170–1
Dent (publishers), 180, 336
Devil's Chair, the, x (map), xiii,
    11–12, 23, 121, 122, 128, 135–6,
    300, 333

'Diafol' (*GA*), 121, 128, 135, 136
Dial, the, 180
Dialect (see MARY WEBB)
Dickens, Charles, 25, 36, 66, 117, 169,
    222, 248–9
Dickens Fellowship and Ball, the, 248
Dickensian, The, 248
Dickinson, Emily, 209
Doran (publishers), 180, 235
'Dormer House, Forest and Valley'
    (*HDF*), 68, 136, 184–9
Donne, John, 104, 321
Dostoevsky, 18, 76
Doubleday (publishers), 180
Downes, Tom (gardener at
    Maesbrook), 67, 107
Downes, Winifred (bridesmaid of
    MW), xviii, 107, 108
ducks, 20
Dutton, E. P. (publishers), 180, 279,
    300
'Dysgwlfas-on-the-Wild Moors'
    (*SFAS*), 136, 212, 228, 230, 231,
    232, 333

Edel, Leon, xiv–xv, 139
Edinburgh Review, the, 328
Edric, Wild, 23, 163 and n, 264
Eliot, George, 9, 118, 125, 185, 220,
    325n, 326
Eliot, T. S., 165, 210
Ellesmere, x (map), 42, 194, 332, 333
Ellesmere College, 50, 85
Emerson, 44
English Review, the, 177n, 203, 209–10,
    220, 236, 336
Evans, Caradoc, 133, 140, 200, 206,
    212, 220–2, 288, 295–6, 321, 339
Everlasting Quest, The, (see Henry
    B. L. Webb)
Everyman, the, 280n

Fabre, Henri, 235
First World War, 137–9, 146, 147,
    149, 150, 152–3, 154–75, 163n,
    183, 196, 213, 223, 325
'Flockmaster, the' (*GA*), 46, 120 and
    n, 135, 136, 188, 258–9
Ford, Mary (great-grandmother of
    MW), 5
Folklore and legends of Shropshire
    (see MARY WEBB)

Forster, E. M., 144, 183
'Foxy' (*GTE*), 23, 159–60, 165–7
Franklin, John, 271
Frazer, Sir James, 72, 165–6
Freud, Sigmund, 191
Furbank, P.N., 329

Galsworthy, John, 246
Garnett, Edward, 278, 304
Gaskell, Mrs, 185
General Strike, 277
Gibbons, Stella and *Cold Comfort Farm*, xvi, 326–7
Gibson, Wilfred, 59, 207
Gilgamesh, 130, 178, 180–1
'God's Little Mountain' (*GTE*), 160, 168n, 333
Goethe, 18
Golden Bough, The (Frazer), 72, 165–6
Goldsmith, Oliver, 46
Gooding, H. B., 108
Goodwin, Geraint, 280, 281–2, 314, 327
Gosse, Sir Edmund, 299
Gould, Gerald, 178, 234–5, 334
Grange, The, x (map), ch. 2, esp. 19–22, 28, 38–9, 272
Grant-Watson, E. L., 282
Gray, Thomas, *Elegy*, 64
Greene, Graham, 25
'Grotto, the' (*HDF*), 42 and n, 188, 189–90
Grove Cottages (5, The Grove), ix, 246–7, 250–1, 274, 276–7, 279–80, 285–6, 298n, 302–3, 313–15, 317, 324, 325

Haeckel, 72, 95
'Hallowes, Michael' (*HDF*), 99, 100 and n, 105, 184–5, 188, 190–1, 258–9
Hamilton, Hamish, xvi, 278, 304, 322
Hamilton, Harriet Eleanor, 65
Hampstead, xvii, xx, 219, 243, 244, Chs 11 and 12 *passim*, esp. 1, 245–8, 250–1, 272–3, 274, 276–7, 279–81, 285–6, 297–8 and n, 302–3, 312–15, 317; 324–5
Hardy, Thomas, xiv, 24, 35–6, 95, 117, 122, 125, 128, 129, 136, 142, 143, 169, 171, 180, 187, 210, 213, 227, 230, 231, 249, 254, 261, 300, 326, 329, 331, 332

Harraden, Beatrice, 299
Harrison, Austin, 203, 220
Hartley, L. P., 269
Hawkstone, 41–2
Hawthorne, Nathaniel, 136, 144–5, 146, 161
Heine, 92
Herbert, George, 241n
Hodder and Stoughton (publishers), 193, 198
Holden (publishers), 295
Holy Trinity, Meole Brace, xviii, 64, 70, 71, 87, 108
Hope Valley, x (map), 333
Hough Green, Chester, ch. 8, esp. 154, 156, 157, 171; 216, 272, 277
Housman, A. E., 207, 208, 321, 323
Howard, G. Wrenn, 138, 223, 267, 269, 276, 335
Hunt, Violet, 299
Hutchinson (publishers), xvii, 198, 213, 227, 336
Huxley, Aldous, 183
Huxley, T. H., 72, 95

Ightfield, 6, 47, 91
Independent, the, 180
Institut Français, 299

James, Henry, 43, 47, 124–5
James, William, 191
Jefferies, Richard, 36, 55, 103
John, St John of the Cross, 175
Jones, Jennifer, 168
Jones, Tom (Deputy Secretary to the Cabinet), 304, 305
Jonson, Ben, v, 176
Joyce, James, 292
Jude the Obscure (Hardy), 143
Julian, Dame of Norwich, 113, 116–17, 117n, 120, 241, 260, 292
Jung, Carl G., 167n, 188n, 190n, 191, 192, 259, 329–30, 331n

Keats, John, 32, 35, 74
King Alfred School, the, xvii, xx, 215, 219, 239, 242, 243 and n, 244, 283, 297, 315
King's School, The Chester, xvii, 153, 157, 171, 172
King's Shropshire Light Infantry, 137
Kubelik, 83

Lawrence, D. H., 76, 165, 166, 171, 183, 186, 209, 246, 326
Lawrence, Margaret, *The School of Femininity*, 258
Leighton, x (map), xix, ch. 1 *passim*; 47
Leighton Lodge, ix, ch. 1 *passim*, esp. 3–7, 12–13, 15–16, 18
Leinster Square, Bayswater, ch. 10 *passim*, esp. 219, 222, 224, 244
Leith, W. Compton, 101
Lewis, Helen Prothero, 133, 282, 337
Limes, The, Meole Brace, 85, 97–8
Lion Hotel, Shrewsbury, 70
Literary Biography (Edel), xiv–xv, 139
Little Wood, the (Lyth Hill), ix, 69, 99, 174, 177, 193, 211, 215, 225, 227, 309
Liverpool, 37, 86–7
Liverpool Post, the, 132–3
'Llanvihangel, Nesta' (*AWHT*), 136, 290, 291, 293–5
Lloyd George, 157
'Lloyd, John' (*AWHT*) ('Many Mansions'), 29
London Mercury, the, 59, 338
Long Mynd, the, x (map), xiii, 23, 69, 113, 128, 131, 133, 135, 160, 291n, 300
Lordshill, x (map), 168, 333
Lory, Miss Edith, see Minoni
'Lovekin, Gillian' (*SFAS*), 37, 228, 231–4
'Lullingford' (*PB*), 252, 333
Lynd, Robert, 141, 178, 181, 220, 221, 229–30, 280, 323, 334, 339
Lynd, Sylvia, 220, 221, 280, 299
Lyons, Mrs, 22, 33, 48–9, 68, 168
Lyth Hill, ix, x (map), xx, 68, 69, 70, 84, 85, 99, 174, ch. 19 *passim*, esp. 176–7, 182, 193, 199–202, 211–12, 215–16; 224–7, 243, 245, 250–1, 276, 283–4, 291n, 300–2, 308–12, 314

Mabinogion, 19, 72
Macleod, Fiona (William Sharp), 72, 111, 117
McLeod, Flora, 74–5, 96–7, 105, 108, 113, 115, 129
Macmillan (publishers), 178, 276–7
Maesbrook, ix, x (map), 59, chs 4

and 5 *passim*, esp. 63–9, 71, 78, 85, 88, 98, 99, 107, 108, 109, 114; 315
Maeterlinck, Maurice, 26
Mansfield, Katherine, 66, 76, 96, 271
Marble Faun, The, 144–5
Marcel, Gabriel, 325n
Marshall, H. P., 328–9, 339
'Marston, Edward' (*GTE*), 160, 161, 165, 166, 168, 170
Masefield, John, 138
Matthews, Elkin, 241n, 313
Mauriac, François, 47
Maurois, André, 282
Mechthild of Magdeburg, 38
Melrose, Andrew (publisher), 206
Meole Brace, x (map), xviii, xix, 55, 59, chs 4 and 5 *passim*, esp. 63–5, 68, 70–1, 87, 91, 97, 98; 114, 318
Meole Brace Literary Society, 74–5, 98
Meredith, Alice (Sarah Alice Scott), (mother of MW), ix, xx, 3, 4, 6, 7, 9–15 and n, 16, 17, 20, 21, 22, 26, 28, 30, 31, 33, 34, 35, 38, 41, 42, 50, 67, 70, 82, 86, 90, 106–7, 108, 114, 116, 146, 153, 154, 155, 156, 171, 174, 216, 271–2 (death), 277, 335
Meredith, Douglas (George Douglas), (brother of MW), xix, 7, 30, 31, 50, 72, 85, 86, 155, 299, 317, 318
Meredith, George, novelist, 75–6, 269, 322
Meredith, George Edward (father of MW), ix, xix, 3–18, 19–25, 26, 28, 30–1, 33, 38, 41, 42, 44–7, 48, 49, 50, 51, 52, 53, 55, 59, 63–8, 70–1, 73–5, 76, 78, 81, 82, 83, 85–90 (decline and death), 91–3, 95, 96, 99, 100, 104, 105, 106, 108–9, 116, 120, 123–5, 135, 151, 157, 169, 171, 172, 241, 259, 272–3, 277, 315, 335
Meredith, Rev. John Blunt (uncle of MW), 6, 21
Meredith, Kenneth (Edward Walter Kenneth), (brother of MW), ix, xii, xvi, xix, 7, 30, 31, 33, 35, 41n, 46, 49, 50, 81–2, 83–4, 85–7, 106, 107, 108–9, 155, 157, 199, 204, 277–8, 310, 315, 318, 335
Meredith, Mary Blunt (grandmother of MW), 5

Meredith, Mary Gladys, see MARY WEBB

Meredith, Mervyn (John Henry Mervyn), (brother of MW), xix, 30, 34, 85, 97, 155

Meredith, Muriel (Alice Muriel), (sister of MW), xix, 30, 33, 67n, 70, 83, 84, 85, 98

Meredith, Olive (Olive Marion), (sister of MW), xix, 30, 67n, 78, 83, 85, 153, 156, 277, 324

Mew, Charlotte, 209

Meynell, Alice, 209

Milton, 8, 19, 241n, 252

Ministering Children, 27,

Minoni (Miss Edith Lory), 33–6, 41, 50, 53, 54, 55, 65, 67, 85 and n, 91, 248, 315–18

Minsterley, x (map), 131

Mold, Mrs, 201, 202

Morning Post, the, 178

Morris, Tom and family, 152–3, 158, 173, 174

Mortimer, Raymond, 235

Moult, Thomas, xii, 161, 305n, 338

Much Wenlock, x (map), xix, 18, ch. 2, *passim*, esp. 19, 26, 27, 28, 29, 38

Nation and the Athenaeum, the, 178, 213, 264, 270

Neo-Platonists, 101

New Statesman, the, 178, 235, 271

New York Herald Tribune, the, 300

New York Times, the, 295, 300

New York World, the, 300

News Chronicle, the, 221, 241n, 288, 313n

Nicholson, Mrs C. A., 220, 280, 297

Nills, The (Nills Hill), x (map), xx, 152–3, 157, 158, 160, 171, 172, 174, 213

O'Connor, T. P., 270, 295, 334

Origin of Species, The (Darwin), 72

Orwell, George, *Nineteen Eighty-four*, 324n

Oxford, xvi, 4, 6, 155

Parry, Mr (landlord of Rose Cottage), 132n, 152

Pater, Walter, 72, 209

Penrose, Weston-super-Mare, ch. 6 *passim*, esp. 114, 115, 116; 150

Plato, 101

Poe, Edgar Allan, 184

'Polrebec' (*AWHT*), 294–5, 333

'Polrebec, Sir Gilbert de' (*AWHT*), 13, 290–5, 306

Pontesbury, x (map), xx, ch. 7 *passim*, esp. 131–3, 137

Pontesford Hill, x (map), xiii, 63–4, 69, 131, 133–4, 135, 152, 157, 300, 318

Powis, Kathleen, 10, 47

Powys, 145, 283n, 293

Powys, John Cowper and T. F., 326

Poynter, Sir Edward, 'Faithful Unto Death', 37

Prayer Book, the, 296, 337

Presocratics, 101

Priory School, The Shrewsbury, xvii, xx, 172, 174, 181, 203

Prix Femina Vie Heureuse, xi, xx, 299–300, 304, 326

Proust, Marcel, 144

Pugh, Edwin, 149, 204, 222–3 and n, 246–9, 250, 269–70 and n, 288, 299, 334, 340

Pulverbatch, Castle, x (map), 291n, 294–5, 333

Quarry Hill Nursing Home, St Leonard's-on-Sea, 315, 316–18

Ralegh, Sir Walter, 97n

'Reddin, Jack' (*GTE*), 160, 161, 164, 165, 166, 167, 168, 204

Return of the Native, The (Hardy), 136, 187

Revelation, Book of, 66, 164

Rhiannon, Birds of, 77

Richardson, Dorothy, 292

Richmond Park, 11, 15

Riddle of the Universe, The, 72

'Rideout Robert' (*SFAS*), 37, 228, 232–3

Rilke, Rainer Marie, 72, 118, 223

Rose Cottage, Pontesbury, ch. 7 *passim*, esp. 131, 132, 134, 147, 150, 151, 152; 155, 213

Rossetti, Christina, 74, 209

Rossetti, Dante Gabriel, 74

Royal Literary Fund dinner (1928), xi, 322–3

Royalty Theatre, 288
rural novel, the, 118, 128–9, 136–7, 160–1, 169, 234–5, 326–7, 329
Ruysbroeck, 44

Sampson, George, *Concise Cambridge History of English Literature*, 195, 263, 328
Sanders, Prof. Charles, 142, 143, 186, 329, 340
'Sarn, Gideon' (*PB*), 117, 252–3, 255, 256, 259, 265–7, 270
'Sarn Mere' (*PB*), 136, 193–4, 251–67, 332, 333
'Sarn, Prudence' (*PB*), 65, 97, 120, 126, 233, 251–67, 271, 272, 292
Saturday Review, the, 234
Scarlet Letter, The (Hawthorne), 136, 144–5, 161
Scawfell, 325
Scott, Harriett Marian, 9 and n, 335
Scott, Sarah Alice (see Alice Meredith)
Scott, Dr Walter (grandfather of MW), 6
Scott, Sir Walter, 6, 13–14, 66, 169, 326
Scott Funds, the, 9 and n, 131, 150, 174, 239, 277, 324
Sedgwick, Ellery, 250, 275, 280, 281, 327n, 340
Shakespeare, 34, 53, 66, 191 and n, 210
Sharp, William (see Fiona Macleod)
Sheffield, Thomas, 107–8
Sheppard, H. R. L., 186, 304, 323, 340
'Shepwardine' (*GA*), 333
Shipton, I., 328
Shirley, 125
Shomere, 193, 333
Shrewsbury, x (map), 38, 47, 59, 64, 68, 70, 71, 74, 83, 85, 131, 146–50, 152, 153, 155, 172, 174, 201, 211, 215, 219, 274, 277, 285, 301, 310, 312, 318, 332, 333
Shrewsbury Chronicle, the, xix, 22n, 83–4, 274
Shrewsbury library, 71–2, 75n
Shrewsbury market, 146–50, 152
Shropshire, *passim*
Shropshire Folklore (Burne), 72, 134, 263, 338

Shropshire Magazine, the, xvii, 84n, 338
Silences of the Moon, The, (see Henry B. L. Webb)
'Silverton' (Shrewsbury), 47, 148, 333
Sin eater (sin eating) (*PB*), 252, 264, 265–6
Sinclair, May, 191, 220, 223, 270n, 280, 282, 337 ('Knowest Thou the Land?')
Sitwell, Osbert, 282
Smallman, Major, 23
Smith, Sheila Kaye, 326
Southern, Miss (friend of MW), 74, 82, 91, 98, 99
'Southernwood, Stephen' (*GA*), 93–4, 119, 121–2, 125–8, 135, 142, 151, 228, 232, 259, 285, 290, 325
Southport, xix, 36, 37
Spectator, the, xvii, xx, 44, 103, 178, 192, 195 and n, 219, 234, 235–6, 269, 272–3, 337
Spinoza, 81, 241n
Spring Cottage, ix, x (map), xx, 174, ch. 9 *passim*, esp. 176–7, 182, 193, 198–9, 201, 211–12, 215–16; 219, 225–7, 239, 250, 276, 283–4, 300, 301, 309, 312, 325
Springfield Republican, the, 300
St Leonard's-on-Sea, Sussex, xxi, 315–18
Stanton-upon-Hine Heath, x (map), xix, 38, ch. 3 *passim*, esp. 40–2, 44–50, 55; 64, 71
Stephens, Mr (landlord of 5, Grove Cottages), 302–3
Stiperstones, the, x (map), xiii, 11, 12, 23, 69, 113, 128, 131, 133, 135, 152, 160, 318
Storm, Theodor, 117
Story of my Heart, The (Jefferies), 36, 55, 103
Stretton Hill, x (map), xiii, 23, 69, 113, 318
Sufi Quarterly, the, 330–1 and n, 338
Sufis, 58, 61, 108, 207
Sunday Pictorial, the, 36, 236
Sunday Times, the, 324n
Swedenborg, 101
Swinburne, Algernon C., 74
Swinnerton, Frank, 255–6, 260, 280, 328, 334
Synge, John Millington, 117, 261, 288

Taffy (Evans), 288
Tempest, The (Shakespeare), 191 and n
Tenniel, 34
Tess of the D'Urbervilles (Hardy), 35, 169
Thomas, Edward, 235
Thompson, Francis, 80, 207
Thoreau, 193
Thorne, Mrs (neighbour of MW at Lyth Hill), 177, 202, 215, 224, 238, 239, 240, 284, 309, 311, 312, 318, 335
Tilley, Mrs (cook at The Grange), 22
Times, The, 292, 299, 323
Times Literary Supplement, the, 172–3, 178, 180, 213, 220, 270, 292
Toynbee, Arnold, 322
T.P.'s and Cassell's Weekly, 41n, 140, 270, 273, 283, 295–6, 321, 337
Traherne, Thomas, 59
Trevelyan, Prof. G. M., 322, 323
Trevor, St John, 22
Trismegistus, Hermes, 188n

Underhill, Evelyn, 191 and n, 341
'Undern Coppy, Lady of' (*GTE*), 163
'Undern Hall' (*GTE*), 136, 162, 163, 168, 333

Vaughan, Henry, 59, 188
Virgil, 199
Viroconium, x (map), 12–13, 274, 290

Walmsley, Mrs (Finishing School), xix, 36–7, 41
Walton, Izaak, 58, 326
Wastwater, 325
Webb, Ethel (Mrs Shelley), 147, 242
Webb, Henry Bertram Law, ix, xix, xx, 5; appearance, 100, 104, 152, 242, 244, 259; birth, early life, education, 97–8; book of essays, 103–5; character, mind, personality, 98–106, 116, 127, 129–30, 132, 150–1, 171–2, 177, 180–2, 203, 205, 211, 215, 225–6, 236, 240–4, 259, 265, 283–5, 287, 289, 297–8 and n, 300–2, 308, 311, 313, 315, 317–18, 324–5 and n; benefits from MW's royalties, 321, 324–5 and n; fails medical examination for military service in war, 137; health, back injury, 131–2, 137, 203, 239, 283;

market-gardening, 131–2, 146–7; pseudonym, author of historical novels (John Clayton), 324; rate-collector, 151; teaches, at The Limes, Shrewsbury, 97; at Brynmelyn School, Weston-super-Mare, 105, 133–14, 129–30; at The King's School, Chester, 153, 157, 171–2; at The Priory School, Shrewsbury, 172, 174, 181, 203; at the King Alfred School, Golders Green, 215, 219, 241–2, 243–4 and n, 245, 283, 284, 297–8, 301, 315, 324; death, 317, 325; will, 324n; literary work, 130, 177, 178, 181, 206, 324; *The Silences of the Moon*, xix, 98, 100–3, 130, 243; *The Everlasting Quest* (see Gilgamesh), xx, 130, 178, 180–1; *A Mary Webb Anthology*, 317, 325, 336
  and MARY WEBB: meeting, courtship, 98–100, 103–5; engagement, 105; looks after in illness, 106; wedding, 106–9; honeymoon, 113; influence on, 100, 102, 104, 106, 116, 117, 127, 156; poems to, ix, 177 and n, 180; relationship with, life together, 99–100, 101–6, 113, 115–16, 124, 129–30, 131–3, 134, 137, 141, 142, 147, 150–3, 157–8, 171–2, 174, 176–7, 180–2, 192, 194, 203, 205, 206, 207, 212–13, 214–16, 219, 225–7, 236, 239, 240–3, 275, 299, 311, 317–18; deterioration of marriage, 177, 181–2, 203, 225–6, 240–4, 245, 265, 277, 282–7, 289–90, 294, 297–9, 300–3, 307–19
  and Kathleen Wilson (second wife): 283, 284, 297–8, and n 300–2, 325
WEBB, MARY
  appearance, manner, 4, 20, 26, 29, 33–5, 41 and n, 52–4, 56, 68, 69, 73, 75, 100, 102, 104–5 and n, 107, 108, 147, 149, 182, 194, 199, 204–5, 211–12, 220–1, 223, 237–8, 241, 242, 248, 265, 279, 280, 282, 299, 301, 303, 309, 314, 315, 316; birth, christening, xix, 3–5; Celtic ancestry, 6, 72, 75, 162, 212, 322
  character, personality: blend of

Webb, Mary—*cont.*

opposites, complexity, xiii, xiv,
xv, 7, 10, 17, 19, 29, 34, 35, 38,
51, 73, 95, 99, 126, 163, 167,
211–12, 222–3, 227, 242, 260, 293,
294; compassion, sympathy, 4, 10,
23, 27–9, 37, 45, 70–1, 74, 84, 96,
100, 123, 137–9, 146, 150, 158–9,
164–5, 167, 170–1, 183, 196–7, 201,
204, 220, 222–4, 239–41, 277, 285,
297, 329, 330; determination,
strong will power, 9, 10, 26, 30,
33, 34, 35, 76, 81–2, 146, 150, 153,
173, 174, 205, 224, 232, 233, 238,
250, 275, 279, 315; eagerness,
spontaneity, childlike quality, 18,
20, 27, 28, 35, 75, 99, 135, 139–41,
148, 205, 222, 237, 281, 288, 300,
305; exactitude, 9, 33, 99, 103,
145, 146; fears, anxiety, insecurity,
xiv, 39, 49–50, 53–4, 56, 65, 66,
68, 85, 88, 93, 104, 105, 115–16,
125, 134–5, 151–2, 155, 157, 167,
169–70, 172, 181–2, 199, 203, 215,
225–7, 242–4, 265, 275, 276, 282–6,
298, 300–2, 316, 318, 325; fervour,
52, 55, 99, 104, 143; firmness, sense
of justice, business-like, 10, 35, 37,
38, 197–9, 276, 277–8, 285;
generosity, kindness, 28–9, 35, 38,
70–1, 82, 107–9, 150, 173, 180, 199,
201–3, 223–4, 239–41, 246, 247,
273, 277, 278, 280–1, 285, 297,
321; good and evil, awareness of,
15, 32–3, 45, 66, 97, 124, 128, 136,
145, 159, 171, 232, 265–7, 271, 291,
293, 294; independence, 30, 34, 42,
86, 280, 316; insight, intuition, 24,
25, 27, 35, 51, 73–4, 123, 126, 197,
204–5, 220, 238, 248, 286, 306,
312; intensity, xiii, 5, 9, 51–2, 73,
76, 77, 82, 96, 99, 144, 181–2, 238,
244, 255–6, 286; irony, xiii, 182–3,
196, 249, 261, 309–10, 329; joy,
wonder, xiii, xiv, 18, 19, 55–6, 57,
64, 76, 77, 147, 174–5, 208, 230,
306; love of children, maternal
sense, 30–2, 33, 34, 41, 70, 132,
194, 199–203, 233, 239; love,
passion, xiii, 17, 27–9, 35, 38, 48, 54,
97, 105, 107, 124, 125, 126, 132,
134–5, 151–2, 180, 194, 200–1, 203,

207, 227–8, 242, 258–9, 265, 272,
287, 289; nervousness, sensitivity,
xiii, 23, 35, 51–2, 53, 54, 152, 173,
199, 220–1, 222, 237, 242, 280, 282,
284–5, 286, 296, 298, 299, 302,
305n, 313, 315–16; sense of comedy,
humour, xiii, 10, 34, 66, 99, 117,
121, 123, 152, 169, 182, 194, 196,
204, 214, 222, 232, 247, 248–9,
255, 263, 305, 327; sharp
intelligence, 10, 20, 22, 24, 34, 37, 75,
99; sharp senses, perceptions, xiii,
xiv, 5, 17, 20–1, 25, 26–7, 29, 35,
36, 42–4, 48, 54, 57, 59, 64, 100,
118, 123, 128, 142, 144, 185, 193,
211, 231, 257, 293, 315; shyness,
sense of physical inferiority,
self-consciousness, 20, 34, 45, 48,
52, 53, 56, 65, 68, 73, 75, 99, 104,
150, 182, 199, 204, 220, 233, 244,
248, 257–8, 265, 280, 282, 284, 300;
sense of purpose, 75, 76, 203–4,
214–15, 222, 224, 236, 238, 279,
280–2, 290, 292; self-neglect, 51,
76, 81–2, 146, 224, 238, 240–1,
274, 276–7, 279, 283, 286, 297,
302–3, 310–11, 314; superstitious,
136–7, 254, 269; thoroughness, 9,
36, 146, 199; urge towards
wholeness, 11, 17, 25, 32, 51, 55,
73, 95, 97, 123, 124, 140, 144–5,
152, 186, 188, 191, 192, 194,
196–7, 203, 259, 267, 279, 285,
291, 311, 329, 330
criticised, ridiculed, 147, 148,
149, 202, 237, 241, 242, 244, 257,
265, 282, 284, 285, 301
education, reading: 6, 22, 33–4,
35–7, 41, 66, 71–3, 74–6, 79, 81,
116–17, 125, 169, 179, 185, 191,
241n, 260, 263; friendships, 20,
28–9, 34–5, 37, 44, 48, 69–70, 74–5,
78–9, 85, 96, 101, 150, 152–3, 158,
173–4, 177, 203–6, 211–12, 220–3,
236–40, 280–2, 284–5, 299, 303,
314
family, love of, 30–2, 36, 41, 48,
50, 64, 65, 73, 84–5, 272;
relationship with father (see
George Edward Meredith), 4–8,
16–17, 20–5, 28, 30–1, 33, 42, 46–9,
51, 52, 65–8, 71, 73, 76, 78, 81,

Webb, Mary—*cont.*
87–95, 99, 100, 104–5, 106, 123–4,
142, 157, 169, 171, 172, 259, 272–3,
315; relationship with mother, see
Alice Meredith; with Kenneth,
see Kenneth Meredith

financial difficulties during
marriage, 150–1, 152, 174, 201–3,
223–4, 239–42, 248, 250, 268, 271,
274–8, 280, 281, 282, 284, 285,
296–7, 302–3, 313, 321

health, illnesses, xi, xiii, xix, xx;
delicate when young, 26;
vegetarianism, 30, 51, 106, 131, 149,
211, 298, 303; Graves' Disease,
xiii, xix, 51–7 (first severe illness),
54–6, 64–6 (convalescence), 76–9,
81–2, (second severe illness), 83
(recovery), 92, 106, 146, 156–7,
171–2, (depression), 173, 196, 214,
219, 229, 238, 271, 273, 279, 286,
298, 303, 309, 311; pernicious
anaemia, 286, 303, 311, 314, 318;
decline and death, xx–xxi, 271, 273,
277, 279, 286–7, 289–90, 297–9,
300–3, 305–19, 321, 322

hiraeth, 114, 129–30, 156–7, 171–2,
224–7, 243, 245, 246, 272–4, 285,
286

knowledge of Bible, influence on
her writing, 19, 45, 53, 64, 66, 71,
79, 120, 164, 189, 190, 260–1,
269

'Lady Day' (pseudonymn), 95
'Ladysmock', 201–3, 314
manuscripts, 32, 46, 83, 209n, 275,
313–14
market-gardening, 131, 146–50,
152
mysticism, xiii, 8 and n, 18, 20,
27, 32, 39, 43–4, 51–2 and n, 57,
65, 67, 72–3, 79–81, 94–5, 101–2,
116–17, 119–21, 125–6, 127, 129,
140, 142, 144, 145, 150, 169–70,
175, 176, 177, 178–9, 188, 191–7,
203, 204, 205, 207, 214, 234, 241,
256–8, 260, 267, 279, 281, 291, 292,
293, 309, 311, 329–331
Nature: love of, union with, 5,
7–8, 14–15, 26–7, 42–4, 51–2, 54–6,
64–5, 67, 68, 81, 94–5, 100, 101–2,
103, 114, 121, 126, 133, 138–9, 156,

159, 162, 170, 193, 194–5, 219,
234–5, 273, 286, 290, 306, 309, 312,
322, 330–1; love of spring, 46, 52,
76–7, 174–5, 224–5, 306; birds, 5,
26, 56, 66, 68, 70, 77, 103, 177,
219, 306–8, 317; flowers, 5, 20, 32,
43, 44, 56, 64, 67, 68, 70, 96, 108,
150–1, 177, 246, 274, 316–17, 318;
attitude to nature, 8, 17, 43, 54–8,
159, 189, 194–5n, 272–3, 322,
330–1; use of in her writing, 16–17,
46, 54–9, 74, 81, 100–1, 115, 121,
127–9, 142–4, 168, 173, 177, 179,
189, 193–6 and n, 207, 234, 256,
287, 306–8, 310, 330; naturalist's
knowledge, 26–7, 29, 32, 36, 43–4,
53, 58–9, 64, 66, 69, 73, 100, 103,
142, 176–7, 193, 235–6, 248;
opposed to bloodsports, 23, 30,
33, 44–5, 159, 164, 171

other interests: bee-keeping, 26,
82, 131, 199; bridge, 30, 76, 98;
cats, 116, 151; cycling, 42, 49, 52;
embroidery, needlework, 65–6, 89,
90, 151, 222, 241, 299, 314; music,
piano, 37, 70, 83, 86, 151; painting
and drawing, 21, 34; Sunday school
classes, 45, 71, 108; plays, theatre,
32, 34, 41, 288; visiting, 27–9, 45,
47, 70, 96, 107

publishers, her relations with, 97,
145–6, 179, 180, 197–9, 206, 267–9,
275–9, 295, 297

psychology, the unconscious
mind, the creative process, her
interest in, 140–1, 165, 167, 186,
189–92, 194, 209–10, 236, 257,
259, 263, 267, 296, 329, 330

religion, 8, 10, 45, 71, 79–80, 91,
93–4, 101, 117, 120, 127, 156,
169–70, 296

reminiscent of Emily Brontë (see
Emily Brontë)

sense of history, 12–13, 18, 24–5,
47, 254, 274–5, 290–1 and n

Shropshire dialect, knowledge of,
use in her writing, 18, 99–100, 148,
204, 261–2

Shropshire folklore, legends,
superstitions, her knowledge of,
use of in her writing, 18, 23–4 and
n, 70, 72, 119, 122, 123, 134–5,

Webb, Mary—*cont.*

136–7, 162–7, 168, 169, 181, 232, 254, 263–6, 269, 271, 294, 325n, 330

Shropshire landscape and countryside, love of, use of in her writing, *passim*, esp. xii, xiii, 5, 7–8, 11, 12–15, 18, 24–5, 27, 36, 43–4, 48, 51, 54, 64, 68–70, 83, 113, 118–19, 123, 127–9, 130, 133, 135–6, 142–3, 145, 150, 153, 156–7, 160–1, 168, 171, 182, 207–8, 215–16, 227, 231–2, 250–1, 254, 256, 272–3, 294, 309, 312, 318, 330–1

Shropshire locations, place-names, use of in her writing, x (map), xii, xiii, 5, 11–14, 23, 28–9, 42, 47, 67–8, 113, 118, 119, 121–2, 128–9, 135–7, 142, 145, 148–9, 160, 168 and n, 193–4, 208, 212–13, 227, 251, 283n, 291, 294, 330–1, 332–3 (appendix 1)

war, effect of on her: 137–9, 146–7, 152, 154–9, 163–5, 167–8, 169–72, 183, 223

and her literary work: early writings, 22, 32, 34, 42, 45–6, 54–9 (essays), 64–6, 71, 74–6, 77, 79–81, 83–4, 88–90, 92–3, 95–7; early publications, xix, 45, 84, 95–6, 116, 117, 133; essays, articles, reviewing, xi, xiv, xix, xx–xxi, 5, 17, 26–7, 30, 32, 36, 44, 54–9 (*The Spring of Joy*), 65, 71, 72, 77, 81, 97 (*The Spring of Joy*), 100, 101, 103, 132–3, 140–1, 160–1, 175, 180, 188, 192, 195 and n, 203, 209–10 ('The Core of Poetry'), 219, 221, 224, 235–6, 261, 263, 272–3, 274–5, ('Glimpses of Old Shropshire'), 276, 279, 281, 282, 295–7 ('The Poetry of the Prayer Book'), 309–10 ('Irony and Mrs Wharton'), 336–7

NOVELS, xi, xiii, xiv, xviii, 11, 14, 18, 41n, 48, 68, 75–6, 93, 95–6, 113, 117–19, 121, 122–3, 126, 127–8, 129, 136, 140–5, 159, 160–1, 164, 169, 179, 182, 186, 195–6, 206, 213, 222, 227–8, 229, 231, 232, 234, 236, 247, 249, 254–6, 259–62, 267, 270, 271, 273, 278, 290–1, 294–5, 304, 310, 321–31, 334 (appendix 2), 336; *The Golden Arrow*, xiii, xvii, xix, xx, 11–12, 14–15, 17, 41n, 93, 94, 95, 113, 117–29, 132, 134–6, 137, 139, 141–6, 147, 148–9, 151–2, 153, 157, 160, 161, 168, 169, 172–3, 179, 180, 181, 186, 196, 206, 213, 220, 222, 258, 259, 263, 266, 278, 285, 290, 295; *Gone to Earth*, xviii, xx, 7, 23, 45, 103–4, 108, 117, 118, 128, 136, 137, 146, 158–71, 174, 178–9, 181, 183, 186, 192, 212, 213, 229, 235, 237, 263, 265, 266, 278, 291, 310; *The House in Dormer Forest*, xviii, xx, 10, 26, 42, 43, 48–9, 67–8, 82, 86, 93, 94, 99, 100, 105, 106, 114, 120, 136, 180, 182–98, 201, 209, 210, 211, 212–14, 225, 229, 234, 235, 256, 258, 259, 267, 278, 310; *Seven for a Secret*, xviii, xx, 37–8, 136, 145, 212, 225, 227–35, 236, 263, 267, 278; *Precious Bane*, xi, xviii, xx, 5, 24, 27, 41n, 47, 65, 97, 105n, 117, 120, 123, 136, 143, 159, 186, 193–4, 247, 250–71, 276, 278, 279, 282, 290, 292, 295, 297, 299, 300, 303–5, 310, 322, 323, 324 and n, 332; *Armour wherein he Trusted*, xviii, xx, 13, 136, 197, 269, 290–5, 298, 305–8, 310, 313–14, 317, 318, 323

POETRY, xi, xiv, xviii, xix, 5, 13, 14, 16–17, 22, 31–2, 34, 41n, 45–6, 55, 58–9, 64–6, 70, 71, 74, 79–81, 83–4, 88–93, 94, 95, 104, 115–16, 117, 120n, 133, 139, 147, 155, 157, 175, 177, 181, 200, 206–10 and n, 215, 226–7, 236–7, 269, 272, 274, 285, 286–7, 289, 306–8, 311–12, 316, 317, 318, 323, 330–1, 336, 339; poems quoted in full or in extracts: 'Sallow Catkins' 1; 'Viroconium' 13, 274; 'The Plain in Autumn' 14; 'The Messenger' ('The Thought') 18, 331; 'There are the pastures of sleep' 19; 'To G.D.M.' 31; 'Snowdrop Time' 32; 'Spring 1898' 46; 'Nature has opened her gates

Webb Mary, poetry—*cont.*
again' 65; 'The Water Ousel'
66; 'Green Rain' 69; 'Presences'
70; 'Spring in the West' 76; 'The
Heritage' 77; 'The Vagrant'
79–80; 'The Lost Orchard'
80; 'Railway Accident' 84; 'The
Little Sorrow' 85; 'Alder Buds'
88; 'The Wondrous Voice' 89;
'Unfinished Embroidery' 89–90;
'Heavy Silence' 92; 'Hunger'
92; 'The Difference' 92–3;
'Treasures' 93; 'The Door' 95;
'The Grape-Blue Hills' 97
'Reflections' 104; 'Isolde' 115,
289, 316; 'Today' 116, 289;
'The Happy Life' 133; 'August
1914' 138; 'Ah, Do Not Be So
Sweet!' 151, 181; 'An Estray' 154,
156; 'Joy' 40, 175; 'Autumn'
176; 'Colomen' 177, 289, 307–8;
'The Neighbour's Children' 200;
'Sunset' 207; 'The Spir of Earth'
208; 'The Watcher' 215; 'To
The World' 217, 289; 'A
Factory of Peace' 219; 'Absence'
226; 'On the Wild Hill' 226; 'To
a Blackbird Singing in London'
245 'To Mother' 272; 'Safe'
285; 'Farewell to Beauty' 286;
'The Land Within' 63, 247, 287;
'New Year's Eve' 289, 318; 'The
Wood' 307; 'Winter' 311;
'Summer Remembered' 311;
'Goodbye to Morning' 312;
'Lilies in the Valleys' 105, 317;
Poems and the Spring of Joy, xviii,
xix, xx, 5, 19, 26–7, 32, 36, 42n,
43, 54–9, 63, 65, 66, 69, 97,
100–3, 119, 175, 180, 188, 209,
and n, 211, 236–7, 323, 336
SHORT STORIES, xi, xx,
xxi, 25–6, 28–9, 32, 42, 70–1,
95–7, 116, 117, 133, 224, 271,
273–5, 279, 282, 308, 336; 'Owd
Blossom' 25–6; 'Many Mansions'
28–9, 'Blessed Are The Meek'
70–1, 308; 'Palm' 224, 'The
Cuckoo Clock' 275; 'The Sword'
275; 'Mr Tallent's Ghost' 275;
'The Chinese Lion' 275; 'The
Prize' 275

Webb, Captain Matthew, 98
Webb, Dr Thomas Law, 98
Webb, Mrs Thomas, 147, 242
'Weeping Cross' (*SFAS*), 213,
231, 332–3
Weil, Simone, 189
Welby, T. Earle, xiv
Wenlock, Edge, x (map), xiii, 18, 19,
23, 30, 32, 36, 42, 69, 211
West, Dame Rebecca, xvi, 179,
237–8, 270n, 299, 334
West, V. Sackville, 148, 237
West Hill, St Leonard's-on-Sea, 315
Westley Farm ix, 199
Weston-super-Mare, xx, 105, ch. 6
passim, esp. 113–15, 118, 129, 130;
132, 150, 153, 156, 225, 251, 316,
325
Wharton, Edith, 309–10, 337
White, Ethelbert, 279
White, Gilbert, 58, 241n, 326
Whitman, Walt, 18
Wicksteed, Mrs Ethel, 284, 314, 315,
316
Wicksteed, Joseph (Headmaster of the
King Alfred School), 284, 301
'Wilderhope' (*GA*), 120, 121, 122, 128,
135, 136, 332, 333
Wildings of Shrewsbury (publishers),
87, 336
Williams, Sir Ernest Hodder, 179, 198
Wilson, Kathleen, 297–8, 300, 302,
325
Wingfield, Rev. William, 4, 16
Woodlands, The, x (map), ch. 3
passim, esp. 40–1, 44, 46, 48–9,
59; 272
'Woodseaves, Kester' (*PB*), 251, 253,
258–60, 261, 265–6
'Woodus, Hazel' (*GA*), 45, 108, 117,
118, 158–70, 204, 228, 257, 266, 294
Woolf, Virginia, xiv, 140, 237, 271,
292
Wordsworth, William, 8, 27, 216
Wrekin, the, x (map), 3, 13, 14, 18,
23, 40, 69, 113
Wroxeter, 12, 274
Wuthering Heights (Brontë), 326

Yeats, W. B., 101

Zola, Emile, 235

THE AUTHOR

Gladys Mary Coles, an award-winning writer and poet, was educated at the Universities of Liverpool and London. After her postgraduate degree she held a research post at London University and wrote biographies of Elizabethan M.P.s, published in *The House of Commons, 1558-1603* (HMSO, 1981). Following this, she became a full-time writer and freelance lecturer.

The leading authority on her subject, she is President of the Mary Webb Society. In addition to *The Flower of Light*, the first major study of Mary Webb's life and work, Gladys Mary Coles' publications include two editions of Mary Webb's poetry and prose, Introductions to her novels and nature essays (*The Spring of Joy*), and a biographical/critical study (*Mary Webb*) in Seren Books Border Lines Series (1990). She has also written an article on Mary Webb for the *New Dictionary of National Biography*, to be published by Oxford University Press in the 21st Century. Her broadcasts include several features on BBC Radio 4 (including a *Kaleidoscope Special*), and on BBC TV and HTV. She has lectured on Mary Webb across Britain, at universities and colleges, and also at the Cheltenham Festival of Literature, the Dorset Literature Festival, the Cardiff Festival and others, and to the Alliance of Literary Societies.

Gladys Mary Coles, well-known for her poetry, has published eight collections, notably *Leafburners: New and Selected Poems* (1986) and *The Glass Island* (1992; reprint 1994), both published by Duckworth. Her poems are anthologised in the *Faber Book of English History in Verse* (1988), the *Forward Book of Poetry* (1993 and 1994), *Twentieth Century Anglo-Welsh Poetry* (1997), and in various other volumes. She has compiled and edited five anthologies, including *The Poet's View: Poems for Paintings in the Walker Art Gallery* (1996).The winner of numerous major poetry prizes, she has received a Welsh Arts Council Award and the Daily Post Arts Award for Literature.

Brought up in North Wales and Liverpool, Gladys Mary Coles lives on the Dee Estuary and in the Clwydian Hills. She is a lecturer in Imaginative Writing at both Liverpool University and Liverpool John Moores University.